FILM THEORY
GOES TO THE MOVIES

AFI Film Readers
a series edited by
Edward Branigan and Charles Wolfe

Psychoanalysis and Cinema
E. Ann Kaplan, editor

Fabrications: Costume and the Female Body
Jane Gaines and Charlotte Herzog, editors

Sound Theory/Sound Practice
Rick Altman, editor

The American Film Institute
P.O. Box 27999
2021 North Western Avenue
Los Angeles, California 90027

FILM THEORY
GOES TO THE MOVIES

EDITED BY

JIM COLLINS, HILARY RADNER,
and AVA PREACHER COLLINS

ROUTLEDGE

New York • London

Published in 1993 by

Routledge
An imprint of Routledge, Chapman and Hall, Inc.
29 West 35 Street
New York, NY 10001

Published in Great Britain by

Routledge
11 New Fetter Lane
London EC4P 4EE

"Between Apocalypse and Redemption: John Singleton's *Boyz N The Hood*" from *Tikkun, A Bimonthly Jewish Critique of Politics, Culture and Society,* vol. 6, no. 5 (Sept.–Oct. 1991) pp. 74–78.

Printed in the United States of America on acid free paper.

Library of Congress Cataloging in Publication Data

Film theory goes to the movies / edited by Ava Collins, Jim Collins,
  and Hilary Radner.
    p. cm. — (AFI film readers)
  Includes bibliographical references.
  ISBN 0-415-90575-3. — ISBN 0-415-90576-1
  1. Motion pictures. I. Collins, Ava. II. Collins, Jim, 1953–
III. Radner, Hillary. IV. Series.
PN1994.F43915 1992
791.43—dc20   92-19960
                                                     CIP

British Library Cataloguing in Publication Data also available.

For Our Students

Contents

Acknowledgements

We would like to express our unbounded gratitude to a number of people who made invaluable contributions to the preparation of this collection: Ron Hogan, Mark Pilkinton, Ted Mandell, Diane Gibbons, Bill Germano, Seth Denbo, Jason Dewees, Chuck Wolfe, and Ed Branigan. We especially appreciate the efforts of Thomas Schatz, who believed in the project from its inception and has offered advice and engagement at every stage of its development. We would also like to thank all of our contributors, without whom of course this book would not be possible. Finally, we owe a special thanks to our students at Notre Dame for providing the impetus for this collection, and it is to them that we dedicate this volume.

Introduction

Jim Collins, Hilary Radner, and Ava Preacher Collins

What does it mean for "film theory" to go to the "movies"? Film theory as it has been practiced since the late sixties has been in the vanguard in developing the critical approaches that we associate with poststructuralism, but this discussion about how a popular art form works has somehow been severed from the activity of actually going to the movies. In its considerations of issues such as the relationship between film language and subjectivity or representation and gender difference, this cutting-edge theoretical work has focused primarily on film classics and alternative cinemas. The analysis of contemporary movies has, for the most part, been left to the world of popular reviewing—a system that is based on sound-bite value judgments, which precludes consideration of the cultural significance of these texts. Public discussion about the broader implications of movies is usually framed in apocalyptic terms by cultural conservatives on both the left and the right who are eager to see them only as symptoms of an all-purpose moral and intellectual decay. The end result is an especially unfortunate situation in which those texts that have the most powerful impact on how we envision ourselves and each other, on how we imagine our present, past, and future—in short, those movies for which there is the most pressing need for intensive critical analysis—are the ones most often evaluated in terms of thumbs, popcorn boxes, stars, hankies, and Armageddon. The primary goal of this collection is to fill a gap within the field of film studies and within the larger arena of public discourse about popular culture: to take the concerns of film theory out of the academy to the movies, and thereby to reinvigorate theoretical debate with the culture of everyday life.

Movies are part of the taken-for-granted of daily life: we go to the movies, we stay in to watch a movie on tape, we tune in ABC's Monday

Night at the Movies on our TV set. But how do we discern and then describe the multiplicity of meanings that movies generate and how do we take into account the diverse forces that generate movies, that make them meaningful? No one critical approach can provide anything like a comprehensive answer to that question. Auteurist analysis located the production of meaning solely within the mind of the director; audience research posited viewers as free agents that fabricated their own stories of themselves; and traditional "industry" analysis bracketed the whole issue of meaning, seeing film as a system of financial investment and return. All three have provided valuable insight, but when used exclusively they have tended to foreclose rather than expand our understanding of movies as social artifacts invested with different types of significance by directors, viewers, and moneymen simultaneously. This collection is an attempt to describe that complexity, but not through the development of some new critical approach that provides a broader, more synthetic view of the terrain. Rather than coalescing into one big picture, the essays in this collection are an amalgam of views taken from specific perspectives, which suggest the heterogeneity of film-making and film-viewing in the present. In order to describe the heterogeneity of an "Industry" that has fragmented into "niches," and a "Mass Audience" that has given way to "target audiences," we have brought together an unprecedented combination of critical approaches, unprecedented because these approaches—industry analysis, reception theory, critical readings—have too often been conceived of as mutually exclusive. This combination may appear to lack a central unifying theme, and this is precisely our intention—to present a productive cacophony that will capture the dissonant mixture of factors that define New Hollywood and various contemporary American cultures.

One of the main goals of this collection is to present essays that would by the strength of their insights demonstrate the continuing need for *critical readings,* when so much of the field appears content to fade into a safe, depoliticized historicism, or just as disturbingly, into an ethnographic imperialism which rejects interpretation of anything except audiences, and simply abandons any notion of critique. The trend towards historicism within the discipline has proved to be a double-edged sword: on the positive side this historicist sword has cut through many of the worn-out truisms used to chart the development of the medium, providing desperately needed specificity regarding the conditions of production, distribution, and exhibition within particular national cinemas, and replacing the Great Man and Great Movement historical paradigms that have been in place for decades. The other edge of the sword, however, has attempted to sever historical research from interpretation, making the latter appear somehow ahistorical and by extension, less valid as "genuine" knowledge. The end result has been a *new antiquarianism,* in which the ideological dimensions of film analysis regarding the act of constructing historical objects and regarding the place of film studies within the academy are simply ignored in the pursuit of history defined as rare objects. This collection's emphasis on critical readings of contemporary cinema is not a call to "presentism" to offset this historicism, but rather a rejection of that antiquarianism that seeks to delegitimize the sort of engaged interventionist analysis that made film theory such a vital force in the academy during the 1970s and 1980s.

The need for critical readings has also been minimized by ethnographic approaches, which like the new antiquarianism attempt to invalidate interpretive analysis as less genuine than empirical research concerning an audience's reactions and viewing patterns. The contribution of recent scholarship on the constitution of audiences, their tastes, and the ways in which they give meaning to mass-media texts can hardly be overestimated. Such work has provided crucial insights into how films become social facts, acquiring diverse meanings as they circulate. The theoretical foundation of this work depends on a number of interconnected presuppositions: recognizing the power of audiences to decode texts according to local structures of feeling, the determination to grant legitimacy to such decodings, and the refusal to subordinate them to the more sophisticated decoding of critics. But these presuppositions also serve to justify an all-purpose rejection of textual analysis, since such analyses are usually produced by critics who have lost their amateur status and as academics belong to the one subculture not valorized by ethnographic researchers, since they have allegedly lost some sort of primary or naive relationship to images that only the "folk" enjoy. The avoidance of any hierarchizing of decodings has led to a counter-prejudice in which "informed" critical readings have become as suspect as "uninformed" readings used to be. To argue that the former still have a function is not an appeal for a new intellectual vanguardism, but rather a recognition of the specific abilities of academic critics as cultural workers, capable of making vital contributions to our understanding of texts by situating them diachronically within historical traditions and synchronically in reference to other forms of cultural production.

While all the essays in this collection argue in varying degrees of explicitness for the necessity of interpretive critical readings, none of them advocates a simple return to the good old days of film theory in the 1970s when analyses grounded in semiotics, Marxism, and psychoanalysis were making their initial impact on the discipline of film studies. This collection is a continuation of that work, which situated issues of filmic signification in reference to the cultural power relations that shaped film-making practice and film-viewing pleasure (of the lack thereof). But these essays also significantly revise some of those paradigms and introduce others—

cultural analysis in the 1990s is by necessity different from that which was practiced in the mid-1970s because our cultural terrain, both at the movies and within the academy has changed fundamentally in the past two decades.

One of the most significant shifts in emphasis is the refusal to isolate film as a medium unto itself—movies are only one form of popular entertainment, circulating alongside, and making use of, rock music, television, and fashion magazines, all of which factor into filmic signification. This is not to suggest that film was always considered in an artistic vacuum. In classical film theory there were, of course, many attempts to theorize the distinctive characteristics of film in relation to the "other arts," whether theater, literature, or painting. But traditional comparative analyses attempted to isolate essential differences in how meaning was produced. The essays in this volume, on the other hand, all contend that we can understand filmic signification only as it is imbricated in diverse ways with other media, past and present, its circulation within the *array* of cultural production mediating the semiotic and ideological resonance of any text. The emphasis on circulation and "imbrication" signals a move away from a film theory devoted to specifying essential differences to film theories concerned with multiplicity and contingency.

This move distinguishes contemporary theory not just from classical film theory, but also from more recent structuralist and poststructuralist theorizing of the 1960s and 1970s. One can quite easily construct a history of film theory in which the dominant trajectory is really a history of metalanguages developing in other disciplines being applied to film. But the history of film theory is more than just a history of metalanguages; it is also a history of critical master-narratives that provided totalizing paradigms that could, at one and the same time, account for how meaning is/was produced, serve as a basis for critical evaluation by which all films could be judged, explain the artistic potential of the medium as a mode of personal expression, and expose its ideological dimensions as a mode of mass communication and mass consumption. Film theory, viewed in reference to its reigning master-narratives, is a history of foundational discourses that grounded film analysis according to axiomatic principles, whether they originated in phenomenology, psychology, linguistics, or dialectical materialism. Structuralist and poststructuralist film theory may have developed new points of inquiry like the issue of pleasure in the metapsychology of film-viewing, or the connections between signifying practice and gender difference, but this work, more often than not, was also dependent upon foundational master-narratives, whether Oedipal scenarios, or the simulated "hyperreal," all of which provided handy ways of totalizing all forms and all dimensions of filmic representation according to a golden paradigm that once again furnished critics with both a mode of analysis and a basis for automatic evaluation.

Contemporary film theory introduces still more points of inquiry, but continues to question the utility of critical master-narratives. Each of the essays in this volume suggests ways of coming to terms with a multiplicity or variability that is not immediately foreclosed by such master-narratives. The theoretical stakes of these essays are both broader and more specific than previous film theory—broader in their determination to regard film as one form of cultural production thoroughly imbricated in other modes of representation and yet more specific in their concern with particular types of film-making, avoiding any essentialist claims about film-as-a-medium. The emphasis here is on how films *work,* not according to some abstract set of principles, but rather in response to the divergent exigencies that arise when industry, audience, and aesthetic practice are all defined by their relative fragmentation, dispersion, and heterogeneity. These theoretical stakes may appear initially less ambitious, but only in reference to the universalist claims of earlier film theory. While the claims made by the essays in this volume are more modest in reference to that tradition, they are also more impassioned because they redefine the stakes of film theory, moving away from the purer realms of linguistics and philosophy to the pragmatic concerns of cultural identity and professional responsibility.

All of the essays, with one exception, were prepared especially for this volume. While the collection features a number of different critical methodologies, it is in no way intended to be either a smorgasbord of various theoretical approaches, nor a collective enterprise in which all of the essays articulate one particular perspective on popular culture. By common agreement among the contributors, the unifying thread throughout the collection is the need to establish the *personal stakes* of these readings, that the individual chapters should not be conceived of as mere examples of x or y approach, but rather arguments for the necessity of doing this sort of analysis in order to come to terms with our cultural existences.

Some of these essays rework methodologies that are well-established within film study: Thomas Schatz's lead essay on the economic infrastructure of the New Hollywood develops out of industrial analysis; Dudley Andrew reconsiders the category of auteurism in current film cultures; Susan Jeffords' examination of different manifestations of the "new masculinity" considers the exigencies of "gender study" in the nineties; Susan White makes provocative use of psychoanalytic analysis in her critique of *Little Mermaid;* Jim Collins's examination of the state of genericity in the nineties discusses the limitations of traditional genre theory for understanding the complexity of hybrid genre films; and Forest Pyle's essay argues for the utility of deconstructive analysis in understanding the relationship between human and artificial life in *Blade Runner* and the *Terminator* series. Other contributors introduce theoretical issues that until quite recently have been relatively foreign to film study: Ed Guerrero's reading of *Jungle Fever* and Michael Dyson's evaluation of *Boyz N the Hood* emphasize the centrality of race in recent filmmaking and film criticism; Henry Giroux brings the concerns of radical pedagogy to bear on *Dead Poet's Society,* and Ava Preacher Collins's comparative analysis of *Mystery Train* and *Heartbreak Hotel* explores the nature of canon formation in popular film; Cathy Griggers' analysis of *Thelma and Louise* develops the possibilities of critique founded on "queer theory" and its relationship to both representation and audience reception.

These categories are admittedly far too limiting to describe the breadth of these readings since virtually all of the contributors situated their arguments in the intersections between different critical discourses. Jeff Sconce's analysis of contemporary horror films ties the concerns of genre and enunciation theory to question of evaluation and cultural status; Sharon Willis's reading of *Thelma and Louise* reflects on the interconnectedness of theories of gender difference and the function of film as popular fantasy; Janet Staiger's investigation of the meanings generated by *Silence of the Lambs* situates reception study in reference to the gay and lesbian reactions to the film; in her analysis of *Truth or Dare* and *Paris is Burning,* Ann Cvetkovich reflects on the relationships among gender, race, and sexual preference in reference to "masquerade" and representation; Hilary Radner's reading of *Pretty Woman* considers the rewritings of femininity, sexual exchange, and fetishism within contemporary consumer culture. Certain issues emerge as the common themes, or more precisely the common problematics addressed by all of these essays—the complicated nature of cultural identity as it is shaped by gender, race, class, and sexual preference, the changing functions of popular narrative, the development of heterogeneous "cultural literacies," the all-pervasiveness of rearticulation as a means of producing meaning in media-saturated cultures, and the need to confront the institutional changes that have occurred in both filmmaking and film study within the past decade.

Changing the stakes of film theory in this way necessarily involves a reconsideration of the pedagogical dimensions of the practice of film theory, that pedagogical function becoming a theoretical issue in and of itself now that the study of popular culture is inseparable from the ongoing debate over the politics of education. The fact that all of these essays focus on recent, contemporary movies is itself a move towards redefining the goals of the analysis of popular culture. The collection purposely avoids constructing a new canon, opting instead to interrogate the forms of cultural significance that these movies are invested with and to question how those investments reflect what is expected of the medium in the 1990s. In other words, the age-old question concerning how films "mean," which has been central to film theory since its inception, is asked yet again by this collection but that question is framed according to different notions of what constitutes culture and what constitutes meaningful criticism within it.

1

The New Hollywood

Thomas Schatz

Among the more curious and confounding terms in media studies is "the New Hollywood." In its broadest historical sense the term applies to the American cinema after World War II, when Hollywood's entrenched "studio system" collapsed and commercial television began to sweep the newly suburbanized national landscape. That marked the end of Hollywood's "classical" era of the 1920s, 1930s, and early 1940s, when movies were mass produced by a cartel of studios for a virtually guaranteed market. All that changed in the postwar decade, as motion pictures came to be produced and sold on a film-by-film basis and as "watching TV" rapidly replaced "going to the movies" as America's preferred ritual of habituated, mass-mediated narrative entertainment.[1]

Ensuing pronouncements of the "death of Hollywood" proved to be greatly exaggerated, however; the industry not only survived but flourished in a changing media marketplace. Among the more remarkable developments in recent media history, in fact, is the staying power of the major studios (Paramount, MGM, Warners, et al.) and of the movie itself—that is, the theatrically released feature film—in an increasingly vast and complex "entertainment industry." This is no small feat, considering the changes Hollywood has faced since the late 1940s. The industry adjusted to those changes, and in the process its ways of doing business and of making movies changed as well—and thus the difficulty in defining the New Hollywood, which has meant something different from one period of adjustment to another.

The key to Hollywood's survival and the one abiding aspect of its postwar transformation has been the steady rise of the movie blockbuster. In terms of budgets, production values, and market strategy, Hollywood has been increasingly hit-driven since the early 1950s. This marks a significant departure from the classical era, when the studios turned out a few "prestige" pictures each year and relished the occasional runaway box-office hit, but relied primarily on routine A-class features to generate revenues. The exceptional became the rule in postwar Hollywood, as the occasional hit gave way to the calculated blockbuster.

The most obvious measure of this blockbuster syndrome is box-office revenues, which have indeed surged over the past forty years.[2] In 1983, *Variety* commissioned a study of the industry's all-time commercial hits in "constant dollars"—that is, in figures adjusted for inflation—which placed only two films made before 1950, *Gone With the Wind* (1939) and *Snow White and the Seven Dwarfs* (1937), in the top 75.[3] In other words, of the 7,000 or so Hollywood features released before 1950, only two enjoyed the kind of success that has become routine since then—and particularly in the past two decades. According to *Variety's* most recent (January, 1992) update of the all-time "film rental champs," 90 of the top 100 hits have been produced since 1970, and all of the top 20 since *Jaws* in 1975.[4]

The blockbuster syndrome went into high gear in the mid-1970s, despite (and in some ways because of) the concurrent emergence of competing media technologies and new delivery systems, notably pay-cable TV and home video (VCRs). This was the first period of sustained economic vitality and industry stability since the classical era. Thus this post-1975 era best warrants the term "the New Hollywood," and for essentially the same reasons associated the "classical" era. Both terms connote not only specific historical periods, but also characteristic qualities of the movie industry at the time—particularly its economic and institutional structure, its mode of production, and its system of narrative conventions.

This is not to say that the New Hollywood is as stable or well integrated as the classical Hollywood, however. As we will see, the government's postwar dismantling of the "vertically integrated" studio system ensured a more competitive movie marketplace, and a more fundamentally dis-integrated industry as well. The marketplace became even more fragmented and uncertain with the emergence of TV and other media industries, and with the massive changes in lifestyle accompanying suburban migration and the related family/housing/baby boom. In one sense the mid-1970s ascent of the New Hollywood marks the studios' eventual coming-to-terms with an increasingly fragmented entertainment industry—with its demographics and target audiences, its diversified "multimedia" conglomerates, its global(ized) markets and new delivery systems. And equally fragmented, perhaps, are the movies themselves, especially the high-cost, high-tech, high-stakes blockbusters, those multi-purpose entertainment machines that breed music videos and soundtrack albums, TV series and videocassettes, video games and theme park rides, novelizations and comic books.

Hollywood's mid-1970s restabilization came after some thirty years of uncertainty and disarray. I would suggest, in fact, that the movie industry underwent three fairly distinct decade-long phases after the War—from 1946 to 1955, from 1956 to 1965, and from 1966 to 1975. These phases were distinguished by various developments both inside and outside the industry, and four in particular: the shift to independent motion picture production, the changing role of the studios, the emergence of commercial TV, and changes in American lifestyle and patterns of media consumption. The key markers in these phases were huge hits like *The Ten Commandments* in 1956, *The Sound of Music* in 1965, and *Jaws* in 1975 which redefined the nature, scope, and profit potential of the blockbuster movie, and which lay the foundation for the films and filmmaking practices of the New Hollywood.

To understand the New Hollywood, we need to chart these postwar phases and the concurrent emergence of the blockbuster syndrome in American filmmaking. Our ultimate focus, though, will be on the post-1975 New Hollywood and its complex interplay of economic, aesthetic, and technological forces. If recent studies of classical Hollywood have taught us anything, it is that we cannot consider either the filmmaking process or films themselves in isolation from their economic, technological, and industrial context. As we will see, this interplay of forces is in many ways even more complex in the New Hollywood, especially when blockbusters are involved. In today's media marketplace, it has become virtually impossible to identify or isolate the "text" itself, or to distinguish a film's aesthetic or narrative quality from its commercial imperatives. As Eileen Meehan suggests in a perceptive study of *Batman,* to analyze contemporary movies "we must be able to understand them as always and simultaneously text and commodity, intertext and product line."[5]

The goal of this essay is to situate that "understanding" historically, tracing the emergence and the complex workings of the New Hollywood. The emphasis throughout will be on the high-cost, high-tech, high-stakes productions that have driven the postwar movie industry—and that now drive the global multimedia marketplace at large. While one crucial dimension of the New Hollywood is the "space" that has been opened for independent and alternative cinema, the fact is that these mainstream hits are where stars, genres, and cinematic innovations invariably are established, where the "grammar" of cinema is most likely to be refined, and where the essential qualities of the medium—its popular and commercial character—are most evident. These blockbuster hits are, for better or worse, what the New Hollywood is about, and thus are the necessary starting point for any analysis of contemporary American cinema.

Hollywood in Transition

The year 1946 marked the culmination of a five-year "war boom" for Hollywood, with record revenues of over $1.5 billion and weekly ticket sales of 90 to 100 million.[6] The two biggest hits in 1946 were "major independent" productions: Sam Goldwyn's *The Best Years of Our Lives* and David O. Selznick's *Duel in the Sun*. Both returned $11.3 million in rentals, a huge sum at the time, and signaled important changes in the industry—though Selznick's *Duel* was the more telling of the two.[7] Like his *Gone With the Wind*, it was a prototype New Hollywood blockbuster: a "pre-sold" spectacle (based on a popular historical novel) with top stars, an excessive budget, a sprawling story, and state-of-the-art production values. Selznick himself termed *Duel* "an exercise in making a big-grossing film," gambling on a nationwide promotion-and-release campaign after weak sneak previews.[8] When the gamble paid off, he proclaimed it a "tremendous milestone in motion picture merchandising and exhibition."[9]

That proved to be prophetic, given Hollywood's wholesale postwar transformation, which was actually well under way in 1946. The Justice Department's pursuit of Hollywood's major powers for antitrust practices began to show results in the courts that year, and culminated in the Supreme Court's May 1948 *Paramount* decree, which forced the major studios to divest their theater chains and to cease various tactics which had enabled them to control the market. Without the cash flow from their theaters and a guaranteed outlet for their product, the established studio system was effectively finished. The studios gradually fired their contract personnel and phased out active production, and began leasing their facilities for independent projects, generally providing co-financing and distribution as well. This shift to "one-film deals" also affected the established relations of power, with top talent (and their agents and attorneys) gaining more authority over production.[10]

The studios' new role as financing-and-distribution entities also jibed with other industry developments. The war boom had ended rather suddenly in 1947 as the economy slumped and, more importantly, as millions of couples married, settled down, and started families—many of them moving to the suburbs and away from urban centers, where movie business thrived. Declining attendance at home was complemented by a decline in international trade in 1947–1948, notably in the newly reopened European markets where "protectionist" policies were initiated to foster domestic production and to restrict the revenues that could be taken out of the country. This encouraged the studios to enter into co-financing and co-production deals overseas, which complemented the changing strategy at home and fueled the general postwar rise in motion picture imports as well as independent production.

Another crucial factor on the domestic front was, of course, television. Early on, the major studios had met the competition head on with efforts to differentiate movies from TV programs. There was a marked increase in historical spectacles, Westerns, and biblical epics, invariably designed for a global market and shot on location with international casts. These were enhanced by the increased use of Technicolor and by innovations in technology, notably widescreen formats and 3–D. These efforts soon began paying off despite TV's continued growth, as *Fortune*'s Freeman Lincoln pointed out in a 1955 piece aptly titled, "The Comeback of the Movies." Lincoln noted that, traditionally, "any picture that topped $5 million worldwide was a smash hit," and he estimated that only about 100 Hollywood releases had ever reached that total. "In September, 1953, 20th Century-Fox released *The Robe,* which has since grossed better than $20 million around the world and is expected to surpass $30 million," wrote Lincoln, and pointed out that "in the 17 months since *The Robe* was turned loose nearly 30 pictures have grossed more than the previously magic $5 million."[11]

As Hollywood's blockbuster mentality took hold in 1955, the majors finally ventured into television. MGM, Warners, and Fox, taking a cue from Disney and the lesser Hollywood powers already involved in "tele-film" series production, began producing filmed series of their own in the Fall of 1955.[12] And late that year the majors also began to sell or lease their pre-1948 features to TV syndicators. In 1956 alone, some 3,000 feature films went into syndication; by 1958, all of the majors had unloaded hundreds of pre-1948 films.[13] In 1960, the studios and talent guilds agreed on residual payments for post-1948 films, leading to another wave of movie syndication and to Hollywood movies being scheduled in regular prime-time. Telefilm production was also on the rise in the late 1950s, as the studios relied increasingly on TV series to keep their facilities in constant operation, since more and more feature films were shot on location. The studios also had begun realizing sizable profits from the syndication of hit TV series, both as reruns in the U.S. and as first-run series abroad. As the studios upgraded series production and as the preferred programming format shifted from live video to telefilm—despite the introduction of videotape in 1957—the networks steadily shifted their production operations from New York to Los Angeles. By 1960 virtually all prime-time fictional series were produced on film in Hollywood, with the traditional studio powers dominating this trend.

Meanwhile the blockbuster mentality intensified. Lincoln had suggested in his 1955 *Fortune* piece, "The beauty of the big picture nowadays is, of course, that there seems to be no limit to what the box office return may be."[14] The ensuing decade bore this out with a vengeance, bracketed by two colossal hits: *The Ten Commandments* in 1956, with domestic rentals of $43 million (versus *The Robe*'s $17.5 million), and *The Sound of Music* in 1965, with rentals of $79.9 million. Other top hits from the decade included similarly "big" all-star projects, most of them shot on location for an international market:

Around the World in 80 Days (1956; $23 million in rentals)
The Bridge on the River Kwai (1957; $17.2 million)
South Pacific (1958; $17.5 million)
Ben-Hur (1959; $36.5 million)
Lawrence of Arabia (1962; $17.7 million)
The Longest Day (1962; $17.6 million)
Cleopatra (1963; $26 million)
Goldfinger (1964; $23 million)
Thunderball (1965; $28.5 million)
Dr. Zhivago (1965; $46.5 million)

While these mega-hits dominated the high end of Hollywood's output, the studios looked for ways beyond TV series production to diversify their media interests. Besides the need to hedge their bets on high-stakes blockbusters, this impulse to diversify was a response to the postwar boom in entertainment and leisure activities, the increasing segmentation of media audiences in a period of general prosperity and population growth, and the sophisticated new advertising and marketing strategies used to measure and attract those audiences. MCA was the clear industry leader in terms of diversification, having expanded from a music booking and talent agency in the 1930s and 1940s into telefilm production and syndication in the 1950s, eventually buying Decca Records and then Universal Pictures in the early 1960s.

The 1950s and 1960s also saw diversified, segmented moviegoing trends, most of them keyed to the immense, emergent "youth market." With the baby boom generation reaching active consumer status and developing distinctive interests and tastes, there was a marked surge in drive-in moviegoing, itself a phenomenon directed associated with postwar suburbanization and the family boom. With the emergent youth market, drive-in viewing fare turned increasingly to low-budget "teen-pics" and "exploitation" films. The "art cinema" and foreign film movements also took off in the late 1950s and early 1960s, as neighborhood movie houses and campus film societies screened alternatives to mainstream Hollywood and as film courses began springing up on college campuses. These indicated a more "cine-literate" generation—with that literacy actually enhanced by TV, which had become a veritable archive of American film history.

While the exploitation and art cinema movements produced a few commercial hits—Hitchcock's *Psycho* and Fellini's *La Dolce Vita* in 1960, for instance—the box office was dominated well into the 1960s by much the same blockbuster mentality as in previous decades. Indeed, the biopics, historical and biblical epics, literary adaptations, and transplanted stage musicals of the 1950s and 1960s differed from the prestige pictures of the classical era only in their oversized budgets, casts, running times, and screen width. If the emergent youth culture and increasingly diversified media marketplace were danger signs, they were lost on the studios—particularly after the huge commercial success of two very traditional mainstream films in 1965, *The Sound of Music* and *Dr. Zhivago*.

Actually, Hollywood was on the verge of its worst economic slump since the War—fueled to a degree by those two 1965 hits, because they led to a cycle of expensive, heavily promoted commercial flops. Fox, for instance, went on a blockbuster musical binge in an effort to replicate its success with *The Sound of Music,* and the results were disastrous: losses of $11 million on *Dr. Dolittle* in 1967, $15 million on *Star!* in 1968, and $16 million in 1969 on *Hello Dolly,* at the time the most expensive film ever made.[15] Fox then tightened its belt, avoiding bankruptcy thanks to two relatively inexpensive, offbeat films: *Butch Cassidy and the Sundance Kid* (1969; $46 million in rentals), and *MASH* (1970; $36.7 million).

Those two hits were significant for a number of reasons besides the reversal of Fox's fortunes, reasons which signaled changes of aesthetic as well as economic direction in late-1960s Hollywood. With the blockbuster strategy stalled, the industry saw a period of widespread and unprecedented innovation, due largely to a new "generation" of Hollywood filmmakers like Robert Altman, Arthur Penn, Mike Nichols, and Bob Rafelson, who were turning out films that had as much in common with the European art cinema as with classical Hollywood. There was also a growing contingent of international auteurs—Bergman, Fellini, Trauffaut, Bertolucci, Polanski, Kubrick—who, in the wake of the 1966 success of Antonioni's *Blow-Up* and Claude Lelouch's *A Man and a Woman,* developed a quasi-independent rapport with Hollywood, making films for a Euro-American market and bringing art cinema into the mainstream.

Thus an "American film renaissance" of sorts was induced by a succession of big-budget flops and successful imports. Its key constituency was the American youth, by now the most dependable segment of regular moviegoers as attendance continued to fall despite the overall increase in population. Younger viewers contributed heavily to the success of sizable hits like *Bonnie and Clyde* (1967; rentals of $22.8 million), *2001: A Space Odyssey* (1968; $25.5 million), and *The Graduate* (1968; $43 million), and they were almost solely responsible for modest hits like *Easy Rider* (1969; $19 million) and *Woodstock* (1970; $16.4 million). As these films suggest, the older baby boomers were reaching critical mass as a target market and were something of a countercultural force as well, caught up in the antiwar movement, civil rights, the sexual revolution, and so on. And with the 1966 breakdown of Hollywood's Production Code and the emergence in 1968 of the new ratings system—itself a further indication of the segmented movie audiences—filmmakers were experimenting with more politically subversive, sexually explicit, and/or graphically violent material.

As one might suspect, Hollywood's cultivation of the youth market and penchant for innovation in the late 1960s and early 1970s scarcely indicated a favorable market climate. On the contrary, they reflected the studios' uncertainty and growing desperation. Film historian Tino Balio has written about "the Recession of 1969" and its aftermath, when "Hollywood nearly collapsed."[16] *Variety* at the time pegged combined industry losses for 1969–1971 at $600 million, and according to an economic study by Joseph Dominick, studio profits fell from an average of $64 million in the five-year span from 1964 to 1968, to $13 million from 1969 to 1973.[17] Market conditions rendered the studios ripe for takeover, and in fact a number of the studios were absorbed in post-1965 conglomerate wave. Paramount was taken over by Gulf & Western in 1966, United Artists by Transamerica in 1967, and Warner Bros. by Kinney National Services in 1969, the same year MGM was bought out by real-estate tycoon Kirk Kerkorian. This trend proved to be a mixed blessing for the studios. The cash-rich parent company relieved much of the financial pressures and spurred diversification, but the new owners knew little about the movie business and, as the market worsened, tended to view their Hollywood subsidiaries as troublesome tax write-offs.

One bright spot during this period was the surge in network prices paid for hit movies. Back in 1961, NBC had paid Fox an average of $180,000 for each feature shown on *Saturday Night at the Movies;* that year 45 features were broadcast in prime time. By 1970, the average price tag per feature was up to $800,000, with the networks spending $65 million on a total of 166 feature films. That total jumped to 227 for the 1971–1972 season, when movies comprised over one quarter of all prime-time programming. The average price went up as well, due largely to ABC's paying $50 million in the Summer of 1971 for a package of blockbusters, including $5 million for *Lawrence of Arabia,* $3 million for the 1970 hit, *Love Story,* and $2.5 million each for seven James Bond films.[18] Significantly enough, however, these big payoffs were going only to top

Hollywood hits as all three networks began producing their own TV-movies. Hollywood features comprised only half of the movies shown on network TV in the 1971–1972 season, and that percentage declined further in subsequent years, as made-for-TV movie production increased.

The network payoff for top movie hits scarcely reversed the late-sixties downturn, as *The Graduate* in 1968 was the only release between 1965 and 1969 to surpass even $30 million in rentals. *Butch Cassidy, Airport,* and *Love Story* in 1969–1970 all earned $45 to $50 million, carrying much of the freight in those otherwise bleak economic years. *Airport* was especially important in that it generated a cycle of successful "disaster pictures" like *The Poseidon Adventure, The Towering Inferno,* and *Earthquake,* all solid performers in the $40 to $50 million range, though they were fairly expensive to produce and not quite the breakaway hits that the industry so desperately needed.

The first real sign of a reversal of the industry's sagging fortunes came with *The Godfather,* a 1972 Paramount release that returned over $86 million. *The Godfather* was that rarest of movies, a critical and commercial smash with widespread appeal, drawing art cinema connoisseurs and disaffected youth as well as mainstream moviegoers. Adapted from Mario Puzo's novel while it was still in galleys, the project was scarcely mounted as a surefire hit. Director Francis Ford Coppola was a debt-ridden film school product with far more success as a writer, and star Marlon Brando hadn't had a hit in over a decade. The huge sales of the novel, published while the film was in production, generated interest, as did well-publicized stories of problems on the set, cost overruns, and protests from Italian-American groups. By the time of its release, *The Godfather* had attained "event" status, and audiences responded to Coppola's stylish and highly stylized hybrid of the gangster genre and family melodrama. Like so many 1970s films, *The Godfather* had a strong nostalgic quality, invoking the male ethos and patriarchal order of a bygone era—and putting its three male co-stars, Al Pacino, James Caan, and Robert Duvall, on the industry map.

The Godfather also did well in the international market, thus spurring an upturn in the overseas as well as the domestic market. Domestic theater admissions in 1972 were up roughly 20 percent over 1971, reversing a 7-year slide, and total box-office revenues surged from the $1 billion range, where they had stagnated for several years, to $1.64 billion. While *The Godfather* alone accounted for nearly 10 percent of those gross proceeds, other films clearly were contributing; revenues for the top ten box-office hits of 1972 were up nearly 70 percent over the previous year. That momentum held through 1973 and then the market surged again in 1974, nearing the $2 billion mark—and thus finally surpassing Hollywood's postwar box-office peak. Key to the upturn were the now-predictable spate of disaster films, though these were far outdistanced by three hits which, in different ways, were sure signs of a changing industry.

One was *American Graffiti,* a surprise Summer 1973 hit written and directed by Coppola protégé George Lucas. A coming-of-age film with strong commercial tie-ins to both TV and rock music, the story's 1962 setting enabled Lucas to circumvent (or rather to predate) the current socio-political climate and broadened its appeal to older viewers. Two even bigger hits were late-1973 releases, *The Sting* and *The Exorcist* ($78 million and $86 million, respectively). *The Sting* was yet another nostalgia piece, a 1930s-era gangster/buddy/caper hybrid, reprising the Newman-Redford pairing of five years earlier—something like "Butch and Sundance meet the Godfather." The nostalgia and studied innocence of both *The Sting* and *American Graffiti* were hardly evident in *The Exorcist,* William Friedkin's kinetic, gut-wrenching, effects-laden exercise in screen violence and horror. While *Psycho* and *Rosemary's Baby* had proved that horror thrillers could attain hit status, *The Exorcist* pushed the logic and limits of the genre (and the viewer's capacity for masochistic pleasure) to new extremes, resulting in a truly monstrous hit and perhaps the clearest indication of the emergent New Hollywood.

Jaws and the New Hollywood

If any single film marked the arrival of the New Hollywood, it was *Jaws,* the Spielberg-directed thriller that recalibrated the profit potential of the Hollywood hit, and redefined its status as a marketable commodity and cultural phenomenon as well. The film brought an emphatic end to Hollywood's five-year recession, while ushering in an era of high-cost, high-tech, high-speed thrillers. *Jaws'* release also happened to coincide with developments both inside and outside the movie industry in the mid-1970s which, while having little or nothing to do with that particular film, were equally important to the emergent New Hollywood.

Jaws, like *Love Story, The Godfather, The Exorcist,* and several other recent hits, was presold via a current best-selling novel. And like *The Godfather,* movie rights to the novel were purchased before it was published, and publicity from the deal and from the subsequent production helped spur the initial book sales—of a reported 7.6 million copies before the film's release in this case—which in turn fueled public interest in the film.[19] The *Jaws* deal was packaged by International Creative Management (ICM), which represented author Peter Benchley and handled the sale of the movie rights. ICM also represented the producing team of Richard Zanuck and David Brown, whose recent hits included *Butch Cassidy* and *The Sting,* and who worked with ICM to put together the movie project with MCA/Universal and *wunderkind* director Steven Spielberg.[20]

Initially budgeted at $3.5 million, *Jaws* was expensive by contemporary standards (average production costs in 1975 were $2.5 million), but it was scarcely a big-ticket project in that age of $10 million musicals and $20 million disaster epics.[21] The budget did steadily escalate due to logistical problems and Spielberg's ever-expanding vision and confidence; in fact problems with the mechanical shark pushed the effects budget alone to over $3 million. The producers managed to parlay those problems into positive publicity, however, and continued to hype the film during post-production. The movie was planned for a Summer 1975 release due to its subject matter, even though in those years most calculated hits were released during the Christmas holidays. Zanuck and Brown compensated by spending $2.5 million on promotion, much of it invested in a media blitz during the week before the film's 464-screen opening.[22]

The print campaign featured a poster depicting a huge shark rising through the water toward an unsuspecting swimmer, while the radio and TV ads exploited John Williams's now-famous "Jaws theme." The provocative poster art and Williams's pulsating, foreboding theme conveyed the essence of the film experience and worked their way into the national consciousness, setting new standards for motion picture promotion. With the public's appetite sufficiently whetted, *Jaws'* release set off a feeding frenzy as 25 million tickets were sold in the film's first 38 days of release. After this quick start, the shark proved to have "good legs" at the box office, running strong throughout the summer en route to a record $102.5 million in rentals in 1975. In the process, *Jaws* became a veritable sub-industry unto itself via commercial tie-ins and merchandising ploys. But hype and promotion aside, *Jaws'* success ultimately centered on the appeal of the film itself; one enduring verity in the movie business is that, whatever the marketing efforts, only positive audience response and favorable word-of-mouth can propel a film to genuine hit status.

Jaws was essentially an action film and a thriller, of course, though it effectively melded various genres and story types. It tapped into the monster movie tradition with a revenge-of-nature subtext (like *King Kong, The Birds,* et al.), and in the film's latter stages the shark begins to take on supernatural, even Satanic, qualities à la *Rosemary's Baby* and *The Exorcist.* And given the fact that the initial victims are women and children, *Jaws* also had ties to the high-gore "slasher" film, which had been given considerable impetus a year earlier by *The Texas Chainsaw Massacre.* The seagoing chase in the latter half is also a buddy film and a male initiation story, with Brodie the cop, Hooper the scientist, and Quint the sea captain providing different strategies for dealing with the shark and different takes on male heroic behavior.

Technically, *Jaws* is an adept "chase film" that takes the viewer on an emotional roller coaster, first in awaiting the subsequent (and increasingly graphic) shark attacks, then in the actual pursuit of the shark. The narrative is precise and effectively paced, with each stage building to a climactic peak, then dissipating, then building again until the explosive finale. The performances, camera work, and editing are all crucial to this effect, as is John Williams's score. This was in fact the breakthrough film for Williams, the first in a run of huge hits that he scored (including *Star Wars, Close Encounters of the Third Kind, Raiders of the Lost Ark,* and *E.T.*) whose music is absolutely essential to the emotional impact of the film.

Many critics disparaged that impact, dismissing *Jaws* as an utterly mechanical (if technically flawless) exercise in viewer manipulation. James Monaco cites *Jaws* itself as the basis for the "Bruce aesthetic" (named after the film crew's pet name for the marauding robotic shark), whose ultimate cinematic effect is "visceral—mechanical rather than human." More exciting than interesting, more style than substance, *Jaws* and its myriad offspring, argues Monaco, are mere "machines of entertainment, precisely calculated to achieve their effect."[23] Others have argued, however, that *Jaws* is redeemed by several factors, notably the political critique in the film's first half, the essential humanity of Brodic, and the growing camaraderie of the three pursuers.

Critical debate aside, *Jaws* was a social, industrial, and economic phenomenon of the first order, a cinematic idea and cultural commodity whose time had come. In many ways, the film simply confirmed or consolidated various existing industry trends and practices. In terms of marketing, *Jaws'* nationwide release and concurrent ad campaign underscored the value of saturation booking and advertising, which placed increased importance on a film's box-office performance in its opening weeks of release. "Front-loading" the audience became a widespread marketing ploy, since it maximized a movie's event status while diminishing the potential damage done to weak pictures by negative reviews and poor word of mouth. *Jaws* also confirmed the viability of the "summer hit," indicating an adjustment in seasonal release tactics and a few other new moviegoing trends as well. One involved the composition and industry conceptualization of the youth market, which was shifting from the politically hip, cineliterate viewers of a few years earlier to even younger viewers with more conservative tastes and sensibilities. Demographically, this trend reflected the aging of the front-end baby boomers and the ascendence not only of their younger siblings but of their children as well—a new generation with time and spending money and a penchant for wandering suburban shopping malls and for repeated viewings of their favorite films.

This signaled a crucial shift in moviegoing and exhibition that accompanied the rise of the modern "shopping center." Until the mid-1970s, despite suburbanization and the rise of the drive-in, movie exhibition still was dominated by a select group of so-called "key run" bookings in major markets. According to Axel Madsen's 1975 study of the industry, over 60 percent of box-office revenues were generated by 1,000 key-run indoor theaters—out of a total of roughly 11,500 indoor and 3,500 outdoor theaters in the U.S.[24] Though Madsen scarcely saw it at the time, this was about to change dramatically. Between 1965 and 1970, the number of shopping malls in the U.S. increased from about 1,500 to 12,500; by 1980 the number would reach 22,500.[25] The number of indoor theaters, which had held remarkably steady from 1965 to 1974 at just over 10,000, began to increase sharply in 1975 and reached a total of 22,750 by 1990, due largely to the surge of mall-based "multi-plex" theaters.[26]

With the shifting market patterns and changing conception of youth culture, the mid-1970s also saw the rapid decline of the art cinema movement as a significant industry force. A number of films in 1974–1975 marked both the peak and, as it turned out, the waning of the Hollywood renaissance—Altman's *Nashville,* Penn's *Night Moves,* Polanski's *Chinatown,* and most notably perhaps, Coppola's *The Conversation.* The consummate American auteur and "godfather" to a generation of filmmakers, Coppola's own artistic bent and maverick filmmaking left him oddly out of step with the times. While Coppola was in the Philippines filming *Apocalypse Now,* a brilliant though self-indulgent, self-destructive venture of Wellesian proportions, his protégés Lucas and Spielberg were busy refining the New Hollywood's Bruce aesthetic (via *Star Wars* and *Close Encounters*), while replacing the director-as-author with a director-as-superstar ethos.

The emergence of star directors like Lucas and Spielberg evinced not only the growing salaries and leverage of top talent, but also the increasing influence of Hollywood's top agents and talent agencies. The kind of packaging done by ICM on *Jaws* was fast becoming the rule on high-stakes projects, with ICM and another powerful agency, Creative Artists Associates (CAA), relying on aggressive packaging to compete with the venerable William Morris Agency. Interestingly enough, both ICM and CAA were created in 1974—ICM via merger and CAA by five young agents who bolted William Morris and, led by Michael Ovitz, set out to revamp the industry and upgrade the power and status of the agent-packager. For the most part they succeeded, and consequently top agents, most often from CAA or ICM, became even more important than studio executives in putting together movie projects. And not surprisingly, given this shift in the power structure, an increasing number of top studio executives after the mid-1970s came from the agency ranks.

Yet another significant mid-1970s industry trend was the elimination of tax loopholes and write-offs which had provided incentives for investors, especially those financing independent films. This cut down the number of innovative and offbeat films, although by now the critical mass of cinephiles and art cinema theaters was sufficient to sustain a vigorous alternative cinema. This conservative turn coincided with an upswing in defensive market tactics, notably an increase in sequels, series, reissues, and remakes. From 1964 to 1968, sequels and reissues combined accounted for just under five percent of all Hollywood releases. From 1974 to 1978, they comprised 17.5 percent. *Jaws,* for instance, was reissued in 1976 (as was *The Exorcist*), generating another $16 million in rentals, and in 1978 the first of several sequels, *Jaws 2,* was released, returning $49.3 million in rentals and clearly securing the Jaws "franchise."[27]

Another crucial dimension of the New Hollywood's mid-1970s emergence was the relationship between cinema and television, which was redefined altogether by three distinct developments. The first involved TV advertising which, incredibly enough, had not been an important factor in movie marketing up to that time. A breakthrough of sorts occurred in 1974 with the reissue of a low-budget independent 1971 feature, *Billy Jack,* whose director and star, Tom Laughlin, successfully sued Warner Bros. for not sufficiently promoting the film on its initial release. For the 1974 reissue, according to *Variety,* "Laughlin compelled Warners to try what was then a revolutionary marketing tactic: 'Billy Jack' received massive amounts of tv advertising support, an unheard of practice at the time."[28] The film went on to earn $32.5 million in rentals, after generating only $4 million in its initial release. This tactic gained further credibility with the *Jaws* campaign and others, soon becoming standard practice and taking motion picture marketing into a new era.

A second crucial development grew out of the FCC's 1972 Report and Order on Cable Television and the 1975 launch of SATCOM I, which effectively ended the three-network stranglehold over commercial television.[29] Pay-cable services started slowly after the 1972 ruling, but the launching of America's first commercially available geo-stationary orbit satellite—and the August 1975 decision by Home Box Office (HBO) to go onto SATCOM—changed all that. HBO immediately became a truly nationwide "movie channel" and a key player in the ancillary movie market. Cable TV proved to be a boon to Hollywood in another way as well, thanks to the FCC's "Must Carry" and "Prime Time Access" rules which increased the demand for syndicated series and movies. That in turn sent syndication prices soaring, providing another windfall for those studios producing TV series.

An even more radical change in Hollywood's relationship with television came with the introduction in 1975 of Sony's Betamax videotape recorder, thus initiating the "home-video revolution." In 1977 Matsushita, the Japanese parent company of Pioneer, JVC, and other consumer electronics companies, introduced its "video home system" (VHS), setting off a battle for the home-video market. Matsushita's VHS format prevailed for several reasons: VHS was less expensive (though technically inferior), more flexible and efficient in off-the-air recording, and Matsushita was more savvy and aggressive in acquiring "software" (i.e., the rights to movie titles) as a means of pushing its hardware.[30]

While Hollywood's initial response to the "Japanese threat" was predictably (and characteristically) negative, it became increasingly evident that the key home-video commodity was the Hollywood film—and particularly the blockbuster hit with its vast multi-media potential. And there was plenty to drive these new media industries, as Hollywood's blockbuster mentality reestablished itself with a vengeance in 1977–1978. Total domestic grosses, which had reached $2 billion for the first time in 1975, surged to $2.65 billion in 1977 and $2.8 billion in 1978, a 40 percent climb in only three years, with hits like *Star Wars, Grease, Close Encounters, Superman,* and *Saturday Night Fever* doing record business. From *The Sound of Music* in 1965 through 1976, only seven pictures (including *Jaws*) had returned $50 million in rentals; in 1977–1978 nine films surpassed that mark.

While *Star Wars* was the top hit of the period, doing $127 million in rentals in 1977 and then another $38 million as a reissue in 1978, *Saturday Night Fever* was, in its own way, an equally significant and symptomatic New Hollywood blockbuster. The film did well at the box office ($74 million in rentals) and signaled both the erosion of various industry barriers and also the multimedia potential of movie hits. The film starred TV sitcom star John Travolta, the first of many "cross-over" stars of the late-seventies and eighties. The Bee Gees soundtrack dominated the pop charts and album sales, and along with the film helped spur the "disco craze" in the club scene and recording industry. *Saturday Night Fever* also keyed the shift from the traditional Hollywood musical to the "music movie," a dominant eighties form, and was an obvious precursor to MTV.

In terms of story, *Saturday Night Fever* was yet another male coming-of-age film, centering on the Travolta character's quest for freedom, self-expression, and the Big Time as a dancer on Broadway. The age-old male initiation rite had found new life in Hollywood with the success of *The Graduate* and the emergent youth market, and proved exceptionally well suited to changes in the industry and the marketplace during the 1970s. One measure of its adaptability and appeal was *Star Wars,* which charts Luke Skywalker's initiation into manhood in altogether different terms—though here too the coming-of-age story, while providing the spine of the film, is developed in remarkably superficial terms. Indeed, *Star Wars* is so fast-paced ("breathtaking," in movie ad-speak) and resolutely plot-driven that character depth and development are scarcely on the narrative agenda.

This emphasis on plot over character marks a significant departure from classical Hollywood films, including *The Godfather* and even *Jaws,* wherein plot tended to emerge more organically as a function of the drives, desires, motivations, and goals of the central characters. In *Star Wars* and its myriad successors, however, particularly male action-adventure films, characters (even "the hero") are essentially plot functions. *The Godfather* and *Star Wars,* for example, are in many ways quite similar but ultimately very different kinds of stories. Like *Star Wars, The Godfather* is itself a male action film, a drama of succession, and a coming-of-age story centering on Michael's ascension to warrior status by fighting the "gang wars." Both films have a mythic dimension, and are in fact variations on the Arthurian legend. But where *Star Wars* is so obviously and inexorably plot-driven, *The Godfather* develops its story in terms of character— initially Don Corleone, then sons Sonny and Michael, and finally Michael alone—whose decisions and actions define the narrative trajectory of the film.

This is not to say that *Star Wars* does not "work" as a narrative, but that the way it works may indicate a shift in the nature of film narrative. From *The Godfather* to *Jaws* to *Star Wars,* we see films that are increasingly plot-driven, increasingly visceral, kinetic, and fast-paced, increasingly reliant on special effects, increasingly "fantastic" (and thus apolitical), and increasingly targeted at younger audiences. And significantly enough, the lack of complex characters or plot in *Star Wars* opens the film to other possibilities, notably its radical amalgamation of genre conventions and its elaborate play of cinematic references. The film, as J. Hoberman has said, "pioneered the genre pastiche—synthesizing a methology so soulless that its most human characters were a pair of robots."[31] The hell-bent narrative careens from one genre-coded episode to another—from Western to war film to vine-swinging adventure—and also effectively melds different styles and genres in individual sequences. The bar scene early on which introduces Han Solo's character, for instance, is an inspired amalgam of Western, film noir, hardboiled detective, and sci fi. Thus the seemingly one-dimensional characters and ruthlessly linear chase-film plotting are offset by a purposeful incoherence which actually "opens" the film to different readings (and readers), allowing for multiple interpretive strategies and thus broadening the potential audience appeal. This is reinforced by the film's oddly nostalgic quality, due mainly to its evocations of old movie serials and TV series (*Flash Gordon, Captain Video,* and so on), references that undoubtedly are lost on younger viewers but relished by their cineliterate parents and senior siblings.

Like *Jaws*, Lucas's space epic is a masterwork of narrative technique and film technology. It too features an excessive John Williams score and signature musical theme, and Lucas's general attention to sound and audio effects was as widely praised as the visuals. Indeed, while the film was shut out in its major Oscar nominations (best picture, director, and screenplay), it won Academy Awards for editing, art direction, costume design, visual effects, and musical score, along with a special achievement award for sound effects editing. And although *Star Wars* was the twenty-first feature to be released with a Dolby soundtrack, it was the first to induce theater owners to install Dolby sound systems.[32] There were countless commercial tie-ins, as well as a multi-billion dollar licensing and merchandising bonanza. And strictly as a movie franchise it had tremendous legs, as this inventory of its first decade well indicates:

May 1977   *Star Wars* released
July 1978   *Star Wars* reissue #1
May 1979   *Star Wars* reissue #2
May 1980   *Star Wars* sequel #1: *The Empire Strikes Back*
Apr 1981   *Star Wars* reissue #3
May 1982   *Star Wars* available on videocassette
Aug 1982   *Star Wars* reissue #4
Feb 1983   *Star Wars* appears on pay-cable TV
May 1983   *Star Wars* sequel #2: *Return of the Jedi*
Feb 1984   *Star Wars* on network TV
Mar 1985   *Star Wars* trilogy screened in 8 cities
Jan 1987   "Star Tours" opens at Disneyland[33]

The promise of *Jaws* was confirmed by *Star Wars*, the only other film at the time to surpass $100 million in rentals. *Star Wars* also secured Lucas's place with Spielberg as charter member of "Hollywood's delayed New Wave," as J. Hoberman put it, a group of brash young filmmakers (Brian DePalma, John Landis, Lawrence Kasdan, John Carpenter, et al.) steeped in movie lore whose "cult blockbusters" and genre hybrids elevated "the most vital and disreputable genres of their youth . . . to cosmic heights."[34] Perhaps inevitably, Lucas and Spielberg decided to join forces—a decision they made, as legend has it, while vacationing in Hawaii in May 1977, a week before the release of *Star Wars*, and during a break between the shooting and editing of *Close Encounters*. Lucas was mulling over an idea for a movie serial about the exploits of an adventurer-anthropologist; Spielberg loved the idea, and he convinced Lucas to write and produce the first installment, and to let him direct.[35]

The result, of course, was *Raiders of the Lost Ark*, the huge 1981 hit that established the billion-dollar Indiana Jones franchise and further solidified the two filmmakers in the New Hollywood pantheon. Indeed, whether working together or on their own projects—notably Spielberg on *E.T.* and Lucas on the *Star Wars* sequels—the two virtually rewrote the box-office record books in the late 1970s and 1980s. With the release of their third Indiana Jones collaboration in 1989, Lucas and Spielberg could claim eight of the ten biggest hits in movie history, all of them surpassing $100 million in rentals.[36] Seven of those hits came out in the decade following the release of *Jaws,* a period that Hoberman has aptly termed "ten years that shook the world" of cinema, and that A.D. Murphy calls "the modern era of super-blockbuster films."[37]

Into the 1980s

The importance of the Lucas and Spielberg super-blockbusters can hardly be overstated, considering their impact on theatrical and video markets in the U.S., which along with the rapidly expanding global entertainment market went into overdrive in the 1980s. After surpassing $2 billion in 1975, Hollywood's domestic theatrical revenues climbed steadily from $2.75 billion in 1980 to $5 billion in both 1989 and 1990. And remarkably enough, this steady theatrical growth throughout the 1980s was outpaced rather dramatically by various "secondary markets," particularly pay-cable and home video. During the 1980s, the number of U.S. households with VCRs climbed from 1.85 million (one home in 40) to 62 million (two-thirds of all homes). Pre-recorded videocassette sales rose from only three million in 1980 to 220 million in 1990—an increase of 6,500 percent—while the number of cable households rose from 19.6 million in 1980 to 55 million in 1990, with pay subscriptions increasing from 9 million to 42 million during the decade.[38]

This growth has been a tremendous windfall for Hollywood, since both the pay-cable and home-video industries have been driven primarily by feature films, and in fact have been as hit-driven as the theatrical market. Through all the changes during the 1980s, domestic theatrical release remained the launching pad for blockbuster hits, and it established a movie's value in virtually all other secondary or ancillary markets. Yet even with the record-setting box-office revenues throughout the 1980s, the portion of the Hollywood majors' income from theater rentals actually declined, while total revenues have soared. According to Robert Levin, president of international motion picture marketing for Disney, the domestic box office in 1978 comprised just over half (54 percent) of the majors' overall income, with a mere 4 percent coming from pay-cable and home video combined. By 1986, box-office revenues comprised barely one quarter (28 percent) of the majors' total, with pay-cable and home video combining for over half (12 percent and 40 percent respectively).[39] Home-video revenues actually exceeded worldwide theatrical revenues that year, 1986, and by decade's end cassette revenues alone actually doubled domestic box-office revenues.[40]

Another crucial secondary market for Hollywood has been the box office overseas, particularly in Europe. While the overseas pay-TV and home-video markets are still taking shape, European theatrical began surging in 1985 and reached record levels in 1990, when a number of top hits—including *Pretty Woman, Total Recall, The Little Mermaid,* and *Dances With Wolves*—actually did better box office in Europe than in the U.S.[41] And *Forbes* magazine has estimated that the European theatrical market will double by 1995, as multiplexing picks up in Western Europe and as new markets open in Eastern Europe.[42]

With the astounding growth of both theatrical and video markets and the continued stature of the Hollywood-produced feature, the American movie industry has become increasingly stable in the late 1980s. What's more, the blockbuster mentality seems to have leveled off somewhat. In the early 1980s, one or two huge hits tended to dominate the marketplace, doing well over $100 million and far outdistancing other top hits. From 1986–1990, however, the number of super-blockbuster hits dropped while the number of mid-range hits earning $10 million or more in rentals increased significantly, as did the number returning $50 million or more— still the measure of blockbuster-hit status. From 1975 to 1985 ten films earned $100 million or more in rentals; there have been only four since. Meanwhile, the number of films earning $50 million or more has climbed considerably. From 1965 to 1975, only six reached this mark; from 1976 to 1980 there were 13; from 1981 to 1985 there were 17. From 1986 to 1990, 30 films surpassed $50 million in rentals.

As the economic stakes have risen so have production and marketing costs. The average "negative cost" (i.e., money spent to complete the actual film) on all major studio releases climbed from $9.4 million in 1980 to $26.8 million in 1990. Over the same period, average costs for prints and advertising rose from $4.3 million per film in 1980 to $11.6 million in 1990.[43] The rise in production costs is due largely to two dominant factors: an increased reliance on special effects and the soaring salaries paid to top talent, especially stars. The rise in marketing costs reflects Hollywood's deepening commitment to saturation booking and advertising, which has grown more expensive with the continued multiplex phenomenon and the increased ad opportunities due to cable and VCRs. The number of indoor theaters in the U.S. increased from about 14,000 in 1980 to over 22,000 in 1990, which meant that widespread nationwide release required anywhere from 1,000 to 2,700 prints, at roughly $2,500 per print. But the primary reason for rising marketing costs is TV advertising, particularly for high-stakes blockbusters. In 1990, for example, well over $20 million was spent on TV ads alone for *Dick Tracy, Total Recall,* and *Die Hard 2.*[44]

While this may seem like fiscal madness, there is method in it. Consider the performance of the three top hits of the "blockbuster Summer" in 1989, Hollywood's single biggest season ever. In a four-week span beginning Memorial Day weekend, *Indiana Jones and the Last Crusade, Ghostbusters II,* and *Batman* enjoyed successive weekend releases in at least 2,300 theaters in the U.S. and Canada after heavy TV advertising. Each of these pre-sold entertainment machines set a new box-office record for its opening weekend, culminating in *Batman's* three-day ticket sales of $40.5 million. In an era when $100 million in gross revenues is one measure of a blockbuster hit, it took *Indiana Jones* just 19 days to reach that total; it took *Batman* 11. And like so many recent hits, all three underwent a "fast burn" at the box office. Compare these week-to-week box-office revenues on Hollywood's two all-time summer hits, *E.T.* (1982) and *Batman,* which well indicate certain crucial 1980s market trends.[45]

	wk 1	2	3	4	5	6	7	8	9	10
E.T.	$22m	22	26	24	23	23	19	19	16	15
Batman	70	52	30	24	18	13	11	8	5	4

E.T. earned another $100 million at the box office, which in 1982 was its only serious source of domestic income, while *Batman* was pulled from domestic theatrical for the home-video market—where it generated another $179 million in revenues.[46] Few recent films match *Batman's* home-video performance, and for that matter, few match its box-office legs, either. In 1990, no saturation summer releases except *Ghost* and *Pretty Woman* had any real pull beyond five weeks, although a number of films (*Total Recall, Die Hard 2, Dick Tracy*) grossed over $100 million at the box office.

The three top hits of 1990, *Home Alone, Ghost,* and *Pretty Woman,* bucked the calculated blockbuster trend and demonstrated why Hollywood relies on a steady output of "smaller" (i.e., less expensive) films which, mainly via word of mouth rather than massive pre-selling and promotion, might emerge as surprise hits. Such "sleepers" are most welcome, of course, even in this age of high-cost, high-tech, high-volume behemoths, and they invariably are well exploited once they begin to take off—as were those three surprise hits of 1990. And each undoubtedly will spawn a sequel of calculated blockbuster proportions, with the studio hoping not only for a profitable follow-up but for the kind of success that MGM/UA had with *Rocky,* a modest, offbeat sleeper in 1976 that became a billion-dollar entertainment franchise.

Many have touted the three 1990 hits as a return to reason in Hollywood filmmaking, including Disney production chief Jeffrey Katzenberg in a now legendary interoffice memo of January 1991. Katzenberg warned of "the 'blockbuster mentality' that has gripped our industry," and encouraged a return to "the kind of modest, story-driven movie we tended to make in our salad days."[47] The memo was leaked to the press and caused quite a stir, but scarcely signaled any real change at Disney or anywhere else. *Variety* subtly underscored this point by running excerpts from the memo directly below an even more prominent story with the banner headline, "Megabudgets Boom Despite Talk of Doom." That story inventoried the numerous high-cost Hollywood films "still being greenlighted," including several at Disney.[48]

In one sense, Katzenberg's memo was a rationale for *Dick Tracy,* the 1990 Disney blockbuster that cost $46 million to produce and another $55 million to market and release, with $44 million spent on advertising and promotion alone. Those figures were disclosed some two months before Katzenberg's memo and startled many industry observers, since by then the film had run its theatrical course and returned only about $60 million to Disney in rentals. But Hollywood insiders (including Katzenberg, no doubt) well understood the logic, given today's entertainment marketplace. As one competing executive told the *New York Times,* Disney had to "build awareness" of the Tracy story and character not simply to sell the film, but to establish "the value of a new character in the Disney family . . . so that it could be brought back in a sequel and used in Disney's theme parks."[49]

The future of the Tracy franchise remains to be seen, but one can hardly fault Disney for making the investment. Lip service to scaleddown moviemaking aside, Hollywood's blockbuster mentality is more entrenched now than ever, the industry is more secure, and certain rules of the movie marketplace are virtually set in stone. The first is William Goldman's 1983 axiom, "nobody knows anything," which is quoted with increasing frequency these years as it grows ever more evident that, despite all the market studies and promotional strategies, the kind of public response that generates a bona fide hit simply cannot be manufactured, calculated, or predicted.[50] The studios have learned to hedge their bets and increase the odds, however, and thus these other rules—all designed not only to complement but to counter the Goldman Rule.

The most basic of these rules is that only star vehicles with solid production values have any real chance at the box office (and thus in secondary markets as well). Such films nowadays cost $20 to $30 million, and will push $50 million if top stars, special effects, and/or logistical difficulties are involved. The next rule concerns what is termed the "reward risk" factor, and holds that reaping the potential benefits of a hit requires heavy up-front spending on marketing as well as production. A corollary to this is that risk can be minimized via pre-sold pictures, and today the most effective pre-selling involves previous movie hits or other familiar media products (TV series, pop songs, comic books). An aesthetic corollary holds that films with minimal character complexity or development and by-the-numbers plotting (especially male action pictures) are the most readily reformulated and thus the most likely to be parlayed into a full-blown franchise.

Another cardinal rule is that a film's theatrical release, with its attendant media exposure, creates a cultural commodity that might be regenerated in any number of media forms: Perhaps in pop music, and not only as a hit single or musical score; note that *Batman* had two soundtrack albums and *Dick Tracy* had three. Perhaps as an arcade game, a $7 billion industry in 1990; note that *Hook* and *Terminator 2* both were released simultaneously as movies and video games. Perhaps as a theme park ride; note that Disney earns far more on its theme parks than on motion pictures and television, and that the hottest new Disney World attraction is "Toon Town," adapted from *Who Framed Roger Rabbit?*[51] Perhaps as a comic book or related item; note that the Advance Comics Special Batlist offered 214 separate pieces of *Batman*-related paraphernalia.[52] Perhaps in "novelized" form, with print (and audiocassette) versions of movie hits regularly becoming worldwide best-sellers; note that Simon and Schuster, a Paramount subdivision and the nation's largest bookseller, has devoted an entire division to its Star Trek publications.

These rules are evident not only in today's multimedia worldwide blockbusters, but also in the structure and operations of international corporate giants that produce and market them. Competing successfully in today's high-stakes entertainment marketplace requires an operation that is not only well financed and productive, both also diversified and well coordinated. John Mickelthwait of the *Economist* has written that an entertainment company "needs financial muscle to produce enough software to give itself a decent chance for bringing in a hit, and marketing muscle to make the most of that hit when it happens."[53] Thus there has been a trend toward "tight diversification" and "synergy" in the recent merger-and-acquisitions wave, bringing movie studios into direct play with television production companies, network and cable TV, music and recording companies, and book, magazine, and newspaper publishers, and possibly even with games, toys, theme parks, and electronics hardware manufacturers as well.

So obviously enough, diversification and conglomeration remain key factors in the entertainment industry, though today's media empires are much different than those of the 1960s and 1970s like Gulf & Western, Kinney, and Transamerica. Those top-heavy, widely diversified conglomerates sold out, "downsized," or otherwise regrouped to achieve tighter diversification. Gulf & Western, for instance, sold all but its media holdings by the late 1980s and changed its corporate name to Paramount Communications. Kinney created a media subsidiary in Warner Communications, which also downsized in the early 1980s—only to expand via a $13 billion marriage with Time in 1989 (to avoid a hostile $12 billion takeover by Paramount), thereby creating Time Warner, the world's largest multimedia company and a model of synergy, with holdings in movies, TV production, cable, records, and book and magazine publishing. Because movies drive the global multimedia marketplace, a key holding for any media conglomerate is a motion picture studio; but there is no typical media conglomerate these days due to the widening range of entertainment markets and rapid changes in media technology.

Conglomeration has taken on another new dimension in that several studios have been purchased by foreign media companies: Fox by Rupert Murdoch's News Corporation in 1985, Columbia by Sony in 1989, and MCA/Universal by Matsushita in 1990. The Fox purchase may have greater implications for TV than cinema, given the creation of a "fourth network" in American and its expansion into Europe. The Sony and Matsushita buyouts take the cinema-television synergy in yet another direction, since this time the two consumer electronics giants are battling over domination of the multi-billion-dollar high definition television (HDTV) market. Columbia and MCA gave the two firms sizable media libraries and active production companies, which may well give them an edge in the race not only to develop but to sell HDTV.

The Sony-Columbia and Matsushita-MCA deals are significant in terms of "talent" as well. Beyond the $3.5 billion Sony paid for Columbia, the company also spent roughly $750 million for the services of Peter Guber and Jon Peters, two successful producers (*Batman, Rain Man,* et al.) then under contact to Warners. This underscored the importance of corporate and studio management in the diversified, globalized, synergized marketplace. Indeed, the most successful companies in the mid-to-late 1980s—Paramount, Disney, Warners, and Universal—all enjoyed consistent, capable executive leadership. Successful studio management involves not only positioning movies in a global multimedia market, but also dealing effectively with top talent and their agents, which introduces other human factors into the New Hollywood equation. These factors were best indicated by the role of Michael Ovitz in both the Sony and Matsushita deals. Co-founder and chief executive of CAA, Ovitz is the most powerful agent in Hollywood's premiere agency. He was a key advisor in the Sony-Columbia deal, and in fact he packaged *Rain Man* during the negotiations and later helped arrange the Guber-Peters transaction. And Ovitz quite literally brokered the Matsushita-MCA deal, acting as the sole go-between during the year-long negotiations.[54]

Ovtiz's rise to power in the New Hollywood has been due to various factors: CAA's steadily expanding client list, its packaging of top talent in highly desirable movie packages, and its capacity to secure favorable terms for its clients when cutting movie deals. In perhaps no other industry is the "art of the deal" so important, and in that regard Ovitz is Hollywood's consummate artist. He also is a master at managing relationships—whether interpersonal, institutional, or corporate, as the Columbia and MCA deals both demonstrate. And more than any other single factor, Ovitz's and CAA's success has hinged on the increasingly hit-driven nature of the entertainment industry, and in turn on the star-driven nature of top industry products.

The "star system" is as old as the movie industry itself, of course. "Marquee value," "bankable" talent, and "star vehicles" have always been vital to Hollywood's market strategy, just as the "star persona" has keyed both the narrative and production economies of moviemaking. In the classical era, in fact, studios built their entire production and marketing operations around a few prime star-genre formulas. In the New Hollywood, however, where fewer films carry much wider commercial and cultural impact, and where personas are prone to multimedia reincarnation, the star's commercial value, cultural cache, and creative clout have increased enormously. The most obvious indication of this is the rampant escalation of star salaries during the 1980s—a phenomenon often traced to Sylvester Stallone's $15 million paycheck in 1983 for *Rocky IV.*[55] Interestingly enough, many (if not most) of the seminal New Hollywood blockbusters were not star-driven; in fact many secured stardom for their lead actors. But as the blockbuster sequels and multimedia markets coalesced in the early 1980s, both the salary scale and narrative agency of top stars rose dramatically—to a point where Stallone, Arnold Schwarzenegger, Bruce Willis, Michael Douglas, Eddie Murphy, Sean Connery, and Kevin Costner earn seven or even eight figures per film, having become not only genres but franchises unto themselves, and where "star vehicles" are often simply that: stylish, careening machines designed for their star-drivers which, in terms of plot and character development, tend to go nowhere fast.

Not surprisingly, the studios bemoan their dwindling profit margins due to increased talent costs while top talent demand—and often get—"participation" deals on potential blockbusters. CAA's package for *Hook* gave Dustin Hoffman, Robin Williams, and Steven Spielberg a reported 40 percent of the box-office take, and Jack Nicholson's escalating 15 to 20 percent of the gross on *Batman* paid him upwards of $50 million.[56]

While studio laments about narrowing margins are understandable, so too are agency efforts to secure a piece of the box-office take for their clients, particularly in light of the limited payoff for stars and other talent in ancillary markets and in licensing and merchandising deals. And given the potential long-term payoff of a franchise-scale blockbuster, the stars' demands are as inevitable as the studios' grudging willingness to accommodate them. As Geraldine Fabrikant suggests in a *New York Times* piece on soaring production costs: "Some studios can more easily justify paying higher prices for talent these days because, with the consolidation of the media industry and the rise of integrated entertainment conglomerates that distribute movies, books, recordings, television programming and magazines, they have more outlets through which to recoup their investments."[57]

The Economics and Aesthetics of the New Hollywood

This brings us back, yet again, to the New Hollywood blockbuster's peculiar status as what Eileen Meehan has aptly termed a "commercial intertext." As Meehan suggests, today's conglomerates "view every project as a multimedia production line," and thus *Batman* "is best understood as a multimedia, multimarket sales campaign."[58] Others have noted the increased interplay of moviemaking and advertising, notably Mark Crispin Miller in a cover story for the *Atlantic,* "Hollywood: The Ad." Miller opens with an indictment of the "product placement" trend in movies (a means of offsetting production costs which, as he suggests, often brings the narrative to a dead halt), and he goes on to discuss other areas where movies and advertising—especially TV advertising—have begun to merge. Like TV ads, says Miller, movies today aspire to a total "look" and seem more designed than directed, often by filmmakers segueing from studio to ad agency. And now that movies are more likely to be seen on a VCR than a theater screen, cinematic technique is adjusted accordingly, conforming with the small screen's "most hypnotic images," its ads. Visual and spatial scale are downsized, action is repetitiously foregrounded and centered, pace and transitions are quicker, music and montage are more prevalent, and slick production values and special effects abound.[59]

While Miller's view of the cinema as the last bastion of high culture under siege by the twin evils of TV and advertising displays a rather limited understanding of the contemporary culture industries, there is no question but that movie and ad techniques are intermingling. In fact, one might argue that the New Hollywood's calculated blockbusters are themselves massive advertisements for their product lines—a notion that places a very different value on their one-dimensional characters, mechanical plots, and high-gloss style. This evokes that New Hollywood buzzword, "high concept," a term best defined perhaps by its chief progenitor, Steven Spielberg, in an interview back in 1978: "What interests me more than anything else is the idea. If a person can tell me the idea in twenty-five words or less, it's going to be a good movie."[60] And a pretty good ad campaign as well—whether condensed into a 30-second movie trailer or as a feature-length plug for any number of multimedia reiterations.

This paradoxical reduction and reiteration of blockbuster movie narratives points up the central, governing contradiction in contemporary cinema. On the one hand, the seemingly infinite capacity for multimedia reiteration of a movie hit redefines textual boundaries, creates a dynamic commercial intertext that is more process than product, and involves the audience(s) in the creative process—not only as multimarket consumers but also as mediators in the play of narrative signification. On the other hand, the actual movie "itself," if indeed it can be isolated and understood as such (which is questionable at best), often has been reduced and stylized to a point where, for some observers, it scarcely even qualifies as a narrative.

Critic Richard Schickel, for instance, has stated: "In the best of all possible marketing worlds the movie will inspire some simple summarizing graphic treatment, adaptable to all media, by which it can be instantly recognized the world over, even by subliterates."[61] The assembly-line process in the studio era demanded that story ideas be progressively refined into a classical three-act structure of exposition, complication, and resolution. But nowadays, says Schickel, "Hollywood seems to have lost or abandoned the art of narrative. . . . [Filmmakers] are generally not refining stories at all, they are spicing up 'concepts' (as they like to call them), refining gimmicks, making sure there are no complexities to fur our tongues when it comes time to spread the word of mouth." Schickel argues that all genres have merged into two meta-categories, comedies and action-adventure films, both of which offer "a succession of undifferentiated sensations, lucky or unlucky accidents, that have little or nothing to do with whatever went before or is about to come next," with a mere "illusion of forward motion" created via music and editing.[62]

Schickel excuses his "geriatric grumble" while demeaning "youthful" moviegoers for their lack of "very sophisticated tastes or expectations when it comes to narrative," and his nod to audience fragmentation along generational lines raises a few important issues.[63] To begin with, younger viewers—despite "grownup" biases about limited attention spans, depth of feeling, and intellectual development—are far more likely to be active multimedia players, consumers, and semioticians, and thus to gauge a movie in intertextual terms and to appreciate in it a richness and complexity that may well be lost on middle-aged movie critics. In fact, given the penchant these years to pre-sell movies via other popular culture products (rock songs, comic books, TV series, etc.), chances are that younger, media-literate viewers encounter a movie in an already-activated narrative process. The size, scope, and emotional charge of the movie and its concurrent ad campaign certainly privilege the big screen "version" of the story, but the movie itself scarcely begins or ends the textual cycle.

This in turn raises the issue of narrative "integrity," which in classical Hollywood was a textual feature directly related to the integrity of both the "art form" and the system of production. While movies during the studio era certainly had their intertextual qualities, these were incidental and rarely undermined the internal coherence of the narrative itself. While many (perhaps most) New Hollywood films still aspire to this kind of narrative integrity, the blockbuster tends to be intertextual and purposefully incoherent—virtually of necessity, given the current conditions of cultural production and consumption. Put another way, the vertical integration of classical Hollywood, which ensured a closed industrial system and coherent narrative, has given way to "horizontal integration" of the New Hollywood's tightly diversified media conglomerates, which favors texts strategically "open" to multiple readings and multimedia reiteration.

These calculated blockbusters utterly dominate the movie industry, but they also promote alternative films and filmmaking practices in a number of ways. Because the majors' high-cost, high-stakes projects require a concentration of resources and limit overall output, they tend to foster product demand. This demand is satisfied, for the most part, by moderately priced star vehicles financed and distributed by the majors, which may emerge as surprise hits but essentially serve to keep the industry machinery running, to develop new talent, and to maintain a steady supply of dependable mainstream product. Complementing these routine features, and far more interesting from a critical and cultural perspective, are the low-cost films from independent outfits like Mirimax and New Line Cinema. In fact, the very market fragmentation which the studios' franchise projects are designed to exploit and overcome, these independents are exploiting in a very different way via their small-is-beautiful, market-niche approach.

Mirimax, for instance, has carved out a niche by financing or buying and then distributing low-budget art films and imports like *sex, lies and videotape, My Left Foot, Cinema Paradiso,* and *Tie Me Up, Tie Me Down* to a fairly consistent art film crowd. New Line's strategy is more wide-ranging, targeting an array of demographic groups and taste cultures from art film aficionados and environmentalists to born-again Christians and wrestling fans. If any one of New Line's products takes off at the box office, it's liable to be a teen pic like *Teenage Mutant Ninja Turtles,* which returned $67 million in rentals in 1990. While fully exploiting that hit was a real challenge for a company like New Line, an even bigger challenge, no doubt, was resisting the urge to expand their operations, upgrade their product, and compete with the majors—an impulse that proved disastrous for many independent companies during the 1980s.[64]

Thus we might see the New Hollywood as producing three different classes of movie: the calculated blockbuster designed with the multimedia marketplace and franchise status in mind, the mainstream A-class star vehicle with sleeper-hit potential, and the low-cost independent feature targeted for a specific market and with little chance of anything more than "cult film" status. These three classes of movie have corresponding ranks of auteurs, from the superstar directors at the "high end" like Spielberg and Lucas, whose knack for engineering hits has transformed their names into virtual trademarks, to those filmmakers on the margins like Gus Van Sant, John Sayles, and the Coen brothers, whose creative control and personal style are considerably less constrained by commercial imperatives. And then there are the established genre auteurs like Jonathan Demme, Martin Scorsese, David Lynch, and Woody Allen who, like Ford and Hitchcock and the other top studio directors of old, are the most perplexing and intriguing cases—each of them part visionary cineaste and part commercial hack, whose best films flirt with hit status and critique the very genres (and audiences) they exploit.

Despite its stratification, the New Hollywood is scarcely a balkanized or rigidly class-bound system. On the contrary, these classes of films and filmmakers are in a state of dynamic tension with one another and continually intermingle. Consider, for instance, the two recent forays into that most contemptible of genres, the psycho-killer/stalk-and-slash film, by Jonathan Demme in *The Silence of the Lambs* and Martin Scorsese in *Cape Fear*. Each film took the genre into uncharted narrative and thematic territory; each was a cinematic tour-de-force, enhancing both the aesthetic and commercial value of the form; and each thoroughly terrified audiences, thereby reinforcing the genre's capacity to explore the dark recesses of the collective American psyche and underscoring the cinema's vital contact with its public.

Besides winning the Oscar for "Best Picture of 1991," *Silence of the Lambs* emerged as a solid international hit, indicating the potential global currency of the genre while raising some interesting questions about the New Hollywood's high-end products vis-à-vis the American cultural experience. With the rapid development of multiplex theaters and home video in Europe and the Far East, and the concurrent advances in advertising and marketing, one can readily foresee the "global release" of calculated blockbusters far beyond the scale of a *Batman* or *Terminator 2*, let alone a surprise hit like *The Silence of the Lambs*. This may require a very different kind of product, effectively segregating the calculated blockbuster from the studios' other feature output and redefining the Hollywood cinema as an American culture industry. But it's much more likely that the New Hollywood and its characteristic blockbuster product will endure, given the social and economic development in the major overseas markets, the survival instincts and overall economic stability of the Hollywood studios, and the established global appeal of its products.

2

Reclaiming the Social: Pedagogy, Resistance, and Politics in Celluloid Culture

Henry A. Giroux

We live in an age in which the new conservativism that has reigned in the United States for the last decade has consistently struggled to depoliticize politics while simultaneously attempting to politicize popular culture and the institutions that make up daily life. The depoliticizing of politics is evident, in part, in the ways in which the new conservative formations use the electronic technologies of image, sound, and text not only to alter traditional systems of time, space, and history, but also to displace serious political issues to the realm of the aesthetic and the personal.[1] In this context, discourses of style, form, and authenticity are employed to replace questions concerning how power is mobilized by diverse dominant groups to oppress, marginalize, and exploit large portions of the American population. Understood in ideological terms, the depoliticizing of politics is about the attempt to construct citizens who believe that they have little or no control over their lives: that issues of identity, culture, and agency bear no relationship to or "acknowledgment of mediations: material, historical, social, psychological, and ideological" (Solomon–Godeau, xxviii). Hence, the depoliticizing of the political represents a complex, though incomplete, effort by the new conservatism to secure a politics of representation that attempts to render the workings of its own ideology indiscernible. That is, dominant groups seize upon the dynamics of cultural power to secure their own interests while simultaneously attempting to make the political context and ideological sources of such power invisible.

In the current historical conjuncture there is an ongoing attempt by the forces of the new right to replace the practice of substantive democracy with a democracy of images. At the same time, the discourse of responsible citizenship is subordinated to the marketplace imperatives of choice, consumption, and standardization. This is particularly true with respect to public schools. The Reagan/Bush Administrations have drastically cut financial support for public school programs, systematically attempted to reprivatize the public school sector by sponsoring legislation that would allow public money to be used to support private schooling, and linked educational reforms to the needs of big business.[2] Moreover, the new conservatives have made schooling an intense site of struggle in their efforts to eliminate non-canonical and subordinate cultures as serious objects of knowledge.[3]

The struggle over the economic and political apparatuses of the state has largely been extended principally by new conservative formations to the sphere of culture.[4] Contrary to the conventional left thinking, as Laclau and Mouffe have pointed out, the greatest challenge to the right and its power may be lodged not in the mobilization of universal agents such as the working class or some other oppressed group, but in a cultural struggle in which almost every facet of daily life takes on a degree of undecidability and thus becomes unsettled and open to broader collective dialogue and multiple struggles.

What has become important to recognize is that the new conservative bloc, while firmly controlling the state and its major apparatuses, has turned its attention during the Reagan/Bush era towards the wider terrain of culture and identified as visible targets higher education, public schooling, the art world, and rock music.[5] This is evident in the right-wing blitz organized around issues such as pornography, political correctness, and multiculturalism and testifies to a new level of hegemonic struggle over the institutions and discourses through which a politics of representation is directly linked to the production of mobile fields of knowledge, shifting and multiple social identities, and new cultural formations. The war being waged by the new conservative bloc is not simply over profit or the securing of traditional forms of authority, it is over the emergence of decentered and diverse oppositional discourses, such as feminism, postmodernism, and postcolonialism, that have begun to call into question all of the grand narratives of modernism with its unfettered conviction in science and technology as the engine of progress, its unflinching belief in the humanist subject as the unified agent of history, and its adamant insistence that Western culture is synonymous with the very notion of civilization itself. What is interesting regarding these struggles is that they not only pose an emerging threat to the dominant order, but they also offer a new set of discourses and strategies that are being taken very seriously by the new right. The dominant conservative formations in the United States appear haunted and besieged by the emergence of the discourses and cultures of difference that refuse to remain silent or confined to the margins of history, power, and politics. This new politics of cultural difference has important implications for redefining the notions of hegem-

ony, resistance, and struggles over forms of self and social representation.[6]

Within the paradox of the reality of depoliticization, the politicization
of culture, and the emerging politics of difference, hegemony has to
be read as always fractured, contradictory, and decentered. Moreover,
domination does not present itself as a universal practice, exhausting
those it oppresses. In actuality, hegemonic power can only be understood
in its specificity, in its constant attempt to restructure and refigure its
strengths and weaknesses, and in its continual attempt to recuperate
forms of resistance that are as ongoing as they are different. I believe
that it is precisely in what Jim Collins has called the decentered
power struggles that constitute both hegemonic and counter-hegemonic
movements that new opportunities present themselves for deepening the
pedagogical as a form of cultural politics.

In what follows, I want to examine how the pedagogical can be
taken up as a form of cultural production that reworks the relationship
between cultural texts, teachers, and students. On the one hand, this
means developing a theoretical case for using popular cultural texts
such as film, television, advertisements, music videos, and mass
circulation magazines as serious objects of knowledge related to the
power of self-definition and the struggle for social justice. Equally
important is the necessity to refuse to take up popular culture within
a liberal pedagogical model that reduces its use to a discourse of
relevance or the narrow, methodological imperative to teach the conflicts.[7] On the other hand, I want to reassert the importance of critical
pedagogy as a form of cultural practice which does not simply tell the
student how to think or what to believe, but provides the conditions
for a set of ideological and social relations which engender diverse
possibilities for students to produce rather than simply acquire knowl
edge, to be self-critical about both the positions they describe and the
locations from which they speak, and to make explicit the values that
inform their relations with others as part of a broader attempt to produce
the conditions necessary for either the existing society or a new and
more democratic social order.[8]

As part of examining the relationship between popular culture and
critical pedagogy, I want to avoid using a binary framework that
locates schooling in a context which focuses either on how schools
monolithically reproduce the dominant social order through particular
forms of social and cultural reproduction or how students contest the
dominant society through various forms of resistance. Instead, I want
to analyze radical pedagogy as a theoretical discourse that helps to
illuminate how cultural texts can be understood as part of a complex
and often contradictory set of ideological and material processes through

which the transformation of knowledge, identities, and values takes place. Such texts like schools, in this sense, produce narratives, desires, and subjectivities that are far from homogeneous and in turn encounter students whose own subjectivities are constructed in multiple, complex, and contradictory ways.

Central to such a task are at least three important issues. First, there is the task of redefining teachers as cultural workers, that is, as educators committed to a political project and normatively based discourse that expands the possibility for radical democracy; second, there is the issue of reclaiming, without romanticizing, popular culture as a complex terrain of pedagogical struggle; third, pedagogy must be viewed as the deliberate attempt to produce knowledge, forms of ethical address, and social identities.[9] More specifically, a pedagogy of the popular would take as its objective the interrogation of traditional positivist and modernist notions of the curriculum and canonicity, the rupturing of the universalized view of identity as a privatized consciousness, and the elimination of the view that cultural difference is a threat to civic democratic culture. I will attempt to take up some of these issues by analyzing a class I taught on education and the politics of identity, focusing primarily on the use of the film, *Dead Poets Society*.

Popular cultural texts such as *Dead Poets Society* should be analyzed within the discourse of political economy and transnational capitalism, within social reading formations that inscribed such texts with overdetermined meanings, one being that their function is to entertain rather than signify. Such texts must be analyzed as commodities that implicate even as they are taken up in order to subvert the very system that produces them. But most importantly for my purposes, films such as *Dead Poets Society* are neither the bearers of monolithic themes, nor should they be read simply as sites of conflicting ideologies. On the contrary, rather than reducing such a text to the reified terrain of relevance and teaching the conflicts, it should be posited as a site of struggle over how representations mean differently and what the consequences of such differences might be if they are to matter as part of a wider theoretical, ethical, and political discourse. Secondly, *Dead Poets Society* can be engaged not only to deconstruct how it represents a particular view of the political, but also how it functions to secure specific forms of affective investments. What is it in films such as *Dead Poets Society*, for instance, that mobilize specific desires, identifications, and needs? And finally, how might students engage this film critically as part of a broader discourse of ethics and politics that promotes a deeper understanding of the historical and cultural locations from which they might speak, act, and struggle?

Pedagogy, Resistance, and Celluloid Culture

During the Fall of 1991, I taught an undergraduate class for teachers in training on curriculum and secondary education. The class consisted of mostly white, middle- and upper middle-class students. Most of the work we had been analyzing in the class consisted largely of exposing the role that schools play in the process of social and cultural reproduction. I wanted to go beyond this type of analysis by introducing students to films and other texts in which both teachers and students exhibited forms of resistance in the classroom. One assignment consisted of having the students choose a popular cultural form which addressed the issue of pedagogy and schooling. At issue here was having the students analyze the relationship between their own experiences in schools and those portrayed in popular cultural forms. The class largely decided to focus on Hollywood films, and finally choose to view two films, *Dead Poets Society* and *Stand and Deliver*.

In one sense *Dead Poets Society* was an exemplary film to use pedagogically because it had been suggested by some students as a text which embodied much of what was perceived as the political and pedagogical principles encouraged in the course. That is, the film was comprehended as "living out" the perceived requirements and practices of critical teaching. What became apparent to me was that my students' initial motivations in choosing the film had less to do with an analytical reading of the text than it did with an investment in the film that was largely affective. According to my students, *Dead Poets Society* was valuable as an exemplary model of critical pedagogy because it staked out a terrain of hope, and offered subject positions from within which they could project an image of themselves as future teachers; an image that encouraged *them* to identify themselves as agents rather than as mere technicians. As some students pointed out, the film made them feel good about themselves as teachers-in-the-making.

In my view, the film presented a model of liberal pedagogy, in part, by mobilizing popular sentiment through what Larry Grossberg has called an "affective epidemic." That is, even though the film takes as its central narrative the issue of resistance, its structure undermined a critical reading of its own codes by establishing a strong emotional affinity between the viewers and the progressive teacher portrayed in this film.

The pedagogical challenge presented by *Dead Poets Society* was grounded in making clear the multiple and often contradictory ways in which it ruptured and supported dominant codes regarding issues of knowledge, pedagogy, and resistance. Deconstructing this film was not meant as a pedagogical exercise in canceling the affective and meaning-making investments students brought to it. Nor was my pedagogical approach meant as an attempt to provide a definitive ideological reading of the film. On the contrary, I wanted to address how the mobilization of meaning and affective investments within the film's form and content functioned as part of a broader cultural and pedagogical practice that was neither innocent nor politically neutral. What has to be recognized here is a central dilemma faced by educators who engage the popular as part of a broader pedagogical project. The dilemma is constituted by the need to challenge the structures of meaning and affect within delegitimating the importance of the varied investments mobilized within the students' response to the film. Hence, I wanted to take up the film as a cultural form which produced knowledge in the service of particular forms of authority, proffered conditions for agency which privileged some groups over others, and revealed contradictory and partial insights regarding how oppression works through various aspects of schooling.

Canonicity, Pedagogy, and Resistance in *Dead Poets Society*

Dead Poets Society (1989), directed by Peter Weir and written by Tom Schulman, is set in a boys boarding school, Welton Academy. The opening shots of the film portray Weldon Academy as an exclusive prep school, situated in a picture-postcard setting that tries hard to emulate the beauty and peacefulness of the English countryside. The school itself has all the aesthetic trappings of an Ivy League college. The architecture of the school is monumentalist and Gothic. The students, teachers, and parents are from the ruling class. The parents and students move easily within a cultural capital that signifies privilege, wealth, and power. Social identities in this film are constructed within an unspoken yet legitimating discourse that privileges whiteness, patriarchy, and heterosexuality as the universalizing norms of identity. Precisely because it exists outside of the context of racial difference, whiteness as a basis of privilege in *Dead Poets Society* becomes "invisible" because there is no context to render it visible as a dominant racial category, as a mark of power and identity that refuses to call attention to itself.[10] Set in 1959, the "whiteness" of the faculty and students is an historically accurate representation; however, *Dead Poets Society* suspends the dynamics of historical contingency and specificity within a reactionary nostalgia. An aura of universality radiates through this film which expresses its cultural and political narratives within a mythical, timeless age when the messy relations of democracy, cultural difference, and social struggle were kept in place, or at least out of sight; when aesthetics took precedence over politics, and students (of privilege) were safely cushioned within monastic borders removed from the potentially antagonistic relations of everyday life. The politics and aesthetics of nostalgia in this film mobilize affective identifications and investments in order to secure the authority of a particular history, "that story which institutionally seeks to legitimate a continuum of sense, which as [Walter] Benjamin insisted, has to be blasted apart" (Chambers, 78).

In the opening address to the parents and students of Welton, the headmaster celebrates Welton's record of academic achievement, pointing out that over 75 percent of its graduates go on to attend Ivy League schools. There is no pretense here. Welton is less concerned about teaching its students how to think than it is in preparing them to assume positions of power. Within this context, pedagogy defines itself through a ruthless instrumentalism removed from the progressive goals of creating the conditions for critical agency, ethical accountability, and the obligations of democratic public life. As the film shifts to portray the dynamics of classroom life, it becomes clear that the curriculum is a no frills version of high-culture canonicity, and the pedagogy used by the all-white, male teachers emphasizes a numbing combination of discipline and transmission as the prevailing pedagogical practices.

Initially, the students appear to embrace fully this anesthetized reactionary environment. For instance, on the first day of school they trade stories about having gone to summer school in order to get the edge over their classmates. We see that the routinization and authoritarianism of the school appears to shape every aspect of their lives unproblematically; they appear to be academic zombies living out the projections and wishes of their successful fathers. Moreover, every other older male figure at the school who figures prominently as a surrogate father reinforces the same unproblematic relation to the competitive milieu. It's hardly surprising, then, that before the semester classes ever begin a number of boys decides to form a study group that will meet *that* very evening. (Tania Modleski has suggested a potential, though repressed, homosexual bond between men and boys in this film; it is not, however, liberatory as realized by Weir.)

An unsettling of sorts occurs with the appearance at Welton of a new English teacher named Mr. Keating, played by Robin Williams. Framed against the deadening pedagogy of his peers, Keating appears to be witty, unconventional, and courageous. In his first meetings with the class, he ruptures traditional pedagogical standards by having them rip out the introduction to their poetry book, which equates reading poetry to the same logic one would use to measure the heights of trees. This is not merely deconstruction, this is a textual assault that attempts to relocate poetry within the interests and voices the students actually bring to the class. Keating doesn't simply want them to read poetry, he wants them to understand it as a form of cultural production. According to him, poetry is about the relationship between passion and beauty. He tells his students

"The powerful play goes on and you may contribute a verse." For Keating, poetry offers the basis not for social empowerment but self-empowerment.

Keating wants to resurrect the humanist subject within an aesthetic of resistance, and eschews any notion of resistance which calls into question how the operations of power work to promote human suffering, and social injustice, and exploitation. Keating's invocation to his students "Carpe diem, lads! Seize the day! Make your lives extraordinary" is expressed in forms of pedagogical resistance that celebrate the privatized ego of ruling-class boys without any reference or analysis of how dominant social forms work subjectively to make these students complicit with the hierarchies of domination that inform the organization of the school, the curriculum, and the social formations that influence a wider society, to which Keating never alludes.

Resistance in Keating's pedagogy suggests a strangely empty quality. He has students stand on their desks so they can see the world from another position. Looking at the room from the top of their desks has an ironic twist to it since most of these students will be looking at the world when they leave school from the pinnacle of power rather than from the horizontal spaces that most people occupy at the bottom of the social and economic pyramid. On another occasion, Keating takes his students to the school courtyard and asks them to march in different strides. The pedagogical lesson taught in this case is that they must learn how to swim against the stream, to find "their own walk." In one celebrated scene in the film, Keating makes a particularly shy student get up before the class, asks him to close his eyes and free associate on a phrase from Whitman, "I sound my barbaric Yawp over the roofs of the world." The boy stutters, Keating whirls the student around and encourages him to speak to the metaphor. The boy finally attempts to articulate a poem and his classmates respond with resounding applause. In this instance, the audience is positioned to see Keating as a sensitive, caring teacher, who creates a space for the student that is metaphorically safe for the student *and* the audience.

In *Dead Poets Society*, resistance demands no sacrifices, no risks, no attempt to deconstruct the relationship between the margins and the centers of power. On the contrary, resistance in Keating's pedagogy serves to depoliticize and decontextualize since it is only developed within a romanticized aesthetic. In fact, even Keating doesn't appear to understand how he is complicitous with dominant relations of power. If he does possess such recognition, it is likely couched in a conventional bourgeois resignation guided by the conviction that poverty and suffering will always be with us; in fact, they may even be good for the soul. He appears to represent the classic modernist teacher whose pedagogical sensibilities have been spawned by Enlightenment thinking, with its narratives of unending progress, faith in a unified social world, and the power of an unencumbered individualism. Keating wants to be loved but is incapable of recognizing that resistance is less the production of a vapid and aesthetic individualism rooted in the traditions of British high culture than it is a call for solidarity and collective action. This is largely due to the aesthetics surrounding his epistemology, his particular "style" of coming to know something that obscures deeper political and social issues. In fact, as soon as Keating's unorthodox teaching methods appear to threaten the legitimating ideology of the school, he resorts to the discourse of accommodation rather than resistance. For example, when Keating is blamed for the suicide of one of his students, he refuses to challenge the trumped-up charges on the part of the headmaster, Mr. Knowland, and accepts his fate passively by simply leaving the school. As soon as politics crosses over into the realm of power and politics, Keating presents himself as incapable of acting on his own behalf. His pedagogical call to make one's life extraordinary reveals itself as rhetoric that limits rather than expands the capacity for human agency and struggle. There is nothing extraordinary in Keating's failure to resist at the end of this film.

Another major subtext of the film centers around the influence that Keating has on a group of students in his English class who discover that as a former student of Welton Academy Keating founded the Dead Poets Society. The students immediately query Keating about the society and what it meant and are told that Keating and a group of friends found a cave off campus and read the poetry of the Romantics in order to "suck the marrow out of life [while] letting poetry drip from our tongue." With the sensitive Neil Perry as their leader, a group of Keating's admirers proceed to recuperate the Dead Poets Society. It is here that the boys begin their own journey of resistance. They violate school rules by meeting in a cave off campus. Initially, they meet to read the Romantic poets, they then resort to reading their own poetry, smoking, playing musical instruments while emulating beat poetry, and bringing some girls to the cave. In one of the final cave scenes, a member of the group proclaims that he wants to be called Nuwanda, and in a striking display of colonialism takes on the identity of the Other as the provence of the primitive, exotic, and romanticized warrior. Other acts of resistance that inform the boys' behavior unfold when Neil Perry defies the wishes of a particularly stern father to concentrate on his course work by taking a role in a local play; another student, Knox Overstreet, boldly pursues a public high school cheerleader at the risk of being beaten up by her boyfriend; and Charlie Dalton puts a notice in the school newspaper signed by the Dead Poets Society calling for the admission of women to Welton Academy.

The dynamics of power and student resistance collide around two issues. In the first instance, Dalton is berelated and paddled by Mr. Knowland, the headmaster, for standing up at a school assembly and mocking him by announcing that the headmaster has a call from God. Dalton, who is from a wealthy family, takes his punishment but refuses to give the headmaster the names of other members of the Dead Poets Society. Neil Perry, a pivotal character in the firm, is torn between the individualism encouraged by Keating and the tyrannical demands imposed on him by his father. Finally, when his father discovers him acting in the school play, he pulls Neil out of Welton and threatens to send him off to a military school the next day. Neil leaves Welton and shortly afterwards commits suicide. There is a curious twist here. Neil Perry comes from a family that is lower middle class; his father constantly justifies his own imperious manner by arguing that he wants Neil to have the education and social status he never had the chance to experience. Neil in this context becomes the Other, the class-specific misfit who lacks the wealth and privilege to take risks, to move easily within the demands and imperatives of ruling-class culture. The message of *Dead Poets Society* seems clear in this case. Resistance for members of this class of "climbers" is not only out of place, it ultimately leads to self-destruction. On the other hand, Charlie Dalton challenges the authority of the headmaster, gets expelled from Welton, and yet there is no doubt because of his wealth and family position that his life will not be altered drastically. He belongs to the culture of the winners, resistance is simply harmless play, in which one can afford to engage when one moves in circles of privilege. In this context, risk translates into an aesthetic, an inconvenience or maybe an interesting story to be repeated later by an adult recalling his own resistance as simply part of a rite of passage engaged in within the hallowed traditions of an oppressive but pragmatic form of schooling.

As played out in *Dead Poets Society,* resistance is more often than not an emotional breach of convention and received social realities; it has more to do with a particular change in personal disposition towards an event than changing the structural conditions of events themselves. Resistance here is used as a form of cultural negotiation rather than social transformation.[11]

Following Neil Perry's suicide, the headmaster in an attempt ward off any negative publicity for the school uses Keating as a scapegoat. In the investigation that follows, the group of boys who idolize Keating are obliged to sign statements indicating that he forced them into resurrecting the Dead Poets Society, filled their heads with heretical thoughts, and was directly responsible for Neil's decision to appear in the school play, disobey his father, and thus commit suicide. With the exception of one member of the group all of the boys sign the statement, rat on their teacher, and continue with their lives at Welton as if nothing had happened. In the final scene of the film, Keating comes back to his office to collect his personal belongings. He has to pass through his English class which is now being taught by Knowland, the headmaster. As he is about to exit, some of the boys in the class as a gesture of nonconformity stand up on their respective desks as a show of support for Keating. He smiles at them and says "thank you boys." Hence, in the end, resistance, betrayal, and repressive authority are reworked and reconciled in a discourse of politeness which cancels out dominating relations of power and those who are complicitous with it. Keating remains the well-mannered man until the end, confirming the idea that resistance does not permanently change the world but merely interrupts it only to return us to the canonical past in which tradition, patriarchy, and Eurocentricism continue to provide a sense of order and continuity. The relationship between power and knowledge in Keating's pedagogy of resistance betrays itself by claiming that the alternative to stuffy textbooks is British and American Romanticism of the 19th Century—not the socially engaged literature of the day.[12]

One of the most pernicious subtexts in the film is organized around the construction of gendered subject positions in which women are represented in terms that are misogynist and demeaning.[13] Understood in these terms, *Dead Poets Society* does more than ignore structured inequalities in the wider society, depoliticize resistance, and naturalize how the canon is used to produce racist and class-specific practices. It also legitimates gendered social practices through various images and representations in which sexual identity is inscribed in various forms of sexist domination. This is most obviously evidenced in the relegation of women in this film to either trophies or appendages of male power. In one glaring example, Keating tells the "boys" that one of the central purposes of poetry is to "woo women." In this case, resistance as a form of "hip" pedagogical posturing is structured through the legitimation of sexist social relations. This lesson is certainly not lost on Keating's boys. While meeting in the cave, one of the boys reads a poem that is written on the back of a *Playboy* centerfold. Resistance for Keating's boys appears to support rather than rupture their own patriarchal identities. On another occasion, the girls who are brought to the cave are treated as if they are too dumb to recognize or understand the poetry of the Romantics. Following a similar logic, Knox's courtship with the public school cheerleader serves to reduce her to a reified object of desire and pleasure. Even the call by Keating's "resisters" to admit girls to Welton Academy transparently reveals itself as an opportunity for the boys to get more dates, to offset their academic work with sexual pleasure. In the end, resistance, knowledge, and pedagogy come together in *Dead Poets Society* to harness identity and power to the misogynist interests and fortunes of patriarchy. Within this coming-of-age narrative, whiteness reasserts itself through the logic of cultural racism, class discrimination, and the objectification of women. This is not merely a foreshortened view of gender relations within prep school culture, it is an active assertion, a politics of representation, in which resistance is incorporated as a pedagogical practice that actively produces sexism as part of its own legacy of power and domination.

Pedagogical Authority and the Politics of the Popular

In order to structure a position from which students might understand how their own subject positions are partly constructed within a dominant Eurocentric assemblage of liberal humanism mobilized within configurations of meaning and desire, I used the presentation of *Dead Poets Society* to raise important questions about the ideological interests at work in forms of textual authority that foster particular reading practices. In taking up this issue I framed my discussion of the film with my students around a number of important pedagogical concerns. These included: how are readers' choices defined and limited by the range of readings made available through the representations mobilized by particular forms of textual authority? How do power and authority articulate between the wider society and the classroom so as to create the condition at work in constructing particular discourses in the reading of this film? The tension I had to confront was how to address the power of hope and agency provided by the discourse of liberal humanism without destroying a sense of pedagogical possibility (Simon).

For me the pedagogical challenge presented itself in trying to engage the film as a mode of writing, which took the form of allowing the students to make the "texts" mean differently by reorganizing the systems of intertextual, ideological, and cultural references in which it was constructed historically and semiotically, and in relation to wider social events. In the first instance, this meant giving students the opportunity to analyze the plurality of meanings that informed the film. This was done by having students view the film from the perspective of their own experiences and histories by writing short, critical papers, which they then duplicated and shared with the rest of the class for dialogue and comment. It was at this point that the students' initial affective investments in the film were mediated critically by other texts, presented to the class, and dialogically voiced and challenged. As well, I introduced magazine and newspaper reviews along with my own written commentary on the film. The pedagogical issue here centered on both having the teachers' voice heard, but at the same time providing the conditions for such a voice to be engaged and challenged. Roger Simon has referred to this pedagogical moment as the reaffirmation of both critical authority and the struggle over the sign. He notes that such a struggle has to be ongoing, because if it stops, learning itself stops.

Once students analyzed how the film can be read differently to mobilize different forms of affect and meaning, diverse points of identification, they were given the opportunity to analyze how *Dead Poets Society* might be understood within the larger framework that informed the course. This suggested analyzing how the film mobilized particular, if not contradictory, relations of domination and possibility, and how such relations articulate with some of the conservative educational reform policies advocated by the Bush Administration. Within this frame, a number of students addressed how *Dead Poets Society* could be understood within some of the current problems regarding issues of race, class, and gender. For instance, students discussed how the film might be taught as part of an anti-racist pedagogy and how the film both excludes cultural differences and erases whiteness as a privileged racial category. The class also discussed how this film reproduced patriarchal relations and how it might be read from a variety of feminist discourses. Of course, there were students whose positions did not change, and who actively argued from a liberal humanist discourse. These students were able to affirm and defend their positions, without being subjected to a form of pedagogical terrorism which would put their identities on trial.

Finally, the class took up the related issues of identity, class, and cultural differences by watching *Stand and Deliver* (1988, directed by Ramon Menendez), which portrays a math teacher, Jamie Escalante (Edward James Olmos), similarly engaged in an act of resistance. Here, however, the setting is a contemporary public school in the barrio in East Los Angeles. Fighting the lethal conditions of overcrowding, lack of resources, and institutional inertia (read as racism), Escalante wages a one-man war against the system in order to "save the barrio kids." Escalante combines a form of pedagogical wizardry and authoritarianism in challenging both the students and the school. He speaks to his students in both Spanish and English, and he affirms their cultural capital while extending their expectations of success and possibility. Inspiring them to reach beyond the inequities and discrimination that routinely structure their daily school experiences and aspirations, he introduces them to the alien world of Calculus, which signifies high academic status and is the mark of a privileged cultural currency in the school curriculum. As the film unfolds, Escalante's notion of resistance translates into getting the students to study hard, pass the Advanced Placement Test in Calculus, and hopefully get a chance to go on to college.

I think *Stand and Deliver* is ultimately a very conservative film. That is, it appropriates elements of a progressive pedagogy to affirm the problematic goal of teaching for the test and legitimizing canonical knowledge rather than getting "students to think critically about their place in relation to the knowledge they gain and to transform their world view fundamentally by taking the politics of knowledge seriously" (Mohanty, 192). On the other hand, *Stand and Deliver* does spark serious questions about racial discrimination, the specificity of the cultural context of teaching, and the importance of teachers and students engaging in the process of negotiation and translation in order to engage both the language of everyday life and to go beyond it as part of a broader attempt at self- and social empowerment. But like *Dead Poets Society,* the film does not link resistance to recognizing the "materiality of conflict, of privilege, and of domination" (Mohanty, 206). Resistance in both films provides a trace of what it means to push against authority, but neither film takes up adequately what it might mean to name and struggle against institutional practices within rather than outside of history, politics, and power. While the students' response to *Stand and Deliver* was taken up more critically because of its concerns with race, class, and identity, it raised once again the crucial issue of how desire is mobilized by film narratives.

In engaging these two films, it became clear to me that the binarism that often structures the relationship between meaning and pleasure was ruptured. Those students who initially took up either of the films in terms of desired images of themselves as a future teacher reworked that particular image not by canceling out the importance of desire, but by extending its possibilities by developing a transformed sense of agency and power.

Reclaiming the Popular

Any attempt to reclaim the popular in the service of a critical pedagogical practice runs the risk of at least three serious reactionary interventions. First, the popular or everyday is often used by mainstream and liberal educators merely to reaffirm the textual authority of canonical texts. Second, humanistic discourses sometimes use the popular as if it were an unproblematic mode of discourse and style, as if student voices in and of themselves lend authority that needs no further discussion or analysis. Third, there is the risk of colonizing the popular in the interests of subordinating it to the discourse of pedagogical techniques.[14]

The category of cultural worker used throughout this chapter refigures the role of educators within a discourse that takes a subject position, a standpoint that argues that without a political project there can be no ground on which to engage questions of power, domination, and the possibilities of collective struggle. This suggests a political project that goes beyond merely discursive struggles. Such a project also attempts to transform non-discursive and institutional relations of power by connecting educational struggles with broader struggles for the democratization, pluralization, and reconstruction of public life. With all apologies to the new conservativism, this is not an endorsement of that strange "species" of discourse popularly known as political correctness but a refusal to erase the political as an essential sphere of pedagogical practice.

If the popular is not to be used to reassert the validity of dominant texts and power relations, it must be viewed as part of a broader process of cultural production that is inextricably linked to issues of power, struggle, and identity. In this case, the popular does not derive its importance as an exotic text brought in from the margins of everyday life. On the contrary, it is used to raise questions about how its exclusion from the centers of power serve to secure specific forms of authority. The political currency of popular culture is not to be determined within a binarism that simply reverses its relationship to high culture. The more important task for cultural workers is to reconstruct the very problematic that informs the high vs. popular culture distinction in order to understand more specifically how cultural production works within and outside of the margins of power in texts actively engaged in the production of institutional structures, social identities, and horizons of possibility. For example, educators might use films, videos, or television within an English class so as to draw attention to the relevance of certain canonical works for everyday life. This approach does not challenge canonicity, it merely serves to make it appear more relevant.

Another use of the popular rests with the assumption that the use of rock music, popular films, and current novels represent a discourse of authenticity that resonates with the "real" experiences that constitute student voices. This position not only wrongly posits experience as something that is unriddled with contradictions but also treats students voices as texts whose authenticity dispenses with the need to make them the object of critical interrogation, mediation, and theoretical inquiry. Paul Smith captures this sentiment well:

> Deriving from the liberal-progressivist educational tradition which reached its acme (or nadir) with the call to relevance in the late 1960s, whatever increased interest there is in [such texts] often leads teachers to use them to facilitate students in expressing or assessing their own experiences. The logic is that the nearest access that most students have to culture is through and in mass culture and that their interest and participation in that realm can be turned toward self-expression and self-consciousness. In this process, so the argument goes, students will see their own experiences reflected and thus be more satisfied with the classroom experience than if they were taught canonical texts. (p. 33)

What Smith is rightly criticizing is not only a prevailing form of anti-intellectualism, but also a view of pedagogy that romanticizes student experience by removing it from the historical, institutional, and discursive forces which shape it in multiple and contradictory ways. Moreover, such a discourse locates experience within an individualist ethos that renders its social grounds and collective obligations invisible. In this case, relativism overrides the concerns of social justice, and individual views outweigh the consequences of the actions that follow from them on the broader public sphere. Finally, it is important to resist the pedagogical practice of treating the cultural text solely as an ever-expanding site of meanings, interpretations, and translations. While the reading of any cultural text can be reduced to the bad faith of textual essentialism or the one right meaning and must be avoided, it is imperative to recognize that popular texts must be read differently and politically; the readings of cultural texts must be understood within the larger dynamics of historical and social formations that struggle over such texts as sites of meaning and possibility. [15] Similarly, both cultural texts and the readings that circulate within, above, and against them must be examined as part of a broader discourse that takes up the circuits of power that constitute the ideological and material dynamics of capitalism (or any other social and economic system).

Conclusion

Rather than assuming that the popular is simply out there beyond the margins of disciplinary knowledge, ensconced in the play of everyday life waiting to be rescued as a serious object of knowledge, I want to conclude by addressing more directly the relationship between pedagogical authority and the appropriation of popular texts such as Hollywood films. Put another way, how can a notion of pedagogical authority be used to justify engaging what is problematically constituted as the popular in the first place? To be sure, it is important for cultural workers to use pedagogical authority in an emancipatory fashion to engage popular culture, to question and unlearn the benefits of privilege, and to allow those who have generally not been allowed to speak to narrate themselves, to speak from the specificity of their own voices. At the same time, it is in the service of reactionary interests for teachers and students to redefine authority as a legitimating discourse that opens up dialogue around the terrain of popular culture, but in doing so fails to interrogate how the dynamics of race, class, and gender, in particular, structure pedagogical projects in which everyday life is appropriated as part of a wider politics of containment. Needless to say, this does not always happen without struggle or resistance, but the issue here is how does one locate oneself as a cultural worker or educator within a notion of authority that legitimates engaging particular forms of popular texts without committing at the same time a form of pedagogical terrorism? How does one legitimate a notion of pedagogical authority that does not justify forms of voyeurism, looking, and appropriation that mimic the legacy of colonialism?

Raising this postcolonial caveat is not meant to suggest that progressive and left cultural workers who take up a directive notion of authority locate themselves by default in the discourse and practice of authoritarianism. On the contrary, authority needs to be reworked and struggled over as part of a wider effort to develop the pedagogical conditions necessary to make the invisible visible, expose how power is mobilized in the interests of oppression, and challenge the very terms of dominant representations. This suggests a notion of authority, popular culture, and pedagogical practice that combines a discourse of hope with forms of self- and social criticism while reclaiming a politics of location that recognizes how power, history, and ethics position, limit, and enable the cultural practices we engage in as educators. At issue here is an emancipatory notion of authority that should be fashioned in pedagogical practices rewritten in terms that articulate the importance of creating the conditions for students to take up subject positions consistent with the principles of equality, justice, and freedom rather than with interests and practices supportive of hierarchies, oppression, and exploitation. Central to this notion of authority is the need for critical educators to develop those spaces and practices that engage but don't erase the identities, compassion, or willingness of students to challenge the discourses of authority. The legitimation for such authority is as self-critical as it is deeply political, as multi-accentual as it is committed to working within and across cultural and social differences to produce the basis for diverse critical public cultures that expand rather than restrict a democratic society.

To reclaim the popular within a committed view of authority is not meant to smother students under the weight of a suffocating form of political correctness. On the contrary, it is to engage the popular as part of a broader circuit of power relations, assert multiple notions of subjectivity without erasing agency, and expand the possibilities of multiple readings of texts while making visible how representations work so as to mobilize both the dynamics of domination and emancipatory struggles. In addition, there is the need for cultural workers to expand the boundaries of historical and semiotic analyses by making the pedagogical more political by addressing and transforming the conditions that will undermine relations of domination while simultaneously creating spaces of resistance, hope, and collective struggle.

Works Cited

Aronowitz, Stanley and Henry A. Giroux. *Postmodern Education: Politics, Culture, and Social Criticism*. Minneapolis: University of Minnesota Press, 1991.

Bennett, Tony. "Really Useless 'Knowledge': A Political Critique of Aesthetics." *Theses Eleven* 12 (1985), pp. 28–51.

Bennett, Tony. *Outside Literature*. New York: Routledge, 1990.

Chambers, Iain. *Border Dialogues: Journeys into Postmodernity*. New York: Routledge, 1990.

Collins, Jim. *Uncommon Cultures: Popular Culture and Post-Modernism*. New York: Routledge, 1989.

Dyer, Richard. "White." *Screen* 29:4 (1988), pp. 44–64.

Ferguson, Russell. "Introduction: Invisible Center." Ed. Russell Ferguson, Martha Gever, Trin T. Minh-ha, and Cornel West. *Out There: Marginalization and Contemporary Culture*. Cambridge, Mass.: MIT Press, 1991, p. 9–14.

Fukuyama, Francis. "The End of History?" *The National Interest* 16 (Summer, 1989), pp. 3–18.

Giroux, Henry A. *Schooling and the Struggle for Public Life*. Minneapolis: University of Minnesota Press, 1988.

————. *Border Crossings: Cultural Workers and the Politics of Education*. New York: Routledge, 1992.

————. "Paulo Freire and the Politics of Post-Colonialism." *Journal of Advanced Composition* 12:1 (1992), pp. 15–26.

Giroux, Henry A. and David Trend. "Cultural Workers, "Pedagogy, and the Politics of Difference: Beyond Cultural Conservatism." *Cultural Studies* 6:1 (1992), pp. 51–72.

Giroux, Henry A. and Roger Simon, eds. *Popular Culture, Schooling, and Everyday Life*. New York: Bergin and Garvey, 1989.

Graff, Gerald. "Teach the Conflicts." *South Atlantic Quarterly* 89:1 (1990), pp. 51–68.

Grossberg, Lawrence. *We Gotta Get Out of This Place: Popular Conservatism and Postmodern Culture*. New York: Routledge (1992).

Grossberg, Lawrence, Cary Nelson, and Paula Treichler, eds. *Cultural Studies*. New York: Routledge, 1991.

Hall, Stuart. *The Hard Road to Renewal: Thatcherism and the Crisis of the Left*. London: Verso: 1989.

Henricksen, Bruce. "Teaching Against the Grain." *Reorientations: Critical Theories and Pedagogies*. Ed. Bruce Henricksen and Thais E. Morgan. Urbana: University of Illinois Press, 1990, pp. 28–39.

Kaye, Harvey. *The Powers of the Past: Reflections on the Crisis and the Promise of History*. Minneapolis: University of Minnesota Press, 1991.

Laclau, Ernesto and Chantal Mouffe. *Hegemony and Socialist Strategy*. London: Verso, 1985.

McLaren, Peter. "Critical Pedagogy: Constructing an Arch of Social Dreaming and a Doorway to Hope." *Journal of Education* 173:1 (1991), pp. 9–34.

Modleski, Tania. *Feminism Without Women: Culture and Criticism in a "Postfeminist" Age*. New York: Routledge, 1991, pp. 137–140.

Mohanty, Chandra T. "On Race and Voice: Challenges for Liberal Education in the 1990s." *Cultural Critique* 14 (Winter, 1989–90), pp. 179–208.

Rutherford, Jonathan. Ed. *Identity, Community, Culture, Difference*. London: Lawrence and Wishart, 1990.

Simon, Roger I. *Teaching Against the Grain*. New York: Bergin and Garvey, 1992.

Smith, Paul. "Pedagogy and the Popular-Cultural-Commodity-Text." *Popular Culture, Schooling and Everyday Life*. Ed. Henry A. Giroux and Roger Simon. New York: Bergin and Garvey, 1989, pp. 31–46.

Solomon-Godeau, Abigail. *Photography at the Dock: Essays on Photographic History, Institutions, and Practices*. Minneapolis: University of Minnesota Press, 1991.

West, Cornel. "The New Cultural Politics of Difference." *October* 53 (Summer, 1990), pp. 93–109.

3

Pretty Is as Pretty Does:
Free Enterprise and the Marriage Plot

Hilary Radner

What's going to happen to the Cosmo girl in the nineties? I think she'll
be better than ever reaching out for life and love and achievement . . .
not expecting anything to be handed to her, but expecting everything.
—Helen Gurley Brown

My foot slid into the glass slipper. I was Mrs. Elvis Presley.
—Priscilla Presley in Elvis and Me
(1988 TV movie)

Transforming Sexual Exchange

In the general uproar surrounding feminism old and new, one issue is
usually overlooked: the terms of heterosexual practice have undergone
radical and undeniable transformation. In *Re-making Love: The Feminization of Sex,* Barbara Ehrenreich, Elizabeth Hess, and Gloria Jacobs comment on this *de facto* sexual revolution:

> Between the mid-sixties and the mid-seventies, the number of women
> reporting premarital sexual experience went from a daring minority to
> a respectable majority; and the proportion of married women reporting
> active sex lives "on the side" is, in some estimates, close to half. The
> symbolic importance of female chastity is rapidly disappearing. (2)

Pretty Woman, the 1990s version of the weepie with an unexpected happy
ending to dry audience tears, whose success confirmed the importance of
the women's market, is remarkable in that it accords little symbolic or
any other importance to female chastity.[1]
Pretty Woman, in which a corporate raider woos and wins a Hollywood

hooker, demonstrates how the changes in heterosexual behavior have demanded a renegotiation of what feminist critics have called the marriage plot upon which the women's novel has largely depended. The traditional marriage or romance plot is about: "finding validation of one's uniqueness and importance by being singled out among all other women by a man" (Brownstein, xv). In the female *Bildungsroman,* the novel of maturation, "her quest is to be recognized in *all* her significance," externalized by her status as bride, the chosen one (Brownstein xv). In this 1990s renegotiation of the story in which woman finds her identity (and of the heterosexual contract that underlies that identity), suggests structural changes in the dynamics of gender and exchange, which have resulted in a repositioning of the representation of the feminine within the social fabric. When looking at *Pretty Woman,* we can no longer state with any authority that the symbolic function of women is to be exchanged among men.[2] To quote the motto of Vivian, the film's heroine played by Julia Roberts: "We say who. We say when. We say how much."

In the 18th-Century novel, as feminist critic Nancy Miller explains, the classical marriage plot required that:

> The daughter must be exchanged but she must also remain in *her place.* The daughter must marry but she must remain within the family, chaste and willing to circulate, but only and necessarily in accordance with the law of the father. (*The Heroine's Text,* 149)[3]

In this system of representation, the woman's value was guaranteed, though not solely determined by, her virginity, referred to as her virtue, her chastity. Thus to be virtuous was represented by absence, the absence of sexual desire and sexual knowledge. In this context, sexual knowledge, and by extension knowledge in general, was the sign not of value but of "damaged goods." Crucial to this system of value was the ideal of two separate spheres, the public and the private.[4] As women came to work outside the home, and acquired economic independence from the family (as they came to make their own decisions rather than following the wishes of the father, head of that family) new categories and structures of femininity and its attendant virtues emerged and new stories, of which *Pretty Woman* is one, came to be told in which the heterosexual contract was of necessity figured differently. It is in the history of the "single girl," singled out as the new paragon of consumer culture, that we see the initial articulation of a new female *Bildung.*

The Working Girl Emerges

In the 1960s, a hinge point in the development of new femininities, women writers such as Helen Gurley Brown, now editor-in-chief of *Cos-*

mopolitan magazine, sought to evolve a technology of feminine sexual practice outside marriage in which nubility is reproduced through the articulation of the woman as consumer of both goods and sexual pleasure. In *Sex and the Single Girl,* Helen Gurley Brown conflates the categories of woman/girl in the category of working girl—the term girl maintaining the woman's status as nubile—marriageable—past her youth. Earlier books[5] and women columnists such as Diana Vreeland, who wrote for *Harper's Bazaar* for thirty years before becoming editor-in-chief at *Vogue* during the 1970s, set the parameters of the consumer-defined feminine ideal that reaches its full flowering under the cultivation of Gurley Brown and her cohort.

As a best-seller, the work of Gurley Brown represents a democratization of the category of single woman across class-lines and emphasized reproducing femininity through consumer practices that were accessible to all "pink" collar workers, regardless of their class origins.[6] For the "single girl," marriage was one of a number of paths that depended on the development of her heterosexual status through which the single girl might realize her ambitions. Thus, Gurley Brown rewrote venture capitalism for a specifically feminine subject.[7] However, as earlier handbooks such as Marjorie Hillis's *Live Alone and Like It* (1933) demonstrate, from the 'teens on (more obviously in the 1920s and 1930s), there was an increasingly marked emphasis on consumerism within feminine culture.[8] This consumer-oriented feminine culture was directly associated with the rise of movies as an entertainment form that crossed class-lines.[9] Thus it would be a mistake to think of the "Single Girl" as emerging fully formed in the 1960s; rather we see that these new public femininities evolved over time through a significant intertextuality, as part of the general uneven development characteristic of cultural change.

In addition to emphasizing the importance of good grooming, the standards of which were set in the first half of the 20th Century by the movies and movie magazines, and which are consistently tied to consumer-product usage (a double consumerism), Gurley Brown and later the notorious "J.," author of *The Sensuous Woman,* who extends Gurley Brown's precepts to their logical conclusion in 1972, distinguish themselves and their historical moment by legitimating the orgasm as the currency of sexual exchange. Helen Gurley Brown in her entrepreneurial capacity sees sexual exchange as integral to the single girl's mode of investment and return. Brown admonishes:

> Sex is a powerful weapon for a single women in getting what she wants from life, i.e., a husband or steady male companionship. Sex is a more important weapon to her than to a married woman who has other things going for her—like the law! (70)

Thus the technology of sexiness developed by Brown has as its goal to maintain, paradoxically, the "single girl's" marriageability. Sexual expertise replaces virginity as the privileged object of exchange outside the law of the family. Though, marriage is still assumed to be the single woman's goal, Gurley Brown's work manifests a shift in the notion of a woman's value. Her value is now overtly and inextricably tied to the representation of a specific heterosexual practice as sexual knowledge rather than sexual innocence, represented as such within an arena characterized by the interpenetration of public and private in which a woman is always working. This new heterosexual contract was renewable; there was no permanent tenure for the wife. Gurley Brown warns:

> A man can leave a woman at fifty (though it may cost him some dough) as surely as you can leave dishes in the sink. He can leave any time before then, and so may you leave him. . . .(5)

Thus within the terms of this contract, the wife must maintain her marriage-ability to remain married. And if she does remain marriageable she too has the right to negotiate for a better contract, another partner, should she so desire. The success of Gurley Brown's revamping of *Cosmopolitan* for the single woman in the mid-sixties, and the number of magazines that followed in its wake targeting the same demographic category (*Working Woman, Self*, etc.), as well as a shift in emphasis from the married (or soon-to-be married) woman to the working woman in magazines such as *Harper's Bazaar, Vogue, Glamour,* exemplify the increasing importance of generating a feminine template that functions as such within the public arena, the office, the workplace.

In an era in which more than fifty percent of all women work outside the home, the 1980s and 1990s have seen the intensification of this new femininity that identifies itself within a public sphere. This new femininity defines itself and its pleasures (its libidinal economy) on a marketplace in which her capital is constituted by her body and her sexual expertise, which she herself exchanges. She is not exchanged by men, but acts as her own agent—as a "free" agent within a grid of relationships defined by office hierarchy and the "deal." Women's magazines, self-help books, women's novels, not to mention Lifetime television, are all eager to offer women a new paradigm for feminine behavior modeled on the principles originally set forth by Helen Gurley Brown.

The "Pretty" in Pretty Woman: Sex Appeal and Fashion Sense

Pretty Woman, its narrative, its success, exemplify the pervasiveness of the new femininity of the single girl, the working girl (here in the full sense of the word). [10] Thus, *Pretty Woman* offers significant insight into the new public femininity and two issues that determine this new femininity as such: 1) the film's relationship to a feminine heterosexuality that destabilizes the public/private division 2) the film's relationship to the technology of the self-as-feminine-consumer, articulated in the film's explicit and implicit connection to women's magazines and the fashion industry. In the film "Pretty Woman" becomes "pretty" when she learns to shop. The free market is, thus, "fixed" through compulsory heterosexuality and commodity consumption. Importantly, Gurley Brown devotes the larger bulk of *Sex and the Single Girl* to the problem of embodiment in which the task of the "single girl" is that of embodying heterosexuality through the disciplined use of makeup, clothing, exercise, and cosmetic surgery, which will enable her to change herself from a "mouse" to into a "glamor puss." This process of embodiment is taken up in *Pretty Woman* through the trope of shopping. Vivian in her capacity as heroine transforms herself from "working girl" to lady of leisure, by acquiring a new wardrobe, her table manners notwithstanding. Vivian shares with Gurley Brown's single girl the need to couple consumer knowledge and sexual knowledge in order to be valuable, in which the sign of value, the moment at which value is legitimated, is marriage, "the fairy tale" for which Vivian holds out at the end of the movie, the goal of every single girl, the moment at which" . . . she is transformed: her outward self reflects her inner self, she is a bride, the very image of the heroine" (Brownstein, xv). The privileged moment of marriage cannot be realized through marriage to any man, the groom must be a prince of men, which translates to a very wealthy man within the world of *Pretty Woman* and *Cosmopolitan* magazine.

The Marriage Plot

It is the new "value" of the woman, determined through her mastery of the "arts" of seduction, sexual gratification, and consumer display, that both demands a fundamental reworking of the marriage plot, and yet preserves the story as one in which eroticism and ambition are inevitably and inextricably linked, in which feminine ambition can only be realized through marriage to the right man. Public discussions of *Pretty Woman* have emphasized its connection to the Cinderella story [11] and its reactionary nature as a invocation of the traditional marriage plot. Yet if we think about the issue of "value" within heterosexual exchange we can easily see that this new romance plot reflects new terms of value and new structures of feminine sexual identity that are in keeping with Ehrenreich's description of female behavior. This rewriting enables *Pretty Woman* to function as the story of a female *Bildung* that attempts to accommodate the marriage or romance plot of the traditional women's novel to the double demands of a structure of representation in which a woman's value is measured by her sexual expertise and her appearance as the feminine-consumer-self.[12] The relationship between Cinderella and the marriage plot may seem self-evident;[13] certainly it has served as the basis of the women's romance at least since Richardson's *Pamela*. (Pamela, it will be recalled, is a servant who marries—after surviving threats to her virtue—Mr. B., her master and would-be seducer, thereby saving herself from a life of drudgery and servitude.) *Pamela* not only offered 18th-Century readers a model of proper female behavior (not to mention providing valuable information on how to marry well),[14] it also served as a model for 18th-, 19th-, and 20th-Century writers of female romances—from Fanny Burney to Georgette Heyer.[15]

Yet if both Pamela and Vivian are rewritings of the Cinderella figure, they have very little in common except that they both marry wealthy men. Pamela, unlike Vivian, is distinguished through her accomplishments, and most notably her chastity, in which her ability to withhold what Mr. B. wants is her principle attraction. Thus she is characteristic of what feminist scholar Nancy Armstrong has defined as the domestic ideal, in which a middle-class private paragon of feminine virtue, of economy, good sense, and restraint, was held up against the undesirable aristocratic model of expenditure and public display. Vivian's function, on the other hand, is to be on display as part of her job as "beck-and-call girl," to occupy the position of a trophy that externalizes her employee's status, a trophy that is always there at hand. That and her sexual willingness distinguish her, at least in part, from other women in her "boss's" life and also from earlier heroines of the marriage plot, Pamela in particular. Nonetheless, she, like Pamela, will be "saved" through marriage.

Thus, within the classical marriage plot Vivian is an anomaly, though her story preserves the conventions and forms of the narrative in which a poor girl marries a rich man who protects her from the vicissitudes of a life of poverty and unhappiness. Tania Modleski defines the classic formula in her benchmark book *Loving with a Vengeance: Mass-Produced Fantasies for Women*, commenting on the sentimental novels of the 19th Century:

> (T)he heroine, who is often of lower social status than the hero, holds out against his attacks on her "virtue" until he sees no other recourse than to marry her. Of course, by this time he wants to marry her, having become smitten with her sheer "goodness." (16)

Given the sexual decorum demanded of the heroine in these romances, we may well ask what are the signs of Vivian's value, what is her "goodness"? In what way is she a model for feminine behavior like Pamela who "holds out" until she gets her man? The full title of the Richardson novel is *Pamela, or Virtue Rewarded*; for what is Vivian being rewarded?

As I have noted above, Vivian is a paragon of sexual knowledge rather than chastity, and it is her sexual expertise rather than her virginity that initially constitutes her value—that brings her to Edward Lewis's (Richard Gere) attention. It is not an accident that Vivian and her friend Kit refer to Cinderella as "Cinda-fuckin'-rella," a term that speaks to the differences between Vivian and earlier paragons. What eventually constitutes her "goodness," that which persuades Edward that he must in fact keep her, is a complicated issue. For although Vivian is not chaste, she does have "moral values," a firm sense of decency and fairness towards others. This is what Edward, a corporate raider, lacks and what he needs Vivian to teach him: Edward is a rake in the 18th-Century sense, but one who rapes companies instead of women. It is Vivian who will bring him back to the fold of a capitalism regulated by the law of the family and patriarchal responsibility. She will teach him how not to "fuck over" workers.

In *Pretty Woman,* the new heterosexual contract is not, then, based on female chastity. Rather it is based on the "world's oldest profession," on the exchange of female sex for male property. In the new heterosexual contract this most unstable, because temporary, of exchanges between male and female is made stable. Vivian becomes Edward's "beck-and-call girl" on a permanent basis: Marriage is stable employment in the service area in which Vivian already holds a temporary position. Although this hard-edged materialist aspect of Edward's and Vivian's agreement is masked or narrativized through a sentimental story of "love" (signaled by the kiss that comes to replace sexual services as the couple's medium of exchange—at one point Vivian even refuses Edward's money), the initial terms of the agreement really never change. Vivial deliberately and aggressively (unlike Pamela who was the pursued rather than the pursuer) seeks employment, first temporary and then permanent, with her employer.

The film sets out the nature of this contract early on; Edward agrees to pay Vivian three thousand dollars for a week of her services. She challenges him: "Baby, I'm goin' treat you so nice you're never goin' want to let me go." Edward accepts the challenge, retorting: "Three thousand dollars, six days, and Vivian, I *will* let you go." It is at this moment that the narrative stakes are defined, are made clear as part of the mechanism of the couple's contractual agreement. In terms of this conflict, the film reaches its point of no return when, at the end, Edward must choose between marrying Vivian and losing her. Although Edward at first makes the wrong decision, he quickly changes his mind in the nick of time and proposes marriage to conclude the story (or at least we assume that is what he is doing though the words are never actually spoken).

Pretty Woman's narrative structure is somewhat unusual in that the subplot involving Edward's takeover is resolved well before the film's end.

In a decision that presages that ending, Edward abandons "speculation" to return to a production-oriented capitalism, in which his goal becomes to rebuild rather than to take apart the company he has recently acquired. In so doing, Edward reaffirms the symbolic law of the family, in which he becomes the responsible father to his workers. He is assimilated into the corporate family complete with a surrogate patriarch in the person of the company's previous owner, James Morse (played by the venerable Ralph Bellamy), who claims he is "proud" of Edward, sealing the new pact between family and business. The reason for this premature plot resolution is hardly mysterious, though, because it functions to validate Vivian's worth for us; she is the source of his professional transformation. Once he is made "good" again he can become the source of her return to respectability, and to the family she once abandoned when she took up prostitution for a living. Thus though the final denouement is brief, it works within the logic of the narrative because the spectator has already witnessed Edward's reform.[16] The step from reformed capitalist to devoted husband is a short one in the film's textual system because the film asks us to read this as a sign of Vivian's "goodness," her worthiness, and her right to wife-status and legitimacy in the world of the family. Thus, Edward's remark that he and Vivian are "similar creatures" because they "both screw people for money" is an explicit statement of the narrative equation Edward's reform/Vivian's redemption. (Yet—and it is hard to avoid a cynical qualifier when it comes to *Pretty Woman*—from the point at which Vivian issues her challenge, we must question the extent to which she does fall in love with Edward. Does she simply raise the stakes in her takeover strategy? Has she stopped "screwing" for money, or has she started "screwing" for more money? That Vivian succeeds in her takeover, a takeover in which it is the loser, Edward, who appears to claim the spoils of victory by asking her to marry him, is only a sign of how well she has done her job, how completely she has won.)

Certainly Edward's reform seems evidence of the sincerity of Vivian's position. The film reminds us, however, that this is not another Cinderella, or even a Horatio Alger, story. The film does not end with Julia's and Edward's reconciliation. In fact the film concludes by returning to the image of a street person, a Rastafarian who "be Cool," who early in the film, as Edward drives around lost in Hollywood and Vivian wanders towards her fateful meeting with him, shouts out to passersby:

> Welcome to Hollywood. Everybody comes to Hollywood got a dream. What's your dream? What's your dream? Hey mister, hey, what's your dream?

At the end of the film, he returns with a reminder of the status of the tale that we have just seen unfold:

Welcome to Hollywood, what's your dream? Everyone comes here.
This is Hollywood, Land of dreams. Some dreams come true, some
don't, but keep on dreamin'. This is Hollywood, always time to dream,
so keep on dreamin'.

The film, thus, provides us with a frame that underlines the implausibility
of its plausibility, of its narrative logic and conventions. Sigmund Freud's
well-known dictum, quoted by Nancy Miller to explain the logic of
women's fiction, bears repetition here: "Unsatisfied wishes are the driving
power behind phantasies; every separate phantasy contains the fulfillment
of a wish and improves upon unsatisfactory reality" (47). Miller points
out that women's fantasies in the form of women's fiction work, just as
men's fantasies, to collapse the "either/or antinomy, ambitious/erotic" to
make "co-existence possible" ("Emphasis Added," 356). To return to the
problem of the film's ending, the film offers a "dream" in which there is
no contradiction between ambition and eroticism, between Horatio (or
Hortensia) Alger and Cinderella), between prostitution and conjugal love:
this is its fantasy that as fantasy speaks the implausibility of its story,
its "impossible relationships," to quote Edward's musings on his own
situation.

Thus the story of *Pretty Woman* exemplifies Constance Penley's definition of "a psychoanalytic idea of fantasy," which offers a framework
through which "the subject participates in and restages a scenario in which
crucial questions about desire, knowledge, and identity can be posed, and
in which the subject can hold a number of identificatory positions" (480).
Story-as-fantasy is best understood not as a single monolithic "wish-
fulfillment" but as a representation of "multiple (if contradictory) subject
positions" (480). The use of the prostitute figure within the marriage plot
is emblematic of this circulation of "wishes."[17]

Redeeming the Prostitute

The film's rewriting of the figure of the prostitute creates a hinge
moment between the heterosexual contract and Edward's return to the
patriarchal fold (his identification with the father and the patriarch). The
sexual freedom, the freedom of exchange that Vivian represents, is also
a moment of departure for the articulation of a masculine fantasy[18] that is
regressive, a pre-Oedipal fantasy of helplessness. This pre-Oedipal fantasy, in which Edward is Vivian's "baby," runs counter to the overt story
of Edward's correct Oedipalization, his identification with patriarchal
responsibility.[19] The "beck-and-call girl" is the woman who unselfishly
fulfills Edward's needs, who lets her desires be regulated by his. It is
precisely their failure to conform to these needs that Edward deplores in
his ex-wife and ex-girlfriend. Edward wants a woman who is always in

place for him, in the place he wants, as though she were the unmediated extension of his desire, returning him to the edenic moment in which the child imagined that he was as one with the mother, before his ontological separation from the source of his sustenance and pleasure. Thus a male interviewee explains to the sociologist Lillian Rubin that he avails himself of the services of prostitutes because "there's . . . times when it's a relief not to have to listen to somebody's directions about what she wants, and to be worrying all the time about her making it too" (Rubin, 132). In terms of Vivian's and Edward's initial contract, there is then no difference between prostitution and marriage in this romance plot. As a prostitute, Vivian is paid in hard cash, and goods; this is her most obvious return on her investment in Edward.

The crudeness of this exchange is masked in the film not only through the development of the "love story" that revolves around the kiss but through the aestheticization of the prostitute, most obviously through the inclusion of scenes from the tragic opera, *La Traviata,* as one of the film's most significant intertexts.[20] Because Vivian appreciates opera, because she weeps at the death of Violetta, Vivian's innate "value," her own status as aesthetic, is confirmed. In the same way, her capacity to laugh at "Lucy's" naïveté on television is a sign of Vivian's innocence, as though the effects of these objects transferred the quality from the source to Vivian herself. To use Edward's words again: opera becomes part of her "soul." At another level, the parallel drawn between Vivian and Violetta gives to the contemporary prostitute the status of a tragic heroine. Violetta's unhappy fate, a fate that Vivian shares in an earlier, discarded, version of the film's screenplay, is the result, however, of a personal sacrifice that Vivian is never called upon to make. (At the request of his father, Violetta sends her lover away so that his sister may marry, knowing that as a fallen woman she herself will never become a bride. Just before she dies of consumption, the father and son return, this reconciliation bringing Violetta back into the family, legitimating her sacrifice, erasing the stain of her profession through death [Clément, 65].) The significance of this parallel is illuminated by Cathérine Clément's description of the opera's heroine. Violetta, claims Clément, was "a good girl":

> . . . one possessing those mysterious, innate qualities of the soul that the bourgeoisie recognizes among its own kin: a certain sense of duty, a generosity with money, an acute sense of kinship, and an indefinable air of the homebody making the heroine of prostitution seem like a housewife who has strayed into the kitchens that are cooking up evil. (61)

Certainly the above description applies perhaps even more obviously to Vivian than to her tragic counterpart. And like *La Traviata, Pretty Woman* is about the "conflict between the family, its property interests and the parallel world of prostitution" (Clément, 64). The proximity of these two stories lends Vivian a pathos that she would not otherwise have, in a sense sanctifying the institution of prostitution in ways that are not justified by the narrative of the film itself.

Within the logic of the film's narrative of investment and return, Violetta's story has a different meaning; one might say that for Vivian, Violetta—like Skinny Marie pulled out of a dumpster at the beginning of the film—offers a cautionary tale: What happens when a young woman invests her capital unwisely. If Violetta returns to the family and its sanctity through death, the new heterosexual contract permits Vivian another solution. The film implies that the prostitute who upholds capitalism regulated by the law of the father can be saved by that same law. Redeeming the prostitute thus enables *Pretty Woman* to reconcile masculine pre-Oedipal desire (Edward's need for a "beck-and-call girl") and the Law of the Father within the same narrative. Vivian is recuperated within the family, finding her correct place again from which she has mistakenly erred—even if she has not been idle in her wanderings, even if it is Edward who profits from her accumulated capital. If this does not seem like a fair return on Vivian's investment (to be spared death hardly seems enough for a new paragon), it is because half of the story, the dream, the fantasy, has yet to be told.[21]

The play between ambition and erotic pleasure, between domesticity and sexual desire, are not the only contradictions that the film attempts to resolve in its "wish-fulfillment." Another crucial issue is best summed up by the contradiction implied through the double injunction that the single girl must represent desire for the masculine subject while simultaneously acting as the agent of her own desire—must reenact the specular image of consumer desire and yet assume agency and autonomy in the context of her own wishes. Certainly Vivian's cash balance has been improved. But if Edward reaps the sexual profits from their contract, where is her pleasure located? If the story, the narrative as a series of events linked through cause and effect, reproduces a fantasy of ambition and eroticism, it is the spectacle of the film, the mise-en-scène of Vivian as an object of visual display that throws into relief the problem of representation and agency, in which Vivian most clearly becomes the agent of her own pleasure.

Cinderella's Foot

To clarify the significance of the role of the feminine-as-spectacle let us return to our initial Cinderella plot. To talk about a marriage plot and the Cinderella story is to make a parallel that leaves out a meaningful detail. Cinderella is a young woman who is mistreated, and even more fundamentally misrecognized, whose hidden virtue is externalized in the form of small feet. This process of externalization is crucial in that it enables the story to represent qualities, i.e. compassion, diligence, discipline, etc., that are visually unrepresentable. Thus, not only do her small feet enable her husband to recognize her as the right choice, they are also the guarantee of other intangible qualities. The prince saves the young woman from her life of drudgery, elevating her to his station—the station in life to which she was always suited by her nature signaled to us through her small feet. If 18th- and 19th-Century marriage plots tend to emphasize "virtue" rather than small feet, Vivian as the new Cinderella returns us to a feminine model in which appearance is again fundamental, in which it is the entire body that comes to play the role of the foot in the fairy tale.

Feet, and the foot fetish, of course, evoke even to the populace at large, a paradigm of sexual perversion in which, in the most literal sense, the man can't "get it up" unless the woman is wearing appropriate foot gear—an accurate description of Cinderella's prince, if we see marriage as standing in for the sexual act.[22] Within the paradigm, the shoe is the fetish—the important element—not the foot; within the popular imagination there has thus been a slide from the object to that which it "covers."[23] The shoe can circulate freely—any woman can wear it—as long as it appears as though she were not "any" woman, that is, as though she were "pretty woman."[24]

This contradiction is exemplified by the fact that though Vivian is sexually adept and knows a great deal about cars, and ties, unlike Pamela she is without "education"; her transformation from prostitute to a woman of privilege is effected solely through her ability to purchase and wear fashionable garments—to "look good" in fashionable clothing. This is her most obvious skill, the necessary complement to her willing expertise in the bedroom. Fashionable clothing takes the place of the glass slipper. In *Pretty Woman*, the capacity to wear the glass slipper has been transformed into the capacity to wear fashionable clothing. And it is through the representation of her entire body that the woman, Vivian, as image, is taken as the fetish. The magical qualities of the glass slipper are transferred or rewritten as the fashionable body, signaled to us as such by Vivian's looks. It is Vivian's good looks that enable Edward to choose her. Of all of Vivian's efforts to please Edward, to be at his beck and call—she performs any number activities from fellatio to playing chess and picnicking in the park—it is her appearance in her hat and gloves, in her red evening gown, in her linen walking shorts, that best defines her for him and for us; that tells the spectator in a rhetoric defined through clothing that she is a princess in disguise, uncovered in her coverings.

The issue of fetishism has been crucial to the development of feminist theory, and there are as many theories of the fetish as there are theorists. The importance of the fetish as a concept specific to film theory is due to the fact that this concept addresses two fundamental issues of visual culture simultaneously, the problems of signification and visualization. The fetish is an essentially visual concept, in particular a visualization of desire; hence, it functions very aptly within a visual system of narrative signification such as film to represent desire (which is basically an abstract, rather than a visual concept). Also as a consumer object (such as a shoe), the fetish is a visual representation of the coincidence of consumer culture and desire. Thus the fetish foregrounds the issues of visual representation, desire, and consumer culture as three crucial avenues of inquiry in the area of film theory.

In her essay "Visual Pleasure and Narrative Cinema" a significant moment in the evolution of feminist film theory, Laura Mulvey, was perhaps the first to draw film scholars' attention to these issues, to the relations between visual pleasure, representation, and gender, and to the central function of the fetish as a mise-en-scène of desire within the cinematic field.[25] The importance of this article lies in the way it underlines the connections between a politics of representation and a politics of gender in which the feminine only appears, according to Mulvey, as a response to masculine desire. Drawing upon classical Freudian theory, Mulvey delineates two modes of representation: the voyeuristic mode, which hinges on the sadistic desire to control the feminine, and the fetishistic scopophilic mode,[26] which operates through disavowal. Both voyeurism and fetishism depend on a displacement of desire into visual representation, into the desire to see, a desire that can be realized, if only metaphorically, through the gaze of a spectator in terms of visual pleasure.

According to Mulvey, both voyeurism and fetishism operate as "two avenues of escape from . . . castration anxiety" for "the male unconscious" (64). As the voyeuristic object, the feminine is associated with a pleasure that "lies in ascertaining guilt, . . . asserting control, and subjecting the guilty person through punishment or forgiveness" (Mulvey, 64). Fetishism works through disavowing the possibility of castration as it is represented by the feminine. Her lack (the fact that she does not have a penis) is disavowed through "the substitution of a fetish object," for that object of desire that is simultaneously an object of anxiety because it symbolizes the threat of castration (her genitalia read as the absence of the penis but also as the sign of her femininity). Similarly, the entire "represented figure itself" can be transformed "into a fetish so that it becomes reassuring rather than dangerous. . . ." (64).[27] Thus for Mulvey, "(F)etishistic scopophilia builds up the physical beauty of the object, transforming it into something satisfying in itself" (64).[28] Mulvey describes the female film star as fetishistic object in the following terms:

> The beauty of the woman as object and the screen space coalesce; she
> is no longer the bearer of guilt but a perfect product, whose body,
> stylized and fragmented by close-ups, is the content of the film and
> the direct recipient of the spectator's look. (65)

For Mulvey, at least in this early article, the representation of the feminine in film is always articulated in terms of masculine voyeuristic or fetishistic pleasure. Many later feminists have accurately pointed out that this is an incomplete understanding of the representation of femininity and its pleasure within cinematic narrative; though the notions of fetishism and femininity offered by Mulvey do not constitute a universal template that explains visual pleasure, her work offers a significant, if incomplete, insight into the specific inscription of femininity within a film such as *Pretty Woman*—precisely because of the film's construction as a mise-en-scène of desire articulated through the rhetoric of feminine culture.

Full-Body Fetishism and the Feminine Consumer

The above definition of the fetish speaks to the representation of the feminine as she is incarnated in Vivian, most obviously in terms of her transformation into Pretty Woman which occurs after her shopping spree, underlined (should we as spectators fail to recognize the importance of this moment) by the voice-over song "Pretty Woman." The approving looks that Vivian encounters in her triumphant parade through Rodeo Drive serve to emphasize her newfound completeness. The film departs from the model described by Mulvey[29] in that it uncovers and integrates into its narrative an explanation of the process of fetishization. The story of Vivian is the story of how to become the fetish. Within the narrative the film charts Vivian's progress from voyeuristic object to fetishistic object. *Pretty Woman* self-consciously investigates that process whereby the woman might become the fetish, to control the gaze of the male (rather than being controlled), earn money, and carve out for herself some small arena of private pleasure.

The crucial role of the gaze in confirming Vivian's movement from one position to the other is clearly represented, visually figured, in the scenes, among others, which depict Vivian's entrances and exits through the lobby of the Regent Beverly Wilshire Hotel, where Edward occupies the penthouse during his stay in Los Angeles. These scenes are notable in that each inscribes characters whose function is to demonstrate for the spectator the proper way to look at Vivian. When Vivian returns from her shopping spree she is greeted with glances of approbation and pleasure from the inhabitants of the hotel lobby, and in particular Barnard Thompson, the hotel manager (Hector Elizondo). This warm welcome is in direct contrast to the stares of frightened disapproval her initial appearance evoked when Edward tried to hustle her in under wraps—his raincoat covering her, hiding what should not be seen and thus drawing attention to the fact that she had something to hide—that she was guilty—the object of voyeuristic scrutiny. These entrances and exits mark the stages of Vivian's transformation, culminating in her apparition as a princess on the way to the ball; dressed in a red evening dress, white gloves, and jewelry worth a quarter of a million dollars, she accompanies Edward to the opera. Vivian is not, by virtue of her red evening dress, "Skinny Marie," whose death at the beginning of the film signals the difference between the position of voyeuristic object that she initially occupied—in which death would have been her inevitable reward—and the position she now occupies as fetish object.

Vivian's Victory Procession

These sequences that document Vivian's joyous transformation also delineate the limitations of Mulvey's theory, in that this theory cannot take account of her jubilation—one that certainly mirrors the approving jubilation of Vivian's spectators but that is also represented as her own, the pleasure of a feminine subject. The empowerment that this position offers is perhaps most clearly represented through Vivian's return to the shop that had originally refused to serve her, denying her access to the fetishized body. The shop women have made a "big mistake" in Vivian's terms because they have lost a great deal of money by refusing to serve her. But Vivian's triumph goes further. The shop women in their eagerness to serve provide independent verification of her transformation. The first dress that Vivian purchased with the help of the hotel manager and his saleswoman friend proved Vivian's potential for transformation; however, until her big shopping spree she remained a working girl, a call girl perhaps, no longer a street walker, but still a lady of the night, if one on the way up. One little black dress is not enough—Vivian needs a wardrobe,[30] which she can only acquire with Edward's credit card, and, more importantly, his authority. Edward's money is not enough to confer legitimacy on Vivian; she must be accompanied by him, he must speak for her before she can really shop. It is clearly Edward's position that gives Vivian her position in the previous store, the store in which she undergoes this transformation. Though Edward authorizes her transformation in the same way that he authorizes her use of his credit card, once the transformation is complete, the wardrobe acquired, Vivian no longer needs Edward. She acquires autonomy through the admiring subservient gaze of the shop women. Her pleasure, however, goes beyond this moment of recognition. Her excessive delight in the monument of her consumer Self produces a pleasure that is narcissistic, an excess that is autoerotic, that depends on her own knowledge of her "prettiness," as well as the admiring glances of her audience. This pleasure constitutes part of the profits of her transactions, of her heterosexual contract.[31]

I interject here a personal anecdote, which occurred during the months following the release of *Pretty Woman,* because it well illustrates this pleasure-in-her-own image implied in the position of the fetishized feminine. An acquaintance and I were indulging ourselves, shopping in one of Chicago's "better" department stores. While I was engrossed in the private negotiation of what is politely described as lingerie, my companion wandered off into the hinterlands of more expensive dresses and suits. A woman arrayed in an elaborate day suit notable in its display as expense paraded before a three-paneled mirror mesmerized by her own reflection and the reflected gaze of a man, her companion, and that of an attentive saleswoman. Upon noticing the gaze of my friend, the gaze of a woman alone, apparently not "chosen", wearing jeans and high-tops, the preferred customer announced jubilantly to her now-augmented audience: "I feel just like Pretty Woman." The irony of this moment derives as much from the fact that this woman could easily have been paying for her own outfit as from the fact that it is this complicated conjunction of gazes, including her own as she gazes at herself in the mirror, that guarantees her pleasure, rather than a single monolithic masculine gaze described by Mulvey. Thus her own pleasure is enacted within a structure of surveillance held in place from a number of vantage points. This overdetermined conjunction of multiple gazes both constrains and enables her pleasure as a narcissistic moment that does not challenge the heterosexual contract.

The importance of this reading of the film and its position within feminine culture is illustrated by another anecdote. During my first viewing of the film, two women seated behind me, who had obviously seen the film before, spent much of their time discussing their favorite outfits—especially during the crucial shopping scene in which Vivian appears wearing an array of ensembles. The women's taste did not necessarily coincide with that of the narrative; however, the pleasure of their viewing seemed to derive from the possibilities of choice (or more accurately, its fantasy) that the film offered. The encoding of these choices within fashion magazines emphasizes the pleasures of transformation as a narcissistic moment that the woman performs for herself. In a two-page spread for *Vogue* featuring Julia Roberts in which she re-presents her roles as Pretty Woman, the caption in red running the full length of the spread reads:

"When I started dressing differently, suddenly I was different" (396–397).[32] The power, its attractiveness for women, of the fetishistic moment is that though it appears to construct itself for the masculine scopophilic gaze (from the position of the masculine subject), this same moment can easily be rewritten through the rhetoric of feminine consumer culture as a narcissistic moment (from the position of the feminine subject).

If this sounds like an edenic scene of perfect wish-fulfillment that accommodates all contradictions, it is only because we have not followed the path of analysis to its final conclusion—there is yet another turn of the screw before we can return to our point of departure as our moment of closure. The spectacle of transformation that the film offers its viewers has always already taken place. Vivian's comedy of abjection enveloped in Edward's raincoat is precisely that: an enactment, a masquerade, that is always unmasking itself as part of its comedy played broadly for laughs. Her perfection as body (she looks as if she is wearing stockings even when she is not) protects Vivian, transforming the potentially dangerous gaze into a sight gag played for the film-viewer's pleasure (Edward enjoys it too, even if he cannot admit that he likes it) and her profit. From the first moment Vivian's body, or rather her bodies, occupy the screen, she is displayed as the spectacle of the fetishistic feminine described by Mulvey above.[33] At the same time, the obvious use of body doubles marks the fetish body as phantasmatic, a purely representational rather than performative function, that signals the gap between fantasy and consumer practice. Of course, the effect would be the same whether or not a body double was used, but the use of a body double underlines the way in which all images reproduced through the conventions of photographic technique and psychological editing as a process of segmentation and condensation are phantasmatic.

A sequence of eleven shots near the beginning of the film (in fact the credits are not yet over), is representative of this phantasmatic mise-en-scène of the fetishized body. In this sequence, the first time Vivian appears in the film, it is not Julia Roberts we see, but her double. In this first shot of Vivian(s), we are presented with a woman's derrière in a black-lace bikini, "v-kini" in the vocabulary of women's lingerie. The torso slowly turns toward the camera, drawing the spectators' gaze to the "V" of the "kini," which points, as it were, to that which it covers. The camera then tracks up the torso, right to left, reframing in close-up, along the arm and hand (silencing an alarm clock) while the woman's head remains hidden under a pillow. Julia Roberts appears in shot 2 of this sequence, but only in a series of poorly resolved snapshots tacked to a wall, her features barely distinguishable, in which another figure, we assume that of a man, is either obliterated or cut out. Shot 3 returns us to the body double, a high-angle shot of a bust cupped in a black-lace "uplift bra." Again, though we see a blonde wig, the woman's face is not visible. Shot 4 offers us hands incased in bracelets. Shot 5 is a close-up of Edward, full-face glancing momentarily into the camera, as though he were the subject of the images that preceded him, that these images retrospectively inscribed his point of view, that they were his fantasies. Shot 6 is a long shot of the car Edward is driving, certainly nowhere near Beverly Hills, his ostensible goal, but moving him toward the moment at which he will take the place now empty in Vivian's snapshots. In the next two shots (7 and 8) we watch as Vivian continues her preparation: her hands repairing her boot with a felt-tip pen, her hand zipping up the boot as the camera travels up the boot to the top of the leg in a baroque, almost parodic, recreation of the fetishistic moment, again from right to left, always reframing in close-up, this parallel movement implying equivalence among body parts. Finally, in shots 9 and 10 we see a segment of Julia Roberts' face, in which the jump between 9 and 10, basically the same shot, emphasizes the unreal nature of the sequence. The sequence closes with a long shot of the Lotus, the car Edward is driving, as it speeds through the night, still lost but still traveling inexorably towards its destination. Not until the next sequence do we see a full-body shot of Julia Roberts as Vivian.

As if to underline the phantasmatic nature of their encounter, the body double intervenes again a little later in the film during the first meeting of Edward and Vivian. In this sequence, Edward hesitates, unwilling to meet Vivian's price for "directions." His gaze lingers on her derrière (that of the double) framed by the car window, which "view" apparently convinces him of her value, since he subsequently agrees to her price and their adventure begins. The use of the double in these two sequences illustrates how a fetishistic regime reinscribes feminine lack or inadequacy through the impossibility of the image it offers the spectator. These sequences also illustrate the close alliance between fetishism and voyeurism, in which the segmentation of the female is both a glorification and a metaphoric mutilation, a carving up, of the same body.

The fascination with the body double as the metaphor of the phantasmatic cinematic body characterizes the film-viewer's self-consciousness, the position of disavowal that he or she always occupies vis-à-vis the film's fantasy as the scene of desire.[34] Typically, though the film's producers took pains to hide the "doubles," the fact was seized upon by the media. The following headline is characteristic: "Those sexy curves super-star Julia Roberts flaunts in her Pretty Woman poster aren't hers!" (*Examiner*, 10). Thus the composite body that represents the fetish body emblemizes not only its status as fantasy but the self-conscious status of that fantasy for the film-viewer,[35] in which the image both simultaneously offers the fantasy and signals its impossibility. Even Julia Roberts is not in and of herself adequate to her own image, which must be created through an excess of bodies.[36] She needs help. Claims one of her doubles: "Julia was grateful to have someone else make her look good" (*Examiner,* 10). Importantly, it is precisely at the beginning of the film, before Vivian's consumer transformation, that Roberts most clearly calls upon the help (the phantasmatic excess) of the body double, because, of course, these are the scenes in which we see her in the least amount of clothing. Underlying her subsequent transformation is the knowledge that Vivian possesses, instead of the small foot, the fetish body endowed with the same magical qualities that create the perfect match between shoe and foot for Cinderella. The fact that Bloomingdale's catalogue sells "Pretty Woman" boots, referring to Vivian's earlier incarnation before she formally becomes Pretty Woman, suggests how the recognition of fantasy is assimilated into the vocabulary of fashion as a technique of masquerade, in which the gap between image and performance is the measure of fantasy and desire for the viewer.

Pretty Woman, its attempt to reconcile a politics of sexual parity with the conventions of the marriage plot, to imagine a fantasy in which a woman always receives a just return for her investment without relinquishing her right to the pursuit of happiness, might indicate why, as the popular writer Sally Quinn claims: "many women believe that their needs are better understood by the Helen Gurley Browns of the world than by the Germaine Greers" (25). I hope, however, that this reading of the film also points to the dangers of taking this statement at face value, of positing Helen Gurley Brown as the authentic voice of popular resistance or the tool of a male conspiracy. The heritage of feminist film critics such as Laura Mulvey is two-fold: it speaks to us of the necessity of paying attention to popular culture and of the folly of dismissing it as mere entertainment. If critics such as Laura Mulvey have drawn our attention to the films of the past, *Pretty Woman* may be telling us that it is also time to look at the stories contemporary culture tells us today. It cannot be mere coincidence that Dorothy C. Holland and Margaret A. Eisenhart concluded, after an eight-year close-focus ethnographical study of college students entitled *Educated in Romance,* that:

> women were not so vulnerable to the threat of a ruined reputation; a different component of the cultural idiom of romance and attractiveness was important. But the results were very similar; women faced constant evaluations of their worth on the basis of their sexual appeal to men, and they made life "decisions" in the shadow of that reality. (21)

As we have seen, *Pretty Woman* tells the same story, in which, as Nancy Miller puts it, "the female *Bildung* gets stuck in the bedroom" (*The

Heroine's Text, 157). Let us not forget that it is precisely these material conditions and the culture that it produces that feminist criticism must address if it is to maintain any political viability.

Works Cited

Armstrong, Nancy. *Desire and Domestic Fiction: A Political History of the Novel.* New York: Oxford University Press, 1987.

Banner, Lois. *American Beauty.* New York: Knopf, 1983.

Brown, Helen Gurley. *Sex and the Single Girl.* New York: Bernard Geis, Random House, 1962.

Brownstein, Rachel. *Becoming a Heroine: Reading About Women in Novels.* New York: Viking Press, 1982.

Collins, Ava Preacher. "Redressing Cinderella." Unpublished paper. M.M.L.A., 1991.

Collins, Jim. *Uncommon Cultures: Popular Culture and Post-Modernism.* New York: Routledge, 1989.

Cleland, John. *Fanny Hill, or, Memoirs of a Woman of Pleasure.* New York: Penguin, 1985.

Clément, Catherine. *Opera or the Undoing of Women.* Trans. B. Wing. Minneapolis: University of Minnesota Press, 1988.

Dowling, Colette. *The Cinderella Complex: Women's Hidden Fear of Independence.* New York: Summit Books, 1981.

DuPlessis, Rachel Blau. *Writing Beyond the Ending: Narrative Strategies of Twentieth-Century Women Writers.* Bloomington: Indiana University Press, 1985.

Ehrenreich, Barbara, Elizabeth Hess, and Gloria Jacobs. *Re-making Love: The Feminization of Sex.* New York: Anchor Press/Doubleday, 1986.

Ewen, Stuart and Elizabeth Ewen. *Channels of Desire: Mass Images and the Shaping of American Consciousness.* New York: McGraw-Hill, 1982.

Examiner. "Oh no, Joe—Say it isn't so: That's not Julia Robert's body—it's Donna's." March 26, 1991, p. 10.

Freud, Sigmund. *On Creativity and the Unconscious.* Trans. I.F. Duff. New York: Harper and Brothers, 1958.

Hansen, Miriam. "Adventures of Goldilocks: Spectatorship, Consumerism and Public Life." *Camera Obscura:* 22 January, 1990, pp. 50–71.

Hillis, Marjorie. *Live Alone and Like It: A Guide for the Extra Woman.* New York: The Sun Dial Press, 1933.

Holland, Dorothy C. and Margaret A. Eisenhart. *Educated in Romance: Women, Achievement and College Culture.* Chicago: University of Chicago Press, 1990.

Hurst, Fannie. *Back Street.* New York: A.L. Burt Company, 1931.

"J." *The Sensuous Woman.* New York: Lyle Stuart, 1969.

Kaplan, Louise. *Female Perversions: The Temptations of Emma Bovary.* New York: Doubleday, 1991.

Laplanche, Jacques and J.-B. Pontalis. *The Language of Psycho-analysis.* Trans. Donald Nicholson-Smith. New York: W.W. Norton and Company, 1973.

Laqueur, Thomas. "Orgasm, Generation, and the Politics of Reproductive Biology." *The Making of the Modern Body*. Ed. Catherine Gallagher and Thomas Laqueur. Berkeley: University of California Press, 1987.

Leach, Edmund. *Claude Lévi-Strauss*. New York: Viking Press, 1974, 1970.

Lévi-Strauss, Claude. *Structural Anthropology*. Trans. C. Jacobson and B. Schoepf. New York: Basic Books, 1967, 1958.

Mannoni, Octave. *Clefs pour l'Imagainaire ou L'Autre Scène*. Paris: Éditions du Seuil, 1969.

Marcom, John, Jr. "Dream factory to the world." *Forbes*. April 29, 1991, pp. 98, 100–101.

Mei, Huang. *Transforming the Cinderella Dream*. New Brunswick: Rutgers University Press, 1990.

Miller, Nancy K. "Emphasis Added: Plots and Plausibilities in Women's Fiction." *The New Feminist Criticism: Essays on Woman, Literature, and Theory*. Ed. Elaine Showalter. New York: Pantheon, 1985.

————. *The Heroine's Text: Readings in the French and English Novel, 1722–1782*. New York: Columbia University Press, 1980.

Modleski, Tania. *Loving with a Vengeance: Mass-Produced Fantasies for Women*. New York: Methuen, 1982.

Mulvey, Laura. "Visual Pleasure and Narrative Cinema" (1975). *Feminism and Film Theory*. Ed. Constance Penley. New York: Routledge, 1988, pp. 57–68.

Quinn, Sally. "The Death of Feminism." *Washington Post National Weekly Edition*. January 27–February 2, 1992, p. 25.

Penley, Constance. "Feminism, Psychoanalysis, and the Study of Popular Culture," in *Cultural Studies*. Ed. by Lawrence Grossberg, Cary Nelson, and Paula Treichler. New York: Routledge, 1992, pp. 479–500.

Richardson, Samuel. *Pamela, or Virtue Rewarded*. New York: W.W. Norton, 1958.

Rubin, Lillian. *Erotic Wars: What Happened to the Sexual Revolution?* New York: Farrar, Straus and Giroux, 1990.

Variety. "Top Rental films for 1990." January 7, 1991, p. 8.

Vogue. "Woman of Character." April 1990. pp. 394–399, 421.

4

The Unauthorized Auteur Today

Dudley Andrew

Breathe easily. *Epuration* has ended. After a dozen years of clandestine whispering we are permitted to mention, even to discuss, the auteur again.[1] Since 1990 *Hors Cadre* has devoted an entire issue to "L'Etat de l'auteur"; *Film Quarterly* has published James Naremore's "Authorship and the Cultural Politics of Film Criticism"; and Rutgers has brought out Timothy Corrigan's *A Cinema Without Walls,* a book that reads like a compendium of contemporary directorial talent and that includes a specific chapter on the status of the auteur today.[2]

No matter what each of us thought, or thinks, of ideological criticism, it was ruthless when it came to proper names, most ruthless of all toward those names that authorized naming in the first place: Truffaut, Rohmer, and behind them, André Bazin. Without trying to settle scores, I am happy to call attention once more to what may be Bazin's most significant insight into the medium he so loved: the cinema, he felt, was congenitally impure. No effort to purify it could long succeed: not the Dadaists of the twenties nor the Lettrists of his own day, not the Cinema-Verité movement of the sixties nor the political avant-garde that after 1968 marched in step with the changing of the guard at *Cahiers du Cinéma.*

In fact, *Cahiers* in its first years had religiously pursued purity, latching onto Sartre's notion of "authenticity," where an individual authors his or her life in choice and where writers and filmmakers authenticate their work in style. Even though auteurism had been fostered as a way of recovering a large number of otherwise disposable studio-made movies, it carried with it the aura of elitism emanating from the French ciné-clubs of the postwar years and from festivals where auteurs were annually inducted and honored as individuals with strong (invariably masculine) personalities producing art capable of transcending its conditions of production and reception. The *Cahiers* critics promised to rectify the distracted attention of earlier audiences with a reverential viewing of films that in some cases they treated as sacramental objects, harboring the genuinely spiritual values conferred on them by their makers. As we will see, this sentiment toward cinema continues to be entertained today in France, though in a sophisticated and self-conscious manner.

Bazin, it is usually forgotten, was a drag on this policy, suspicious of its vocabulary.[3] He was most likely to mention an auteur in conjunction with a genre or a national trend or a social movement. When he allowed himself to indulge in the excesses of existential auteurism, as in his essay *"Le Journal d'un curé de campagne* and the Stylistics of Robert Bresson,*"* he multiplied the names of authors. Recall this remarkable sentence from that more remarkable analysis: "The sound of a windshield-wiper against a page of Diderot is all it took to turn it into Racinian dialogue."[4] Bazin faced up to the question of adaptation and translation with all the economic, and ideological ramifications these terms imply. In this cultural ecology the auteur certainly played the most noticeable function but nevertheless was treated as a function within a system of forces. To stop one's analysis at the auteur, as Bazin accused his friends at *Cahiers,* was to stop inquiring of the cinema.[5] It was to fetishize an imagined purity of spirit or core of being beneath the images of a film. Bazin's taste for impure cinema, for hybrids and eccentricities, would have salivated at this volume's Table of Contents, and at postmodern cinema generally. For despite his commitment to the integral humanism of Rossellini and Renoir, no one was more adept than he at teasing out the multiple strands woven into any film experience. The author may have been primary for him, but only as a tortion in the knot of technology, film language, genre, cultural precedent, and so forth, a knot that has in the past decades grown increasingly tangled.

Structuralism came to study systematically the textual knot and to suppress the search for its human source. Language alone could be credited with authoring those linguistic configurations we call texts. Peter Wollen discussed Hawks and Ford not as complex men with worldviews but as names for certain regularities in textual organization, although in the first (1969) edition of *Signs and Meaning in the Cinema* he still felt required to append his pantheon of rich auteurs, holding it up against that of Andrew Sarris. By the time of the second edition (1972), flush with Foucault, he retracted the retrograde appendix. Still, Wollen's structuralism (which he compares to meteorology and implicitly to chemistry) made room for the individual as "catalyst," that is, as an element, innocuous in itself, having the potential to initiate a complex reaction when dropped into the proper mix of other elements.[6] This scientist analogy did not keep Wollen from proclaiming the primacy of interpretation, of "reading the codes," and from confessing that some films yield nothing when read deeply while others (the great films?) reward such reading by supporting a supplement of meaning read into them. The auteurist in him was sustained by this belief in the importance of locating in the confused and contradictory activity of texts those structures that, under analysis, invariably precipitate out when the same catalyst is known to have been employed. We name these structures "von Sternberg," "Fuller," "Cukor," and so on. Isolating the auteur's signal within the noise of the text carried for Wollen a strategic function, by initiating further analyses to disentangle other signals—other codes—that contribute to the textual (dis)organization. Critics may begin by appreciating the intentions and achievements of a bold individual, but persistent structural analysis should lead them to distinguish numerous other factors (codes of genre, studio, technicians, culture) that support or more often vie with that of the director. The vibrancy of the text, its fertility as a site for productive reading, outlives the illusory vibrancy of some genius standing behind or before the text.

The two editions of Wollen's important book, the first reluctantly auteurist, the second Foucauldian, stand as mileage markers in the short trail of academic film studies, a trail that we know leads quickly to psychoanalysis, ideological critique, and the study of audiences in popular culture. One might call this a tiresome tale of academic fads, were it not for the fact that the identical issues (the status of the auteur, the discipline of the system, competition within the text, and competition within audiences) can be seen at play in real-world cultural arenas. With the demise of the confident studio system, American films joined those of other national cinemas in more readily displaying the tensions that went into their making and the anxieties that attended their reception. In the late sixties one can monitor cinema systems and their disruption worldwide. Let's look to Japan in 1968 where the notorious Seijun Suzuki affair staged a drama of business and expression as colorful as in a Kabuki play.[7]

When a Tokyo ciné-club announced its intention to hold a retrospective of most of Suzuki's forty B-movies, his studio, Nikkatsu, pulled the prints from circulation and fired the director ostensibly for making incomprehensible films. At issue, as the subsequent court proceedings brought to light, was the right of a studio to shape the appeal of its products. The elite reception to which Sukuki would have been treated in this retrospective undermined the regulated flow of images in the culture industry.

In the years following the trial the studio has been vindicated in that ciné-clubs have lost the substantial cultural weight they attained in the late sixties. Today they are invoked as a warm memory of a more innocent, more human age. On the other hand, the ciné-club proved to be a vanguard of a general uprising, for it breached the ramparts of the studio walls by declaring its right to use films in any way it might choose. The fragmentation of the mass audience into uncoordinated subgroups has been the story of global culture since 1980 and it is the story of postmodernism as well, with well-known consequences for the intentions of authors, agents, and even governments.

Suzuki constitutes a preeminent case because of the ostensibly apolitical nature of his films. Nikkatsu was concerned not so much about the power of auteurs and their renegade texts but about that of audiences to break up the meaning of texts and to break up the system Nikkatsu believed it controlled. This same shift became evident in the West in the 1970s with the canon-bashing that occurred in the wake of feminism and multiculturalism: while a great many films and some new auteurs may have climbed into the pantheon, they have done so at deflated value. For the most advanced cultural critics have sold their stock in auteurs and even in texts, buying heavily into audiences and the cultures they comprise.[8]

But the Suzuki story continues; today he is indeed a genuine force in Japanese cinema. Special issues of journals have been consecrated to him. While he no longer turns out three films a year, but more like one every three years, each now causes a stir. Nikkatsu on the other hand is inert. The auteur has outlasted the industry, or rather he has adapted to a fragmented audience, one small but passionate portion of which will pay to see, and see repeatedly, whatever it is that Suzuki signs.

Auteurism, in short, is far from dead.[9] As Timothy Corrigan says, it may

> in fact be more alive now than at any other point in film history.
> . . . within the commerce of contemporary culture it [auteurism] has
> become, as both a production and interpretive position, more critically
> central yet massively different from what it once may have been.
> Since the early 1970s, the commercial conditioning of this figure has
> successfully evacuated it of most of its expressive power and textual
> coherence; simultaneously, this commercial conditioning has called
> renewed attention to the layered pressures of auteurism as an agency
> that establishes different modes of identification with its audiences.[10]

What has happened since the early seventies, since the Wollen book and the Suzuki affair, to produce these different modes of identification? Among other factors, the incessant flow of televisual images has eroded the stability of texts and seeped like an acid to break up the last signs of their authors as authorities who hover over the experience of their work and exert a moral pressure on its interpretation. Auteurs may exist but they do so by the grace of spectators. Today critics feel the need to be concerned with the cultural environment within which a diverse citizenry moves, takes pleasure, and jockeys for position. They must be concerned with Tokyo, London, São Paulo, and Rome, where, out of control, a superabundance of images is taken up willy-nilly by the myriad groups wandering the streets at cross-purposes or to no purpose at all.

Critics like Corrigan, who are fascinated or bewildered by the rapidly shifting movements in culture since Vietnam, recognize the importance of the auteur in the proliferation of texts and meanings, but treat that auteur not as an individual with a vision or even a program but as a dispersed, multi-masked, or empty name bearing a possibly bogus collatoral in the international market of images, a market that increasingly trades in "futures." This reduction of the auteur to a single relay in the economic flow of images has the effect of superimposing representations onto reality, reversing the traditional model. "To begin to write," Edward Said claimed, "is to redirect human energy away from the 'world' to the page."[11] If the cinema had ever been worthy to be taken as a page on which something once begun was written, Corrigan would have us believe this is no longer the case today, that we are in the midst of "A Cinema Without Walls" spilling out into the world. If they once did so, auteurs today turn not away from the world but toward it, and the world, if we dare to speak of it at all anymore, is a salad of possibilities in which images and representations are included as first-order elements. Not long ago one aptly referred to Fellini's "world," or Ingmar Bergman's or John Ford's, indicating thereby an abstracted set of elements systematically interrelated in a structure to be projected on a screen somewhere to the side of the daily life from which those elements were culled. But today, should we speak of Spike Lee's "world," when his is designed to fold itself inside our world? Appearing on talk shows and Nike shoe ads, Lee is familiar in our living rooms, just as pizza and Public Enemy fit comfortably within his films. Indeed those films are likely to be invited into our living rooms on tape. This is more than a matter of new technologies of distribution; it stems from a recognition that nature and culture and the representation of both are increasingly experienced homogeneously. Do tourists today distinguish their trip to the Epcot Center from their visit to Florida?

The global commercialization of culture validates Corrigan's viewpoint, money serving as the great equalizer. Not only does it equalize Spike Lee, Ridley Scott, and Robert Bresson at the Video Rental store, but it places even the most intentional auteur (Coppola is Corrigan's well-chosen example) inside a system that is larger than he, a system that quickly and crudely exchanges his value on the market in its own way. American film critics like Corrigan who once looked to Europe for models of films and criticism, must now be increasingly attentive, like their country itself, to Japan and what it represents in economy and culture. For Japan stands for neon and simulacra, not for texts and authors, despite the proliferation of print in that country. In the postwar era the auteur was the strongest tie linking cinema to the literary function; the auteur proved that Film could be an art, an expression of personal thought and feeling, opposed to the externality of spectacle, opposed also perhaps to the universal appeal of most movies. The mention of literature calls to mind a cinema that is viewed in private, meditatively, one that is reflected upon and discussed and from which ideas may be taken, in short a cinema to be read rather than consumed.[12]

Are even books still read in such a way? To think about the author in Japan is to think nostalgically, to think of Soseki and Tanizaki and the refined world of sensibility that they represented and to which they contributed. Whereas today, in Tokyo's Jonmocho district—the world's greatest concentration of bookstores—magazines and manga increasingly dominate the shelves. Thousands of browsers move from rack to rack, flipping pages. They edge distractedly to the cashier where they riffle through their wallets and exchange thousand-yen notes featuring portraits of Soseki for picture books of humanized robots or more often of robotic nubile girls (drawn or photographed, it hardly matters). A leading critic of Japanese literature concludes his last book with a meditation on post-literacy in the midst of a booming publishing culture.[13] Japanese books are designed to be disposable. In that country the author is recruited into a commerce of swift exchange where even in scholarly writing the tops of ideas are scanned with the rapidity of a simplified line drawing.[14]

Cinema is part of the media economy that has reduced the auteur to a sign, indeed precisely to a signature. But cinema is also a victim of this economy, its carefully painted images losing out on (and to) the electronic pictures flowing like tap water or sewage down twelve or thirty-four or a hundred channels around the globe. Looked at from the perspective of Tokyo, literature and cinema have in common the futile and pathetic struggle to preserve the value of thought, of feeling, of art, in a world that decreasingly cares about such things.

But let me return to Europe where such things are discussed and apparently still cared about. For the auteur has returned to academic respectability today, as Corrigan's book demonstrates, and it has done so thanks to heretical Foucauldians like Edward Said and Gilles Deleuze. Said's sensitivity to the micro-structures of power and knowledge didn't keep him from writing a book called *Beginnings* and from retaining a belief that critical humanism (that is, strategic interventions by individuals) could alter such massive and dispersed ideological formations as the one he identified as "Orientalism." To "begin" a project is not to originate a work, but rather to deflect a flow, to branch off in a direction. This limited sense of novelty retains the power of individual effort and critique while recognizing the greater power of the social system within which anything that makes a difference must begin. We credit this view to the likes of Alexander Kluge and Fernando Solanas. Why not apply it in some degree, too, to a Ridley Scott, whose attempt to branch out from the road picture in *Thelma and Louise* (1991) seems more heroic for its collapse in the film's final chase sequences.[15]

Less moderate than Said, Gilles Deleuze returns to Nietzsche and especially to Bergson in insisting on "the new," on "creative evolution." Deleuze's influential books on cinema depend on auteurs, on their muscular expansion of the repertoire of cinematic representation, and effectively on what we once called their "visions of the world." In a symptomatic moment he locates in the films of Akira Kurosawa a configuration of camera movements that double as a fictive graphic sign—a kanji—for Kurosawa's own name.[16] Always a problematic and very special sign, the signature of the author is a mark on the surface of the text signaling its source. The signature embeds within it—as in hypertext—a genuine fourth dimension, the temporal process that brought the text into being in the first place.[17] The signature moors the film image to a submerged reef of values by means of the slender line drawn by camera or pen. It is visible in the credits of films, in the literal appearance in the midst of their films of auteurs like Hitchcock, and after him of Truffaut, Godard, and Rohmer.

An auteur may be surrounded by the images for which it is claimed he is responsible, while not directing their reading. This would be Deleuze's point regarding Kurosawa and Hitchcock, whose use of the figure of the spiral in *Vertigo* he identifies as a graphic signature as well. The spectator is free to employ these figures as he or she wishes because, for Deleuze, one doesn't "read" a movie anyway, rather one subsists within its duration and its flow, carried by it, but not carried to any pre-given destination. The auteur marks the presence of temporality and creativity in the text, including the creativity of emergent thought contributed by the spectator.

Deleuze's resolute stance against the semiology of cinema may be responsible for the French reassessment of the auteur in terms no longer of literature but of painting. Several of France's most significant films of late take as their subject the creative instant of the artist. Jacques Rivette's *La Belle Noiseuse* and Maurice Pialat's *Van Gogh* confirm the relation between cinema and painting that theorists like Jacques Aumont and Raymond Bellour have been insisting upon, particularly in relation to Godard's recent work.[18] Godard has always understood that the image of the auteur as a writer before a blank page must be followed by the more disappointing image of those pages filled out in a language whose net inevitably surrounds and constricts the expressive impulse that pushes the stylus into the paper. But the image of the painter before an empty canvas retains the lure of pre-linguistic purity, the moment when representation and perception interact in ways that are potentially fresh. *Passion* (1982) takes originality for its subject; *Je Vous Salue Marie* (1984) meditates on the virgin birth by simulating the untrammeled perception of nature. One might consider Godard, Rivette, and even Pialat as special cases, but when a popular success like *Touts les matins du monde* (1991), starring Gérard Depardieu, burrows into the stillness of a Baroque composer before the act of composing, one must credit a significant backlash against the massive successes of American action cinema (*Terminator 2* [1991]) and of the simulations of international postmodernism (*La Femme Nikita* [1991]) that form the backdrop of contemporary culture.[19]

In their theory and films, then, the French remind us even today that properly speaking the author is not one who employs a completed language system but stands as the function that reaches back to the silence before language and draws out in birth pangs an expression shaped to feeling and thought. To read a poem or a novel is to participate again in this struggle for expression, what today we call *écriture,* the quest for the state of wordlessness through words.[20] *Écriture* (and paradoxically these "painting films"[21]) involves temporality and interiority, whereas the postmodern media world is one of pure spatiality and externality, the display—the spectacle—of the social.

The term *écriture* inevitably turns my conclusion toward Marguerite Duras. *Le Camion* (1977) opens with a shot of an intersection. When a truck (*the* truck of the title) centers itself in focus, the credits begin to identify those responsible for this text, including Marguerite Duras as author and director. But where, or which, is the text of those listed as responsible for it? We ask this when the credits are interrupted by a shot of Duras herself reading a written text to Gérard Depardieu. When the truck returns along with the remainder of the credits we are led to realize that this film is an exemplication of a reading that we are intermittently allowed to be present at. No prior literary work is translated by the cinema. The cinema in fact imagines a piece of writing that is simultaneously under construction. The author is present in the text as a cinematic effect.

Atop this fertile image of the auteur in the text, however, we must impose a second image, more recent and far more normal: on the cover of a popular monthly journal a black-and-white photo of a fetching teenager, hat cocked 1930s style, with the caption inviting the reader to open and enter "La vraie vie de Marguerite Duras."[22] In the midst of a biographical assemblage, a crucial page is devoted to the recent adaptation of her most popular novel *L'Amant* (1992). Duras, we learn, wrote a screen version of *L'Amant* at the request of its producer Claude Berri by composing a parasitic novel, *L'amant de la Chine du Nord* that contains references to its possible realization in motion pictures. The second chapter begins: "C'est un livre, c'est un film, c'est la nuit."[23] Producing more "literature," this adaptation only brought her into dispute with Berri and with the film's director, Jean-Jacques Annaud, a dispute whose notoriety has even now become part of the promotion of a film that Duras repudiates. Yet Duras's name and her adolescent photograph are integral to the advertising of this film and presumably to the pleasure of the public standing in line to watch what is in every sense a hybrid artifact.

L'Amant (as writing, text, film, supplemental text, and cultural phenomenon) strains the issues of purity and hybridity with which I began. *L'Amant* requires Duras and requires her absence; this is the paradox of auteurism.[24] We want to believe in Duras, though few authors disappear more mysteriously behind a screen of words. This is a struggle of faith in an atheist world, for the author is surely an analogue of God, the creator and source of the world. With the disappearance of God we are left with the body of the world; so, with the disappearance of the author, we are left with the material body of the text. Since Nietzsche, we have been tempted to play with that body as we choose, for readers exist and the text exists, but the author is an effect of both, an effect, moreover, brought about by distance and invisibility. Nevertheless, despite Nietzsche and the freeplay he ushered in, the word "auteur," and the occasional signs left by whatever this word signals, can thicken a text with duration, with the past of its coming into being and with the future of our being with it.

5

Loose Canons: Constructing Cultural Traditions Inside and Outside the Academy

Ava Preacher Collins

Within the past decade a major government monograph and several high-profile books focused on the topic of canon formation have appeared. In fact it has become a "hot" issue, inextricably bound up with the debates raging around "political correctness," presented in such highly visible fora as a special televised *Firing Line* debate and the pages of *Village Voice*. This hubbub was largely initiated in 1984 by then-Secretary of Education William Bennett's "To Reclaim a Legacy: A Report on the Humanities in Higher Education," which launched the conservative attack on expanded curricula in colleges and universities that had developed in response to feminist and poststructuralist concerns. The publication of Allan Bloom's *The Closing of the American Mind* and E. D. Hirsch's *Cultural Literacy* made clear, to this reader at least, just how marginal the field of film studies still is within education. In the curricular changes these three musketeers of the cultural right demand, film and television studies would surely be among the first to go. Bloom's tirade against rock and pop music and MTV are certainly applicable to film (although he does make a cursory nod to Woody Allen) and to television as entertainment media that distract from legitimate higher educational pursuits. Perhaps more indicative, though, is that Hirsch's literacy list and the expanded *Dictionary of Cultural Literacy* has only sparse and random entries on individual movies and movie stars, and there's not a single entry on film or television even in the technology section. For both authors, film and television are cultural influences that are significantly accountable for eroding literacy, both actual and cultural; they are political and politicized enemies of the canon, against which a renewed notion of the canon must be pointed.

Although the position that Bennett, Bloom, and Hirsch espouse has been thoroughly dissected and effectively dismantled,[1] they do pose a challenge in terms of an issue that must be confronted in almost any discipline, namely that of evaluation. How we go about theorizing evaluation without allowing Bennett, et als. to dictate the critical paradigms to be adopted is problematic, especially since the paradigms they cultivate run counter to the major developments in film study since the late sixties. The dominant criteria that traditionally served as a basis for canon formation in literary studies (which in turn served as the model for textual interpretation and evaluation in film studies)—the text as "well-wrought urn" produced by individual genius, expressing transcendental, timeless, and universal truths—have been dismantled by a film theory that has concentrated on the material conditions of production and reception of texts within specific cultural contexts. But while these theoretical developments have changed the way we interpret texts, they have not produced a corresponding transformation in the way we evaluate those texts. As Barbara Herrnstein Smith notes,

> The past decades have witnessed an extraordinary proliferation of theories, approaches, movements, and entire disciplines focused on interpretive criticism, among them (to recite a familiar litany) New Criticism, structuralism, psychoanalytic criticism, reader-response criticism, reception aesthetics, speech-act theory, deconstructionism, communications theory, semiotics, and hermeneutics. At the same time however, aside from a number of scattered and secondary essays by theorists and critics who are usually otherwise occupied, no one in particular has been concerned with questions of literary value and evaluation, and such regularly go begging—and, of course, begged—even among those whose inquiries into other matters are most rigorous, substantial, and sophisticated. (5)

Film theory, in the vanguard of producing these new forms of interpretive criticism, has also neglected the issue of evaluation, shortsightedly leaving evaluative criticism to the auspices of the conservative right (to the Blooms and NAS members) within the academy, and to the world of popular reviewing outside of the academy. How do we take up the question of evaluation without bracketing more recent theoretical developments, and reverting back to notions of "Romantic auteurism"?[2] On an even more fundamental level, how do we, as scholars and members of the academy dealing with the popular entertainment media of film and television, come to terms with evaluating that which is defined by its very existence outside of the academy—that is, popular culture—without converting it into that which it is not, never was, and never will nor should be?

In other words, how do we frame the question of canon formation in regard to popular culture in such a way that we don't end up adopting specious notions of objectivity and authenticity in order to justify the addition of titles to previously existing master-lists, but rather recognize the ability of "marginal" discourses—those discourses marked precisely by their exclusion from the list of the culture's traditionally esteemed objects—to create their own criteria for evaluation? That popular culture is actively engaged in constructing the terms of its evaluation is the subject of this paper, which will focus on two films, *Heartbreak Hotel* (1988) and *Mystery Train* (1989) that thematize the problem of evaluation of popular culture through their use of and reflections on the figure of Elvis, whose canonization depends on evaluative mechanisms operating outside of the academy, and has become a phenomenon of such magnitude that even scholars cannot ignore it.[3]

In one of the few articles that does address the issue of evaluation in film theory through a consideration of film canons,[4] Janet Staiger suggests a way that film theory can think about the problem of evaluation that is in keeping with its recent agenda, maintaining that "selection by evaluation can be made less dangerous to marginalized groups if such a selection is made with an awareness of the politics of the chosen criteria and with a politics of eliminating power of some groups over others, of centering at the expense of marginalizing classes, genders, sexual orientations, or cultures" (18). But crucial as it is, is this awareness of the political functions of the canon enough? Henry Louis Gates, Jr. warns, "The recent trend toward politics and history in literary studies [and one can read here film studies, as well] has turned the analysis of texts into a marionette theater of the political, to which we bring all the passions of our real world commitments. And that's why it is sometimes necessary to remind ourselves of the distance from the classrooms to the streets. Academic critics write essays, 'readings' of literature [film], where the bad guys (you know, racism or patriarchy) lose, where the forces of oppression are subverted by the boundless powers of irony and allegory that no prison can contain, and we glow with hard-won triumph. We pay homage to the marginalized and demonized, and it feels as if we've righted an actual injustice" (44). We must be mindful of this romanticized vision of our ability as critics, scholars, and teachers to show the sheep the way home once and then expect them to be able forevermore to find it on their own. Our desire to teach "strategies (not interpretations) and the implications of these strategies" to our students in order to keep the oppressed from being oppressed, the marginal from being marginalized overestimates our cultural influence and underestimates our institutional limits. Such a practice still assumes an arena of cultural privilege and condescension to popular cultural forms considered so commodified they can only be res-cued by strategic readings. Academics and the academy are not the only, nor the most powerful, nor necessarily even central cultural agents for combating oppression. Our willingness—indeed, eagerness—to speak for and co-opt the voice of the other (including that of the text) is indicative of our belief that we are the primary agency involved in performing a "socially responsible" re-evaluation of the canon, evidence not of our political correctness, but our pedagogical inequity.[5]

Contrary to appearances, I am not arguing here for the elimination of canon formation altogether since otherwise we are inevitably doomed to reproduce the politics of power intrinsic to canon formation. Canons are expressions of social and political power—a notion which drives classical humanists (e.g., Bennett, Bloom, and Hirsch) to despair, to predictions of a disemboweled educational system, to charges of "political correctness" against those who point out the politics inherent in conservatives' allegedly apolitical and transcendent canon of Western texts. My point is that the political functions of canons may not fully account for their origins, and academic critics are not the sole agents engaged in forming and reforming the canon.

Canon formation is, after all, in no very grand sense a process of collecting and, more specifically, *re-collecting* the artifacts of our shared culture, a process on which the academy holds no patent. I use the word re-collection here in both the sense of gathering together again and of selective remembrance. Canon formation is basically selective remembrance. But to recollect is to bring together again that which was lost or discarded, to find and reincorporate or reconstitute that which was not originally saved (or deemed worthy of saving), but nonetheless was vaguely remembered. Re-collection invests the collected artifact with value (it is worth remembering and saving), but it also bestows a cultural authority on the agency or institution engaged in re-collecting. Various individuals, agencies, and institutions compete for that cultural authority, establishing their own systems of valuation for what should be remembered and how it should be remembered. American culture is characterized by a surplus of evaluative speculation; the most obvious and familiar examples of institutions, agencies, or individuals engaged in such activity alongside film scholars and cultural studies scholars are the various awards presented across the spectrum of the popular arts—the Academy Awards, the Emmys, Grammys, Tonys, etc., as well as journalists' Ten-Best lists of everything from books to fashion. The various aesthetic, technological, social, and institutional criteria used to construct these canons are rarely seriously considered or recognized by the academy, which fashions itself as a cultural gatekeeper that monitors, and thus controls the politics of canon formation.

Less recognized are agencies like the Bradford Exchange, the Franklin Mint, and K-Tel, which create and offer collectible items to decorate homes. These items usually enshrine a nostalgic moment or popular culture icon on a limited-edition plate or china figurine, which are advertised on

TV or by direct-mail brochures for purchase as "investments." The criteria used to decide what goes on these plates is yet another evaluative mechanism of canon formation, but the process of enshrinement itself is so interesting that I'd like briefly to examine it. Recently, the Bradford Exchange released an Elvis "Jailhouse Rock" plate. A moment from the filmed version of one of Elvis's early rock hits, "Jailhouse Rock," is frozen onto the painted surface of the plate. The plate commemorates or re-collects a "classic" moment in rock n' roll history, but the moment is endowed with that classic value precisely by virtue of its presence on that plate; in other words, it is designated an "instant classic" by the very fact of its enshrinement on the plate. But the plates themselves are only offered on a limited basis, creating an enforced scarcity that quite literally creates value for the process of collection and re-collection (of the image the plate captures). A moment or object is wrested from the obscure past as worth re-collecting, and as it is re-collected through the activity of collecting the plates, it enters in to the realm of both cultural capital and economic capital, its exchange rate determining its economic and cultural value. That exchange rate is purposely inflated through planned scarcity, which makes the object and its enshrined moment accessible to only a privileged few. In a very bald way, this is an abject lesson in how canon formation functions, and perhaps its very baldness leads to our amused and scornful attitudes toward it. It too uncomfortably reveals the tie between economic relations of power and cultural relations of power, how one reproduces the conditions of oppression of the other. In this model the economic self-interest is so palpable that it is difficult to discern any particular ideological agenda other than pure consumption, so we feel justified in passing it off as vulgar economic charlatanism. But the political implications are enormous, and begin to provide an insight to why critics and scholars from both the left and the right have systematically attempted to depoliticize the realm of cultural analysis, to make it an unassailable, transcendent activity.

This is not to suggest by any means that popular or alternative canon formation is defined solely by commercial interests. On the contrary, popular texts often engage in revaluation and re-collection, forming ad hoc canons through various devices such as intertextual referencing and appropriation, where texts use and cite other texts in a purposeful manner in order to establish their own positions in relation to preceding traditions. The highly contingent canons that are formed as a result of this operation often reflect strategies of re-collection that deliberately disavow commercial interests, rescuing popular culture from its relegation to the jaws of kitsch, reconnecting it with its roots, providing a history, a complexity, and a voice of resistance that is rarely acknowledged. This process of re-collection as reclamation is nowhere more evident than in Chris Columbus's 1988 film *Heartbreak Hotel*.

The film is set in small-town Ohio in 1972, where Johnny, the protagonist, is a high school student with rock n' roll aspirations. He lives with his little sister and mother—a devoted Elvis fan—in a perpetually vacant hotel, the legacy of the father who abandoned them. After an accident hospitalizes his mother, Johnny decides that the only thing that will "heal" her and make her happy again is a date with Elvis, so he devises an elaborate plan and succeeds in actually abducting the singer after a concert in a nearby town. Elvis's stay at the hotel effects a repudiation of his early seventies Las Vegas persona in favor of the reclamation of his fifties persona.

In the course of this reclamation of the "real" Elvis, an explicit vision emerges of the film's own criteria for bestowing value on particular texts (rock songs, movies, rock stars, etc.) it chooses to re-collect. The film separates the wheat from the chaff according to its own invented criteria of authenticity and allegiance to rock n' roll. Authenticity here is grounded in the connection between the performer and his audience, who are together the true arbiters of value. When Elvis tries to brush off Johnny's assertion that he has lost touch with his renegade, rockabilly roots with a cavalier, "What do you know?" Johnny counters that he knows more than the Colonel (Colonel Tom Parker, Elvis's longtime manager) and "the other fat-asses" who handle Elvis's career, even though in his own words he's a "fucking little nobody from backwater Ohio." What Johnny *can* "read" is that the reception of the text, as much as its production, is essential to determining its value, that inherent or intrinsic artistic value cannot be assumed. Elvis now (1972) and Elvis then (1956) are two very different phenomena.

In *Heartbreak Hotel's* re-collection of the Elvis story, the 1950s Elvis was "authentic," a rebel who was directly in touch with his audience, as opposed to the seventies Elvis, whose connection to his audience is mediated through his handlers who shield him from that audience. The seventies Elvis is so far removed from his audience that, without any consciousness of the irony of his act, he sends a Cadillac to a woman who cannot attend his concert because she was badly injured in a car accident. The problem with the seventies Elvis is precisely that he is "handled," made "safe." The audience that values the seventies persona is composed of the little blue-haired ladies who collect the Bradford Exchange plates, even though they depict one of his most "scandalous" early rock n' roll songs. The menace represented by that moment—the disruptive, rocking inmates who deserve to be locked up, but threaten to shake down the walls—has been safely contained on a mountable, collectible plate. Elvis himself, the rock n' roll legend, has been engulfed as well by his extravaganza show and his jumpsuit that, as Johnny's sister remarks, "makes him look like he works at a Dairy Queen." If Elvis is to regain his status as a true icon, worthy of worship and adulation—as the King of rock n' roll—he will have to be taken back to his roots, reconnected with Johnny and that youthful audience that has the power to reclaim him for rock n' roll.

To accomplish this, Elvis is abducted both physically and culturally. As an icon or archetype he has to be "taken back" from the clutches of a totally mediated mass culture, reappropriated and re-appropriated (made appropriate again for rock n' roll). A fair amount of screen time is devoted to the struggle to reappropriate Elvis, and it often looks as if he may be unsalvageable. Johnny convinces Elvis to shave off the lambchops and to buy clothes that recall the "old" Elvis, but then Elvis succeeds in a Graceland-style redecoration of the hotel that strips Johnny's room of all his rock posters. But Elvis is gradually recuperated, and we know the process is complete in a validating moment when his life imitates one of his own films.

Early in *Heartbreak Hotel,* Johnny and his mother go to an Elvis double-feature at the drive-in. In the course of one of their conversations, over their shoulders from the back of the car, we watch a scene from the Elvis movie *Loving You* (1957), in which a youthful, impetuous Elvis fights an unappreciative and contentious spectator who derides the very song he requested to be performed. When Elvis re-enacts this scene shot-for-shot and verbatim late in *Heartbreak Hotel,* we know immediately that the old Elvis has been recuperated and is once again true to that earlier rock n' roll image that is the "authentic" Elvis. *Heartbreak Hotel* literally projects the earlier film as a guarantee of that authenticity, replacing one mediated, mass-cultural image—the Las Vegas Elvis—with that of an earlier medi-ated, mass-cultural image—the Hollywood Elvis, the latter distinguished as a marker of "authenticity" because it provides the history to situate and read the meaning of the present scene. Just as Johnny and the youthful rock n' roll audience are the agents who, through "excorporation" (which will be defined and discussed below), have the authority to insert Elvis back in to his rightful place in rock n' roll history, the film *Heartbreak Hotel,* through this kind of intertextual referencing that appropriates the "authentic" image of Elvis, is establishing its own authority as a creator of that history. Importantly, we see here how a popular culture text itself makes distinctions among mass-cultural representations and images, which are not uniform, standardized products that produce in turn a uniformity of effect among consumers, who are unable to distinguish authentic forms of expression.[6] The thematization within *Heartbreak Hotel* of the significance and value of the ability of both text and audiences to make such distinctions necessitates a recognition of the complexity, variability, and creativity of popular culture production, which tends to be dismissed or rejected even in those theoretical models developed to counter a debased notion of popular culture.

For instance, the notion of excorporation which I have been utilizing here is an important permutation of the British culturalist turn to audience studies that challenged the privileging of text as a locus of stable and transcendent meaning production. Such studies in fact opened a door for some of the most productive studies of popular culture to date, but they also perpetuate the very elitist attitudes toward popular culture production that they were intended to alleviate. In defining excorporation, John Fiske argues that the audience primarily determines value—an idea which leads to a curious devaluation of popular texts themselves, and concomitantly, I will argue, an impoverished notion of the possibilities for alternative canon formations. Fiske writes,

> Culture is a process of making meanings that people actively partici-
> pate in; it is not a set of performed meanings handed down to and
> imposed upon the people. Of course, our "freedom" to make meanings
> that suit our interests is as circumscribed as any other "freedom" in
> society—the mass-produced text is produced and circulated by capital-
> ist institutions for economic gain, and is therefore imprinted with
> capitalist ideology. But the mass-produced text can only be made into
> a *popular* text by the people, and this transformation occurs when the
> various subcultures can activate sets of meanings from it and insert
> these meanings into their daily cultural experience. They take mass-
> produced signifiers and, by a process of "excorporation" use them to
> articulate and circulate subcultural meanings. (285)

In this passage, Fiske collapses the two predominant positions of Marx-ist/leftist theorizing of popular culture. The first, issuing from the Frankfurt School theorists, and most clearly expressed by Theodor Adorno and Max Horkheimer, holds that popular culture is the product of a cabalistic culture industry that imposes the ideology of commodification on the masses in order to integrate them into the industrialized social order. Fiske's description clearly adopts this position—mass culture texts are imprinted with capitalist ideology, and can only be "transformed" productively by the audience. In this valorizing of audience activity, Fiske applies the other predominant theoretical model of the left, which views popular culture as a variant of "folk culture," or (in Fiske's own words) an adapted "oral popular culture," that expresses the authentic vision of the working class or oppressed subcultural groups who locate and project their collec-tive voice through the popularizing of texts that only they can effect. Put another way, the "folk" save tainted, commodified mass culture by wrenching it bodily from the corrupt realm of commodification, rearticulating and circulating it within the valorized realm of everyday experience. Popular texts themselves, then, are devalued as industry products that gain value only in audience activations; Fiske sees this as evidence of cultural democracy at work. While this valorizing of audience does overcome the necessity of positing the retrograde opposition of high and low art and the concomitant legitimation of high art that distinguished Adorno's elitist model—which in fact this model was developed precisely to supersede—it is also dangerously essentialist, romanticizing the daily cultural experience of subcultural groups, ignoring the contradictory relations of cultural power that relegate these groups to subcultural status in the first place. Such a view does not usurp or even significantly challenge the foundations of canonical power; the readings and the meanings that these subcultural groups make may express resistance, but a resistance that is contained within the marginalized, dispossessed position these groups occupy, which appears more a site of capitulation to existing power structures than struggle, or true democratic process. The meanings these groups create remain subcultural, oppositional, radically contingent, and ahistorical exactly because they continue to be measured against the supposed stability of the meaning-making structures of "dominant culture."

What I am arguing is that *Heartbreak Hotel* usurps that illusion of stability for itself, exposing in the process the illusionism—the ideology—behind canon formation that masks the contingent, *un*stable political nature of the mechanisms of creating a history and a canon, which in fact involve relations of domination and subordination that can be manipulated by popular culture texts as well as high art texts. In such a view, popular culture texts become players in the hegemonic struggle of cultural power relations, and not just victims to be saved from domination in that struggle. Contrary to Fiske's contention that only the people can make the text into a popular text, I contend that *Heartbreak Hotel* situates itself as a popular text through artistic appropriation, that is quoting or citing an antecedent text in order to activate sets of meanings from that text (here specifically *Loving You*). The text draws its own lines of affiliation that become markers for reading the text.[7] This is not a tactic of saving the appropriated text, but of *situating* the appropriating text, of providing a specific context or tradition for interpreting and placing it. This is acutely illustrated in *Heartbreak Hotel's* appropriation of the *Loving You* scene. Elvis is literally excorporated by Johnny (and, mise-en-abîme, by the actor David Keith, who plays Elvis in a very convincing impersonation), and his look is transformed, but the transformation is not completely believable or convincing, perhaps not even understood until the (again, literally) rejuvenated Elvis replays the *Loving You* scene. Significantly, after this point in the film, Elvis begins to circulate as a member of the community, subculturally, as it were—no longer the mega-star whom everyone in town stands outside the hotel to glimpse or gape at; at a subsequent party at the hotel, everyone finally comes inside to dance and mingle with Elvis. In other words, the excorporation in and of itself, while a decidedly radical and disruptive act (and therefore important as a moment of resistance) is not a guarantee that the text (in this case, Elvis himself) will become "popular"—i.e., take on or circulate any particular meaning for the community either affectively or effectively. Rather, the meaning and value of the texts depends on the re-contextualization or re-articulation of the text either by the mechanisms of the text itself or by the audience or both. In the Fiskean model (indeed in almost all models from the right and the left), such re-contextualization and re-articulation occurs against the backdrop of established, stable preconstituted traditions of Great Texts which provide an original context to understand the re-contextualizing and/or re-articulation. But *Heartbreak Hotel* makes no such appeal to an institutionally stable, *preconstituted* tradition. Instead it constitutes its own ad hoc tradition.[8] It cites an antecedent movie, appropriating it and validating it as a "classic" (an "instant classic" in the true sense of the term) in the very act of appropriation, creating a history and insisting on its status as historical precedent, as durable and worth recollecting in the very act of recollecting it.

Appropriation and excorporation, then, are neutral strategies of meaning production—they are not transformative in and of themselves, but rather affect transformation of the text only in the activations effected within the appropriating or excorporating text or agency. They are strategies that abduct for any text that employs them the very power base at the heart of canon formation; they are two sides of a coin that, among others, determines the cultural value of a text. They are strategies that become powerful and complicated in their activations, which are not necessarily stable and predictable; therein lies the significance of their hegemonic challenge to structures of institutional power like the canon, which have always claimed to own and control such strategies, but can no longer maintain control over cultural production of meaning in the changing cultural terrain of an emerging technoculture that endlessly circulates and recirculates texts and information in unpredictable, shifting forms and patterns for widely varied, heterogeneous audiences.

The Canonization of Elvis

The "Elvis phenomenon," of which *Heartbreak Hotel* is only one extremely minor manifestation, provides an exemplary vehicle for examining the challenges that these strategies represent, especially to the canon, since this phenomenon revolves around issues of canonization in all senses of the word. Elvis been elevated since his death to the level of a saint, a still-reigning King, but exactly what he rules and into which tradition he "fits" is not at all clear. In many ways, what happened to the image of Elvis after he died—its multiplication, increasing presence, distribution, and circulation—parallels as well as being an effect of the emerging technoculture. Greil Marcus's book, *Dead Elvis,* collects, catalogues, and discusses a mind-boggling number of the innumerable proliferations of media images of Elvis that have appeared since his death. Marcus writes,

> When he died the event was a kind of explosion that went off silently, in minds and hearts; out of that explosion came many fragments, edging slowly into the light, taking shape, changing shape again and again as the years went on. No one, I think, could have predicted the ubiquity, the playfulness, the perversity, the terror, and the fun of this, of Elvis Presley's second life: a great, common conversation, sometimes, a conversation between specters and fans, made out of songs, art works, books, movies, dreams; sometimes more than anything cultural noise, the glossolalia of money, advertisements, tabloid headlines, bestsellers, urban legends, nightclub japes. In either case it was—is—a story that needed no authoritative voice, no narrator, a story that flourishes precisely because it is free of any such thing, a story that told itself. (xii)

After Elvis died, his image no longer attached to a specific, living body—an author or narrator—who maintained control over the specific representation and dissemination of that image—was "liberated," became part of the public domain, where it was and still is subject to multiple articulations and rearticulations that ground it in precise ways, all circulated simultaneously by a technologically sophisticated media culture that places competing images, representations, and discourses side-by-side in a kind of "conversation," in which all of those competing "speakers" are trying to convince "listeners," "readers," or "viewers" of the significance of their particular configuration—their canon. *Heartbreak Hotel,* made after Elvis's death, but diegetically situated before his death, ironically capitalizes on the "liberating" of Elvis's image to make a film about the very loss of control over image, and the dire consequences of that loss in terms of creating a particular or specific tradition or history. Within the story, of course, Elvis is able to reassert control, to realign and reconnect himself in this case with his rock 'n' roll past (and not coincidentally, also with his roles as loving father and good husband)—that is, with the specific discursive formation of rock 'n' roll—that the movie endows with a particular value.

But the explosive multiplication of images that is characteristic of the technoculture, and of which the Elvis phenomenon is an exemplar, is usually construed as a direct impediment to evaluation, rarely celebrated as presenting multiple possibilities for interpretation and evaluation even by those studies which ostensibly celebrate that multiplicity. Marcus's book is a case in point. It seems at first a positive diagnosis of the possibilities for building a new "sense of place" for Elvis in this image explosion, embodied in the first instance by the very undertaking of such a project that collects under one cover the multiple articulations of Elvis, from avant-garde artworks to tabloid covers, to give a sense of the cultural "conversation" surrounding Elvis. But Marcus is also part of this "conversation," privileging his own particular discourse of the intellectual rock critic by casting Elvis as a genius in the tradition of Lincoln, Melville, and Faulkner, who expose "the deepest and most extreme possibilities and dangers of our national identity." He was led to understand this alliance by "the sense of mystery in the speeches, the novels, the music. No one knows how to explain the grace of Lincoln's Second Inaugural Address. No one knows how to explain the unholy power of the chapter in *Moby Dick* called 'The Whiteness of the Whale,' the chapter that makes you wish that you too were on the ship, on the hunt. And no one knows how to explain the music . . . " (31).

Marcus is worried that somehow this mystery will be diminished and explained, that Elvis will be "whittled down" in the discussion and marketing of him: "The real Elvis seems more than anything else a question of marketing. There is an audience out there, right here: find it, map it, service it, use it up. The idea of Elvis as a market is the idea that Elvis *can* be used up. What have we seen since Elvis's death? What do we see as the market brings him down to size?" (33). Marcus grudgingly admits that we do see a lot more videos and records and CDs, but mostly, "The country is aware of Elvis as a weird icon: as a T-shirt, a black velvet wall hanging, an emblem of working-class bad taste or upper-class camp, an ashtray, a $200 baby doll with a porcelain head marked down to $125, a commemorative limited-edition dinner plate" (33). Such images, Marcus notes, move us "farther and farther away from the source . . . : Elvis Presley's music"(34). Marcus acknowledges the endless reconfigurations of Elvis's image and story, which are a source of fascination for him. However, Marcus's particular personal re-collection of Elvis is in his musical representation, which is the source of his value. Throughout the book, Marcus cites the songs that he feels are Elvis's best, and firmly situates his musical precursors as the black blues singers of Beale Street and the pentecostal church, establishing a particular tradition that gives a particular meaning and value to Elvis's music. But Marcus assumes that the value and function of that music will remain constant for all audiences (even if the image and story don't), indeed that the audience will remain constant—an idea that has already been problematized, if not debunked by the above reading of *Heartbreak Hotel*. Marcus finally does not acknowledge that as the image and story of Elvis are reconfigured, so is the value of his music reconfigured.

The endless reconfiguration of Elvis's image in all respects is the subject of Jim Jarmusch's film *Mystery Train*. The movie is composed of three distinct sections or "passages," each marked by a title at the beginning and a fade to black at the end, and each passage at some point coincides temporally and spatially with the other two. That is, the stories occur roughly simultaneously and in the same location—all of the characters are in the same hotel in separate rooms—and the simultaneity is revealed by select repeated images, and certain recurring sounds, but the main characters from each section do not meet during the time that they are in the hotel. Jarmusch goes to great lengths to emphasize this narrative simultaneity, which violates traditional linear narrative progression in Hollywood cinema, where simultaneity is usually indicated through parallel editing techniques that finally bring two objects, characters, or images to a point where they coincide, or by split screens that establish the explicit connection between the two spaces. The characters who are connected by marriage or friendship to other characters in a different section never meet up, while those "foreign" characters who unknowingly are connected by having been in the same hotel meet up casually, without recognition of their connection. In *Mystery Train,* then, the narrative connections are revealed only slowly, while the incidental details of the mise-en-scène, such as location shots that show the Memphis skyline, the restaurant and the bar, the black velveteen pictures of Elvis that appear on the wall of each room, the voice of the DJ announcing an Elvis song, and the high-pitched whistle of the train (the mystery train?) passing the hotel provide the immediate connections to link the three sections. But within each section these details circulate very differently, taking on a different value and function for each of the groups of people that encounter them.

Each section revolves around displaced foreigners who end up through lack of familiarity with American culture wandering through some of the seediest, most downtrodden, and obviously dangerous sections of Memphis. The two young Japanese rock fans in the first section, "Far from Yokohama,"are on a pilgrimage to locate the source of rock 'n' roll, to be able to situate the King within a specific American tradition. Jun, the young Japanese male speaks reverentially of Sun Studio, where not just Elvis, but Carl Perkins, Jerry Lee Lewis, and others first recorded. They head for Graceland, but stumble across the seedy-looking Sun Studio, which proves a baffling and disappointing experience since they cannot understand the rapid-fire, Southern-accented monologue of the guide. Jun's disappointment extends to the city of Memphis, which Jun complains could be "Yokohama with sixty percent of the buildings gone," but his companion Mitsuko takes real pleasure in the foreignness of this city, stressing that this is Memphis, and America, which unlike Yokohama, has Elvis. Later, in their hotel room, where the picture of Elvis on the wall substitutes for the lack of a TV set, Mitsuko calls Jun over to look at her "important discovery" in her scrapbook. She places a picture of Elvis on the page next to a picture of a middle Eastern king, and the two bear a striking resemblance of each other. Then she turns the page and compares the Elvis photo to a Buddha, then to the Statute of Liberty, and finally to Madonna (whose photo has obviously been designed to create that resemblance)—and the resemblance in each case is striking. Jun, impressed out of his inscrutability for the first time, mutters, "Elvis was more influential than I thought." In this scene, they find what they could not locate at Sun Studio—a source of Elvis's attraction, which is precisely in his lack of fixity, the different ways he has been articulated and can be rearticulated, and the radical variability of those rearticulations.

Here, the circulation of images and icons, their lack of fixity in time or place is foregrounded to emphasize what Jun and his girlfriend have "discovered"—that Elvis is a floating signifier, influential whenever and wherever he is invoked in order to create or become representative of a new tradition. His image can be combined and recombined at will, and each recombination functions differently and takes on a new significance. Thus, Elvis takes on significance according to the particular context into which he is inserted, but he also lends a significance to that new context that also rewrites the tradition. His significance, his popularity, the root of the pleasure that his myth provides, resides precisely in this ability perpetually to displace Elvis, and for Elvis perpetually to displace whatever tradition he is inserted into, in time as well as in place, for his image to circulate as freely as the innumerable fans who willingly displace themselves to travel to Memphis to pay homage to his "influence." Shortly after Mitsuko shows Jun her discovery, he stands by the window as the train rumbles by, musing on how "It's cool to be 18. It's cool to be far from Yokohama. It's cool to be in Memphis" which, he recants, is not at all like Yokohama. He begins to revel in this trip on the mystery train that both takes away and brings back, and in the possibilities of this sense of displacement, this state of transit, the ability to make distinctions without necessarily anchoring those distinctions in one tradition or another, letting them float.

The one anchor that drags on this expanded sense of evaluation is commodification—appropriating the representation(s)to make money, to capitalize oppressively on belief and evaluation in order to dupe the viewer or listener. The second passage, "A Ghost," lays out the internal conflict in such a notion. A young Italian widow finds herself with time to kill while she waits for the flight that will take her and the body of her (mobster?) husband back to Italy. She finds herself a foreigner adrift in an unfamiliar commodity-pushing Memphis, being bilked out of money at every turn. After being beguiled into buying a stack of magazines she doesn't want, she ends up in a restaurant, where she is approached by a hustler who claims he has something to give her. He spins a tale about a hitchkiking Elvis, gives her a comb, and then says that Elvis said she should give him a $20 delivery fee. She is disgusted by his obvious hucksterism and apparently not taken in, but gives him the money to get rid of him (and ends up paying for his coffee as well). But later she tries to repeat the story to her quintessentially American roommate Dede (who has duped her into paying for the room), who stops her, explaining that the story is a well-known hustle. But then Luisa has a vision; a ghostly Elvis appears in her room, and the hustler's story, for both Luisa and the audience takes on an new aura of possibility. Even in a commodified culture where Elvis stories are circulated endlessly for money in the very magazines that Luisa carts around, but does not read, the connection between commodification of the image or story (where the product is considered inauthentic because it is produced primarily for monetary gain and not out of some conviction or intention to impart cultural "truth") and the authenticity of the "vision" it produces is conflicted. Is this vision a projection of her unconscious, her own act of excorporation, a way of making the story "real" or significant, or is it an authentic ghost, a true ghostly appearance? It hardly matters; she believes in the vision enough for it to keep her awake all night.

The last section, "Lost in Space," involves the bodily appropriation of Elvis. Joe Strummer (a real-life member of the band The Clash) plays Johnny, the recently laid-off, but perpetually displaced English working-class stiff, whose life unwittingly duplicates the underside, tabloid "reality" of Elvis's life. Johnny "becomes" Elvis, both a real Elvis (an impersonator, taking on the young, pre-mega-star Elvis persona) and the "real" Elvis of the tabloids—both another Elvis and an Other Elvis. He, too, is conflicted about this rearticulation of Elvis and the re-collection he inspires in others through it. He sports an Elvis hairstyle, inspiring his friends to call him Elvis, which he detests. Like the real Elvis, this Elvis hangs out with black friends, lives with a girlfriend who everyone believes he has married though he hasn't, and who is now leaving him, drinks to excess, sports a gun that he finally shoots someone with—but unlike Elvis he cannot escape the consequences of such behavior, and he will pay dearly for the shooting if he is caught. This particular Elvis is so steeped in the Elvis tradition that he cannot escape the "reality" of the representation he has adopted, and when he reaches *Mystery Train's* version of the *Heart-*

break Hotel, his first act, significantly, is to turn to the wall the ubiquitous Elvis picture that is present in even the seediest, most uninhabitable room in the hotel. The picture is redundant because Johnny represents him, has become a "real" Elvis, providing the means of re-collecting him and his influences that the picture usually provides.

By this third passage, the viewer fully understands the simultaneity of the events in each passage, how all of these particular appropriations of the Elvis myth circulate at the same time, and in the same place, modifying each other, but resonating very differently for each of the "foreigners," who are very much taken in by the myth, but also take the myth in and rearticulate it in their own particular re-collection of it (with Mitsuko's being the most literal re-collection). In Jarmusch's film, the image of Elvis is, like the characters, in transit, foreign, an Other until appropriated, taken in and rearticulated by the characters according to the variable criteria that each employs, and those rearticulations function variably for the characters as well.

Ironically, this analysis of *Mystery Train,* which dwells on the inability to capture Elvis in traditional narrative forms, or to situate the phenomenon that is Elvis in any one tradition, inserts that phenomenon into yet another tradition—academic discourse—and that tradition will necessarily be re-configured as a result, even though it may not be willing to acknowledge that reconfiguration. Academic discourse as an institution has certainly claimed itself impervious in the past to the influences of other institutions, while claiming rights of domain over others, pressing its values as transcendent, unchanging, and universal. Unfortunately, the canon debate is still often cast in these terms, with the power of the canon as a pre-constituted entity believed not subject to the influence of other institutions—that is, non-politicized and non-contingent, not in general circulation socially or culturally. Any idea of reforming this idea of the canon simply presupposes its power as a pre-existent entity under the auspices of a predominant institution—the academy—which is in fact only one institution among many, with its own specific values that may or may not be taken up by other institutions. Value is fundamentally variable, both within institutions and among them, and any attempt to fix it within narrow traditions in one in-stitution simply does not respect the way that values, texts, and institutions circulate within the culture. The canon debate needs to be recast in order to reflect this circulation, the influence these values, texts, and institutions have upon each other once a forced and illusionary separation ceases to be maintained. Perhaps our first task, then, is to board the *Mystery Train* in order to learn to acknowledge the social and cultural conditions under which we formulate and apply evaluative criteria, and to recognize their variety, complexity, and mutability within institutions and as institutions.

Works Cited

Andrew, Dudley. "Dialogue." *Cinema Journal* 25:1 (1985), pp. 55–58.

Aronowitz, Stanley and Henry A. Giroux. "Schooling, Culture, and Literacy in the Age of Broken Dreams: A Review of Bloom and Hirsch." *Harvard Educational Review* 58:2 (1988), pp. 172–194.

Bennett, William. "To Reclaim a Legacy: Text of Report on Humanities in Higher Education." *Chronicle of Higher Education,* November 28, 1984, pp. 16–21.

Bloom, Allan. *The Closing of the American Mind: How Higher Education Has Failed Democracy and Impoverished the Souls of Today's Students.* New York: Simon and Schuster, 1987.

Bloom, Harold. *The Anxiety of Influence.* New York: Oxford University Press, 1973.

Collins, Jim. "Appropriating Like Krazy: From Pop Art to Meta-Pop." *Modernity and Mass Culture.* Ed. James Naremore and Patrick Brantlinger. Bloomington: Indiana University Press, 1991, pp. 203–223.

Fiske, John. "British Cultural Studies and Television." *Channels of Discourse.* Ed. Robert C. Allen. Chapel Hill: University of North Carolina Press, 1987, pp. 254–289.

Gates, Jr., Henry Louis. "Whose Canon Is It Anyway?" *New York Times Book Review.* February 2, 1989, pp. 1, 44–45.

Gendron, Bernard. "Theodor Adorno Meets the Cadillacs." *Studies in Entertainment.* Ed. Tania Modleski. Bloomington: Indiana University Press, 1986, pp. 18–36.

Giroux, Henry A. and Roger Simon. "Critical Pedagogy and the Politics of Popular Culture." *Cultural Studies* 2 (1988), pp. 294–320.

Marcus, Greil. *Dead Elvis.* New York: Doubleday, 1991.

Mast, Gerald. "Dialogue." *Cinema Journal* 25:1 (1985), pp. 51–53.

Rorty, Richard. "That Old Time Philosophy." *New Republic.* April 4, 1988, pp. 28–33.

Scholes, Robert. "Three Views of Education: Nostalgia, History, and Voodoo." *College English* 50 (1988), pp. 320–341.

———. "Aiming a Canon at the Curriculum." *Salmagundi* 72 (1986), pp. 101–117.

Smith, Barbara Herrnstein. "Contingencies of Value." *Canons.* Ed. Robert von Hallberg. Chicago: University of Chicago Press, 1984, pp. 5–39.

Staiger, Janet. "The Politics of Film Canons." *Cinema Journal* 24:3 (1985), pp. 4–23.

———. "Reply to Dudley Andrew and Gerald Mast." *Cinema Journal* 25:1 (1985), pp. 62–65.

6

Spectacles of Death: Identification, Reflexivity, and Contemporary Horror

Jeffrey Sconce

A columnist in *Premiere* magazine reports overhearing the following conversation in a video store. Two teenage girls argue over which movie monster they would prefer to be killed by, Jason of *Friday the 13th,* Michael of *Halloween,* or Freddy of *Nightmare on Elm Street.* One girl makes the case against Freddy:

> "Jason or that *Halloween* guy, they just kill you and you're dead. That's all you have to worry about. Freddy makes you a nervous wreck and *then* kills you and *then* turns you into a face sticking out of his chest!"
> "Yeah, but he's so *funny.*"
> "Only because you're watching the movie! If you were *in* the movie and he was chasing you, you wouldn't be thinking, like, 'What a funny guy!' You'd be screaming and yelling and trying to get away, just like the kids in the movie!"[1]

At this point, the *Premiere* writer interjects himself in the conversation to ask about Norman Bates. "Who?" the girls ask. "The guy from the *Psycho* movies." "Oh, him. He stinks," offers one girl. "He's just an old guy."

This anecdote of horror's generation gap typifies the low critical esteem most film commentators have for the contemporary horror film, especially the subgenre of the "slasher" movie. Despite their commercial success and stylistic variety, such films remain a target of indiscriminate ridicule by the film cognoscenti. Often, this derision is aimed as well at the teenage target audience for these films, which critics routinely characterize as a legion of brain-dead pubescent zombies docilely filing into the nation's multiplexes for each new "teenie-kill" release.

As a convenient doormat of popular film criticism, "slasher" movies provide a formulaic reference point for critics to compare other, more "worthy" horror films. Consider, for example, a *Rolling Stone* review for the art-house horror success, *Henry: Portrait of a Serial Killer* (1987). Speaking of the slasher cycles of the 1980s, this critic writes, "Those films offer supernatural villains and cardboard victims; they're easy to shake. Not so *Henry*. The film is no masterpiece, but it is spare, intelligent, and thought-provoking."[2] By comparison, the *Nightmare on Elm Street* films would no doubt be labeled loud, stupid, and mind-numbing. The *Nightmare* series surrounds its carnage with wall-to-wall special effects and raucous heavy-metal anthems such as "Bring Your Daughter to the Slaughter." *Henry,* on the other hand, is refined and tasteful, "theatrical in the best sense" as one writer phrases it.[3] As the film gained notoriety on the art-house circuit during 1990, film reviewers consistently celebrated the movie in terms of its "intelligence" and stark "realism." One left the theater provoked into thinking about the complexities of human evil rather than simply humming Iron Maiden tunes.

The dismissal of "slasher" films and the simultaneous critical promotion of *Henry* raises two interrelated questions. First, if "slasher" films are so bad (as in poorly made), why would teenagers flock to the cinema repeatedly to watch other teenagers get sliced and diced by a menagerie of seemingly immortal psychos? A writer for *Film Comment* offers what has become the preferred explanation. "In most slasher movies the symbolic identity of the killer is obvious and inflexible. Whether he's named Jason or Freddy, he's the incarnation of adult authority come down to punish guilty teens for sexually precocious behavior."[4] I would argue that most critics employing this specious "slasher as superego" argument have never actually sat in a theater with a bunch of teenagers to watch one of these films. For one thing, it makes little sense that young couples, at the theater either legitimately to watch a film or covertly to make out in the back row, would continually choose movies that promised such grave retribution for sexual experimentation. Secondly, as anyone who has watched one of the *Nightmare on Elm Street* films in a theater knows, few people in the audience actually care about the films' ever-increasing pile of murdered teens. The real hero is Freddy, who appearances on screen are met with cheers, whistles, and wild applause. As the conversation between the two girls at the video store suggests, some teenagers have a difficult time identifying with the "cardboard victims" on the screen at all. Clearly, Freddy "what a funny guy!" Krueger is the main point of interest for these viewers.

The second question concerns the taste of the "elite" audience of critics and cinephiles that promoted *Henry* as such a superior horror film. Why would a "sophisticated" audience, one presumedly accustomed to more respectable fare, suddenly champion so passionately this ghoulish story of an ex-con roaming the streets of Chicago in search of random victims to stab, shoot, bludgeon, and decapitate? What is it about this particular film that made serial killing an acceptable premise for a movie? While Freddy won over his audience with humor, Henry seems to have captured the imagination of film critics with his soft-spoken charm. Some writers fell completely under Henry's sway, such as a reviewer for the *Village Voice* who noted, "Henry's just about the nicest guy in the picture. He's polite, a gentleman."[5]

Freddy and Henry are both brutal and relentless agents of death. As celebrity serial killers, each stars in a "body-count" film, a movie that structures its narrative progression around a series of increasingly gruesome murders.[6] What distinguishes the films and their subsequent critical reputations is the cultural context of their release and circulation as well as the actual style of their "execution." The first *Nightmare* film appeared in 1984 and was directed by Wes Craven, who had established his reputation in the genre during the 1970s with such notorious films as *Last House on the Left* and *The Hills Have Eyes*. Appearing in the wake of John Carpenter's *Halloween* and Sean Cunningham's *Friday the 13th,* the film and subsequent series were quickly relegated to the "slasher" ghetto (although a reviewer for the *New York Times* did note that the Freddy series featured "the most intelligent premise in current genre films," but added that the movies did not "take advantage of their potential"[7]). By and large, the *Nightmare* series came to be seen as a highly formulaic and thus uninteresting group of films, thin on plot and heavy on special effects, pumped out at regular year-and-a-half intervals for a teen audience that didn't expect much in the first place.

While for most critics the *Nightmare* films represented the work of a semi-respected horror auteur reduced to mindless exploitation formula, John McNaughton's film was instead a low-profile exploitation project that quickly garnered growing critical esteem. Financed by a Chicago video company in search of cheap product, the film had a difficult time finding theatrical distribution (essential for a successful video release) because of its commercially prohibitive "X" rating. The film's fate began to change with a screening at the prestigious Telluride Film Festival in 1989, which attracted a more sympathetic audience of critics who championed the film for its restrained direction and disturbing tone. Although McNaughton himself was concerned the film might be "too arty for the blood crowd and too bloody for the art crowd,"[8] the movie nevertheless embarked on a successful city-by-city release, usually playing at the local art-house, rather than the local drive-in.

As the differing cultural and critical status of the two films suggests, Freddy and Henry serve as the organizing centers of two radically different horror films championed by two completely separate audiences. Put simply, "slasher" films, despite being continually reviewed and reviled by middle-aged film commentators writing for the mainstream press, are not in fact made for middle-age film commentators writing for the mainstream press. As the *Premiere* columnist demonstrates, these critics find it inconceivable that there could be a single sentient being not intimately familiar with and appreciative of Hitchcock's *Psycho*. For the most part, such critics are completely baffled and befuddled by the appeal of more recent horror films. Conversely, the lack of toy merchandising, collector's cards, and pinball machines featuring the likeness of "Henry," coupled with the film's high visibility in the literature of "elite" film culture, would suggest that *Henry* is aimed at an audience other than young teens, in this case a more exclusive and cinematically literate viewership.

Obviously, the films differ inasmuch as the *Nightmare* series obeys certain conventions of the teen exploitation picture while *Henry* relies on familiar devices of "art" cinema. But the difference between the two films goes beyond these simple surface considerations of style, beyond the presence or absence of teen victims and a heavy metal soundtrack. Perhaps the most fundamental and important difference between the movies is the relationship each film constructs between the viewer, the serial killing protagonist, and the unfolding spectacles of death that mark each film as "horror." The films employ separate and radically different strategies of identification, each specific to its own target audience, for the construction of the viewer's involvement with the film's images, characters, and story.

At the same time, the films share highly "self-conscious" forms of narration. An important textual feature of both films is a foregrounding of the storytelling process. As David Bordwell writes, "Narration . . . relates 'rhetorically' to the perceiver. . . . To what extent does the narration display a recognition that it is addressing an audience? We can call this the degree of *self-consciousness*."[9] I would argue that both the *Nightmare* series and *Henry* are acutely aware of the specific social audience they are addressing, and this extreme self-consciousness of narration is vital to the relations of identification each film constructs for its audience. In the pages that follow, I want to compare how *Freddy's Dead* (the last of the *Nightmare on Elm Street* series) and *Henry* encourage these differing modes of identification through highly self-conscious narrational forms, and how, in turn, these modes of identification provide a form of cinematic pleasure unique to each audience group, teenagers in the case of *Freddy's Dead* and cinephiles with *Henry*. I would argue these different forms of audience identification lie at the heart of the lowly critical status afforded the Freddy series by adult film culture, and influence as well the simultaneous valorization of *Henry* as an example of a "quality" horror film. By examining how each film encourages a different form of audience identification, we can see that the valuation of films, as often as not, is a judgment made about a particular audience group. Examining these generational "taste" wars in detail, however, requires first providing at least a cursory overview of the concept of "identification" as it has been traditionally articulated in film studies.

In his pathbreaking study of psychoanalysis and the cinema, *The Imaginary Signifier,* Christian Metz begins with a simple question, "With what does the spectator identify during the projection of the film?" Though the question may be simple enough, the answers and theories this question has generated are most complex. A central concept that is of relevance in this context is that of "enunciation." Debates concerning enunciation in the cinema are complicated, and the positions staked out by various theorists hotly contested. Enunciation theory, as it developed and flourished in the mid-1970s, was an often unstable and always volatile combination of Lacanian psychoanalysis, the linguistic theories of Emile Benveniste, and the Marxist aesthetic strategies of Bertolt Brecht. Any attempt at a summary of this complex (and unfinished) project is thus doomed to be partial and distorted.[10]

That caveat aside, theories of enunciation basically attempt to explain the nature of the discursive relationship between the viewer and the cinematic text; that is, how the film addresses and positions the viewer in relation to the image. "Identification," in this sense, refers to the process whereby the cinematic spectator, as a socially constructed subject, makes sense of the spatial and temporal manipulations of the cinematic image to produce a "realistic," "real-seeming," or at least comprehensible story. To use a purely linguistic model, films are "spoken" messages. Enunciation theory, in large part, examines "who" speaks in this textual arrangement, "what" is spoken, and how this process of enunciation engages and guides the spectator's subjectivity.[11]

Many theorists have argued that a central goal of Hollywood narrative cinema, as a socially and historically specific representational system, is to erase or at least obscure all marks of its enunciation. Most movies, through conventions of editing, camera work, lighting, and other formal parameters, present stories that seem to be without a source and that present themselves as unmediated reality. Of course, movies do not present actual "reality," but instead provide a representation of a certain "ideological" realism. "Psychological editing," as it is often called in Hollywood cinema, is the process by which images are shot and ordered so as to confirm and conform to our culture's way of viewing the world. In this form of enunciation, theorists argued, the role of the "enunciator" is concealed (through the conventions mentioned above) to place the spectator in a pleasurable position of seeming mastery over this visual field. The spectator thus "identifies" with the visual field, not as a constructed message, but as a self-generating reality for which he or she appears to be the sole, intended subject.

Metz refers to this phenomenon as "primary cinematic identification," describing the constant, unfolding relationship the spectator maintains with the cinematic image as a film's story progresses.

> We are not referring here to the spectator's identification with the characters of the film (which is secondary), but to his preliminary identification with the (invisible) seeing agency of the film itself as discourse, as the agency which *puts forward* the story and shows it to us. Insofar as it abolishes all traces of the subject of enunciation, the traditional film succeeds in giving the spectator the impression that he is himself that subject, but in a state of emptiness and absence, of pure visual capacity.[12]

One of the preeminent pleasures of the cinema, then, is this illusion of mastery over a perceptual field that seems to be without a source, that positions the spectator as its own subject. "In other words," writes Metz, "the spectator *identifies with himself,* with himself as an act of pure perception . . ."[13] observing "a story from nowhere, that nobody tells, but which, nevertheless, somebody receives. . . ."[14]

Theorists argued that movies are able to produce this illusion so forcefully because they accommodate processes of subjectivity already present in the spectator. This is where the contribution of psychoanalytic theory becomes important in understanding "enunciation." One of the central projects of psychoanalytic theory is to explain how social and cultural relationships produce subjectivity in individuals. Psychoanalysis argues that our conscious and unconscious minds are not "pre-given" in a form of subjectivity that is intrinsic, essentialist, and ahistorical, but are instead produced by our entrance into social formations and symbolic systems that pre-exist our consciousness. Consciousness (and "reality") are thus socially, culturally, and historically specific.

Once we recognize that subjectivity is socially produced, we can see that the production of consciousness is a profoundly *political* process, as are the mechanisms of "enunciation" in the cinema that reward us for seeing and interpreting the world in a certain way. The cinema, as Laura Mulvey states, embodies "preexisting patterns of fascination already at work within the individual subject and the social formations that have molded him. . . . As an advanced representation system, the cinema poses questions of the ways the unconscious (formed by the dominant order) structures ways of seeing and pleasure in looking."[15] The seemingly "natural" way of presenting the world in cinematic enunciation is thus a process inscribed with ideological values. It is not value neutral, but is instead a means of representing the world that is inseparable from certain ideological "ways of seeing" that are implicitly and explicitly naturalized as the only way to see. For example, in discussing the viewer's identification with a movie's characters, what Metz would term "secondary identification," Mulvey argues that the pleasures afforded by Hollywood cinema are voyeuristic and often sadistic, placing women as objects to be contained and controlled by the male gaze. Again, this is a type of representation that is often seen as completely "natural" when in fact it is socially determined. Because narrative cinema is a political form of "seeing and pleasure in looking," many theorists argued that films are an important component in maintaining repressive social relations which continue to replicate themselves both in the consciousness of individual subjects and in the cultural artifacts of society as a whole.

In their political attacks on classical Hollywood narrative and the characteristic modes of identification it offers spectators, many critics and filmmakers called for an avant-garde film practice that did not seek to hide its marks of enunciation and thus defamiliarized these characteristic ways of seeing the world. They championed a radical cinema that foregrounded cinematic technique, that drew attention to a film's status as a politically constructed discourse. Robert Lapsley and Michael Westlake provide a useful summary of this approach:

> The favored line of argument went as follows: spectators took films as transparent renderings of the real when in fact they simply produced a reality effect; films were able to do this by effacing all signs of their production; the only way, therefore, of breaking this ideological hold was through films organized so as to foreground their work of production, i.e. self-reflexive texts.[16]

In short, these critics called for narrational forms that were extremely "self-conscious," that refused to provide Hollywood's characteristically transparent yet ideologically refracted "window" on reality. Central to the debates over radical film practice was the work of Bertolt Brecht and his concept of "distanciation."[17] Again, crudely defined, distanciation is a means of creating an "anti-illusionist" aesthetic. Those who adopted Brecht's theories in the cinema felt that if viewers were made aware of the discursive relationship between the film and the spectator, they would be able to maintain a certain distanced and critical engagement of the film. They would think about the politics of representation rather than simply be absorbed within a representational system that produced an ideological version of "reality." One of the keys in producing distanciation was thought to be the use of self-reflexive techniques such as direct address of the camera; violations of conventional continuity editing; non-naturalistic acting, lighting, and set design—in short, anything that compromised conventional forms of spectator identification by forcing the spectator into contemplating his or her relationship with the film as an ideologically constructed discourse.

Do self-reflexive devices and self-conscious narrational forms always have this effect? When a film foregrounds its spectator relations, does that automatically and uniformly disrupt a viewer's primary identification with the image or secondary identification with a character in the story? Not necessarily. As Jim Collins writes,

> The recognition of a source outside of the self producing the image does not mean that the spectator must bolt from the theater screaming "lies, lies, it's all a lie," any more than a literary narrator's "dear reader" remarks shatter the reader's involvement with a novel. . . . Popular narrative since the 19th century has seldom been frightened to admit its status as a "tale," and has generally shown few signs that the recognition of the source might preclude spectator/reader involvement. If anything, it is the definite recognition of the source— whether it be a specific author, genre, or school, etc.,—that is in large part responsible for a given text's popularity.[18]

Whereas initial work on enunciation and identification abstracted these processes across virtually all narrative cinema as a uniform effect, subsequent work has emphasized that these processes must be examined film by film within an historical context and in relation to specific social audiences.

One of the most puzzling cases in such a project is the horror film. Few genres have been as important as horror in examining issues of identification and spectatorship in the cinema. This is perhaps because no other genre so explicitly foregrounds the issues of vision and power inherent in the cinema as a whole. Nowhere are the politics of seeing and not being seen more palpable and even downright bloody than in the horror film. And yet the processes of identification at work in horror remain difficult to isolate, describe, and predict. As Carol Clover notes in her study of the slasher film:

> The processes by which a certain image (but not another) filmed in a certain way (but not another) causes one person's (but not another's) pulse to race finally remains a mystery—not only to critics and theorists but even, to judge from interviews and the trial-and-error (and badly imitative) quality of the films themselves, by the people who make the product. The process of suture is sensed to be centrally important in effecting audience identification, though just how and why is unclear.

Nor is identification the straightforward notion some critics take it to be.[19]

Clover and others note that the horror viewer often quickly shifts character identification in these films, alternately entertaining the positions of both "Red Riding Hood *and* the wolf."[20] Clover is particularly fascinated with the slasher film's ability to problematize identification according to gender. Without necessarily resorting to self-reflexive intervention, these films are frequently able to make male viewers identify with female characters and female viewers with male characters at certain points in the story, a fact which Clover sees as an at least potentially promising "visible adjustment in terms of gender representation."[21]

What is perhaps most remarkable about *Freddy's Dead* and *Henry: Portrait of a Serial Killer,* however, is the way each film uses self-conscious narration and even explicitly self-reflexive devices to *encourage* rather than question or subvert certain patterns of identification in the viewer. In both of these films, the self-reflexive techniques thought by many theorists to challenge dominant modes of enunciation and identification are used instead as a means of *intensifying* certain forms of viewer identification. Moreover, the form and effect that this self-conscious narration and reflexivity take is determined in large part by each film's socially (and generationally) distinct audience. In both cases, reflexivity is used as a snare, a textual feature designed to attract a specific type of viewer marked by a certain sociology of taste, teens for *Freddy's Dead* and cinephiles for *Henry.*

Consider the following scene from *Freddy's Dead,* one that at first glance would seem to be a textbook case of self-reflexive distanciation. In this scene, yet another carload of witless teenagers have installed themselves in the house on Elm Street. On the couch, a stoner sits staring at a television with a broken screen. No sooner have his friends left him alone than the stoner hears the strains of Iron Butterfly's "Inna Gadda da Vidda" filling the room. He stares at the television in amazement. Where before there had been only a busted screen now stands Freddy Krueger against a backdrop of psychedelic colors. Freddy motions for the stoner to follow him. Getting up from the couch, he is sucked into the TV by Freddy's magic powers. But once inside the TV, the happy hallucination ends as the stoner suddenly finds himself the object of prey in a deadly video game. At various points in the chase, both Freddy and the stoner transform into video game characters; that is, each becomes a small two-dimensional figure scurrying across the TV screen. As is Freddy's habit, he torments the stoner teen before killing him, this time by forcing him to negotiate the characteristic obstacles, hazards, and tortures of a Nintendo game. Eventually, both Freddy and the teenager emerge from this video realm and back into the three-dimensional space of the house. But video logic still applies. Freddy sits with a "powerglove," a video game accessory that allows the player to control all functions with one hand. With this device, Freddy puts the stoner through the paces, making him pogo through hallways and up and down stairs, repeatedly crashing his head into the ceiling (à la Super-Mario) until at last dead. At one point, Freddy fiendishly invokes the Nintendo tagline, *"Now* I'm playing with power!'"

In this highly self-reflexive and comic meditation on the spectator relations of the series as a whole, a passive teen sits transfixed before the screen, lured by Freddy into a zone of dynamic spectacle where he is eventually killed. On the one hand, it would be easy to read this particular scene as an indictment of contemporary youth culture, an adult condemnation of a generation interested only in drugs and video stimulation. Within the reading strategies adopted by teens themselves and encouraged by the scene's self-consciously comic address, however, a more probable reading is one of parody. Indeed, when Freddy first commandeers the television set, he invades a moralistic "This is your brain—This is your brain on drugs" commercial. "Looks like a frying pan and some eggs to me," Freddy says sarcastically after beaning the guy in the commercial with the skillet. For an audience of young teens, the stoner's eventual death by drugs, rock 'n' roll, and arcade addiction is funny precisely because of its hyperbolized treatment of the hazards of teen culture. Narrational self-consciousness in this case serves as an ironic commentary on the film's presumed viewership, a commentary that allows teens in on the joke.

Does this self-reflexive model of viewership (transfixed teen sucked into mindless spectacle) force the film's viewers to assess their ideological position as teenage consumers of visual narrative in the late 20th Century? Probably not. Does this scene encourage teenage viewers to identify with Freddy, even as he dedicates himself to the eventual extermination of all living teens? Perversely, the answer would seem to be yes. When the stoner first sees Freddy dancing in the television, a point-of-view shot aligns the spectator's vision with that of the doomed teen. Thus, as Freddy beckons with his psychedelic dance, he motions to the spectator as well. Although the viewer is at least momentarily placed in the position of the stoner teen through point-of-view shots, he or she certainly does not identify with him. The audience, after all, knows something that the stoner does not, namely, that this particular teen is about to buy the farm in spectacular fashion. In this direct address of the spectator, Freddy does not threaten or frighten the viewer (as we would expect of most movie monsters), nor does he rupture the chain of identifications that allows the viewer to follow the story. Instead, he promises to honor the generic contract negotiated across the entire film series, one that promises to subject a nameless series of dim-witted teens to incredible spectacles of death. In effect, Freddy is signaling to the viewer that the anticipated visual pyrotechnics are about to begin.

Fans of Freddy certainly do not attend these films expecting or hoping for a compelling narrative. There is no mystery as to what is going to happen in these films, nor is suspense really at issue. Romantic subplots among the doomed teens, frenetic last-minute rescues, and even Freddy's perfunctory "death" at the end of each film are just so much window-dressing to surround the core attraction of these films—episodes of intense visual excitation. Conventional notions of narrative, such as they exist, function only to link the five or six ingeniously staged kill sequences, "set pieces" that became increasingly elaborate as the series progressed through the 1980s. This sequence of the stoner's death not only encapsulates the spectator relations of the *Nightmare* series as a whole, then, but also foregrounds the dizzying visual plasticity that serves as the identifying feature of these films. The very premise of the *Nightmare* series (Freddy's ability to enter dreams and kill the dreamer) ensures repeated confrontations such as this, where a wise-cracking Freddy, much to the viewer's delight, has the absolute power to manipulate time, space, and matter.

Within the *Nightmare* formula, it is easy to see why Freddy is the star protagonist and chief point of identification rather than the menaced teens. Freddy is all powerful while the teens are just so much fodder for Freddy's gory choreography. Most of the teenagers in the series are flatly drawn "types," blank to the point that they repel even the most rudimentary form of character identification. Freddy, meanwhile, is the only character who gets any decent lines in the picture. Most importantly, Freddy continues from film to film. The teenagers do not.[22]

This is not to say that teenagers emerge from the theater saying to themselves (or more ominously, to their dates), "Gee, Freddy's really cool. I wish I could be just like him." The identification at work here is more complex than viewers simply aligning their interests and sympathies with Freddy (I am definitely *not* arguing that the teen audience for these films is comprised entirely of aspiring serial killers). Instead, what Freddy proffers in his appearances on screen are episodes of accelerated perception and dazzling spectacle. Since Freddy's domain is that of dream logic, quite literally anything can happen when he is at the center of the narrative. Under his command, unfortunate teens sprout roach arms, drown in pools of blood, collide with phantom school buses and even have their heads miniaturized and served as meatballs on a Freddy pizza.

If we refer back to Metz's theory of the cinematic spectator as "identifying with himself as an act of pure perception," we can see why the *Nightmare* films might have such durable appeal. As episodes of spectacle punctuated by brief narrative links, the *Nightmare* series' entire structure is designed to promote and indulge these episodes of intense visual excitement. In this sense, viewers identify with Freddy not so much as a character but as a facilitator, the dynamic "source" of the phantasmagoric imagery. The self-reflexivity of this scene (and others in the series) does call attention to the film's process of enunciation, but ironically, it focuses this attention onto the character of Freddy, who serves the unique function of a cinematic enunciator actually contained within the film's story world.

All films depend on primary cinematic identification. The viewer must make this identification and assume a certain subject position for the images to be "meaningful." The *Nightmare* films are distinct in that their "pleasure" operates almost entirely at the level of primary identification. Secondary identifications with characters and a subsequent investment in the narrative simply are not important or even necessary. In this sense, the *Nightmare* films are not unlike another popular youth visual entertainment medium—video games. Both reward viewers for acute perception and nimble subjectivity in relation to constantly transforming perceptual data, usually based on a minimal narrative premise. Both are also often incomprehensible to the adult community. The reference here to Freddy and his stoned victim as video characters is thus both apt and perhaps even a bit calculated. The scene confirms that having the skills of good Tetris player is probably more valuable in either watching or eluding Freddy than possessing a highly developed sense of narrative acumen.

What rattles the cages of adult film culture, as epitomized by the movie reviewers who continually deride these films, is that the *Nightmare* series is so unabashedly devoted to pure and seemingly pointless visual stimulation. These movies have little need or regard for qualities of narrative causality, probability, and complexity, textual features that this "sophisticated" community holds so dear. Consequently, these films become ripe targets for abuse by a film community committed to more "sober" and "realistic" filmmaking.

This is especially apparent when one looks at the press coverage surrounding *Henry,* a "quality" film which critics were most adamant about distinguishing from other contemporary horror fare like the *Nightmare* series. Speaking of director John McNaughton's handling of a certain scene in *Henry,* for example, Dave Kehr writes admiringly,

> McNaughton betrays a trust—the basic agreement between horror-film maker and horror-film patron—that style will always act as a buffer, transforming act into effect, substance into flourish. That transformation does not happen in *Henry,* and the results are nearly unbearable.[23]

In other words, while garden-variety slasher films disguise "substance" with overblown "style," *Henry's* gritty realism "delivers the goods" and produces genuine horror (Kehr's mistake here is not realizing that "style" *is* the "substance" of these other films). Critics took care to note that McNaughton's film is a "portrait" of a serial killer, a realistic study in character and not a sensationalistic exercise in bubbling latex. Kehr's comments are typical of writers who celebrated *Henry's* chief stylistic strength as being, paradoxically, its "absence of style." But this "absence of style" that seems to equal "realism" is only perceptible when contrasted against a field of more "spectacular" slasher films. Both press and promoters were quick to make such comparisons. "He's no B-movie monster in a hockey mask," writes the reviewer for *Rolling Stone*.[24] Or, as the advertising material for the film's video release states, "He's not Jason. He's not Freddy . . . He's real."

Of course, creating a film that seems to exhibit an "absence of style" is in itself a stylistic decision. *Henry's* bleak "realism" is just as manipulative a formal treatment of the material as Freddy's elaborate stalk-and-slaughter sequences. Throughout *Henry*, director McNaughton consistently represents his protagonist's crimes in a way that contrasts sharply from prevailing representations of murder and violence in contemporary horror films. Thus, in contrast to the baroque manipulations of time, space, and teens that characterize each death sequence in *Freddy's Dead*, *Henry* begins with a close-up of the inert face of a woman. The camera pulls back slowly to reveal that the woman is dead and lying in a field, a knife slash across her abdomen. The only sound on the audiotrack is that of the insects in the field around the corpse. The shot is deliberately static, quiet, and of an uncomfortable duration, presenting a confrontational image that sets the tone for the overall film.[25] Repeatedly in *Henry*, death appears not as a dynamic spectacle but as a gruesome tableau.

In fact, for the entire first-third of this film about a serial killer, the viewer does not witness a single murder. Instead, the viewer only sees the bodies Henry has left in his wake. On the soundtrack accompanying these static studies in death is the sound of the struggle between Henry and his victim. McNaughton, in other words, uses asynchronous sound and image to convey the actual murder aurally while portraying visually only the murder's bloody aftermath. In each of these scenes, the camera slowly circles the now-motionless body as the soundtrack records the sounds of Henry stabbing, shooting, or strangling the victim.

What is particularly striking about these early murder scenes, and important as well in producing a certain form of identification in the cinematically literate spectator, is each tableau's sense of calculated execution. Because of their marked contrast to the dynamics of other horror films, these scenes are not simply examples of "self-conscious" narration, but of self-consciously "artistic" narration. They speak to an audience presumably sensitive to representational strategies (and presumably fed up with slasher fare), and ask to be read as an artistic decision in the representation of violence. What is seen by critics as frugal "realism" is in fact a function of pronounced technique and calculated directorial intervention.

Small wonder, then, that this film would be championed so vociferously by film critics and art-house cinephiles. Unlike the *Nightmare* films, *Henry* is a horror film tailor-made for such an audience's proclivity to engage formal strategies of representation critically, to step back and consider a film, not only in terms of affect, but in terms of its construction. *Henry* is a film with an artistic agenda, and is thus attractive to an audience that prides itself on its ability to decipher and interpret cinematic strategies of representation.

Henry's quite self-conscious address of a cinematically literate audience is especially apparent in the film's most graphic murder sequence. Much like Freddy's scene with the teenage stoner, this sequence presents a highly self-reflexive analysis of the spectator's relationship to the horror image. In this scene, Henry and his sidekick Otis watch a videotape they have made of themselves killing a suburban family. The spectator sees the entire murder played out in "real time"; that is, we watch the unedited tape with Henry and Otis on their television set. Interestingly, most popular press reviews of the film seemed compelled to provide a laboriously detailed account of this scene's action and structure, explaining aspects of its formal construction and emphasizing its affective impact. Almost all agreed that this scene was the most important and provocative in the film, a point that was emphasized by the number of people each critic claimed to see walk out of the theater at this moment in the movie. Peter Travers's account is emblematic:

> In the film's most terrifying scene, the one that prompts the walkouts, Henry and Otis attack a suburban family and videotape the deed. "Take her blouse off," Henry tells Otis, who is grabbing the struggling housewife. "Do it, Otis. You're a star." Cinematographer Charlie Lieberman . . . turned a camcorder over to Rooker [who plays Henry] to shoot this scene as Henry would. The video footage—grainy, unfocused, crazily angled—makes the carnage joltingly immediate. It's a stomach churner. . . . Otis replays the murders at home in slow motion, savoring even the moment when he tried to have sex with the woman he just killed, only to be stopped by Henry.[26]

Invariably, critics discussing this scene concentrated on the video camera as a device for enhancing "realism" and "immediacy," even as they distanced themselves as critics to make that observation. Kehr labels it a moment of "cinema degree zero," adding that "the video image tells us that there is already no hope of rescue, that the action is over and cannot be altered. And the absence of cutting . . . tells us nothing will be spared, but also (and somehow more threateningly) that nothing will be artificially enhanced or exaggerated for our enjoyment."[27] Throughout the critical discourse surrounding this scene, there is an obsession with discussing it as technique. It is admired as a form of explicit manipulation of both the medium and the audience. "The viewer is trapped in the dead-eyed stare of the videocam, forced into a position of passive endurance."[28]

One might argue that when the camera pulls back from the TV set and shows us Henry and Otis camped out on the couch watching the murders in slow motion, there should be a chilling moment of self-recognition as the viewer considers how voyeurism and sadism are so strongly linked both in this specific scene and in the horror film in general. If such self-recognition does occur, it would be a classic example of distanciation, the spectator made critical and self-aware of the politics of representation through a self-reflexive device (perhaps the people who fled the theater at this point had such an experience). But the incessant attention to technique and effect in the critical accounts of this film suggest that another form of identification may be at work, at least for the small segment of the audience responsible for writing about the film. In its self-conscious and even self-reflexive address of the "elite" movie-goer, *Henry* encourages the spectator to identify with the film's director. This is not necessarily an identification with the flesh-and-blood body of John McNaughton, but with the director as an abstract author of the text, as the implicit teller of the tale. A pleasure provided in such an identification is one of spectatorial prowess, a confirmation of one's critical understanding of cinematic signification. It is a quite different pleasure, obviously, than allowing oneself to be taken along for a spectacular ride as in the *Nightmare* films. Observing and evaluating a narrative in terms of technique necessitates maintaining a certain critical distance, which itself becomes the foundation of the "so-phisticated" viewer's pleasure. We might say that the critics and cinephiles watching *Henry* convert their primary cinematic identification with the image into a form of secondary identification with character, only the character with whom they identify never appears on the screen, but is instead the artistic "enunciator" whose presence is felt in the text, paradoxi-cally, as the pronounced intervention of stylistic "restraint."

The scenes described here present two audiences watching murders on two television sets in self-reflexive portraits of horror spectatorship that suggest two possible modes of viewer identification. The "pleasures" afforded by each type of identification differ also; indeed, these pleasures may very well be defined in opposition to one another. Perhaps Freddy has enjoyed such popularity in American youth culture over the past decade because his power to combine vicious wit and visual weirdness resonates with a generation more attuned to spectacle than narrative, who prefer the spectacular over the normative. In contrast to *Psycho's* Norman Bates, the privileged horror figure of "elite" film culture who asks to be read as a "complex" character operating in a tightly and cleverly plotted narrative, Freddy serves as a functional gateway to fragmented and almost random episodes of intense visual stimulation.

At the same time, the "sober" pleasures afforded by *Henry* are only possible when the film is situated against a backdrop of more "spectacular" horror films. As a consequence, the cinephiles and critics who praise *Henry* are either implicitly or explicitly damning the viewing pleasures in the *Nightmare* films. Their appeals to issues of originality, character, and realism over formula, sensationalism, and special effects represent an effort to promote a certain cultural agenda and aesthetic, one that many middle-aged critics no doubt view as increasingly besieged by the "crass" tastes of younger movie-goers.

Considering the extreme differences of structure and identification in *Freddy's Dead* and *Henry*, is there a certain point when it becomes futile to describe them both as "horror" films? And if one or the other is not a horror film, what is it? In his book on horror, Noël Carroll defines the genre as follows:

> . . . art-horror is an emotional state wherein, essentially, some nonor-
> dinary physical state of agitation is caused by the thought of a monster,
> in terms of the details presented by a fiction or an image, which thought
> also includes the recognition that the monster is threatening and im-
> pure. The audience thinking of a monster is prompted in this response
> by the responses of fictional human characters whose actions they are
> attending to, and that audience, like said characters, may also wish to
> avoid physical contact with such types of things as monsters. Monsters,
> here, are identified as any being not now believed to exist according
> to reigning scientific notions.[29]

Applying Carroll's definition to these two films presents a number of interesting problems. If teenagers experience exhilaration more than fear in the spectacular visual excesses of the *Nightmare* movies, are they still horror films? If the audience does not identify with the actions and responses of the "fictional human characters," but instead eagerly awaits the demise of these characters at the hands of Freddy, is that still a horror film? If Henry is not a monster according to Carroll's definition, since he is only human, does that exclude *Henry* as a horror film? And finally, even if we grant Henry monster status, are the cinephiles who attend to his carnage strictly in terms of stylistic technique and narrational manipulation actually experiencing a horror film?

I bring up these questions to point out how difficult it is to systematize the textual features of a genre or to categorize readings and responses for a given film, much less to begin making evaluative judgments over "quality." What is at stake in valuing one film or another, or even in attempting to define systematically a group of films, is a struggle over cultural meaning and power. Just as representation, enunciation, and identification are political processes, so too are the cultural classification and evaluation of texts. To say one film is "good" horror and the other is not, or even to say that one film *is* horror and the other is not, presents a situation where a critic occupying a certain social and cultural position passes judgment on the viewing experiences and values of other social groups. There can be no indelible essence of horror contained in a checklist of textual features, and judgments as to "quality" of horror films must be tempered by a recognition of the political construction of "taste." Do men and women find the same films to be horrific? How many men compared to women, for example, would say *Fatal Attraction* is a horror film? What are the political stakes in saying one group is right in this classification and the other is wrong? Many social audiences may prefer the action horror of John Carpenter over the intellectual horror of David Cronenberg. What are the political stakes in saying one director's films are "inferior" to the other, when the judgment being made is ultimately as much about audiences as about films?

If we think back to the conversation at the video store, we can catch a glimpse of such a cultural struggle at work. On the one hand, there is the economic power of the teenagers, whose tastes rule the contemporary marketplace in film (and video). Their buying power and tastes make the dominance of the slasher film possible. Then there is the representational power of the columnist from *Premiere,* tied to a critical establishment of frustrated tastemakers who often abhor the prevailing tastes of the entertainment marketplace and who yearn for a cinema of old. His attempt to make fun of these teenage girls in a national publication by exposing their ignorance of *Psycho* and their disdain for a classic character like Norman Bates ("He stinks!") is a promotion of one aesthetic over another, one set of evaluative criteria over another.

But as the philosophical debate between these teenage girls over favorite movie monsters demonstrates, contemporary teen audiences do not necessarily watch horror the same way that their parents did. While one girl can imagine what it would be like to be Freddy's prey and wants no part of it, the other girl focuses instead on Freddy's visual ingenuity and inexhaustible supply of one-liners. When finally forced by her friend to entertain a different mode of identification and put herself in the place of the terrorized teens on screen, her only comment reaffirms her allegiance to a cinema of overwhelming vividness. "If I have to be murdered," she tells her friend, "I'd rather be murdered by a guy with imagination."[30]

7

Hardware and Hardbodies, What Do Women Want?: A Reading of *Thelma and Louise*

Sharon Willis

If summer, 1991 witnessed the spectacle of a modest female buddy film, *Thelma and Louise*, sharing considerable intense media attention with the most expensive blockbuster in Hollywood history, *Terminator 2*, it is because the former ignited an equally explosive spectacle, one that overflowed its frame into the popular press, where it intersected with a debate about women and violence. Like *Fatal Attraction* (1987), *Thelma and Louise* plugged into ambient anxieties about sexual difference, and men's and women's places as organized by the "battle of the sexes." And like *Fatal Attraction, Thelma and Louise* troubled borderlines that contemporary popular critical discourse continues to code as fragile: those between art and life, fantasy and agency, cinematic fiction and the life stories we tell ourselves.

Debates around the film all turned on the question of its status as a feminist statement. Within this framework, objections emerging from feminist and anti-feminist quarters took several forms. A range of critics took issue with the firm's depiction of men. In a rhetoric clearly borrowed from feminism, but crudely reduced, they found the film guilty of male-bashing. Richard Johnson of the *Daily News* found it: "degrading to men, with pathetic stereotypes of testosterone crazed behavior" (quoted in Richard Schickel, "Gender Bender," *Time* [June 24, 1991], 52). Focusing on the film's women as negative and dangerous models of feminist assertiveness, critics called the film everything from "a PMS movie, plain and simple" (Ellen Goodman, also quoted in Richard Schickel, "Gender Bender," 52), to "basically a recruiting film for the NRA" (Richard Johnson, quoted in *People* [July 24, 1991], 94) to "a fascist version of feminism" (John Leo in *U.S. News and World Report,* also quoted in *People* [July 24, 1991], 94). All of these arguments depend firmly on an overestimation of the film's few moments of violence, and a conviction that the film should be read as a political tract, whose exemplary characters are representative of and for feminism. From another perspective, some feminists criticized the film for the pessimism they saw in its driving its heroines off a cliff at the end. Margaret Carlson: "As a bulletin from the front in the battle of the sexes, *Thelma and Louise* sends the message that little ground has been won. . . . They become free but only wildly, self-destructively so—free to drive off the ends of the earth" ("Is This What Feminism Is All About?," *Time* [June 24, 1991], 57). This anxiety about self-destructiveness as a political dead-end was widely shared, and John Simon's is only one exemplary comment: "The filmmakers think that . . . feminist liberation, even if hurtling into destructive excess, is somehow glorious, which is surely the way benighted moviegoers are encouraged to view it" ("Movie of the Moment," *National Review* [July 8, 1991], 48).

Violent responses to the film's "violence" are related to a common fascination with the increasingly visible "battle of the sexes" in popular culture, but they also attribute to the image the power to shape spectator consciousness more or less directly through the identifications it encourages. However, only an oversimplified assessment of the complex processes of identification, one that imagines it to flow seamlessly into imitation, allows us to elide the question of fantasy in readings that implicitly rely on a notion of "politically correct" images and stories.[1] An analysis equal to the complexity of the psychic operations involved in identification has to acknowledge, first of all, that identification is not a state, but a process, and that as such, it is likely to be mobile and intermittent, rather than consistent. We will do better to think of viewer identifications as scenarios, rather than fixations. Hardly confined to identifications with characters, then, these scenarios may equally well fasten on situations, objects, and places. Finally, a more complicated analysis would not imagine that fantasmatic identifications forged at the movies are acted out, and acted out as directly imitative behavior. And this is because identification is not necessarily mimesis, and because identifications need not be based on consciously perceived or desired resemblances; indeed, they may come as a surprise, a disruptive moment whose effects are partial, provisional, and unpredictable.[2]

Anxious interpretations of spectator identification that expect that women's viewing pleasures will translate directly into aggressive attitudes and behavior towards men in daily life themselves have their source in fantasy. Moreover, they highlight the very cultural pressures they work to foreclose. These readings activate and seek to manage the fantasies of women's rage and autonomy coming together in figures of dangerous feminine power that seem to preoccupy the culture. Simultaneously related to women's impact as consumers, and to the impact of feminism on mass marketing, these fantasies are beginning to shape images that work to produce a feminine audience, whose anxieties and desires they speak, and speak in ways that remind us that the question "what do women want?" is still wide open. This feminine audience itself is figured as out-of-control, as Thelma and Louise are, in men's and women's, and feminist and non-feminist discourse alike.

Men critics frequently expressed a certain fear and anxiety about feminist identifications with women as the subjects of violence and rage, while women critics, whether they defended or attacked the film, always seemed compelled to address the crude question of role models, and always at some point fell back on personal anecdote, on their private temptations to identify. For example, women seemed obsessed with the most cartoonishly piggish male, the driver whose truck Thelma and Louise blow up in the film's central and monumentally spectacular image of feminine rage. Thus, Margaret Carlson claimed this fantasy as her own in *Time:* "The movie may not have the impact of *Fatal Attraction,* but the next time a woman passes an 18-wheeler and points her finger like a pistol at the tires, the driver might just put his tongue back in his mouth where it belongs" (57). And *Newsweek*'s Laura Shapiro savors the following anecdote that foregrounds the fantasy's enactment in daily life: "Last week four women who had seen the film were walking down a Chicago street when a truck driver shouted an obscenity at them. Instantly, all four seized imaginary pistols and aimed them at his head. 'Thelma and Louise hit Chicago,' yelled one" ("Women Who Kill Too Much," *Newsweek* [June 17, 1991], 63). What allowed so many women critics to take this film so personally? The answer must lie in the film's openness to the fantasmatic scenarios one can bring to it.

However, the public critical recourse to real-life performance consistently recognizes the fantasmatic drive of the film's pyrotechnic spectacle only to shut it down immediately in order to fixate on a stable, if imaginary, antagonism between men's anxieties and women's vicarious pleasures. But to accomplish this, it must eschew irony and forget the difference between fantasy and agency that is at the heart of the film itself. In doing so, such readings touch on a commonly shared critical anxiety about the film's implausibilities. Framing the film as generically realist, Stanley Kauffmann exemplifies that response, arguing that the script is "burdened with contrivances" ("Stanley Kauffmann on Films," *New Republic* [July 1, 1991], 28). "The wild ride of *Thelma and Louise* was meant to be a vicarious release for all women who feel anger at the world of men. But, though there are bull's-eyes along the way, the film's artifices clutter up its original honest intent" (29). Such a drive to regulate the film according to plausibility suggests that the desire for it to work as a feminist parable or prescription also serves an agenda of containment. For this drive depends on forgetting that the film's spectacle is made of the play between plausibility and fantasy, a play organized around the figure of a body, but a body catapulting across the landscape in a car, indissociable from motion, from the drive forward, the drive forward into loss.

While this play gathers around the women's driving bodies, monumentally clothed in the car that is iconic of automotive and consumer history, it also saturates the landscape draped around them. This is a landscape in which a woman's gaze becomes panoramic and volatile. Emphatically fantasmatic, the film reminds us that one of the effects of driving is to render landscape as image, as cinematic flow. In this landscape a woman's gaze can become the avid consumer of the male body, as the film's most intensely eroticized spectacles capture the hitchhiker JD's buttocks for Thelma's gaze, and the spectator's that is appended to it, going along for the ride, so to speak. Saturated with unreal color, this landscape is marked as a screen for special effects. Frequently veiled by uninterrupted sheets of even rain—director Ridley Scott's signature—this geography bears numerous cultural markers. Not only does it recall the special effects landscape of Scott's *Blade Runner* (1982), but its artificial rain calls up the deliberately whimsical atmospherics of commercials. If the film seems to revel in its own production of artifice, then the critical detour through identifications and personal stories must implicitly rehearse the subject's pleasure in constructing herself as an image, an image staged and performed. Indeed, such a detour should remind us of the ways we mimic Louise's implausible route to circumvent Texas on the journey from Arkansas to Mexico, the detour that circumscribes the "heart of the matter," the personal history that is at once obscure, empty, and structuring.

At every turn, the film displaces its energy from narrative justification and explanation to other, less comfortable seductions—those of the road, the traveling, the speed of motion, and those of the image. Readings of the film that are determined to decide its political meaning depend upon stubborn forgetfulness that its fantasmatic machinery produces displacements that overthrow any and all resolutions and explanations. For example, the overdiscussed violence that turns a simple weekend vacation into a journey of no return is Louise's murder of the man who attempted to rape Thelma in the parking lot of the Silver Bullet Bar.[3] But we consistently forget that Louise shoots him, not in the heat of rage when she intervenes to prevent the rape, but rather, in a calm pause afterwards, when he insists upon having the last word with this verbal challenge, "Suck my cock!" She kills him, then, not for what he does, but for what he *says,* a far thinner pretext.

Nevertheless, discussions of the film have insisted tenaciously enough on giving Thelma and Louise a narrative reason for winding up on the lam;

they have been sexually victimized. But the film continually highlights the shakiness of this excuse for a headlong flight with no destination beyond the going (as the heroines insist, "Let's not get caught, let's keep going"). Meanwhile, we often forget the displacement embedded in the plot turn that definitively precipitates Thelma and Louise over the edge of no return, the armed robbery that cannot be fully explained by a logic of sexual abuse. Thelma becomes a robber because the hitchhiker with whom she has spent the night has stolen all the money the two women have to their names. Here is another incident of victimization: seduction and abandonment compounded by the theft. Except that Thelma reads the event as a fortunate one: she has had her first good sexual experience. Within historically conventional Hollywood terms where women are cata-pulted out of domesticity by the acts of sexual violence they endure, or by giving in to the violence of their own desire, Thelma is punished for her lust and pleasure. But she doesn't read it that way. The punishment seems lost on her. Instead, this moment becomes her occasion for incorpo-rating JD's theatrically scripted robbery routine. Later, we watch Thelma perform as JD, repeating this routine exactly as he had demonstrated it for her. And all of this is mediated through a cut to the store's video surveillance camera; Thelma becomes an image before our eyes, and through the explicit theft of a man's posture, words, and persona.

The film's most compelling fantasies keep emerging through this kind of cross-gender identification. These are the ones that are thrown off, that escape a narrative logic of cause and effect. *Thelma and Louise* is about a long erratic drive, alternately wandering and speeding toward an impossi-ble destination along the arc of a detour. And the detour becomes the whole trip, a trip projected across the space between two images—the snapshot Louise takes at the beginning of the trip and the final still that permanently suspends the women in their Thunderbird. The snapshot memorializes a "before" image, women dressed up and made up for an outing. This is the image the film's journey undoes, as the women strip down to tee-shirts, cast off all the accoutrements of glamor, of conven-tional feminine masquerade. Ending with a still image that answers to the first one as its "after," and the film puts an ironic spin on the genre of "before" and "after" pictures that advertise diets and beauty makeovers to the female consumer. Finally, this is a film about the motion between two still moments, the route from image to image. And here, the whole film seems to come down to Thelma's lusty appreciation of JD's buttocks as he walks away from their car. "That's him goin'," she tells Louise, "I luuuuve watchin' him go." This is a film that wants us to be able to say the same: we love watching it go, not watching it get somewhere.

If our readings take the film's conclusion, or its heroines' destination, to decide its meaning, then we repress the partiality and disruption that make its journey so compelling. Such are the readings that pronounce the film dangerous and wrong-headed because it invites women to take on wholesale the tired old clichés of Hollywood masculinity and male bonding that prevail in the history Westerns, road movies, and action films. For women to embrace and celebrate feminine versions of these clichés, the very clichés that men increasingly reject, such readings argue, advances nothing and merely inverts the current gender imbalance in representation. But this argument skips over the process by which the film parades the takeover of these clichés, a process that foregrounds the posturing involved. And this posturing has at least two effects. It remobilizes for women viewers the pleasures of fantasmatic identifications with embodied agents of travel, speed, force, and aggression, pleasures that we have historically enjoyed in a cross-gender framework, but this time offering room for a different mix of desire with that identification. At the same time, the spectacle of women acting like men works to disrupt the apparent naturalness of certain postures when performed by a male body.

A similar insistence on deciding a conclusive meaning, it seems to me, handicaps any argument that suggests *Thelma and Louise* advocates or encourages violence. Such arguments implicitly propose that representations of violence conclude with violent or aggressive behavior in the world. But, we might productively ask, what if violent fantasy does not translate simply into violent real-life agency, what if it in fact works as much to deflect it or contain it? Or what if it works to master our ever-growing anxieties, as a culture, about becoming the *objects*, not the *subjects*, of violence in everyday life?

Thelma and Louise's impossible suspension as an image hanging over the abyss, monumentalized in their last kiss, stresses the film's demand to be read as fantasy, and as fantasy that reworks elements of a vast image repertory embedded in a history and continually marked by effects of cultural circulation.[4] To participate in the drive to decide, once and for all, for or against *Thelma and Louise*, to push the journey to its conclusion, or to freeze and fix the volatility of the fantasies it generates will lead us to "get what you settle for," in Louise's words. Rather, I'd like to preserve this volatility by locating *Thelma and Louise* in some kind of cultural matrix, a matrix traced both through the "routes" of my childhood consumer education, and through the current cultural play with the signs of gender.

And these routes have something to do with women and cars. For, finally, this is a story about women and cars. As the screenwriter Callie Khouri remarks: "I just got fed up with the passive role of women. They were never driving the story, because they were never driving the car." What happens when women drive cars, instead of adorning men's cars, instead of sitting, fixed and still, draped across them? What happens when women wear cars, instead of clothes? What happens when women strip down for a purpose that exceeds, bypasses, or falls short of sexual display?[5]

The tremendous discussion surrounding *Thelma and Louise* suggests that I am not the only woman fascinated by unruly red hair, or by driving and its myths. These are, finally, the two anchors on which my fantasies about *Thelma and Louise* are tethered, and which allow the film to fall within a nexus of volatile mythologies and identifications that unevenly relate gender to driving.

Thelma and Louise mobilizes a set of childhood-viewing memories from the moment of my early image literacy. And these memories articulate an uneasy liaison between the television serial reruns by which I was most fascinated, *I Love Lucy* and *Route 66*. Lucy was seductive in her aggressive violation of feminine norms, as her frenetic body and raucous voice consistently played against glimpses of her beauty in repose to break the frame of glamor coded as the female body fixed for spectacle. *Route 66*, for me, was about the spectacular stillness of the seamless road trip endlessly circling on itself as each episode repeated the same scenario. Each time the two buddies arrived at the appointed hour in the same kind of town, and produced or witnessed the same story of loss, retrieval, and loss—only to move on at the end of the hour. Now if these two series became the vehicles of my desire, fantasy, anticipations, and early nostalgias, it was not by any simple identification, but rather through the partiality, failure, and disruption of identification that crossed and re-crossed the divide of sexual difference.

As I watch *Thelma and Louise,* my childhood apprehension of sexual difference as it was staged in driving comes back to me. Our cars and the roads we drive are on one of the few arenas where it is acceptable, and even anodine, to act out aggression. It is in the car, in the flow, or blockage of traffic that we feel safe performing a theatrics of contained aggression through gestures and speech that we wouldn't risk face to face; we posture and feign, car to car, as we jockey for position with other drivers. Riveted in my identifications with both of my parents in this private theater that was the car, I absorbed the "auto-motivations" behind their postures of driving aggression. My mother's willfulness on the road operated in open defiance of an internalized voice that she often ventriloquized: the voice of the surveying male driver repeating the critical jokes about women drivers that circulated so widely in the sixties of my childhood. My father, on the other hand, took driving as an occasion for the pleasure of posturing with a stereotypical masculine bravado that I never saw him staging anywhere else. How easy for the signals, the lines of identification to get crossed amid the pleasure and excitement of this private show where fantasies of violence never led to its execution, where the parade, and the story of it were the main event.

In contemporary popular culture, I want to suggest, our viewing habits, like our driving habits, reflect destabilizing play with conventional mythologies of sexual difference, offer an arena of play and experiment with gender posturing, and this is where *Thelma and Louise* intersects with an array of contemporary representations, like *Terminator 2* and *La Femme Nikita*. "Killer Women: Here Come the Hardbodies" bellows the headline that the July 29 issue of *New York* magazine boldly emblazons above its cover photograph of Linda Hamilton all pumped up and dressed in combat gear for *Terminator 2*. The ambivalence at the core of these images lies at the heart of popular culture's increasing obsession with lethal women. Is this the answer to the question, "what do women want?" Hardbodies? If so, whose question is this? Are these bodies products of a masculine imagination—its deepest anxieties, and its secret, perhaps masochistic desires? If hardbodies is the answer to women's questions, then whose hardbodies do we want? Men's, women's, or our own? Is women's fascination desiring or identifying, narcissistic or anaclitic, benign or aggressive?

If so much discussion of *Thelma and Louise* pivoted on violence, it is because the film stages a violence that is neither thematized nor represented on the screen. This is the violence of representational struggle, both in private fantasy and in public discussion. At the fantasmatic level, the film pries gender away from sexuality, pries feminine masquerade loose from effects of glamor and sexual seduction, makes the body into its own costume. This is the effect of cinematic representations of women who no more actively *want* than, say, Rambo or the Terminator, or Mel Gibson's Martin Riggs in *Lethal Weapon,* all of whose smoothly muscled carapaces make their very bodily presence a mute thrust of demand. In destabilizing contrast to their male precursors, these new presentations of the muscled female body stage a form of drag based on a masculinity that aggressively displays its difference from an anatomical base. They thus parade an interruption: where we expect them to exhibit the mark of sexuality for consumption, instead we see the body as costume.

One of the more compelling pleasures of this film, for me, is the radical change in the women's body language—posture, gait, and gesture—, a change that went along with the shift from dressy clothes to tee-shirts and jeans. This dramatic transformation cannot be read, however, as a revelation of the "natural" body underneath the feminine masquerade of the housewife or service worker. Rather, the prominence of this bodily transformation sets the film in an associative chain of recent images of women clearly "reconstructed" on screen, like Sigourney Weaver's Ripley in *Aliens* (1987), and most recently and spectacularly, Linda Hamilton's Sarah Connor in *Terminator 2*. These revised embodiments of femininity stress the body's constructed character as costume, a costume that asks us to read it both as machine and as masculinity.[6]

These images remind us of consumer culture's obsession with managing and transforming the body through exercise, with constructing bodies as sculpture, as fashion, as clothing. Exercise inscribes the subject's will to mastery on the body, just as it reinscribes the sexual difference that we continually restage in our private and public lives. Playing on these everyday consumer practices today's cinematic images of transformer women tend to highlight the doing. These are displays about doing as well as showing, where gender identity is not simply what we *are*, or something we *possess*, but something we *do* as well.[7]

Thelma and Louise suggests that we need to reconceptualize feminine desires, and to shift our framework so that it can accommodate not only need or want, but also demand. At the same time, we need to acknowledge the conflicts and contradictions that inhabit our fantasies, and to recognize the aggressive and violent components of our identifications. As we take pleasure in the recent visibility of fantasies that move us, fantasies we can imagine ourselves authoring, we also begin to glimpse the burdens and pains that are bound up with that pleasure. As feminine subjects of fantasy begin more and more to produce representations for popular consumption, women are emerging in our collective imagination as agents of culture and of fantasy, and not just their objects. Since fantasies are complex and contradictory, and since they are embedded, as we are, in a specific moment in a cultural history, this greater access to representational production will no doubt continue to expose the anxious and negative side of even our most exciting, progressive, or jubilant visions. In the context of the violent debates about *Thelma and Louise,* it might be safe to say that our popular representations—themselves consumers of our collective wishes, anxieties, and fantasies—are speaking us in a way that we don't seem quite ready to claim, or even to own up to. If we want the pleasure of the ride they offer us, we need an analysis of fantasmatic identifications that is up to speed with these representations. And this involves the violence and the pleasure of imagining sexual identity not as cause but as effect.

Works Cited

Julie Baumgold. 1991. "Killer Women." *New York*, July 29: 24–29.

Judith Butler. 1990. *Gender Trouble: Feminism and the Subversion of Identity*. London and New York: Routledge.

Margaret Carlson. 1991. "Is This What Feminism Is All About?" *Time*. June 24: 57.

Jim Jerome. 1991. "Riding Shotgun." *People*. June 24: 90–96.

Stanley Kaufmann. 1991. "Stanley Kauffmann on Films." *The New Republic*. July 1: 28–29.

Richard Schickel. 1991. "Gender Bender." *Time*. June 24: 52–56.

Laura Shapiro. 1991. "Women Who Kill Too Much." *Newsweek*. June 17: 63.

John Simon. 1991. "Movie of the Moment." *National Review*. July 8: 48–50.

Susan Willis. 1991. *A Primer for Daily Life*. London and New York: Routledge.

8

Thelma and Louise and the Cultural Generation of the New Butch-Femme

Cathy Griggers

Repetition and Difference

In one textual lineage, *Thelma and Louise*—one of 1991's more contro-
versial and unusual summer releases—fits in a chain of recent popular
Hollywood films featuring "nightmare" female leads and narratives about
female revenge fantasies. In this context, the film, directed by Ridley
Scott and starring Susan Sarandon and Geena Davis, can be placed in a
lineage with movies such as *Body Heat* (1981, Kathleen Turner), *Black
Widow* (1987, Debra Winger and Teresa Russell), *Fatal Attraction* (1987,
Glenn Close), and *The Grifters* (1990, Angelica Huston), each of which
presented mass audiences with a tacit cultural nightmare—a contemporary
vision of feminine sexuality that's gotten out of hand (unrepentant hus-
band-murderers in *Body Heat* and *Black Widow,* a vengeful mistress in
Fatal Attraction, and a narcissistic, cold, seductive mother in *Grifters*).
Like all dreams, nightmares are a cultural form of memory and imagination
in which irreconcilable differences are worked through. Resolutions—to
the extent that these differences can become manifest, that is spoken and
visible, in dreamwork—are very much a matter of formal composition:
image and linguistic selection from the cultural archive and arrangement
based on metonymy and metaphor, or displacement and condensation. In
other words, what can be spoken in any nightmare, or in any filmic
representation of a popular cultural nightmare, reflects something of what
cannot. But only something. Never the whole story. And what the some-
thing-that-can-be-spoken masks, more than anything else, is the fact that
there is no whole story. There never was.[1]

In another discursive context, *Thelma and Louise* can be placed in the textual lineage of the road/buddy film, a genre that has always had a special relation to subcultures. *Easy Rider* (1969), *Butch Cassidy and the Sundance Kid* (1969), and *Road Warrior* (1982) are examples of road films that went mainstream, popularizing the motorcycle-gang subculture, old-West frontier outlaws, and post-apocalyptic cyber-punk culture (with a low-tech twist) respectively. An African-American road film that was far more difficult to mainstream—because its black outlaw hero was much more threatening to popular white audiences—was *Sweet Sweetback's Baadasssss Song* (1971), a Melvin Van Peebles creation that gave screen-time not only to the black-urban subculture but also to an angry, young male protagonist who has given up trying to adjust to the existing white, U.S. social order.

In the history of narrative structures, the road narrative traces all the way back through the history of the novel (*Don Quixote* being perhaps the most famous print version) and has roots in Greek Menippean satire and carnival (Bakhtin). Like any modern genre, the road narrative's forms are never pure, but a hybrid of forms produced by various cultural determinants and undergoing continuous variation. One of the satiric functions of the genre has always been to purvey a contemporary social scene and to expose its most problematic aspects, providing a narrative *raison d'être* for taking readers and viewers on a journey out into the streets, through brothels, dens of thieves, etc.—exposing the subcultural underside of everyday life.

My reading of *Thelma and Louise* accommodates both of these textual traditions, both the filmic representation of a cultural anxiety and the satiric road film. The reading does not, however, begin or end within either of these two traditions, but subverts them in order to privilege another textual tradition organized around the pleasures of camp. In this regard, the reading I present here of *Thelma and Louise* exemplifies the complex and variable process by which cultures produce signification and by which cultural subjects produce meanings from signs—that is, the process of semiosis.

Cultural Semiosis: Codes and the Production of Meaning

Thelma and Louise's genre categorization is as complicated as the film's gender categories. In this regard, *Thelma and Louise*—without any help from the audience—refuses to be entirely "straight." It's not your typical summer women's film, not because its cultural anxieties are too nightmar-ish (the rape scene followed by the revenge-murder is certainly horrifically realistic), but because those anxieties are taken beyond the domestic scene and put out on the open road. It's not a typical road film, however, because its heroes aren't male. Furthermore, the pleasures evoked in a fantasy of "friendship bonding" and escape common to the "buddy" film take a new twist when set in the terrain of femininity. In this sense, the film demonstrates that expectations can be established by the repetition of generic typologies, but because any given text might exceed or fail these parameters in various ways, these typologies don't determine any final meaning. This is the first basic principle of cultural semiosis, or the production of signification: 1) *the text is not the fulfillment of a code or genre, but is crisscrossed by multiple codes* (Barthes). What *Thelma and Louise* makes visible is that *bodies,* like texts, are also crossed by multiple regimes of signs. Thus a second and third principle of cultural sign-production follows from this first postulate: 2) *meaning (like identity) is not determined through reference to a single code* (such as the code of femininity) but through an assemblage of multiple codes and in the context of a performance, and 3) *the determinate meaning from the range of possible meanings of any assemblage of signs is produced by the reader/ viewer,* shaped by her representational and social experiences.

The meaning of this film, therefore, has everything to do with the social history of its female audience. In a socio-historical context, *Thelma and Louise* takes on its particular meaning in relation to women's changing social status and gender roles in the political economy of the United States after the Second World War. Thelma and Louise's age is generally that of the white, post-war baby-boomer. Thelma is unhappily married, and Louise is single, reflecting the changing status of marriage for many women who grew up in the U.S. in the postwar period. Louise is a lower-income worker in the food service sector with some access to cultural capital; over the years she's accumulated a few signs of lower middle-class status (she owns her own car, for example, is independent, and has a savings account of $6,700). Thelma is a lower middle-income housewife. Their class status and environment have not provided them with a college education or a profession. And, like millions of women in the U.S. of the baby-boomer generation, neither of them has children—a situation that has helped make reproduction, birth control, and abortion rights a heated and controversial contemporary issue. One need only note that by 1988, 16% of the U.S. female population between the ages of 30 and 34 were single (never married), and almost 11% were divorced. The number of single women who had never married in this age group as a percentage of the total population rose from 6.2 in 1970 to 16.1 in 1988. And in 1988, the population of women in this age bracket totaled nearly 11 million. Furthermore, in 1988 in the U.S., married couples with no children totaled over 27 million, while female householders with no children totaled over 4 million (*U.S. Bureau of the Census,* 1990).

The notion of "aberrant readings" further complicates our understanding of the production of meaning, for clearly there is a range of possible meanings that a given reader/viewer can generate in the reception process. The identification of sub-versive texts (or subtexts within a given work) depends upon who is reading, and while certain narrative strategies may attempt to contain subversive readings, they can never be completely controlled because they exist in the eye of the beholder.

The reading of *Thelma and Louise*r that follows is one such reading. It begins with a signifying absence in the popular media's coverage of the film, exemplified in *Time* magazine's *Thelma and Louise* cover issue (June 24, 1991), which featured a close-up photograph of Geena Davis and Susan Sarandon in matching men's white T-shirts with rolled-up sleeves under the caption: "Why *Thelma and Louise* Strikes a Nerve." Nowhere in the discussions of the controversy stirred by the film is the issue of lesbianism mentioned. And nobody talks about Thelma and Louise's kiss.

Specifically, the reading that follows is guided by an aesthetics of *camp*—one (sub)versive reading practice that has a well-delineated history. According to critic Sue-Ellen Case, in regard to gay and lesbian identities, the camp aesthetic is motivated by a survival tactic of dissembling. Camp's discursive strategy—from the point of view of either the producer of a given text or the reader/viewer—is to subvert the dominant, straight discourse of naturalism or realism from which queer subjects are typically excluded (Case, 60).[2]

The Kiss

In the semiotics of lesbian eroticism, the kiss is usually how everything starts, and in *Thelma and Louise* this entry point into the lesbian erotic register is how the film finally ends. Thelma and Louise, after leaving behind them a trail of mayhem, are trapped by state troopers at the Grand Canyon. Refusing to surrender, they kiss and drive off the ledge into oblivion. For me, this is where the narrative of *Thelma and Louise* actually begins.

The road narrative has brought its characters to this moment—desperate ecstatic—just as the film has brought its audience to this point. Though the duration of the physical exchange between Thelma and Louise is far shorter than the typical Hollywood kiss, the scene's auditory track is coded with swelling non-diegetic music and its visual track with extreme close-up shot-reverse-shots—conventions for signifying an erotic exchange.[3] In the film, the kiss is followed by a falling. *Kiss and die.* Thelma and Louise are floating afterwards—below them death awaits, expansive, a canyon of empty air, a finite moment of infinite possibility. *They could care less.* The kiss is the final dare, perhaps, or better, a letting go until there's nothing left but the momentary clasping of hands, limbs, *for however long it lasts.* But don't be mistaken; these women are already falling when they kiss. They don't die because they kiss, rather they kiss because they're going to die.

The kiss between women is a complexly regulated occurrence in popular representation where it is appearing more and more frequently, and where various narrative strategems work to contain or at least deflect its dangerous surplus of expenditure and value. Typically it surfaces as an image, often in the context of some bizarre narrative scenario (my favorite: Debra Winger practicing poolside mouth-to-mouth resuscitation on Teresa Russell in *Black Widow*), but always providing a certain amount of visible pleasure or anxiety—the return, perhaps, of the not-so-repressed. The kiss (Louise makes the first move, but not before Thelma announces "I can't go back . . . let's keep goin' ") exceeds the economy of both the film's dominant narrative (the road film) and of the dominant social body (heterosexual femininity). Thus it exacts a certain price in order to circulate within mainstream representation—the familiar death sentence demanded of characters when the subversive narrative generating them threatens to go too far.[4] But the kiss also exists, and this must be made quite clear, not only *in spite of* but *because of* these dominant economies—individualism, adventure, the salary wage, and housekeeping are not foreign elements in the cultural generation of the new butch-femme.

The "meaning" of the symbolic death sentence for the lesbian subtext has long been a critical issue for lesbian literary theory, which has thoroughly scrutinized the containment strategy at work in the coupling of lesbian erotic narratives with a romanticized notion of suicide epitomized in Radcliffe Hall's *The Well of Loneliness*. Often in the case of contention between a subnarrative and dominant narrative in a given film, formal aspects (such as the aesthetic, compositional, and temporal technique of the freeze frame) become the supervalent signposts of excessive meaning (the fetish)[5] precisely when the subnarrative's hermeneutic code (the plot), which functions in the realist text as the code of *truth*, is most regulated.[6] In other words, formal play at the level of the signifier becomes one means of foiling the dominant narrative's manifest rule of law and order.[7] The erotic subtext surrounding Thelma and Louise, for example, is disengaged at the end of the film from the plot's death sentence by both the freeze frame and the replay of earlier clips from the film appearing immediately after the freeze frame and running for the duration of the credits (creating a loop in time, a return to the moment before loss—the emotive function of the fetish-sign).

Between subjection to a hetero-phallic law and the ecstasy of the abyss, Thelma and Louise choose the abyss with very little hesitation. For some viewers, this choice may signify an aporia, may be the site at which their reading can no longer regenerate itself. But for other viewers, Thelma and Louise's symbolic choice may seem fairly uncomplicated and familiar.

This reading will be in the name of the latter viewers, and will take Thelma and Louise's kiss as the beginning, not the end, of a love story—a writerly move that refuses the containment strategies of straight femininity's narrative, and that will serve to remind one that the determinate meaning of any text is in the rewriting that occurs when a given reader reads.

Refusing the death sentence, then, I won't take Thelma and Louise's abysmal ending as my imperative. Quite the contrary. Not heeding the law of linearity and its "truth," I will take their kiss and the frozen flight that follows—the moment between ecstatic female bonding and death—as the authorizing signs to read the film's narrative as a lesbian love story, a coming out story, a depiction of gender-role difficulties in woman-woman relations, and a social inquiry into the cultural generation of the new butch-femme.[8]

The "aberrant" reading I'll do here relies on partial identifications and a non-linear rewriting of the narrative, a method particularly fetishized in camp readings. This state of reading is so cultivated in some lesbian communities that its most extreme exemplification is what I call the "fetish camp video club," where individuals using home-video equipment re-edit "favorite" films for home-viewing, looping erotic scenes and removing tragic endings—thereby increasing the texts' fetishistic surplus value and expenditure. A classic example of such altered favorites is Tony Scott's campy vampire flick *The Hunger* (1983), which pairs Susan Sarandon and Catherine Deneuve in some very hot lipstick scenes, but which ends catastrophically for the lesbian subtext. This practice is an example of *excorporation*—a process by which subordinate cultures make their own culture out of the resources and commodities provided by the dominant system" (Fiske, 15). While this example may be extreme, I'd like to premise that partial identifications and non-linear rewritings of narratives are generally "normative" for any readership, if perhaps less cultivated. Such a premise must be pursued if the category "normative/aberrant" is to bear any meaning whatsoever in regard either to text reception or sexuality.

Cabin Fever

The narrative begins with two characters—a housewife and a working woman—both with a case of ennui. These femmes are no spring chickens. They've been around long enough to know they haven't been far enough—not yet. And so they've got cabin fever—the desire to get out and to get away—if only for the weekend. Or so they think. But they will never come back from this trip.

They have cabin fever for different reasons. Thelma is fed up with housework, Louise with the salary-wage exchange. Tips don't make up the difference. There's something missing, something left unmarked in the political economy of both the contemporary working single-woman and the domestic housewife. This excess is not mediated in either case by the negotiations one can make over the division of labor in childbearing and childrearing. Thelma and Louise, like over 30 million women in the United States, are childless well into their reproductive years. This state of childlessness makes it easier for them to embark on their journey, and easier for them to fail to return. Nor is that something "else" that's left unfulfilled by housework or the salary-wage exchange satisfied by the surplus value they themselves fulfill in relation to their men—what they give of themselves at no cost and for no return to make the salary-wage exchange for the male worker more bearable. In other words, the surplus value of "free" domestic labor helps to make up for what's inadequate in the male worker's salary wage.[9] Thelma and Louise's dissatisfaction with this feminine function—to provide the system of commodity logic with the surplus value it needs to continue to cut its profit on the backs of its men—is the original impetus for their fever, for their nomadic desire to find if not more space or a better one, then another space, a different one. But in order to do this, they'll have to move, and once they make a move, once they hit the road, they'll be unable to stop.

The return of pleasure they'll get from the flight, the surplus value and expenditure that will make the social exchange for them more bearable, can only come by slipping the stasis of their authorized social roles. This pleasure is imminently dangerous, because the general political economy, which is a masculine political economy, will be devalued by it. Their men will be more miserable than they already are, and the Law will recognize these women as the definition of a *bad example*—a threat to the existing social order. In a system of exchanges that existed before they arrived, Thelma and Louise's desire for more pleasure, and their decision to act on this desire, will bring them toil and trouble. Cabin fever will lead them on a nomadic flight where they will quickly lose what in exchange value is left for a woman of the lower middle class or on the fringes of the lower middle class: home, or the small possessions that can be had in lieu of real property (clothes, a car), and the pseudo-protection of their bodies by their men and by the Law. In exchange, they will get each other, for a time, and the real, and imaginary, adventures of excess erotic expenditure.

Thelma and Louise go together on this journey because it's clear that's all they have—each other. And they realize that's enough. They've waited around long enough for their men to save them to be happy to have a weekend together. Nothing so grandiose or romantic or expansive after all, their relation is built of the material, tangible opportunities of what they can get now—Louise's convertible, the key to a friend's cabin, and each other. They're happy and excited—they feel adventurous although they know the adventure is small. But it's what they have that's their own to share—the open road, the weekend, and cabin fever. Thelma skips the part where she asks her husband's permission for this small space. Louise's man is too busy having adventures of his own to be anyone's gatekeeper. And so the road film begins.

Packing

But not before packing. Packing is Thelma and Louise's first excess—not because they take too much (they're femmes after all)—but because they have so much fun doing it. Thelma is seriously prone to overpacking: she even packs a pistol (a phallic simulacrum), the only material object her husband has given her that will prove useful on her journey. Many of the objects she packs, however, are the accoutrements of femininity, most of which she will have to abandon, or will want to. But Thelma and Louise don't know that now; they're having fun pretending they can travel light and still take it all—or take enough. Comfort is as important as practicality. They have their scarves, their shades, their lipstick, and their camera. Some small pleasures. They're still parked just beyond the driveway, yet the trip has already begun. They take their photograph together as if to document their accomplishment: they've packed; they're ready to go; they brought everything they need. . . .

Packing, however, implies from the start a problematic self-sufficiency, because its economy is caught somewhere between a notion of returning home and a remaindered nomadism. Gender is an incontrovertible factor in the function that the figure plays in the cultural repertoire of signs. Typically, men carry luggage that women overpack. And in a more psychic register, Pandora *is* Pandora because she has *a box*. So that worse than having to carry a woman's luggage is the prospect of opening and unpacking all the psychic baggage of femininity attached to the signs it contains. It's in this psychic register, of course, that Thelma *has* to pack the pistol that will allow this summer women's film to become the nightmare adventure it becomes. And it's specifically the psychic register of the self-empowered, phallic female, signified by the pistol, that drives Thelma and Louise, and the narrative, to the lesbian erotic. Louise is the first to claim the pistol and the masculine power it signifies in the revenge-murder scene, but it goes without saying that Louise's appropriation of phallic power is partially provided by Thelma's excess desire: she gives the pistol to Louise, she wants Louise to have it, to use it. And later she takes it for her own.

Men

Thelma and Louise, as a form of social satire, brings to the screen surface of its audience's social consciousness a spectrum of negative stereotypes of men. These stereotypes include the piggish and domineering husband, the non-committal and narcissistic lover, the rapist (sociopath, woman-hater), the irresponsible but sexually attractive adolescent outlaw (the good-time boy), the "officer" (a man invested in authority), the infantile but aggressive truckdriver (the public sexual-harassment offender), the cold and punitive FBI officer (a bad imago of the Father/ Law), and the paternalistic Detective Slocum (the Good Father who's *so* good he can break the law without hesitation, entering Louise's apartment illegally with a credit card). This type, the sympathetic but paternalistic authority, turns out to be the most dangerous because he believes in his own ability to "do the right thing" in regard to the women. Enticing Louise to stay too long on the phone with his sympathetic ear and his well-intended reassurances, Slocum is the one who puts the two women in the hands of the feds—not realizing the role he plays in systematically closing off the lines of flight that allow Thelma and Louise to feel they are "alive."

Each of these stereotype's appearance on screen is the impetus for a feminine revenge fantasy. The film gives each stereotype what's coming to him—some sooner than later. The piggish husband is finally left at home with his empty beer cans, pizza, and dirty dishes, reduced to watching his "wife," Thelma, executing armed robberies on videotape. Louise finally shows her wandering man what it's like to sit and wait forever, and refuses his long-awaited marriage proposal. Meanwhile, the sociopathic, misogynist rapist is murdered with his pants down and the words "Suck my cock—" still hanging on his lips. The officer who's invested in masculine authority is locked in his own trunk, but not before he's allowed to shake, whine, and whimper for mercy as Thelma tells him to treat his wife better than her husband treated her. The sexual-harassing truckdriver is threatened with death, humiliation, and the loss of his rig. The FBI officer is left with his mouth gaping in disbelief as Thelma and Louise thumb their noses to the Law, demonstrating they'd rather die than submit. And Detective Slocum, in his turn, is imaged impotently running after the women's speeding car at film's end—in slow motion—witness finally to the role he himself plays in the perpetuation of violence against women. Even the good-time boy, who's an attractive worm, has to go to jail—but not before taking a hard scolding from the good Detective (*Daddy*) in which he's told that *he* is responsible for whatever ill-fate befalls Thelma and Louise now that they're on the road minus the money he stole from them.

The only non-negative image of a man in *Thelma and Louise* is the young black bicyclist who appears out of nowhere smoking reefer (the nomad)—a man who has his own reasons for being out on the road.

Savings Account

Louise has a stash, almost 7 grand, and without it the narrative couldn't come to completion. The savings account, or the promise of it, is a prerequisite for the flight that leads to becoming lesbian. Louise calls it "our future." In the political economy, access to the space of sexual preference is money-coded. This is why before the Second World War lesbianism proper was class-coded (i.e., something *those* girls do *and admit to* because they have no status to lose, a sign of a working-class background) while lesbian eroticism was a class privilege (i.e., something Vita Sackville-West and Violet Treyfusis could *afford* to do, but would never do seriously enough to trade scandal for social status, family, wealth, and inheritance, etc.). The relation of economic dependence to the social construction of heterosexuality which Wittig (1992) critiques from a materialist perspective also explains why the generation of the postwar, female baby-boomers' entry into the workforce is the cultural generation of the new butch-femme and her entry into mainstream representation.

Thelma allows the money to slip away. Victim to the good-time boy's thievery, she squanders Louise's life savings in a single evening.[10] The savings account, along with the independence that it represents, is the most serious bone of contention between Thelma and Louise during the course of the narrative. Early on, Louise is the financial manager of their trip for both herself and Thelma, since Thelma is entirely dependent on her husband or the kindness of friends (like Louise) and strangers for her money (she has forty dollars and some change on her after the attempted rape). Thelma, not used to handling money, handles it extremely poorly. Louise first treats this dependency with quiet resolution, but the turning point of the film and of the coming-out subtext is when Thelma releases Louise from the butch position of sole financial provider. At the moment that Louise is ready to despair and end the journey, Thelma takes the pistol, takes on the signs of phallic power (Thelma's style of dress becomes noticeably butch for the rest of the film), and decides to rob a store, setting the narrative back on the road again. After repeated requests from Louise to "stop flaking out," Thelma gradually gives up her "feminine" dependency on those around her, including Louise, and begins making her own decisions—including the decision to "keep going" and stay with Louise at any cost.

Lipstick Trouble

Lipstick appears and disappears as a sign of feminine identity and as a femme-sign throughout *Thelma and Louise*. In the film's two crisis moments, trouble with lipstick signifies trouble with either feminine identity or the social contexts and consequences of femininity. In the rape scene, for example, Thelma's innocently applied lipstick—here a marker of traditional, straight femininity—becomes a sign of her potential status as victim and object of denigration. By the end of the scene, her face is smeared with lipstick and mascara; her mask is ruined, a sign that traditional femininity has failed her. The rape is stopped only by Louise's timely intervention, and that intervention depends crucially on Louise having Thelma's pistol and having herself had the experience of being raped.

Lipstick, along with eye-makeup and hair products, is a classic signifer of the social materiality of femininity's masquerade. Thelma and Louise's relation to lipstick is connected not only to their gender roles and their struggle with identity, but also with the material, social circumstances that shape the contours of their femininity and masculinity—both of which are in constant flux and which flow in direct correlation to what their social environment will allow or will demand as they pursue their line of flight. In the second crisis moment of the film, when Thelma has lost the $6,700 ("our future") and Louise contemplates ending the nomadic flight that will lead them to the kiss and to a final ecstatic bonding, Louise throws her lipstick out of the car—a sign not of freedom but of despondency and despair. Lipstick is a signifier not only of the women's relations to men and to the social body, but also of their relations to each other. The degree to which Louise can maintain her femininity in a given situation depends on the degree to which Thelma can give up some of hers. The femme-butch line of flight requires a constant adaption and variation. Indeed, the scene that follows Louise's lipstick-despair is Thelma's coming-out scene: on closed-circuit TV while Louise sulks in the car, Thelma goes butch—undergoing a corporeal transformation into the pistol-wielding lipstick dyke. This transformation perks up Louise right away. Later in the film as the chase intensifies, Thelma, with more road dust on her face than makeup, announces to Louise, "Something's crossed over in me and I can't go back—I just couldn't live."

Not restricted to strict codes of femininity or masculinity, these dust-covered and sunburnt *mamettes* are crossbreeds. Empowered with their machines (pistols and car), wearing blue jeans, boots, T-shirts, and a just-so touch of lipstick, they signify the multiple and contradictory regimes of signs from which they construct, day to day, a sense of identity. On a diminishing frontier of cultural identity where gender is a survival response to an environment both hostile and still potentially expansive, Thelma and Louise, as bodies of signs, are hybrids, incomplete interminglings, and open contradictions.

The Becoming-Butch Blues

Out on the road all night, tired and barely able to look each other in the eye, hiding from the Law and sipping from their bottle of booze to stay awake with a diminishing hope of ever really making it to the imaginary land of a *better-life,* both Thelma and Louise show unmistakable signs of the becoming-butch blues. For Thelma and Louise, becoming butch—a psycho-social and virtually bodily process visually documented in the film—is as much an outcome of a material and social condition as a sexual preference. This social process of becoming-lesbian is the crucial insight of *Thelma and Louise*—an insight that its road-narrative structure might well make more visible than an "explicitly" lesbian coming-out film like *Desert Hearts* (1986) because of its *movement*—its ability to take its characters out of one temporal and social register on a line of flight through a variety of social situations and signifying regimes. The film represents not *a* private moment of choice, but a history of choices that leads down a certain path.

Thelma and Louise, as prototypes of the mainstreaming of the new butch-femme, don't become butch because they're lesbians; they become lesbian because they've already become butch to survive. And surviving in this context means staying alive while escaping the traps of the dependent housewife, the bad marriage, the innocent victim, and the single-working woman who's going it alone and not getting enough. Lesbian identity is represented in this film as a social condition rather than an "innate" sexual orientation. In placing sexuality (signed by the kiss) *after* its cultural production, *Thelma and Louise* reminds its audiences that identity in the body is an outcome of the social production of identity as a body of signs constructed out of the real, material options one has at hand. And for more and more women who are discontented with the exchanges normative femininity offers them, becoming the new butch-femme is not only one very viable alternative. It is often an adventure many find themselves on— a journey that began innocently enough with a friend, driven by a desire for a better space, a little more independence, a refusal of unjust or even unsatisfactory social exchanges, and a taste for the pleasures of surplus erotic expenditure.

Works Cited

Bakhtin, M.M. *The Dialogic Imagination.* Ed. Michael Holquist. Trans. Caryl Emerson and Michael Holquist. Austin: University of Texas Press, 1981.

Barthes, Roland. *S/Z*. Trans. Richard Miller. New York: Farrar, Straus, and Giroux, 1974.

Case, Sue-Ellen. "Towards a Butch-Femme Aesthetic." *Discourse* 11:1 (Fall–Winter, 1988–89), pp. 55–73.

Coulson, Margaret, Branka Magas, and Hilary Wainwright. "The Housewife and her Labour under Capitalism'—A Critique." *New Left Review* 89 (1975), pp. 59–72.

Fiske, John. *Understanding Popular Culture*. Boston: Unwin Hyman, 1989.

Gardiner, Jean. "Women's Domestic Labour." *New Left Review* 89 (1975), pp. 47–58.

Reid, Mark Allen. "The Black Action Film: The End of the Patiently Enduring Black Hero." *Film History* 2:1 (1988), pp. 23–36.

Sebeok, Thomas. "Fetish," *American Journal of Semiotics* 6:4 (1989), pp. 51–66.

U.S. Bureau of the Census. *Statistical Abstract of the U.S.: 1990* (110th Edition). Washington, D.C. 1990.

Wittig, Monique. *The Straight Mind*. Boston: Beacon Press, 1992.

Žižek, Slavoj. *Looking Awry: An Introduction to Jacques Lacan through Popular Culture*. Cambridge, Mass.: MIT Press, 1991.

9

Taboos and Totems: Cultural Meanings of *The Silence of the Lambs*

Janet Staiger

By the fifth week of the release of *Silence of the Lambs* (1991), the debates over the film had solidified into a set of propositions: 1) that whether or not Jonathan Demme had intended to create a homophobic film, the character of the serial murderer had attributes associated with stereotypes of gay men; 2) that in a time of paranoia over AIDS and increased violence directed toward gays in the United States, even suggesting connections between homosexuals and serial murderers was irresponsible; but 3) that the character of Clarice Starling played by Jodie Foster was a positive image of a woman working in a patriarchal society and, thus, empowering for women viewers. The diversion in views produced a consequent division: two non-dominant groups, some gay men and some feminists (both straight and lesbian), found themselves at odds over evaluating the film.

The controversy further escalated when several activists "outed" Jodie Foster. "Outing" is the recent practice by some people to declare publically that certain individuals are homosexual or bisexual[1] even though those people have not chosen to make their sexual preferences known. The argument for doing this is that it is hypocritical for famous people to remain private about such preferences if they participate in public activities which perpetuate homophobia. Rather they should help promote gay rights.

Foster's outing produced in the most vitriolic counter-analysis the claim that Foster was being outed because she was a strong woman and that she was being "offer[ed] up [by gay activists] as a sacrifice in the furtherance of gay visibility."[2] "You don't have to look far," the woman argued, "to find a reason why a culture with screen idols such as Marilyn Monroe and Judy Garland would object so vociferously to an actress like Jodie Foster.

Like their straight brothers, the gay men who condemn Jodie Foster and *Lambs* are out to destroy a woman who doesn't put male interests first and doesn't conform to their idea of what a woman should be. Under the guise of promoting gay consciousness, they're falling back on the same reliable weapon that men have used for centuries against women who claim a little too much for themselves—they're calling her a dyke."

Although other women were not so strong in their condemnation of Foster's outing, all thirteen of those women whose views of the movie, *Silence of the Lambs,* I had available to me expressed praise for the film. These included at least two lesbians, one of whom criticized Larry Kramer of ACT UP for his "patronizing" attitude toward Foster, trying to treat her as a "disobedient daughter."[3]

Whether Foster is or is not a lesbian or bisexual "in real life" is not the point of this essay. Whether the character she plays in *Silence of the Lambs* is or is not a lesbian is also not at issue here. What I shall be pursuing instead is the ultimate *stitching* together of gay and woman that became the "climax" of the discussion. I shall argue that this possibility, while not inevitable, is grounded in its reception context and process. What I shall be doing here is what I call historical reception studies. This research attempts to illuminate the cultural meanings of texts in specific times and social circumstances to specific viewers, and it attempts to contribute to discussions about the spectorial effects of films by moving beyond text-centered analyses.

Because I wish to give you an application of this rather than an extended theoretical argument, I will simply lay out several hypotheses informing my research:

1) Immanent meaning in a text is denied.

2) "Free readers" do not exist either.

3) Instead, contexts of social formations and constructed identities of the self in relation to historical conditions explain the interpretation strategies and affective responses of readers. Thus, receptions need to be related to specific historical conditions as *events.*

4) Furthermore, because the historical context's discursive formation is contradictory and heterogeneous, *no* reading is unified.

5) The best means currently available for analyzing cultural meanings exist in poststructuralist and ideological textual analyses. These methods, of necessity, draw upon multiple theoretical frameworks and perspectives such as deconstructionism, psychoanalysis, cognitive psychology, linguistics, anthropology, cultural studies Marxism, and feminist, ethnic and minority, lesbian and gay studies. They do so with a clear under-

standing that the connections and differences among the frameworks and perspectives must be theorized.

Consequently, historical reception studies work combines contemporary critical and cultural studies to understand why distinct interpretive and affective experiences circulate historically in specific social formations. In a case study, the following steps might occur:

1) An object of analysis is determined. This object is an *event*, not a text: that is, it is a set of interpretations or affective experiences produced by individuals from an encounter with a text or set of texts within a social situation. It is not an analysis of the text except in so far as to consider what textually might be facilitating the reading.

2) Traces of that event are located. Here I shall be using primarily traces in the form of printed prose and images, but when available, oral accounts would be very good sites of additional evidence. The print and images include about twenty reviews, news articles, letters to papers, advertisements, illustrations, and publicity which circulated in the major mass media.

3) The traces are analyzed textually and culturally. That is, as new historians elucidate causal processes to explain conjunctions called "events" and then characterize the social significance of these events in relation to specific groups of people, so too does this research. Furthermore, the analyses avoid categorizing receptions into preferred, negotiated, or resistant readings. Rather the processes of interpretation are described since more richness in explanation can be achieved than by reducing readings to three specific generalizations.

4) Finally, the range of readings is considered not only by what seems possible at that moment but also by what the readings did not consider. That is, structuring absences are as important as well.

My project will be to work toward explicating the event of the "sacrificial" outing of Jodie Foster. I shall argue that, although this event might be explained simply through contemporary U.S. stereotypes of lesbians— i.e., a strong woman must be a lesbian—or even because of informal oral communication circulated by gays and lesbians about Foster's sexual preferences, the possibility of making such an inference was facilitated by the critical response *Silence of the Lambs* received. Furthermore, Foster's outing is symptomatic of current cultural taboos and totems. Thus, calling Foster a lesbian is more overdetermined linguistically, psychoanalytically, and culturally than it might appear.

In this initial study of the event, three specific reading strategies occur.[4] These are: 1) the construction of binary oppositions with deployments of high and low, good and bad attributions; 2) the use of metaphor and analogy; and 3), most pertinent to the event, the hybridization or grafting of incompatible terms together. This practice is activated from the prior two strategies and even finds its motivation from one of the dominant metaphors in the discourse.

Taboos

Perhaps because many writers have gone to film school or because thinking in oppositions so colors our everyday lives, reviewers of *Silence of the Lambs* often structured their plot analyses around a central binary opposition. The most obvious opposition was one between Hannibal "The Cannibal" Lecter and Jame "Buffalo Bill" Gumb. One reviewer notices that Lecter is upper class and witty while Gumb is a "working-class lout."[5] The reviewer even emphasizes how this sets up an audience to sympathize with the "good" Lecter and to find disgusting the "bad" Gumb. He critically summarizes, "Lecter: rich, wise, clever, helpful, and funny. Gumb: working-class, stupid, dense, and dull. Lecter: straight. Gumb: gay. Lecter: abstract evil; Gumb: evil incarnate." David Denby characterizes the Lecter/Gumb opposition as between "an unimaginable vicious genius; the other merely rabid and weird."[6] Another reviewer writes that the film has "two villains who represent quite different incarnations of evil. Buffalo Bill a grotesque enigma, has absolutely no redeeming virtues. But Lecter is strangely sympathetic, a symbol of muzzled rage."[7]

Important to this evaluation is that Lecter's victims are bureaucrats and authority figures, such as the census taker whose liver he ate with a nice Chianti. Meanwhile, Gumb goes after young, overweight women. Additionally, of course, Gumb is played as effeminate—something remarked upon by several reviewers who also acknowledged the gay community's concern about the film.

Binary oppositions are commonly deployed in ways such that the two terms in the opposition are not equal. Peter Stallybrass and Allon White in *The Politics and Poetics of Transgression* argue that cultural oppositions often duplicate themselves in various discursive realms.[8] That is, hierarchies reproduce themselves across various symbolic systems such as psychic forms, the human body, geographical spaces, and social orders. To justify these figurations, one symbolic system will refer to the other to warrant its ordering. An obvious example would be the equation commonly made between the head as exalted and the lower anatomy as base; the physical body is written over by a metaphysical discourse.[9]

This hierarchization of binary oppositions functions analogically to legitimate Lecter's cannibalism. Thus, the class attributions, choice of victims, and socialized behavior patterns are read not merely as oppositions but ones with values attached which reinforced each other. Viewers routinely enjoyed Lecter, particularly as played by Anthony Hopkins. *Variety*'s reviewer symptomatically jokes: the "juiciest part is Hopkins."[10] Lecter, of course, offers an interesting problem since he breaks a taboo which would so normally be described as the horror for a film.

Can we explain the spectators' acceptance of this transgression beyond the functioning of the textual array of values attached to the binary oppositions? Freud writes in *Totem and Taboo* that taboos are occasionally breached only to reassert the boundaries authenticating them. One instance of such a breach is the ritual eating of something considered taboo. Such a thing might even be the plant or animal which the tribe considers to be its totem. Totems stand as symbols for the group.

But according to Freud, they are also causal explanations. The totem is the tribe's origin, the "father" of the tribe. Thus, Freud links the ritual eating of totems to the Oedipal story and argues that what has been established as out-of-bounds (e.g., killing one's father) is in the ritual the symbolic consumption of the totem's character. A current example of such a ritual act, Freud writes, is the Christian communion. Drinking wine and eating bread is devouring one's own kind. Lecter, of course, foregoes the more oblique symbolism: he actually eats members of the tribe but for the same purpose.[11] Lecter's ingestation of his own kind, authorized as the incorporation of the bodies of authority figures and legitimated through socially originated hierarchies of binary oppositions, provides both textual and contextual determinations for spectators to accept, and even find pleasure in, his destruction of boundaries.

Consequently, and as part of the weirdly disconcerting pleasure of the event, the reviewers make all sorts of jokes about accepting the broken taboo as if they too wish to participate in the ritual. These jokes occur in the form of puns, doubly validating as they are by puns being a lawful disruption of traditional meanings. For example, Denby writes: "The horrors of the scene are brought off with, well, taste."[12] Another reviewer notes, "Buffalo Bill is famous for killing women, skinning them and leaving the cocoon of an exotic moth in their mouths. Lecter made his name by eating the flesh of his victims raw. All of that may sound a little hard to swallow."[13] One columnist gives Demme a "C− in Mise-en-Scène 101 for the way he fleshes out (so to speak) the villainous Jame Gumb on screen."[14] Notice that all of these wisecracks are made apologically, because they do, indeed, open fissures in social categorizing. Headlines are particularly susceptible to word play, and the discursive motif continues there. Examples include: "Overcooked Lambs," "Skin Deep: Jonathan Demme's Chatter of the Hams," and "Gluttons for Punishment."[15]

Thus, a very powerful and significant binary opposition between Lecter and Gumb is constructed and circulated by viewers of the film. A second structuring binary opposition is proposed by Denby and J. Hoberman who point out that Clarice Starling has several fathers with which to contend.[16] Hoberman expands the comparison: Crawford, the FBI agent, is her daytime dad who is rational; Lecter, her nighttime father, is a "charismatic suitor."[17] This reading of the film as an incest story is transformed in other reviews. As one writer suggests, *Silence of the Lambs* can be seen as about Starling who is "changing, trying to formulate an identity."[18] Interpreting the film as an Oedipal passage for Starling is reinforced *visually* by iconographic materials published with the reviews. Most illustrations were supplied by Orion in its publicity kit. These feature Lecter standing behind Starling with Crawford behind both of them. Some illustrations cut out Crawford; others left him in. All three people face forward so that Crawford and Lecter seem to be peering over Starling's shoulder.

Reading *Silence of the Lambs* as an initiation/Oedipal story fits in an eerie way a discussion of the slasher genre by Carol Clover. She argues that in this genre women are victimized by psychopathic killers. However, she continues that it would be an error to assume that slasher pictures are simply cases of misogyny. For one thing, we ought not imagine that gender characteristics determine viewer identification.[19] This is particularly important with cinematic representation in which the physical body is often so powerful as an immediate signifier of gender. Furthermore, viewer identification does not necessarily remain stably located to a single character throughout a film. For instance, Clover believes that in slasher movies identification seems to alter during the course of the picture from sympathizing with the killer to identifying with the woman-hero. Clover also argues that the (apparently male) monster is usually characterized as bisexual while the woman-hero is not so simply a "woman." She is often "unfeminine," even tracking the killer into "his underground labyrinth."[20]

The ultimate confrontation in the slasher film, Clover believes, is between a "shared femininity" and a "shared masculinity" in which the monster is castrated. Thus, the woman-hero is able to appropriate, referring to Linda Williams's work, "all those phallic symbols' " of the killer's. Moreover, and important here, the woman-hero is "a congenial double for the adolescent male" who is now negotiating sexual identity. The woman hero is a safe identificatory substitute for a male, with the repressed plot about male-to-male relations. The woman-hero is thus a "homoerotic stand-in."

Psychoanalytical discourse is widespread, and Hoberman, among others, is familiar with it. Thus, the historical discourse of psychoanalysis may be abetting his reading the film as an Oedipal crisis for Starling, one that ends "happily." Starling is permitted to join the FBI; Lecter rewards her with unfettered independence from threats by him. Furthermore, and most significantly, Starling kills Gumb, symbol of aberrant sexual behavior, thus overtly denying homoeroticism while permitting it to exist in the apparently heterosexual Crawford-Starling pair.

Thus, one way some reviewers seem to have read the film is Starling-as-Masquerading-Woman who accedes into patriarchy. However, another way exists to understand parts of the interpretive reception of *Silence of the Lambs*. To explore that I need to draw out further the second interpretive strategy: the functions of metaphor and analogy.

Totems

We can assume that some reviewers of the movie read the original novel which is thus part of the potential context for interpreting the film. The novel employs a rather hackneyed device: the various characters are linked to animals, with a theme of natural preying.[21] At the first meeting between Crawford and Starling, Crawford describes Lecter's behavior: "It's the kind of curiosity that makes a snake look in a bird's nest" (6). Starling, of course, is thus forewarned. Later, added to Lecter's attributes is the classic connection of the snake being the devil: "Dr. Lecter's eyes are maroon and they reflect the light in pinpoints of red" (16); his tongue flickers in and out of his face (144). Thus, the metaphor builds a set of parallelisms: body attributes equal snake equals devil; therefore, evil.

The animal motif as metaphor and category for social cognition, perhaps set up by having read the novel, perhaps from Starling's name itself—or from the title of the film—perhaps from habit, permeates reception discourse about *Silence of the Lambs*. Lecter is a "cobra"[22] who lives in a "snake pit of an asylum."[23] He makes "hissing, vile, intimate remarks to women."[24]

The initiation theme crisscrosses with this motif. Starling is described as "molelike" for her penetration of the killers' habitats. She descends into the "dungeon-like bowels" of the prison;[25] she raids the "basement of death."[26] Stuart Klawans points out that Starling must overcome all sorts of obstacles: the initial course in the opening shots, a "labyrinth of offices," "a mazelike dungeon."[27]

But Starling is not always, or usually, the one doing the preying. "Lecter plays cat and mouse with Clarice."[28] For viewers, Starling can become the totem animal with whom she identifies: *she* is the "lamb in wolves' territory."[29] Also crossing is the devil association. Starling "must defend herself at all times, lest [Lecter] eat her soul."[30]

Social discourses are never uniform nor logical even as they try to map hierarchies across semantic categories. In the reception of *Silence of the Lambs*, Lecter's meaning is mobile; some times on the top, other times on the bottom. This inversion is most obvious when he is positioned not to counsel but to threaten Starling. The photographs of the series of father figures with Starling could be read another way. Some men reviewers took Starling to be a woman-victim. Could readers perceive Starling as a woman in danger?

In a discussion of the representation of the naked female body, Margaret R. Miles points out that by the 15th century, a common visual motif is the positioning of a woman in a frontal pose with the figure of Adam, her lover, standing behind her.[31] Or, Adam is transformed into the Figure of Death and the woman dances with him. Or in even more threatening and troubling images, Death copulates with the woman in sadomasochistic brutalism. These images are reminiscent of representations of vampirism, a later connection of animals, eating, sexuality, and death. Miles argues that their significance is the patriarchal connection of woman with sin, sex, and death. But she also notes that "Julia Kristeva has stated that [while] 'significance is inherent in the human body,' . . . little more can be said about *what* is signified until one examines the meanings of bodies in their particular religious and social contexts."[32]

Hauntingly, then, another theme in the critical reception of the film is the ambiguous threat of Lecter to Starling as woman-victim. When they discussed it, many reviewers did take the threat to be sexual in some way. Added to this was the suggestion of pandering by Crawford who sends Starling to Lecter hoping, as Vincent Canby puts it, "to arouse his interest."[33] This reading, however, does not mean that Starling is necessarily being read psychically as female, with the sexuality as heterosexual—in fact it would be repressed polymorphous sexuality—but it does open the space for such a reception. This opens for discussion another feature in the array of interpretations.

Minotaurs and Moths

Women who discussed the film in the public discourse that I surveyed liked *Silence of the Lambs* and seemed especially to sympathize with Starling. Julie Salamon describes Starling as "an attractive woman of unexceptional size doing what used to be thought of as a man's job. . . . She is a rare heroine, a woman who goes about her work the way men do in movies, without seeming less a woman."[34] Amy Taubin praises the movie as a "feminist film" which "suggests that [sexuality and sexual role] fantasies can be exumed and examined, and that their meanings can be shifted." Taubin goes on to invert traditional mythology: after describing Starling's discussions with Lecter as "the meeting of Oedipus and the Sphinx," she claims that the pleasure of the film is "the two-hour spectacle of a woman solving the perverse riddles of patriarchy—all by herself."[35]

Again, Starling is being placed in the narrative position traditionally given to a male. However, in Taubin's scenario, Lecter is not the patriarchal father. Rather, Lecter must fit in the slot of the Sphinx, the monstrous hybrid with the upper torso of a woman and the lower torso an amalgamation of animal body parts. Although symptomatically its gender is unknown, the Sphinx has traditionally been associated with the "maternal." Interestingly, however, no other reviewer surveyed suggested that Lecter had any feminine traits, perhaps because by contrast he seemed masculine compared with Gumb.[36]

Another monstrous hybrid is also mentioned in the reviews. Hoberman retitles the movie "Nancy Drew Meets the Minotaur." The Minotaur is a double inversion of the Sphinx, for its lower body is that of a human male while its head is that of a bull.[37] Thus, the human body halves that define the two beasts are reversed as well as the genders. Furthermore, the Minotaur is absolutely knowable as male since the lower portion of its body is entirely visible—the area legitimated by medical discourse as that which defines and describes sexual difference.[38] This Minotaur association is reinforced through the labyrinth metaphors mentioned earlier.

The third reading strategy is hybridization, the grafting together of irreconcilables. The associations with these particular mythical beasts are some evidence of this. Note, in particular, that what is grotesque is not the blurring of boundaries or even their transgression, which is the case for Lecter's cannibalism in which he ingests another and takes on its attributes. Rather what is disturbing is the all-too-apparent, the *see-able,* combination of disparate semantical categories: human/animal. Again, Hoberman's discourse is particularly insightful. About Gumb, he writes, "[Buffalo Bill] is a jarring billboard of discordant signs—a figure stitched together like the Frankenstein monster."[39]

Hoberman's vocabulary, then, gives us the thread to another pattern of interpretation motivated by the text and mobilized by the historical context. Gumb received his nickname because he skins his victims and sews those skins together to make himself an outfit. Literally stripping the women of their outer raiment, Gumb tries to fashion himself into the woman he desires to be. All of the reviewers decide he is the ultimate monster.

Working from Kristeva's thoughts about the abject, Barbara Creed has recently argued that the horror to be confronted in some films is not just the phallic mother but, finally, the archaic mother of the imaginary, pre-Oedipal experience.[40] The monstrous horror is not the castrated female but the maternal authority which threatens the "obliteration of the self."

Many of the reviewers observe that Gumb's behavior is readable as effeminate, leading to the inference, despite lines of dialogue, that he is homosexual. As the reviewer for the Los Angeles *Reader* puts it, Gumb has a "swishy stage-homosexual posturing."[41] This association seems to be emphasized and commented upon by a sketch accompanying a *Village Voice* article in which Gumb holds a needle and thread while Starling has a pencil and paper. Again, Starling is face forward in the foreground with the threat behind her, looking toward her. No matter her gender, Gumbo's is by cultural categories feminized.

Also reinforcing this threat of the engulfing maternal monster is Gumb's totem: the death's-head moth, so named because the markings on its back resemble those of a skull. It is this animal which he wishes to imitate in its transformation into beauty; it is this totem which he shoves down his victims' throats. Klawans observes that Jack the Ripper is considered to be the first serial killer, whom Klawans notes arrives when women start living on their own in the city.[42] Furthermore, to make his self apparent, to construct his own identity, the serial killer will repeat his signature at each crime scene. By "pattern, [the killer] writes in code with his victims' bodies."[43] The film, then, meticulously follows common lore about such behavior. The death's-head moth functions symbolically to write "Gumb" on the bodies of women. According to the movie plot, Gumb did this as well to forecast his forthcoming transformation and new link to the identity "woman." Holding the moth in their mouths, the women's interiors are now exteriorized—their skins gone but their bodies the cocoon for a new beauty.

This association of moth, maternity, and monster is strongly prepared for extratextually, so the fact that viewers responded to it is not surprising. For *Silence of the Lambs,* the moth was a major motif in the advertising campaign through the posters of it covering Starling's mouth.[44] But the ad's image does not have the moth *in* Starling's throat. It would not be visible. It covers her mouth, hiding an orifice. In this film, and in symptomatic displacement, inversions have existed all over the interpretational landscape. Outsides become insides both in Lecter's cannibalism and Gumb's scripting his forthcoming transformation.

Furthermore, the moth is *stitched* across her mouth. Starling is figured and readable as a hybrid monster as well. If she is easily thought of as an individual in search of her identity, she, like Gumb, can be associated with the moth. She is interpretable as part of his clan. But this stitching is across the mouth, leaving Starling, like that of so many victims, silenced.

Recall that readers have also equated Starling with the lambs she tried to save from slaughter. After death, lambs have two functions: they can be eaten; their hides can be worn. In both cases, the sacrifice is incorporated by the killer—internally via swallowing and externally via masquerading as an other. In both cases, difference and identity are threatened. Klawans writes, why is the audience being worked over in *Silence of the Lambs?* "The best answer . . . and it's a good one—is that the protagonist is a woman. She might even be a lesbian." Other *male* writers also publicly regarded this a distinct possibility prior to the outing of Foster.[45] Thus, although Starling *is* a woman, she may not be a "*normal*" woman. We thus have a complete quadrant of gender and sexual preferences available in the film: Lecter: heterosexual male; female victims: (heterosexual) females; Gumb: homosexual male; Starling: homosexual female. Reading Starling as a lesbian, however, is not a direct result of textual evidence but an inference from the interpretive strategies and the discursive context of the film.

Mary Douglas writes in *Purity and Danger* that social pollution comes from threats to the political and cultural unity of a group.[46] Social pollution anxieties can be rewritten over the human body in a concern for its orifices since body openings "are connected symbolically to social preoccupations about exits and entrances."[47] In my analysis of this public discourse, the most apparent danger was from incorporating or transgressing traditional oppositions. Douglas believes that one way to cancel such a social pollution is a confessional rite.

As the release date for *Silence of the Lambs* neared, Orion and the producers used the Hollywood strategy of attracting attention to it by giving several benefit shows. One party was for the AIDS Project in Los Angeles. In the United States in 1991, this gesture of concern cannot be disassociated with the public assumption that AIDS is primarily a disease of gay men and lower-class drug-users. Gay activists immediately read the event as a pollution rite: "They [are attempting] to launder the film by using . . . an organization whose clients are mostly gay to offset criticism."[48] To gay activists, the act of trying to imply concern for homosexuals was thus an inverted confession of the homophobia of the film.

This event occurred extratextually and prior to the film's opening. Thus, its existence determined the reception of the film for many viewers. When the film went on to do good box office, the intensity of the threat increased. For gay activists, an external threat—wide reinforcement of the notion that effeminate men are psychopathic serial killers—was not only being ignored by massive numbers of audience members but likely being, again, incorporated into public mythologies. Thus, some gay activists chose to blur the line which is so often crossed: the difference between fiction and real social life.

Notice that gay activists did not try to argue that *Starling* was a lesbian. Like Orion, they made the argument that the movie had some (obscure) value to social life. Like Orion, they made the argument extratextually: *Jodie Foster* was a lesbian. In a time in which homo- or bisexuality is threatened as a personal identity—threatened not just by social stereotyping but by real physical threats from homophobic violence—"sacrificing" Foster seems logical. That is, pointing out the hypocrisy of the filmmakers by arguing that Foster had not yet come to terms with her own identity and sexual preferences was necessary if society was ever to come to terms with its notions of "monsters."

As I have indicated, Foster might well have come under attack simply because of stereotypes of the strong woman as a lesbian as well as informal oral communication about her, but motifs in the advertising and film, combined with reading strategies by its viewers, reinforced the credibility of the accusation by those who chose to out her. Starling's gender is ambiguous. She is easily read as a "son" in a patriarchal identity crisis; she is easily read as "unfeminine," tracking archaic mothers in their lairs; she is easily read as a hybrid—a moth-person. And within a structural square of oppositions and inversions, her position is the most "other": not heterosexual, not male. She could be the lamb sacrificed in punishment for the film's expressed homophobia and repressed polymorphous sexuality.

Of course, other people pointed out that those choosing to out her were in an odd way accepting the notion that being called a lesbian would be humiliating. And that, in any case, Foster was being denegrated or patronized just as women so often are in our culture. As I mentioned earlier, women—both straight and lesbian—uniformly defended her and the movie as a positive, powerful representation of a female.

In closing I wish to underline what I have been doing theoretically. This study is an attempt to indicate how contemporary theoretical frameworks can be useful in determining the cultural meanings (with the plural emphasized) of a specific text. What I have not done is to try to unify the text or the readings by asserting that one reading or set of oppositions or displacements is more viable than another. I have tried to provide the *range* of readings and to give an initial account of what might explain that range.

Additionally, my *primary* evidence for the cultural meanings of the events was not derived from a textual reading of the film. It came from public discourse. From that discourse, mediated though it is, I determined what textual, extratextual, and social determinants might account for the readings in my sample. I did not, although I might have, discuss significant absences in the discourse, a critical one being "blood," which is obviously significant considering how AIDS is transmitted.

Determining the cultural meaning of a text is full of assumptions and pitfalls. Interpreting interpretations is viciously circular. Additionally, the discourse I used in public and therefore already suspect. It is by no means representative of its culture—although I would be willing to argue that it has some relation to it as well as an effect on it. Given these (and other) problems, however, I still believe that research of this sort is helpful in a project of trying to understanding how individuals interpret the world and how they use discourse to shape, or reshape, that world. While I have made no decision about the political gesture of outing, I do believe I need to work toward understanding what acts of resistance such as that one mean in my social formation.

What this investigation has reaffirmed for me, then, is that at this time homosexuality, bisexuality, or ambiguous sexual preference is threatening to a wide range of readers. Gumb's death as an "unnatural" person is met with a sigh of relief. "Sick" though the movie's ending may be, Lecter's continued career as a cannibal of authority figures is met with a shaky laugh of pleasure. Maybe this is because Lecter's act of murder is one that dominant culture takes to be a normal ritual of incorporation: father to son, not the hybriding of monsters such as men who sew rather than model themselves after appropriately masculine authority figures.

10

The Powers of Seeing and Being Seen: *Truth or Dare* and *Paris Is Burning*

Ann Cvetkovich

I want to juxtapose the films *Truth or Dare* (1991) and *Paris Is Burning* (1991) in order to consider whether, contrary to the claims of many feminist film theorists, being the object of the gaze, and more specifically the *feminine* object of the gaze, can be a position of power. Both films focus on the spectacle of femininity; *Truth or Dare* moves between Madonna's offstage life and her performance in the lavish production numbers of the Blond Ambition tour, while *Paris Is Burning* provides access to both the comments and the performances of the black and Latino gay men whose participation in Harlem drag balls often takes the form of dressing as women.

Despite the differences between the mainstream cultural circles in which Madonna moves and the racially and sexually marginalized world of the drag balls, the two films speak to one another in significant ways. The men of the drag-ball scene aspire to the glamor, fame, and presumed power of female movie stars, fashion models, and performers. As Venus Xtranvaganza puts it, "I would like to be a spoiled, rich white girl. They get what they want whenever they want it, and they don't have to really struggle with finances." For feminists who emphasize the oppressive nature of the ideal of femininity that Venus finds so appealing, it may come as a surprise that white femininity could be the object of fantasy. Yet deluded as Venus's ambitions might be, they contain an element of truth, reminding us of the privileges of straight, white, middle-class women relative to the men who frequent the drag balls. As one of the richest and most successful women in the music industry and as a highly visible media celebrity, Madonna seems to confirm the fact that power and privilege are available to at least some women. At the same time, she seems to envy the world of the drag balls, borrowing, for example, one of the competitive categories as inspiration for the song and the video "Vogue." Prominent in *Truth or Dare* are the gay men of color who are her dancers; in fact, José Gutierrez, one of the featured dancers, appears briefly in *Paris Is Burning*. Although it can be argued that Madonna turns to such subcultures only to appropriate them, thus perpetuating the long history of white mainstream culture's colonization and domestication of African-American culture, it is clear that the world of the balls has for her the aura of transgression, play, and hipness. At the same time as each arguably misrecognizes the other's power, it might be useful to interrogate the structures of fantasy and desire that make a white, straight girl want to be a black, gay boy, and vice versa.

To argue that being the object of the gaze can be a position of power goes against the grain of a central paradigm within feminist film theory. Following Laura Mulvey's "Visual Pleasure and Narrative Cinema," feminists have frequently equated being the object of the gaze with being passive and feminine, and being the subject of the gaze with being active and masculine.[1] Mulvey's call for a "passionate detachment" that would disrupt the pleasures of narrative cinema suggests that only alternative or avant-garde cultural practices can transform the regime of the male gaze. Madonna, on the other hand, serves as an emblem for a feminist criticism that sees possibilities within mainstream culture not only for remaining in control while being the object of the gaze, but for doing so without eschewing femininity. Focusing primarily on Madonna's earlier "Boy Toy" image, John Fiske and E. Ann Kaplan suggest that Madonna expresses a female sexuality or pleasure that is not defined or circumscribed by patriarchal power and that she provides a model of resistance for her young girl fans.[2] Susan McClary argues that Madonna's recent work "deconstructs the traditional notion of the unified subject" and provides "counternarratives of female heterosexual desire."[3]

In keeping with such readings, *Truth or Dare* suggests that Madonna enjoys displaying herself for the visual pleasure of others: the Blond Ambition stage show is all spectacle, built around sets and costumes that combine music with theater and that foreground Madonna's body and the image she presents. The making of a film about the tour suggests, furthermore, that Madonna is not content merely to be watched onstage. She invites the cameras of director Alek Keshishian to pursue her behind the scenes, letting even the most ordinary or intimate moments be filmed and creating impromptu performances for the camera. A woman who likes to be seen, Madonna commands our attention as we watch her being made up, dressed, and pampered by others, watch as she is transformed into the star we see onstage, watch as she manages her performers and staff, watch as she confesses her hopes and fears about the tour, watch as she exposes her family squabbles and tensions. *Truth or Dare* engages with the star system, which produces gossip and scandal as a means of generating publicity, and turns what might seem to victimize the star, especially the female star, into a vehicle for money and power.[4] The media blitz surrounding the film's release suggests that she is happy to use the publicity machine to promote her star status.[5]

Moving between Madonna's Blond Ambition performance and her life offstage, *Truth or Dare* highlights what is already evident from her previous videos and live performances—her ability to assume a variety of roles or poses, no one of which can be considered her "true" self. Especially significant is her ability to play with gender identities; in addition to crossdressing as a man, she alternates between masculine and feminine styles of dress and behavior. The videos for "Open Your Heart," in which she plays a peep show performer who later dresses as a young boy offstage, and "Express Yourself," in which she appears alternately in a man's suit and as a temptress chained at the neck, exemplify this capacity for genderbending. Madonna's feminine guises appear to be roles that she consciously chooses and exploits, rather than a sign of an imposed femininity. She performs "Express Yourself," which opens the tour and is featured near the beginning of *Truth or Dare,* in a man's suit under which she wears a gold Gaultier bustier whose cone-shaped breasts protrude from slits in the suit. The costume combines masculinity and femininity, which are in both cases signified by exaggerated fashion styles. Establishing control over the opening spectacle of the men dancing, Madonna descends from a staircase, pauses to grab her crotch, and then joins her women back-up singers, who are dressed similarly to her. The women display their power over the men, humping them, helping them to get up off the floor, and then finally dismissing them. This opening number sets the stage for her more feminine costumes and poses to be understood as just that—performances. Whether masculinized or feminized, Madonna establishes her own pleasure as center of attention.

Paris Is Burning helps to illuminate Madonna's use of the spectacle of femininity by exploring the attraction of dressing as a woman for purposes of performance. The male drag queens who spend enormous amounts of time and money in order to walk the ball gain power and prestige from their pursuits. What they are imitating is not necessarily "real" women—like Madonna, they emulate female performers, whether Hollywood icons, the stars of television shows such as *Dynasty,* or supermodels from fashion magazines. Madonna's performances are perhaps best understood on the model of gay male drag, which opens up a distinction between being a woman and performing as a woman; whether explicitly imitating a movie star (such as Marilyn Monroe in the "Material Girl" video and the April 1991 *Vanity Fair* photos) or more generally aspiring to the glamor and artifice of pin-up photos and elaborate female costume, Madonna is playing a role or enacting a fantasy.[6] When she adopts feminine costume, she is a woman in female drag. Gay men realize what feminist film critics have come to assert—that representations of beautiful women are not "false" or "artificial" images that disempower or distort "real" or "natural" women but tremendously powerful cultural signs. Both Madonna and the queens of the ball scene recognize the power of the image of the feminized woman. Even if that power ultimately belongs to a capitalist culture that links female sexuality and the commodity, it is too simplistic to see the female icon as merely the sign of exploitation or objectification or to assume that her power cannot be diverted to serve other ends.

Viewed as deliberate artifice, Madonna's and the drag queens' performances of femininity might also be considered subversive because they embody another crucial axiom of feminist theory—the claim that gender is a social construction rather than a natural or biological essence. Mary Ann Doane, for example, develops Joan Rivière's concept of masquerade in order to suggest that the performance of an excess of femininity reveals gender identity to be an artifice. "By destabilizing the image, the masquerade confounds this masculine structure of the look. It effects a defamiliarization of female iconography."[7] Anti-essentialist feminist theory is perhaps best exemplified by Judith Butler's conception of gender as a performance. Butler explicitly invokes "the cultural practices of drag, cross-dressing, and the sexual stylization of butch/femme identities" as instances of the subversive power of gender parody. "In imitating gender, drag implicitly reveals the imitative structure of gender itself—as well as its contingency."[8] Both Madonna and gay male drag queens would seem literally to embody or render concrete the anti-essentialist claim that gender identity is a costume rather than an essence. When they masquerade as hyperfeminine, imitate female stars and icons, or cross-dress, they subversively reveal the instability of gender identity.

Yet, while *Truth or Dare* and *Paris is Burning* might be used to demonstrate anti-essentialist feminist theory and the subversive power of female masquerade and cross-dressing, the juxtaposition of the two films also suggests that gender is less malleable in practice than it is in theory. In the move from specific instances of drag or cross-dressing to a general theory of gender identity, the distinction between a performance that explicitly announces its artificiality and one that seeks to conceal itself, or between performance in the literal sense and performance in the figurative sense, is lost. Although the cultural theorist may celebrate the artifice that drag queens construct, some of the men in *Paris Is Burning* aspire to be "real" not only on, but offstage, to pass as straight, or female, or white, or middle class. The discussion of sex-change operations in the film reveals that gender transformation is more than just a game or a theatrical performance for some of them. For the transsexuals in the film, the desire to be a "real" woman emerges from the desire to escape the problems that come with being black, gay, and poor; a transformation in gender is a mechanism for altering class, race, and sexual identities as well. Not all of the men share this view; as the older-and-wiser Pepper Labeija points out, such aspirations depend on an illusory sense of female power, ignoring the fact that having a vagina is just as likely to invite rape and violence as to bring fame and fortune. The desire to be a "real" woman implicitly rests on an essentialist conception of gender, assuming that social privilege is guaranteed by biological nature. It reestablishes the fixed gender roles that cross-dressing and drag might challenge.

The move from cross-dressing to a theory of gender and sexual identity also runs the risk of effacing the specificity of drag within gay and lesbian subcultures. As Eve Sedgwick puts it, "one might say that gender theory at this moment is talking incessantly about crossdressing *in order* never to have to talk about homosexuality."[9] Sue-Ellen Case has also complained about how lesbian butch-femme performance has been read as an instance of postmodern culture without any attention to its specifically lesbian dimensions.[10] These generalizations overlook the differences among gender performances, and the extent to which some forms of cross-dressing, especially transvestism and transsexuality, are the object of homophobic attack. Discussing Divine, for example, Sedgwick and Michael Moon suggest that cross-dressing constitutes an aggressive reclamation of a body otherwise subject to freak status. Both the flamboyantly excessive drag queen and the carefully deceptive transsexual are threatening to gender and sexual norms in ways that Madonna's experiments in costume and masquerade never are. Even as a cross-dressed woman she falls within the bounds of aesthetically acceptable femininity.

The stakes and risks of cross-dressing are thus quite different for Madonna than they are for the gay men of *Paris Is Burning*. Whereas their costumes transform potentially unacceptable identities, she has much less to hide as a straight white woman, as a celebrity, and as someone whose body conforms to conventional standards of beauty and normalcy. The power and pleasure gained at the drag balls constitute a utopian possibility that has to be read within the context of the participants' relatively disempowered social positions. Madonna, on the other hand, has access to money, time, and power, which she can use to change her identity at will. That she can do so does not necessarily mean that *anyone* can do so, whereas the drag balls arguably make the more radical implication that anyone can be a star (at least temporarily). Moreso than Madonna herself, the balls fulfill the utopian premise of the words to "Vogue": "It makes no difference if you're black or white/if you're a boy or a girl./When the music's pumping it will give you new life/You're a superstar, yes, that's what you are." In addition to putting more at risk in adopting drag, the men in *Paris is Burning* also get far less in return than Madonna, both economically and culturally. There is little financial reward to be had, except for the prospect of modeling or performing success. The boys who go on to become Madonna's back-up dancers may be successful in crossing over into mainstream culture, but they are not Madonna herself, and they are only employed for as long as she finds them useful to her image.

Thus, when drag and masquerade are invoked to exemplify a constructivist theory of gender, they may give rise to the misleading assumption that gender can be transformed as easily as a change of costume, an assumption that reduces complex social and historical forces to acts of voluntarist individualism. As part of the project of historicizing the body and identity, it might be important to ask who has historically had greater access to transformation. While Madonna's relatively unusual status as a woman performer, and the transgressive power of her cross-dressing and masquerade, may be worth noting, comparison with the world of *Paris Is Burning* is an important reminder of her privileges.

Another problem with celebrating Madonna's transformative powers is that, far from escaping or transcending cultural impositions too easily, she might be considered a slave to the demands consumer culture makes of women. It is only the investment of considerable money and labor that produces her perfect image. During a significant amount of her onscreen time in *Truth or Dare,* Madonna is either having her hair or her makeup done. The desire and ability to transform oneself makes one the perfect subject of consumer capitalism, not its opponent. Susan Bordo, for example, has suggested that Madonna's ability to change her body and her image constitutes an "abstract, unsituated, disembodied freedom" that "celebrates itself only through the effacement of the material praxis of people's lives, the normalizing power of cultural images, and the sadly continuing social realities of dominance and submission."[11] Far from demanding fixed or essential identities, contemporary culture seems to embrace and encourage the pleasure to be obtained from a constantly changing image.

Paris Is Burning raises the issue of race in ways that further complicate the politics of gender transformation and performance. Whereas cross-dressing or changing gender is often seen as subversive, changing racial identities has a far different status. To the extent that the men of *Paris Is Burning* seek to pass as white or to imitate images of white femininity, they seem to be subscribing to, rather than challenging, racist ideology. Some of the ball categories, such as Town and Country, Executive Realness, or Military Realness, in which the contestants dress not just as women but as men, have less to do with gender than with race.

The relation between fantasized or performed identities and actual identities may be quite complex, however. For example, the gay man who dresses as a woman is not necessarily trying to be a woman, just as the lesbian who adopts a butch identity is not necessarily trying to be a man. Similarly, to characterize certain styles of dress as "white" or as representing the desire to be "white" may reproduce a concept of "natural" racial identity. Arguing against the claim that black people who straighten their hair are trying to be white, for example, Kobena Mercer argues that "natural" hair is itself a style and that hairstyles that involve straightening may be just as "genuinely" African-American as an unprocessed Afro.[12] By the same token, the imitation of white stereotypes by the ball participants can be read as undoing and transforming those images rather than reifying them. The contestants in categories such as Executive Realness reveal the race and class-based power of certain styles, the appropriation of which defamiliarizes them. Livingston further underscores this appropriation by intercutting scenes from the balls with footage of businessmen on the streets of New York. What might seem like unremarkable scenes from "mainstream" society become images of white middle-class people, whose power and "normalcy" cannot be taken for granted. *Paris Is Burning* suggests that the power to consume is a significant indication of social power, and that the woman who can wear what she wants might be the woman who can do what she wants. The equation of wealth and a beautiful appearance with power, promoted so relentlessly by advertising and consumer culture, is often criticized as a false promise, but the costume balls suggest that it contains an element of truth. Who has the more accurate view of the relation between consumption and social privilege—the middle-class woman who remains unfulfilled despite her ability to shop or the gay black man who considers her to have a power that he doesn't have? It may well be that only those who have money or middle-class privilege have the luxury of thinking that money doesn't buy happiness.

While it might seem to have the opposite effect, the example of *Paris Is Burning* makes it difficult to dismiss the possibilities of self-transformation that Madonna represents. Particularly when issues of class or race are considered, the men of *Paris Is Burning* might seem to be exactly those individuals who are disenfranchised by the illusory and racist ideals that Madonna's image promotes. They do not see themselves in this way, however, and their investment in fashion, consumption, costume, and masquerade as the means to power suggests that the politics of style should not be dismissed as a substitute for other more "genuine" forms of social transformation.

It has been important for feminists to think of ideologies of gender not as monolithically imposed by the dominant culture on passively stupid consumers but as actively adopted, for better or worse, by individuals who have agency.[13] Just as female consumers of mass culture should not be dismissed, it is important not to see the men of *Paris Is Burning* as deluded, as unable to discern the fictional nature of televisions shows such as *Dynasty* or as slavishly emulating the suspect values represented by the lifestyles of the rich and famous or middle-class consumerism. The drag balls in *Paris Is Burning* can be understood as a subculture (in Stuart Hall's sense) that allows for a utopian empowerment unavailable elsewhere.[14] Organized into "houses" presided over by "mothers," the "children" of the balls create communities that sustain them in the face of rejection by family and society. Dorian Corey, one of the older men in *Paris Is Burning,* refers to the balls as an alternative to drugs and crime, as a safe high. Less respectable than more masculine subcultures that form around sports and music, gay male subcultures, like women's subcultures, suffer from the denigration of fashion and consumer culture as trivial or decadent.

Seen through the eyes of the drag queens, the white middle-class woman emerges as a rather more powerful figure than she is within a feminist discourse that attends only to her gender. Their fantasies render her whiteness, and its association with class privilege, more visible. That a specifically female figure comes to stand for social privilege suggests the complex interaction of race, class, and gender differences within the symbolic practices of consumption and fashion, and further indicates that the display and transformation of the body need not be a sign of disempowerment. The position of the beautiful, white, middle-class woman, such as Madonna, in cultural representations is double-edged. The power of her image can obscure and effect the disenfranchisement not only of women who are not white or middle class or straight, but of women who are. But *Paris Is Burning* suggests that to turn from mass cultural fantasy to real people's lives is not necessarily to leave fantasy, consumption, or fashion behind. The rejection of the transformations that both Madonna and the gay men undergo as superficial styles that leave unchanged the race, class, and gender positions that they fixedly occupy underneath their clothing and makeup leaves us with a very old conception of political action. It is important to acknowledge the political significance of femininized, and hence trivialized, cultural practices, such as fashion.

By the same token, the debates about female pleasure that Madonna inspires should not be dismissed. She operates within traditions of performance that produce a double bind for women: if they behave like women, they must flaunt their sexuality and bodies for the male gaze, and if they act like men, they run the risk of failing to do so adequately or succeeding only at the cost of renouncing their gender identity. Madonna refuses the strategy adopted by some feminists of rejecting forms of femininity or sexuality that bear any relation to patriarchal constructs. She performs in the spirit of pro-sex feminism, embracing costume, sex, fashion, and femininity with the aim of defining her own pleasure.

Paris Is Burning suggests that pleasure, fantasy, and sexuality are not separate from the supposedly more urgent concerns of race and class. The role of costume and masquerade within gay male culture authorizes queer possibilities for women as well, enabling an investigation of spectacle in terms other than those that structure analysis of the straight male spectator. Among the pleasures Madonna explores through her imitation of female icons is the relation of the female spectator to images of women. The possibility of a female-female gaze is one that is often overlooked, as theorists interested in positing a lesbian gaze have pointed out.[15] Whether lesbian or straight, the female spectator of Madonna can be said to have a libidinally invested gaze. To question this pleasure as always suspect may be a disabling theoretical and practical move. Providing an example of how dominant culture can be appropriated and reworked, Madonna herself has been appropriated to serve as an icon for lesbians. Her lesbian following represents a feminism that embraces the possibilities of fashion or style.

Given Madonna's and the drag queens' willingness to display themselves for the gaze, we might ask how *Truth or Dare* and *Paris Is Burning* use the documentary form, catering as it does to voyeuristic desires, to mediate between performer and audience. In addition to capturing the visual power of performance, both films seek to uncover the person behind the performer. As documentaries, they implicitly assume that the camera has the power of surveillance, enabling it to investigate and expose the truth of its subjects. Critical of the politics of the documentary form, however, film theorists have questioned the consequences of its capacity to naturalize or efface its processes of representation. The interview format, for example, draws upon realist and empiricist epistemologies that assume that truth can be obtained from the testimony of subjects speaking in their own voices. It rests, for example, on the assumption that Madonna is the greatest authority about herself, or that if we want to know about drag balls we should talk to the participants.

The ways in which the two films either rely on or subvert the documentary's claims to truth vary because of the different social status of their subjects. *Truth or Dare* participates in the tradition of the rock documentary as well as the entertainment industry profile, seeking to reveal the truth about a public figure who has become an object of curiosity and speculation. It provides the voyeuristic pleasure obtained from revelations about the private life of a public figure. *Paris Is Burning* is closer to the genre of ethnography, exploring a subculture that might otherwise be invisible, and presenting the human side of those who might otherwise be considered abnormal or deviant. Voyeuristic pleasure is again potentially engaged insofar as documentary provides audiences with access to a transgressive or marginal culture. Criticism of anthropological ethnography has suggested that it reproduces and installs the power of the investigator. The study of "marginal" subcultures constructs them as such and colonizes potentially threatening or alien subcultures by domesticating them as exotic others. Such criticism might well apply to the racial politics of *Paris in Burning,* insofar as its white middle-class filmmaker, Jennie Livingston, by producing a film for mainstream audiences, colonizes, exploits, or exoticizes her subject. On the other hand, as a lesbian filmmaker exploring a gay subculture, Livingston also opens up debates about the politics of drag and race within gay and lesbian subcultures. Both films, then, raise important questions about the politics of documentary.

As its title suggests, *Truth or Dare* is quite self-conscious about documentary's presumption to tell or discover the truth. Like the players in the game, the star who consents to be interviewed or filmed is often lured into revealing secrets, and it is often sexual behavior that functions as private or personal information. In *Truth or Dare,* as in her media appearances in general, however, Madonna willfully invites the camera's and the public's gaze and dares to reveal all about her sexuality and her body. She thus might be said to circumvent the media's power to exploit or expose hidden truths or the private lives of stars. Rather than being the victim of the camera's gaze, Madonna seems openly to invite it, going to the narcissistic length of commissioning a film about herself and her career. Because she so explicitly acknowledges that "truth" is a token of exchange in a game of seduction, we should be alerted to the fact that we may only be getting the truth Madonna chooses to give us, rather than being privy to secrets and scandals that she is reluctant to divulge. *Truth or Dare* also announces its artificial status visually. It is not naturalist cinéma vérité. The offstage scenes are shot in black-and-white in contrast with the color footage of the performances; the fast-paced editing and cross-cutting suggest a carefully constructed compilation; and Madonna and others repeatedly address the camera directly or indicate their awareness of being filmed.

If the media generated stories about *Truth or Dare* by reporting on its scandalous and transgressive representation of gay sexuality or of Madonna going down on an Evian bottle, it did so with its star's full consent. Madonna is a tease and an expert in media relations; she offers up truth in the form of a new image or new information, but she ultimately controls the flow of information about herself. She thus subverts the documentary's capacity to control her. It is not the audience that constructs the voyeuristic will to truth, but Madonna who posits the secret we then want to pursue. The documentary is structured around what D. A. Miller has called an "open secret"; what matters is not the content of the truth, but the structuring of it as hidden. Madonna incites voyeuristic desire by playing on the construction of sexuality, and female sexuality in particular, as secret and transgressive. Many of her previous videos have been the subject of controversy for their display of sexual transgression: her role as a peep show performer in "Open Your Heart," her sexual relations with a religious saint in "Like a Prayer," her chained body in "Express Yourself," and the bisexuality and explicit sexuality in "Justify My Love." Following in this tradition, *Truth or Dare* makes the most of its prominent display of masturbation and homosexuality. The film's commitment to defending or celebrating homosexuality is thus somewhat ambivalent, since what counts is not so much homosexuality itself as its usefulness as a vehicle for controversy and for Madonna to assert her right to freedom of expression. The scene in which her dancers watch the Gay Pride Parade in New York, for example, is undercut by the one straight dancer, Oliver's, homophobic voice-over. It is also significant that while the film foregrounds the dancers' "hidden" sexual identities, there is no discussion of their racial identities, which are potentially just as controversial or unusual.

If we are prompted to ask what the "real" Madonna is like and whether her fame and fortune bring her happiness, we are given answers to those questions because the film quite consciously constructs them. Ultimately, then, whether as truth or as dare, Madonna's film ensures that she will always win the game. Viewed on camera, her private life is yet another performance, putting in place the desire for more. Since the positing of a "real" person behind the star was only ever a fiction designed to incite the voyeurism that fuels the publicity industry, Madonna's approach to documentary and star profiles can't really be said to cheat in order to avoid telling the truth. Her attitude to publicity stands in contrast to that of Warren Beatty, who scorns her apparent desire to live on camera. She understands that the publicity machine is part of what makes her a successful star, and rather than resist it in the name of authenticity or self-protection, she uses it to her advantage. She refuses to maintain the distinction between public and private life, that Beatty, representing an earlier generation of stardom, upholds. In criticizing Madonna, he disavows his own participation in and dependence upon the media to promote not only his films but his image.[16] Madonna treats the media's investigating gaze as an opportunity rather than a threat, orchestrating her own self-revelation in order to capitalize on the seductive power of secrets.

Unable to find the scandal of Madonna's sexuality anything other than one that she openly invites, the media focused its attention on whether she could be accused of revealing too much, by, for example, inviting the cameras along for her visit to her mother's gravesite. In addition to exploiting the power of sexual indiscretion, the film trades on the other target of the gossip columns—the secret of emotional distress. One of the standard narrative paradigms for media profiles is the search for whether, despite fame and fortune, the star is happy, where happiness is measured in terms of emotional or romantic fulfillment. For example, one of the scenes in *Truth or Dare* consists of voice-over comments by Madonna's friends and co-workers as we watch her alone in her apartment. They speculate about whether she is lonely, whether she is too driven, whether she is understood by those around her. Such narratives are overdetermined in the case of a woman performer, where the implication is that her career success doesn't count as long as her personal life is not happy. Once again, though, Madonna forecloses the scandalous potential of such stories by using the camera as a confessional. The film opens with her intimate acknowledgment that she might have a nervous breakdown at the end of the tour and the camera follows her as she wearily cleans up after a party and goes to bed alone. Complete with revelations about her need to mother her performers, her strained relation with her alcoholic brother, and her failed seduction of a Spanish film star, Madonna becomes her own best analyst, debunking the idea that stars are anything but human. She simultaneously reveals and demystifies her own power. As we watch her much-touted skills as businesswoman and workaholic in action, the means of production of her spectacle are laid bare—it is hard work to produce the magic of her performance.

Although less talked about, *Truth or Dare*'s focus on Madonna's professionalism, rather than on her emotions or her sexuality, may be its most interesting and most revealing feature. Unlike the male stars who are the subject of most rock documentaries, she is not into groupies, drugs, or other forms of excess. (Compare, for example, with Oliver Stone's reverential and masculinist treatment of Jim Morrison in *The Doors* [1991], which romanticizes the tragic inseparability of genius and self-destruction.) Instead, she is highly disciplined and extremely concerned about her body, taking care to get enough sleep, eat right, drink lots of water, protect her overworked voice, and on and on. In addition to being the star of the show, she is also a vigilant boss and manager, overseeing everything from technical details to interpersonal relations. *Truth or Dare* dymystifies both the glamorized and the tragic narratives of stardom. However, when it can't shoehorn her into the narratives of the suffering female star or the decadent female star, the media is all too ready to punish her for being too self-aware, too manipulative, or too untalented.

Despite her privilege, Madonna represents a fairly unusual success story for women in the music business. The world of popular music is still largely dominated by men, and Madonna's success had depended on her ability to borrow from other art forms where women have been more visible, such as film, fashion magazines, and dance. Her willingness to display her body as a locus of spectacle has been viewed with some suspicion, however, by those who see this kind of performance as a poor substitute for "real" musical talent. She is often negatively characterized as someone who is "merely" a good business woman who knows how to sell her limited skills. The assumption that art and business are or should be separate is questionable, and especially so for mass culture. Reception of Madonna seems to be shaped by the double bind that affects many professional women, who are scapegoated both for being too aggressive (that is, too masculine) and for being too sexual (that is, too feminine). Whether or not the freedoms available to her are available to everyone— and they are not—or even desirable, she provides a measure of the nature and extent of mainstream success for women. As a dedicated, yet somewhat ambivalent, follower of Madonna, I watch her as a guide to what possibilities for feminist expression are available within mainstream culture. Much of what I value sexually, politically, and culturally will never be seen on MTV, or *Nightline,* or in a Hollywood movie, but it is interesting to see how Madonna negotiates the still rather restricted opportunities available to women. If Madonna's sex life or intimate feelings are significant, it is in relation to her professional and public life, which *Truth or Dare* tellingly documents.

Paris Is Burning raises rather different issues about the politics of documentary partly because its more marginalized director and subjects risk more than Madonna does. Whereas Madonna is both the producer and the subject of *Truth or Dare* (since she commissioned director Alek Keshishian to film her), the power relations *Paris Is Burning* establishes among its director, Jennie Livingston, a white lesbian, its subjects, the men who perform in the drag balls, and its audience, both gay and straight, and black and white, are considerably more complex. The ethnographer must not control the film too much, thus failing to let its subjects speak for themselves, and at the same time she must not create the illusion of transparent naturalism, thus failing to reveal the film's constructedness. In *Paris Is Burning,* Livingston's directorial presence is evident, for example, in the insertion of images from magazines and footage of white businessmen to illustrate the fantasies of the drag queens, a strategy that underscores how mainstream capitalist culture constructs their desires. Furthermore, the use of titles to underline terms such as "realness," "legendary," or "categories" suggests that the film is intended for an audience unfamiliar with the drag balls, and that the speakers' world is not immediately accessible without translation. For the most part, however, *Paris Is Burning* has been received as a documentary about the drag balls, not as a film about Livingston's conception of them.

Assessment of whether or not *Paris Is Burning* sympathetically or accurately documents its subjects and of what political work this project might accomplish depends on how its audience is constructed. Thus bell hooks, for example, takes the film to task for exoticizing the pain of its subjects and suggests that it encourages white audiences to celebrate rather than criticize the racist fantasies that underlie the desire to cross-dress.[17]

Failing to account for differences of gender and sexuality, however, hooks constructs a monolithically black-and-white audience. In fact, her criticism of male drag resembles homophobic dismissals of drag in general, and pathologizes the ball participants. To assume that one should see the men as disenfranchised or disempowered only plays into stereotypes of both gays and blacks as dysfunctional or perverse. In fact, *Paris Is Burning* presents a far from uniform vision of ball subculture. While it takes the participants' pleasure seriously, it also suggests that the ball subculture cannot entirely protect its members from the larger racist and homophobic culture, nor from the most empty promises of mainstream consumer culture. The film concludes with an account of Venus Xtravaganza's murder while tricking, and with the documentation of voguing's crossover into mainstream visibility, both of which shed a less than celebratory light on the subversive potential of the balls. Moreover, the internal differences among the speakers make it difficult to ascribe a single position or politics to the subculture. The older men, such as Pepper Labeija and Dorian Corey, are often critical of the consumerism and unrealistic fantasies that motivate the younger boys, and it is they, rather than Livingston herself, who overtly provide the terms for analysis and commentary.

Paris Is Burning provides neither an unambiguously celebratory nor an unambiguously critical vision of the drag balls, and it complicates assumptions about the politics of either reading. By focusing on a group which is outside the mainstream of both African-American and gay and lesbian communities, the film suggests the impossibility of generalizing about racial or sexual identity. Furthermore, it might be more useful to assess *Paris Is Burning* not in terms of whether it reveals the "truth" about the men it documents but in terms of the relations it establishes between its maker and her subjects, and by analogy, between the audience and its subjects. Rather than worrying about whether someone outside the culture can accurately document it, we could ask why a white lesbian filmmaker is interested in the ball subculture. *Paris Is Burning* contributes to the work of feminists and gays and lesbians who are emphasizing differences *within* their communities, in an effort to resist a single or monolithic identity politics. Furthermore, at a time when post-Stonewall gay and lesbian political activists are reexamining the movement's attempt to normalize homosexuality and embracing queer identities that are proudly deviant, a film that represents drag queens and transsexuals in a positive light is important.[18] At least as significant as Livingston's race is her gender, for it is by no means to be taken for granted that a white lesbian or a feminist would be interested in gay male drag of any color. Recently, however, as part of a discourse about sexuality that includes discussion of butch-femme roles, sadomasochism, and sex positivity, both lesbians and feminists have been exploring the possibilities of a cultural politics that draws on fashion and style to subvert sexual and gender identities.[19] Placed in this context, *Paris Is Burning* contributes to a lesbian culture that would counter the argument that drag is sexist and draw inspiration from the ball subculture. The point, then, is not whether Livingston, as an outsider to the ball subculture, is qualified to represent it, but what it means for her *as an outsider* to make a connection with it. (In any event, the hazards of ethnography are not necessarily circumvented when the filmmaker is of the same class, race, sexuality or gender as her subjects.) Her work represents the possibility of alliances within the gay and lesbian community of a different kind than that fostered or prevented by separatism, and more specifically signals the new alliances between lesbians and gay men that are producing "queer" identities in the 90s. To see the film in this way is to suggest that it can operate across differences between its audience and its subjects in productive ways. At least as important as the film's vision of a subculture are the questions it raises about how fantasy structures our relations to consumer culture and, conversely, how consumer culture structures our fantasies.

The importance of *Paris Is Burning* in illuminating the subcultures that *Truth or Dare* only hints at cannot be underestimated. It provides a context within which to scrutinize more critically the extent to which Madonna challenges the status quo, and offers access to voices that are largely missing from mainstream culture. At the same time, though, given the ball subculture's investment in consumerism, femininity, and mainstream success, it is misleading to construct a rigid dichotomy between the two films or between mass culture and alternative cultures. As Jackie Goldsby points out, the documentary form provides a rather more marginal forum for the participants than they themselves seek, even though it is "the only genre that will acknowledge this world as it is: colored and queer."[20] Furthermore, although it is structured by power relations, crosscultural contact occurs in both directions. Livingston's fascination with the ball subculture echoes Madonna's fascination with gay and black subcultures. Both films suggest that gay male subcultures, far from being hidden, are rather more central, more of an "open secret," than we might expect, providing a vehicle for the self expression of middle-class white women, both gay and straight.[21] Thus it is important not to see the two films as mutually exclusive, as representing the oppositions of mainstream to margin, white to black, mass culture to alternative culture. The intersections of these worlds suggest a more complex intermingling of gay and straight, white and black, and male and female identities, both "real" and assumed.

11

Spike Lee and the Fever in the Racial Jungle

Ed Guerrero

> Let us then say that we can reinterpret ideologies of difference only
> because we do so from an awareness of the supervening actuality of
> "mixing," of crossing over, of stepping beyond boundaries, which
> are more creative human activities than staying inside rigidly policed
> borders.
>
> —Edward Said

Concerning policed borders, one can often find a film's ideological
perimeters early on in the manner and style in which its opening titles are
rendered. In the case of Spike Lee's fifth production *Jungle Fever* (1991),
the titles and credits are lettered on urban traffic signs and worked into a
montage of streetscapes replete with counterpoised maps of Harlem and
Bensonhurst, and an opening dedication to the slain black youth, Yusef
Hawkins, . . . all set to the theme music of Stevie Wonder's soundtrack.
This flow of sounds, images, and inscribed street signs, combined with
all of *Jungle Fever*'s pre-release media-hype and press packaging, clearly
heighten audience expectations that Lee is going to deal with the politics
of race and miscegenation, the crossing of boundaries, the stubborn defense of territories. Yet, unlike Said's promise of new definitions and
creative possibilities arising from "stepping beyond boundaries," Spike
Lee has something a bit more closed, confrontational, and melancholy in
mind. Symbolizing the fixity of Lee's perspective, the sign that announces
that the production is a "Spike Lee Joint" has a ONE WAY sign distinctly
displayed underneath it. Adding to this visual cue the film's title itself
is templated on the international, red, WRONG WAY traffic symbol.
Moreover, the drift of these opening significations is reenforced by the
film's title which taints the issue of intimate interracial relationships, i.e.,

miscegenation with the metaphor of disease, a fever that one, presumably, is in danger of catching, but that can be cured.

From the start though, if one is to question the subtle but problematic argument in this latest of Lee's features, this questioning must occur against the background of brother Lee's serious contributions to the medium, to the persistent and ingenious ways that he has reinvented and expanded the practice of black cinema in America. Riding the broad popular wave of consumer interest in rap music, hip-hop, youth fashions, and black sports stars, in a very pivotal sense, Lee has shifted mass thinking about black films and filmmaking in some fundamental ways. First, Lee has clearly demonstrated that, to employ a problematic term, blacks can be *auteurs*. That is to say, that a black director, using varied financing strategies (Lee's term is "guerrilla filmmaking"), can make a rapid series of feature films rendering his or her vision of black life, and that these films can be popularly consumed and supported at the box office. Thus, Lee has opened a gap, however small, in the dominant production system's wall of racism and exclusion, suggesting a strategy that, hopefully, many socially defined and marginalized *others* will be able to replicate according to their needs. As importantly, by exploring in his films a number of socially charged issues that have expanded the nation's perceptions about what it means to be black in America, Lee has been able to place elements of the African-American experience at the center of America's popular culture agenda and social imagination. Hot, socially contained or contested issues that Lee has opened up in his films include the sympathetic, sensual depiction of black sexuality; the frank exploration of black-color caste and class hierarchies; the use of narratives rendered from a black point of view and firmly situated in the black world; the cinematic exploration of what Houston Baker, Jr. has mapped as "the matrix of the blues," consisting of vernacular blues sounds, images, and forms in black urban language and music (Baker, 3–14).

Yet upon examining the progress of his work, it also becomes clear that for Spike Lee these powerful issues are double-intentioned. Importantly, Lee's complex, multivalent explorations of the socially repressed, unspoken, and unspeakable issue of "race," have also played into his main profit-making, marketing strategies, in that the more his films assert themselves in the pre-release, public imagination through debate or controversy, the more audience interest they generate, and thus, dollars at the box office. This intense media milieu, along with the press-hyped fears of the racial conflagration that the film was expected to provoke, heralded *Do the Right Thing* (1989). At the time of the film's release, the *Oprah Winfrey Show* and *Nightline* dedicated entire programs to *Do the Right Thing*'s alleged explosive social potential. As well, Lee mugged for the covers of *Newsweek, American Film,* and even managed to find his way onto the cover of the conservative *National Review*. Additionally, the *New York Times* and the *Village Voice* ran at least a dozen articles and reviews between them covering all aspects of the film. To a less intense degree, this pattern has repeated itself with the release of *Jungle Fever*, as exemplified by the affectionate close-up of the film's co-stars, Annabella Sciorra and Wesley Snipes on the June 1991 cover of *Newsweek*. And clearly, we seem to be building towards the same media climate with the Lee vs. Amiri Baraka pre-production tussle over who owns the interpretation of Malcolm X's life.[1]

Lee's astounding success, his increasing commitment to mainstream cinema's narrative conventions, visual language, marketing strategies, and the progressively larger budgets he's managed to accrue over the trajectory of his last three films, all lead to a series of critical questions that are for the purposes of this essay best answered by looking at *Jungle Fever* and interrogating the film's argument, as well as its position in dominant cinema discourse. Generally, one must wonder where the trajectory of Lee's work is headed, whether the determined incursion of his interpretation of "blackness" into mainstream cinema's vast production system and its attendant markets will do anything to challenge Hollywood's racial hegemony. More specifically though, is *Jungle Fever* really counter-hegemonic on the issue of miscegenation? In other words, does Lee's film challenge mainstream cinema's historically hostile stance and taboos against interracial relationships and marriage?

In response to these questions, let us, first, place *Jungle Fever*, and its socially charged narrative about a black male/white female interracial relationship, into an historicized frame by citing a moment from the studio film industry's distant past. During the early twenties, in reaction to a series of star scandals, and in order to avoid government censorship, Hollywood decided to self-regulate by initiating a code of production standards that would appease its critics, church organizations, and a growing middle-class audience of movie consumers. Thus by installing their own hand-picked commissioner, ex-postmaster Will Hays, and negotiating with cleric and civic leaders what commonly came to be known as the Hays Office Code, the studio moguls were able to hold off any attempt at censorship and interference from outside the industry. Reflecting the morals of the times, the Code was tolerant of such necessary box-office moneymaking ingredients as expressions of sex and crime as long as they were morally contained or punished in a film's narrative. But most importantly for this discussion, the Code also upheld the strong sense of racial *apartheid* and paranoia of the times by expressly stating that miscegenation, or the mixing of the races, was to be portrayed as in no way desirable (Miller, 3). Over time, through this system of in-house, self-censorship, most of the tenets of the Code remained in force until the gradual erosion of its puritanical ethos starting with the Motion Picture Association of America's introduction of a liberalized production code in the mid-sixties. Notably though, the taboo against miscegenation, whether explicitly articulated as in the original Hays Office Code or more implicitly just understood and practiced, has remained in force over the long continuum of dominant cinema's reign, from the very inception of commercial film in the U.S. with *The Masher* (1907) or *Birth of a Nation* (1915) right up to the present—with the exception of a few gaps or counter-currents as exemplified by such infrequent productions as *Broken Blossoms* (1919), *Guess Who's Coming to Dinner?* (1967), or *100 Rifles* (1969).

Thus, one must note that in the Freudian sense repression isn't a total or complete process, in that all forms and instances of miscegenation have not been relentlessly or thoroughly kept from the commercial screen. Rather, in those occasional films when miscegenation is dealt with, the issue is articulated through various narrative strategies of containment that filter it through the perspective, values, and taboos of the dominant, white culture. And while these strategies are multitudinous, the most common one is to depict interracial romance as occurring between a white male and an exotic non-white female (rarely the other way around), as in *Sayonara* (1957), *The World of Suzie Wong* (1960), or the much protested by the Asian-American community *Year of the Dragon* (1985). Moreover, consistent with the spirit of the antiquated Production Code, interracial unions usually end in separation or tragedy, with the person of color being eliminated, sometimes sadistically as in *Mandingo* (1975), or more often just killed off as in *Rambo 2* (1985). Even the fatal attraction of the monstrously black King Kong for the blonde, symbolically white-clad Fay Wray in *King Kong* (1933) clearly marks the deployment of this trope. Yet more subtly, when occurring between a non-white man and what is presumed by the dominant imagination to be the object of desire of all races of color, the white woman, interracial unions are often flawed by rendering them between subjects who are distinctly unequal in ways that inversely underscore the superiority of the all-powerful white norm. Consequently, the white woman depicted in unions with non-white men, is devalued in some subtle way. She is plain; she is blank; she is handicapped, etc., thus suggesting that the sign of her whiteness should be in itself enough of a reward for the person of color. In both of Sidney Poitier's miscegenous forays, *A Patch of Blue* (1965) and *Guess Who's Coming to Dinner?*, he is united with white women who are unmistakably devalued or are not his equals. In the former film, Poitier's white girlfriend is blind, and in the latter, while he is an imminent physician and head of the World Health Organization, his fiancée is simply rich, with no accomplishments or qualifications of her own, other than her whiteness. Both films, then, make the point that these uneven matches are the best a black can aspire to when dealing with the sovereign essence of "whiteness." Notably, this strategy is subtly echoed again in *Jungle Fever,* in the extramarital affair between the black architect Flipper and the high-school educated, white, temporary office worker Angie.

The point of this historical excursion through the taboos and repressed fears of Hollywood's filmic psyche, is that, in the present instance, no matter what acclaim Lee has earned as an "independent" or "guerrilla" filmmaker, *Jungle Fever* is strictly a dominant cinema commodity that rigorously upholds every expectation and prohibition of the archaic Hays Office Code on the issue of miscegenation. Despite the film's first appearances as a fresh, controversial, or even a counter-hegemonic incursion into the discursive tangles of America's racial jungle at the site of one of its most sensitive issues, interracial coupling, dating, loving, etc., ultimately *Jungle Fever* renders miscegenation from the dominant cinema perspective, that is, as in no way desirable. When it comes to portraying intimate interracial relations, Lee's film efficiently does what Hollywood films have always done. For Lee has produced a cautionary melodrama about an interracial romance doomed from its inception, a tale that clearly maintains that blacks and whites are better off sticking to their own races and territories. The cleverness and cinematic illusion of Lee's argument lies in the fact that he accomplishes this rationalization of the eroding, dominant social taboo against miscegenation by upholding it from a binary oppositional "black" perspective that is an amalgam of black political ideas ranging from Afrocentricity and black separatism to a subtle refrain of black neo-conservatism always faintly resonant in Lee's films and interviews.[2]

Lee's argument, as it is depicted in *Jungle Fever,* confronts the discerning spectator with some problematic moments. The film comes off as confused on the issue of exactly how "race" is constructed, as evident in some glaring contradictions in the narrative. The first of these inconsistencies arises when the buppie, Flipper, is questioned by Angie about whether or not they should have children. Flipper answers to the effect that this would be a bad idea and states that their children would be a "bunch of mixed nuts." One is left to ponder this comment, as it elicits a reflex and logical counter-question: aren't all American black people, including Flipper's "quadroon" daughter, to use his rather confused and insulting rhetoric, "a bunch of mixed nuts"? The issue here is obvious enough. Flipper's statement explicitly and the film implicitly articulate the premise that there is a *biologically pure* essence of "blackness" somewhere out there in America, generally agreed upon and uniformly upheld by black people. Correspondingly, Lee seems to echo this longing for a pure essence of blackness in the very choice of Flipper's last name which literally is "Purify." Yet given the infinite and irrepressible range of skin tones, hair textures, eye shapes and colors, so on, among the many diverse physical features that make up the characteristics of the vast collectivity known as African-America, Flipper's comment about "mixed nuts," alluding to a supposedly tainted miscegenous type in contrast to a mythical, pure type, has no empirical basis in science or reality.

Notably, Lee's visual sense of the unresolvable black/white tensions and oppositionality of this melancholy discussion is carefully worked out in this moment's mise-en-scène, as Flipper and Angie sit on distant ends of a king-sized bed looking off in opposite directions. A brick wall as background to their medium-framed, shot-reverse-shot dialogue further enhances the distinct feeling that their relationship is contained and going nowhere. In an obvious reversal of the film's advertisement, which plays on the contrasting allure of black and white skin by depicting a close-up of Flipper and Angie's fingers affectionately interlocked, Flipper now sits at a distance, his skin cast as a blue-black shadow while Angie's is translucent white in the light of the window. Both of these visual constructions fetishize and manipulate the contrast of black and white skin, although for different purposes. Interlocking male/black and female/white fingers as a poster advertising the film are a titillating suggestion of erotic, forbidden entertainments awaiting the spectator inside the theater, while the distance between Flipper and Angie in shadow and light carry the film's moral message about the pain and futility of miscegenation.

Rebuttals to Flipper's "mixed nuts" comment abound in Black Cinema, say, in the way that a range of physical types naturally occurs in the concluding photo in Ayoka Chenzira's film *Hairpiece: A Film For Nappy Headed People* (1984), or in the way hybridity implicitly shapes the narrative of Julie Dash'es *Illusions* (1982), which in part deals with a light skinned black woman's negotiations in, and passage through, the white world. Correspondingly, in *Jungle Fever*'s story world, Flipper and Cyrus would only have to look at their light skinned wives to realize how contradictory and out of touch their notion of a mythic physical homogeneity really is. In a related manner regarding the politics of cultural production, it has been argued often enough that there is no pure or transcendent category of "blackness," (or logically, "whiteness,") known exclusively to black (white) people that magically clarifies or overdetermines all texts, identities or transactions in the racial jungle. African Americans, as the name implies, are a heterogeneous formation, expressing a diverse range of opinions and ideas on any given subject (Gates 45).

However, this is not to take up the position of those intellectuals and critics who would theorize blacks as a people with a distinct historical subjectivity out of existence, those who articulate the oppositional and problematic "anti-essentialist" argument that there is no such thing as a cohesive, politically conscious, freedom-seeking, plural matrix of "blacknesses," forged by historical struggle taking the name African-Americans. The experience of being black in this country, the devaluation, racism, and tension generated by the invisible, governing white norm that a black subject has to face daily, would quickly cure one of any such delusion. What is posited here is obvious enough to the most casual sojourner trying to negotiate the paradoxes and dangers of the racial jungle. Put simply, "race" as we know and live it, is an ever-shifting set of *socially constructed* meanings forged out of political struggle (Omi and Winant). And importantly, in the case of African-Americans, "race," for example, as revealed by the construction of the white character—Tar Baby in Toni Morrison's novel *Sula* or Steve Martin's comic protagonist in Carl Reiner's 1979 movie *The Jerk*—is loosely inclusive in its boundaries and community membership, as contrasted to the paranoid exclusion of the reigning collectivity known as "whiteness."

It is a sad reality that the exclusivity of whiteness based on the "one drop" rule remains in *de facto* force in this country to this day, and that it applies exclusively to African-Americans. As the rule goes, if a person has "one drop" of African blood or an African ancestor then that person is considered as black and thus looses the naturalized privileges of whiteness (Davis, 4–6). How often have black people observed whites in casual conversation volunteer that they have a trace of Native American ancestry or blood in their backgrounds as a way to enter or negotiate a discussion of the repressed and volatile subject of "race"? However, such a gesture would, at best, come off as naive to an African-American, for the simple reason that, in the dominant psyche, Native Americans do not raise the same social or political challenge to white privilege and hegemony as does the vastly larger, barely contained and insurgent social collectivity of African-America. This obvious truth has not escaped notice and discussion in black literature. In his short story, "That Powerful Drop," Langston Hughes's character Simple satirically reflects on the absurd finality of the "one drop" formula when he observes that, "If a man has Irish blood in him, people will say, 'He's *part* Irish.' If he has a little Jewish blood, they'll say, 'He's *half* Jewish.' But if he has just a small bit of colored blood in him, BAM!—'*He's a Negro!*'" (Hughes, 201). For the same reason, as Patricia Williams so eloquently points out in her book *The Alchemy of Race,* it is a trauma close to death for many whites to recognize, let alone reveal, that they have any African blood flowing in their veins (Williams, 61). Interestingly enough, Lee understands the pathological nature of such fears, as rendered in his clever soda fountain scene set in Bensonhurst where Italian-American men almost come to blows over the slightest insinuation of African blood in one of their family lines. Conversely then, would Lee prescribe such an exclusive, paranoid view of race for African-Americans? Would he counter the dominant, invisible, yet all-powerful norm of an essential "whiteness" by proposing that African-Americans fall into the equally bogus notion of a binary and essential "blackness"?[3]

Yet in another important way, the absurdity of such a claim, for a *biologically pure* black essence is further undercut by a powerful, if repressed, contradiction worked into the film's narrative. Given black middle-class men's well-documented preference to marry light-skinned African-American women—as revealed in a number of black novels, including Wallace Thurman's 1929 classic of the Harlem Renaissance, *The Blacker the Berry . . . ,* or the "high-toned" heroines and chorus girls of any of Oscar Micheaux's black independent, bourgeois melodramas, and as pointedly rendered in *Jungle Fever* in Cyrus and Flipper's clearly stated preference for light-skinned wives—one must ask *the* critical question and, so to speak, play the child pointing out the emperor's nakedness. Where do all of these light-skinned African-American wives for the black bourgeoisie ultimately come from, if not from some form the process of miscegenation itself?[4]

Lee inadvertently plays with this contradiction, skirting the fringes of the issue when Flipper and his wife argue in the department store where she works and she accuses Flipper of having "finally gone ahead and done it," that is, of trading her in for a white woman. In this scene, which has faint intonations of the "tragic mulatto" stereotype, it is clear that Flipper's wife recognizes the repressed, ultimately miscegenous origins of Flipper's preferences in women, although, here, Lee backs off from thoroughly interrogating the issue. So in the final instance, Flipper and Cyrus are themselves lost in the maze twisted turns, choices, ideologies, and illusions etched into the terrain of the racial jungle, as the film's implicit premise unravels under critical scrutiny.

To say all of this, however, is not to overlook the film's subtle complexities, its clever turns and brilliant moments. In an important sense, *Jungle Fever* contains within it a dialectical, counter-current tension that arises out of Lee's propensity and talent for visualizing sexuality, an element that is consistently explored in all of his films and that he continually works to refine. In this case, Lee's inclination for depicting the erotic has produced perhaps the most frank, seductive rendering of interracial, black-on-white sex on the Hollywood screen to date. Lee's black male/white female sexual panoramas—Flipper and Angie locked in spontaneous coitus on a drafting table at the office, their continual, close-up kisses throughout the film, and their working through a variety of erotic positions in their bare apartment—stand in tempting contrast to the routine, missionary position, lovemaking scenes between Flipper and his wife that open and close the film. Moreover, Lee's moments of black/white eros are light years beyond *Guess Who's Coming to Dinner?*'s one, tame, 1967 interracial kiss. At that time, Sidney Poitier kissing his white fiancée in the back of a taxi was so socially charged that it literally couldn't be fully represented on the screen. This potent black male/white female kiss had to be contained in a smaller frame within the dominant frame of the screen, distanced to a voyeuristic gaze in the taxi cab's rearview mirror. So considering that any film's most powerful ideological argument is usually embedded in the visual, i.e., a film always argues for what it *visually represents* often regardless of a director's intentions, it would seem that Lee's enticing depiction of black/white sex and affection between Flipper and Angie, visually undercuts the argument and outcome of the film's separatist narrative. In a subtle, ironic manner, then, Lee is perhaps spreading the "fever" that he wishes to critique if not cure.

Jungle Fever also makes an insistent appeal for social justice in the stark, editorial way that it renders the limited intellectual horizons of Bensonhurst and its denizens, the neighborhood where Yusef Hawkins was so savagely and pointlessly murdered. The film seems to argue here that racism arises out of an explosive mix of personal bigotry with cultural fear and ignorance. But, Hollywood-style, *Jungle Fever* does not go much beyond this in its analysis of the causes of racism; the film limits its exploration of racism to personal expressions of anger without ever taking on its much more powerful and relevant political and institutional dimensions. In this same manner *Do the Right Thing* is brilliant at rendering the drama of racism in the montage of Puerto Ricans, white cops, Koreans, African-Americans, etc., all shouting racist invective at whatever oppositional group happens to be the focus of their rage. This is the *how* of racism, and it makes good cinematic spectacle. But what is never explored is the much more political *why* of racism, as in why are all of these people so divided from, and angry at each other, and, ultimately, who does this benefit?[5] Certainly *Do the Right Thing* foreshadows the barbaric treatment of Rodney King, and to a degree the counterfeit standard of "justice" applies to the case and the massive L.A. Uprising that followed it. But black cinema must now go beyond the commodified spectacle of racial violence, which always enriches the media and entertainment industries, in order to challenge the institutional foundations that subtly and relentlessly hold America's *apartheid* system in place.

Also *Jungle Fever*'s "war council" of black women, held in Flipper's living room, is a powerful articulation of the film's uncontainable excesses, those usually unspoken social truths, energies, and contradictions that in brief illuminating flashes break through the formal surface of the dominant cinema text to pose some unexpected challenge or set of questions to the "official story." Correspondingly, and in part out of Lee's response to gender-oriented critiques of his preceding films, this was the one scene where Lee surrendered directorial control, letting black women improvise on the subject of black men and white women over the course of twenty-five takes. What emerges here is not the director's monologic stance against race-mixing, as marked by the ONE WAY traffic sign. Rather, the scene communicates the irrepressible heteroglossia of black discourse as these women articulate a wide range of views—from the satirical adoration of the mythical black "Zulu dick," to the social marginality of black men, to varied perspectives on miscegenation, from anger and repulsion to an open endorsement of interracial dating, sex, love. It must also be said to Lee's credit that he adds another layer of complexity to this film in the subtle way he acknowledges these uncontainable social energies he attempts to define and harness, in that he holds out the vague possibility of a successful interracial union in his depiction of a Bensonhurst couple (figured along the lines of dominant formula), a black woman and white man.

By way of a conclusion, something must also be said about *Jungle Fever*'s framing of the term "interracial," which seems to imply the hookup of blacks and whites *solemente*. By overlooking the numerous, varied interracial combinations of "people of color," who as the oppressed or marginalized often share a certain affinity with each other, the film's narrow interpretation of the issue inadvertently supports the political interests of those who would benefit from keeping non-white collectivities divided. Conversely, Julie Dash's *Daughters of the Dust* (1991), in which one of the daughters elopes with a Native American, and Mira Nair's *Mississippi Masala* (1992), about a young Indian woman who falls in love with an African-American man, come as necessary first steps in broadening the range of interracial combinations represented on the commercial screen. Though it is also worth noting that Lee seems to recognize this potential in *Do the Right Thing,* with Mookie's *Puerto Riquenio* girlfriend, Tina, but such possibilities do not emerge in *Jungle Fever.* Ultimately then, Hollywood continues to repress an obvious social truth by not representing interracial relationships as part of the everyday transactions of a society with multiple, overlapping racial boundaries.

As a corresponding insight, the film's sense of narrowness and racial finality also spills over into the issue of gender politics in the stark way that its resolution returns Angie to the grim, oppressive patriarchy of her father's Bensonhurst clan. Thus in the final instance, in accordance with dominant-cinema expectations, Angie is punished for crossing racial boundaries, for mixing. At the same time, though, this scene signals Lee's inability to envision Angie with the potential for a liberated future based on her gender. It is highly implausible that a woman of Angie's adventurous character, whose miscegenous affair can, at least in part, be read as an act of rebellion against all that Bensonhurst has come to stand for (including the violent beating she takes at the hands of her father) would not foresee the possibilities of her freedom beyond the dead hearth and home of racist patriarchy.

Yet in a society that is rapidly pluralizing, and where the invisible, dominating social construct of "whiteness" faces the prospect of being just another large minority past the year 2000, we must push our social vision to imagine what soon will become inevitable: an eruptive, almost infinite variety of *miscegenations* spreading across the political horizon, blurring all binaries and oppositions, subverting the norm, transgressing not only differences of color, but class, gender, and sexual orientations as well. Certainly this is what Mikhail Bakhtin had in mind when he discussed the modern novel (and to extrapolate, narrative cinema) as open-ended and "unfinalized," as working against the strictures and closures of "official culture" (Morson and Emerson). This is certainly what author Toni Morrison, whom Lee admires, has in mind when Sula, her visionary character who transcends the norms of gender and race, an "artist without a canvas," declares on her deathbed that the racially closed and polarized little town that has ostracized her will some day come to love her,

> after all the old women have lain with the teen-agers; when all the young girls have slept with their old drunken uncles; after all the black men fuck all the white ones; when the guards have raped all the jailbirds and after all the whores make love to their grannies; after all the faggots get their mothers; trim; when Lindbergh sleeps with Bessie Smith and Norma Shearer makes it with Stepin Fetchit; after all the dogs have fucked all the cats and every weather vane on every barn flies off the roof to mount the hogs . . . then there'll be a little love left over for me. And I know just what it will feel like. (Morrison, 145–46)

So far, these aren't the kinds of social possibilities that Lee imagines in his films. And it must be said that when staring into the threat of an ecologically exhausted, dystopian future, with most of the world's "consumers" located in industrial, and/or white-dominated nations in a sort of approaching global *apartheid,* the apocalyptic "color line" that W.E.B. Du Bois so brilliantly forecasted, Lee is not wrong to focus his efforts on exploring the limitations, injustices, and tensions of being black in this society. For this is what Spike Lee does best, exploring the cultural tensions and specificity of his interpretation of "blackness" at a particular locale on the vast heterogeneous map of African-America. In this sense Lee is a profound diagnostician of racism in its localized forms and masquerades, as he sees it. Thus any intimation of biological essence that Spike Lee may fall into must necessarily be considered against the ever-present but naturalized background of a hegemonic "white" essence that relentlessly struggles to proscribe all black discourse in this country. However, in order, some distant day, to cure the real fever that plagues the land, which is an overdetermining, paranoid racism that sets all against all, thus poisoning all relations in the society; in order to exit the discursive tangles and snares of America's racial jungle, and to heal this land's fractured territories, we are going to have to spawn black filmmakers who much like Sula, can imagine emergent, irrepressible social combinations and possibilities as well.

Works Cited

Baker, Jr., Houston A. *Blues, Ideology and African-American Literature: A Vernacular Theory*. Chicago: University of Chicago Press, 1984.

Davis, F. James. *Who is Black?* University Park: Penn State University Press, 1991.

Diawara, Manthia. "Cinema Studies, the Strong Thought and Black Film." *Wide Angle* pp. 4–11. 13: 3–4, Black Cinema Issue (July–October, 1991), pp. 4–11.

Gates, Jr., Henry Louis. *Figures in Black: Words, Signs, and the "Racial" Self*. New York: Oxford University Press, 1987.

Hanchard, Michael. "Identity, Meaning and The African American." *Social Text* 8: 2 (1990), pp. 31–42.

Hughes, Langston. *The Langston Hughes Reader*. New York: George Braziller, Inc., 1958.

Lott, Tommy L. "A No-Theory Theory of Contemporary Black Cinema." *Black American Literature Forum* 25: 2, Black Cinema Issue (Summer, 1991), pp. 221–237.

Lubiano, Wahneema. "But Compared to What?: Reading Realism, Representation and Essentialism in *School Daze, Do the Right Thing*, and the Spike Lee Discourse." *Black American Literature Forum* 25: 2, Black Cinema Issue (Summer, 1991).

Miller, Randall, M., ed. *The Kaleidoscopic Lens, How Hollywood Views Ethnic Groups*. Englewood N.J. Jerome S. Ozer, Pub., 1980.

Morrison, Toni. *Sula*. New York: Plume, 1973.

Morson, Gary Saul and Caryl Emerson. *Mikhail Bakhtin, Creation of a Prosaics*. Stanford: Stanford University Press, 1990.

Omi, Michael and Howard Winant. *Racial Formation in the United States*. New York: Routledge and Kegan Paul, 1986.

Said, Edward W. "An Ideology of Difference." In Henry Louis Gates, Jr., ed. *"Race," Writing, and Difference*. Chicago: University of Chicago Press, 1985, p. 43.

Savery, Pancho. "The Third Plane at the Change of the Century: The Shape of African-American Literature to Come." In Lennard J. Davis and M. Bella Mirabella, eds. *Left Politics and the Literary Profession*. New York: Columbia University Press, 1990.

Williams, Patricia J. *The Alchemy of Race and Rights*. Cambridge, Mass.: Harvard University Press, 1991.

12

Split Skins: Female Agency and Bodily Mutilation in *The Little Mermaid*

Susan White

For the female is, as it were, a mutilated male, and the catamenia are semen, only not pure; for there is only one thing they have not in them, the principle of soul.

—Aristotle

"It hurts so much!" said the little mermaid. "Yes, you must suffer a bit to look pretty!" said the old queen.

—"The Little Mermaid"

During the last two decades much has been written about what constitutes a "woman's story." The initial postulation was that the main narrative structures of Western film and literature are utterly dominated by and act to support the premises of patriarchy.[1] In recent years, however, feminist critics have nuanced this argument, recognizing that most stories have more than one tale to tell. Many now claim that women's discourses about their own sexuality and their wills to shape the world permeate both male- and female-authored texts, even if they are are at least partially organized by patriarchal structures.[2] The dominant or hegemonic (ruling) forces of Western society (to which this essay's discussion is limited) work subtly, even microscopically to form women's attitudes about themselves. But non-hegemonic forces (representing minority or counter-cultural views) also work to fashion women's self-perceptions, and can be the source of critiques of hegemony. So even in apparently sexist or racist narratives, some of the real concerns of women and minorities get expressed in subtle, "subtextual" ways. To praise or to condemn any particular narrative as "pro-" or "anti-"woman, whether its author is male or female, becomes problematic. Often, as is the case with the film under analysis in this essay, the best we can do is to pull apart and follow the threads of the work's contradictory ideologies. How, then, do we discern or even conceptualize an "authentic" woman's story? Perhaps we can't: feminist critics are instead coming to see most cultural products as a complex weave of oppression, rebellion, play with existing structures, recuperation, and transformation.

The Little Mermaid, Disney's award-winning and extraordinarily popular 1989 animated feature,[3] addresses the issue of female desire, especially *adolescent* female desire, in the context of a narrated rite of passage—the attainment of adult womanhood. Adapted from Hans Christian Andersen's 1837 fairy tale of the same name, the film depicts a young mermaid longing to be a part of the human world, yearning to be loved by a man, and determined to have the body of a woman at any price. This essay examines how the film version of *The Little Mermaid* vicariously gratifies girls' and women's urges for active participation in the world around them (or in different worlds altogether), while also presenting an image of women as both physically and socially constained. The critical methodology derives from many sources, including Freudian and Lacanian psychoanalysis, whose relevant terms will be discussed below.[4] Along with semiotics (the study of sign systems), structuralism, and Marxism, psychoanalysis is an invaluable aid in understanding just what a film may be "working through"—what social problems are being mulled over unconsciously by the film-going public. Although many feminists scholars have objected to the sexism implicit in Freud's language and theories, most feminist film critics argue for the importance of Freud's work as a *description* of women's roles in 19th- and 20th-Century Europe and America. Psychoanalysis is particularly useful in discussions of attitudes about the male and female bodies, with which the following is largely concerned.

It is easy to see why Disney's mermaid has been popular among little girls "ages three and up"[5]: she is unself-consciously beautiful, physically exuberant, and able to pursue her dreams of love. Both older and very young girls have delighted in following the mermaid through the stages of her maturation. Clearly, the mermaid speaks to something in their experience, or else the video of the film would not be played again and again, a fact that many parents have reported. However, critics have rushed to observe that the film's plot also acts to counter the mermaid's dream of self-realization. Indeed, it is obvious that the film presents a version of womanhood that contradicts the jubilant physical confidence upon which the film's attraction to girls and women seems partly based. The film implies that the sense of freedom necessary to exploration and accomplishment must finally be curbed if one is to become a woman. We are led to inquire, how does the culture that produced Hollywood conspire to make this *loss* an acceptable, even *pleasurable* process, one that little girls want to see again and again? By means of historical and psychological contextualization of the mermaid, I hope to reveal just what the female spectator may get out of stories that, like Disney's *The Little Mermaid*, seem in part designed to reinforce negative stereotypes about women and girls.

In determining whether a narrative reinforces the dominant cultural codes concerning gender, race, and class, or subverts the premises of oppression and inhibition, we must consider the uses to which that narrative is put, as well as its content. Disney's *The Little Mermaid* surely serves a different function for its consumers (primarily pre-adolescent girls) than did the 1837 Andersen story from which it was adapted,[6] and not only because the story was considerably changed by its animators. The cultural stakes and consumer context of the mermaid's tale have altered radically since Andersen wrote his allegory about a mermaid's wish to attain an immortal soul by marrying a mortal man.[7] Even in 1837, however, the Christian (or, at least, religious) allegory cannot have utterly subsumed the mermaid's fervent wish to fashion a woman's body out of her mer-flesh. Surely no girl who has read the story can forget the mermaid's physical heroism, her willingness not only to lose her voice but to feel as though she were walking on knives each time she takes a step on her new legs—for such were the conditions of becoming human in Andersen's story. Similarly, although the cultural burden carried by the mermaid as mythological figure for the past several millenia has changed (harnessed as it now is to specific 20th-Century uses), the echoes of that tradition remain and influence our responses to the mermaid story, as it surely conditioned the responses to Andersen's tale.

The modern mermaid represents a convergence of various mythological strands and social forces. In *Sea Enchantress*, Benwell and Waugh (1965) cite numerous forebears, including the fish-tailed Oannes, Lord of the Waters, one of the great triad of Babylonian gods. The Homeric siren, whose enchanting voice led men to their watery graves at sea, began as a bird-like figure (sometimes confused with the Harpy). These sirens of the Classical Age "gradually lost their bird-like appearance and became mermaids," and were integrated with sailors' fantasies of sea beasts with a human form (46).[8] The pagan mermaid was incorporated into Christian bestiaries as a "warning against sin" (69). She appears, more or less in this capacity, in Dante's *Divine Comedy*, Spenser's *Fairie Queene*, and several of Shakespeare's plays.

The traditional description of the mermaid as a treacherous woman gazing into a mirror as she combs her hair matches Freud's description of the narcissistic woman in "On Narcissism." This dangerous, self-satisfied creature, both feared and desired by men, can be observed in representations from the Biblical Lilith to the *film noir* heroine.[9] It is easy to see the mermaid at almost any point in her career as a projection of male apprehension about and longing for women. But even though the traditional stories, like Freud's discussion, seem to derive from male fantasies, the mermaid's point of view is not entirely lacking in this history. In Andersen's depiction and elsewhere, her longing for both her native element and for what dry land has to offer her is often presented poignantly.

In the 20th-Century's cinematic depictions of the mermaid, both male projection and female desire are easily traceable. A loose survey of film's use and abuse of the mermaid seems to indicate that she generally appears as a figure of transition, a "liminal" figure (Turner), in many senses of the word. A prototypical film of the "male anxiety" genre is *Mr. Peabody and the Mermaid* (Irving Pichel, 1948), which depicts the mermaid as the means by which a man (William Powell) navigates the midlife crisis brought on by his fiftieth birthday and the interest shown in his younger wife by other men. By showing the mermaid as a (temporarily) docile alternative to Mr. Peabody's strong-minded wife, this film takes its place among the numerous post-World War II Hollywood products that express anxiety about the possibility of male fallibility and female independence.

The 1980s and 1990s have featured a resurgence of the mermaid narrative, again as an apparent response to the changing status of women in American and other Western cultures. *Splash* (a Disney/Touchstone film, directed by Ron Howard, 1984) recapitulates *Peabody*'s psychological configuration, except that the male anxiety depicted concerns whether or not a man should get married at all.[10] The film opens with a flashback of the protagonist's brother looking up the skirts of women on board a ferry (checking out their "lower" parts). Perhaps in embarrassed response to his brother's behavior, Alan (played as an adult by Tom Hanks) jumps overboard and encounters a "little mermaid" before reluctantly allowing himself to be rescued by the boat's crew. A psychological reading of the film might claim that because the mermaid has no skirts, or recognizable female sexual organs, Alan paradoxically finds her less threatening than the women with whom his brother is so fascinated.[11] Alan is not ready to confront female genitals. The same mermaid (Daryl Hannah) later appears in New York in adult human form, just as Alan is agonizing over losing his live in girlfriend, who moved out when Alan refused to say he loved her. Although Alan does not at first know that the mermaid *is* a mermaid, she seems to offer the peculiar combination of traits that can command male commitment: exoticism (she is not mute but speaks "mermaid language" until she learns TV English), extreme femininity (she loves to shop), intense sexuality (she appears naked near the Statue of Liberty when she first becomes human in pursuit of her man), and helplessness (she is a "fish out of water" who must be hidden by her sweetheart). Alan's problems are not over, since every trait that attracts him also readily presents itself as dangerous or repellent. Still, this story goes further than does *Peabody* in reconciling itself to potentially powerful women. Alan decides in the end to inhabit the undersea realm with the mermaid, rather than staying on land where she is persecuted by evil scientists. The ocean floor is depicted as woman's territory, and in a reversal of the usual pattern of exogamy, the man gives up his own world to inhabit hers.[12]

Psychoanalysis, as a branch of psychology dealing specifically with sexuality and with the unconscious, may account for film's insistence on the "dangerous and repellent" side of the mer-woman. When, midway through *Splash*, Alan discovers that the exotic beauty who has precipitously replaced his demanding girlfriend is a mermaid, he turns away, clearly horrified. The existence of the tail seems to incite revulsion, bringing to the foreground the disgust men often display in response to female sexual aggression. The phallic dimensions of the tail may reveal, in this context, how female desire has almost always been read in our culture as masculine, improperly feminine (a view heartily embraced by Freud in "Femininity," and "Female Sexuality"). However, the "phallic" tail's "otherness" (its scales, its fishy odor) also seems to evoke the uncanny feeling Freud claims is incited by a boy's view of the female genitals, his (oceanic) place of origin, whose power in his psychic life has been mentally repressed. In his essay, "The 'Uncanny'," Freud notes that the indescribable strangeness we feel in "uncanny" situations is produced by reminders of repressed past experiences. Like any other "fetish" object, the tail would serve simultaneously as a defense against remembering the first traumatic view of the female genitals and a reminder of man's genital origin, his emergence from his mother's body. So, despite its phallic shape, the mermaid's tail is not easily defined as either male or female, as threatening or reassuring.

For the past several years, the mermaid has become a pervasive cinematic symbol of the girl's difficult rite of passage to womanhood. Films including the superb *I Heard the Mermaids Singing* (Australia, Patricia Rozema, 1987), *Mermaids* (U.S., Richard Benjamin, 1990), *La petite sirène* (France, Roger Andrieux, 1990), and even Madonna's 1991 music video, "Cherish," featuring back-up mermaids, and Bette Midler's "mermaid" stage performances, all involve painful "growth" experiences. The loss of virginity, obsessive and unrequited love, the discovery or persistence of maternal betrayal, and the difficulty of finding "appropriate" women to act as role models are dilemmas faced by each of these girls and women. As a fairy tale, *The Little Mermaid* spells out these issues through a highly symbolic and boldly colored mise-en-scène, designed to appeal to very young girls as well as to older children. Following the lead of psychologists who have written on the symbolic meaning of fairy tales,[13] many critics have noted that the mermaid's acquisition of legs may interest little girls because it represents in a very literal fashion her physical attainment of womanhood. Andersen's version emphasizes the painful elements of growing into womanhood, associated with loss (of the tail, of home, of her voice traded away to a sorceress for the legs) and physical agony (each step she takes feels like walking on knives). As Roberta Trites notes,

> [t]he enchantress's image of flowing blood prepares the girl for menarche, while the image of knife-like pain warns the girl about the potentially hymen-breaking phallus. (Trites, 148)[14]

The assumption is, as Bettelheim has said about tales like *Beauty and the Beast*, that girls purge their own fears of these physical and emotional changes by seeing them symbolically represented. But these stories are also cueing girls in very specific ways on what to expect from from the womanhood they face, and both Disney and Andersen present discomfiting alternatives.

Andersen's story is, briefly, as follows: A royal mermaid is enamoured by the human world, because it is exotic, but more importantly, because by marrying a human she can gain an immortal soul. With the help of a sea witch, who appropriates the mermaid's voice as payment and tells her she must win a mortal's love or die, the mermaid's tail is painfully split into legs. Going to the surface, she finds the prince whose life she had once saved, and with whom she is in love. But the prince regards the voiceless girl as a kind of pet, and eventually marries another. The mermaid's sisters offer her a chance to come back to them: they have sold their hair to the witch for a magical knife. All the mermaid has to do is kill the prince and she is free to return to sisters, father, and grieving grandmother. The mermaid refuses. As she dissolves into sea foam, the spirits of the air take the mermaid with them, telling her that she may still become immortal by helping the wretched (cooling them with breezes, etc.). The mermaid kisses the prince's bride good-bye, and disappears.

Disney's animation team wrought many changes upon the story. Like the later *Beauty and the Beast*, the film is a musical, featuring songs of ambition, desire, jealousy, and triumph. The plot is also very different. The mermaid's father (King Triton), benign in Andersen's tale, is in the film violently jealous of his daughter's love for humans, and she must defy him to go to the surface (to which she has free access after the age of fifteen in the story). The grandmother disappears, while the sea witch's character—Ursula—is (literally) expanded: she is fat, sophisticated, flamboyant, wicked, and power-hungry.[15] She is generally accompanied by two eels, who act as her familiars. Ursula forces Ariel (the mermaid) to sign a contract condemning her and her father to eternal captivity if the mermaid fails. When Ariel finally finds the prince, he comes very close to falling in love with her, thanks to the staging abilities of her aquatic sidekicks, a crab and a fish. However, the envious Ursula disguises herself as a lovely brunette (Ariel is a redhead), and uses the mermaid's stolen voice to enchant the prince. Just as the prince is about to marry the witch, a slapstick series of events foils her. Ursula grows as enormous as a dirigible and the prince punctures her with a broken mast, freeing the father, saving Ariel, and, of course, unleashing the typical "happy ever after" scenario. Sixteen-year-old Ariel marries the prince. Nothing is said of her permanent exile from her underwater home.

Obviously, the Disney film considerable "waters down" the Andersen story, as Trites and others have complained.[16] Gone is the pain of acquiring legs, the implicit female bonding between the mermaid and the bride, the story of the acquisition of the soul. Many critics find fault, as well, with the film's depiction of the little mermaid as little more than a happy housewife in the making. Indeed, her main occupation, other than performing for her father in the choir of mermaids (all of whom are his daughters, though there seems to be no mother), is collecting and arranging artifacts lost by humans from ships. These seem to be largely domestic items, such as eating utensils and furniture, though there is also a statue of a man (generic in the story, Prince Eric in the film) later shattered by the jealous father. Indeed, the mermaid in her cave does resemble a girl with her trousseau awaiting the arrival of a princely husband.[17]

In a day and age when high school girls tend to be convinced of their physical inadequacy, are "twice as likely as boys to perceive themselves as fat" (Byrd, A12), and are "building the best body [their] money can buy" through plastic surgery (Doun, B5) at younger and younger ages, it is no wonder that a narrative like *The Little Mermaid* has been widely successful among pre-adolescent girls.[18] The film depicts the process of becoming woman as magically painless, while acknowledging its extraordinary difficulty. *The Little Mermaid* maintains, as it were, a hint of the agony Andersen shows to be involved in acquiring and occupying a woman's body, but depicts it as ultimately insignificant in comparison with the rewards. Thus, when acceding to womanhood means more than ever to carve one's flesh into the appropriate shape, the Disney Corporation's choice to excise the pain and blood from the mermaid's transformation is significant. Unlike Andersen's story, the film might be seen to embody a cultural denial or *displacement* of the plight of women, disguising the real price that living for love and beauty exacts.

Critics are right to be dismayed by *The Little Mermaid*'s simultaneous acknowledgment and erasure of the many pains involved in constructing the proper woman's body. Further, the urgency of the mermaid's wish for the right body indicates that, despite her "rebel" status, it involves a social imperative. The film implicitly vilifies any body that does not fit the paradigm it presents: youth, abundant hair, white teeth, voluptuous breasts (or beefy biceps), and, for women, slenderness. As Trites points out (149), Ariel is almost anorexic in appearance, while the "bad" mother is obese (an delighted with it), the fattest of the Disney villainesses. Ursula seems to have absorbed all the older female characters figuring in the story, indicating that the mother-daughter problem reflected here is a LARGE one, despite Ursula's transformative abilities. As is so often the case in stories about mothers and daughters, Ursula acts as both a "bad mirror" and an overwhelming physical presence. A fascinating moment supporting the theory that the film's subtext is caught up with dictating morphological norms is the one where Ursula describes her supernatural powers to Ariel in an ironic and flamboyant song. As she hovers over a vaporous image of two mer-folk, one male, one female, Ursula sings of her ability to dissolve impediments to love. The wavering virtual image of the mermaid shows an obese body, while the merman is scrawny (the ninety-seven-pound weakling of commercial legend). "This one longing to be thinner, that one wants to get the girl," croons Ursula in her theatrically ironic song, "Poor Unfortunate Souls," and with a fiery "poof!" she transforms the pair. Interestingly, the relative bulk of the two is reversed: the boy is now large and muscular, and the girl willowy and slender. Men "must" be bigger than women. Ariel watches open-mouthed as a cinema-like projection of her own silhouette with legs runs in place, and Ursula tells her she must get the kiss of "true love" within three days. Ursula, it must be said, thinks love is very silly.

While films like *Pumping Iron* (or anything starring Arnold Schwarzenegger, for that matter) indicate that an ethos of suffering for the right body extends to men as well as to women, we must note that important distinctions between these standards persist. The main difference is that the stakes are an order of magnitude higher for women, the proper body being depicted as *the* most important element of her identity. Even in the female-directed, iconoclastic film *Wayne's World* (Penelope Spheeris, 1992), the moral of the story is that the "average" or even unattractive man *can* win the mesmerizing woman. Male *desirability* is still considered much less important than male *desire* in cinema and elsewhere. The transformation of the body towards desirability has involved, up to the present, a process of *weakening* the woman in order to render her sexually desirable, while men are made stronger.[19] In this context, we can hardly blame little girls for seeking the kind of magical solution provided by *The Little Mermaid* to the almost impossible project of growing up, when now more than ever the adult female body must retain the contours of childhood (cf. Nabokov's *Lolita*), while acquiring the secondary sexual attributes of the woman.

Although *The Little Mermaid* "anaesthetizes" the physical pain Andersen describes as part of achieving adulthood,[20] the girl's physical and psychological endurance and loss mark almost every moment of the film. Above all, *sacrifice*, the hallmark of movie womanhood, is written into the Disney version as it is into the tale.[21] Sigmund Freud describes masochism, in the form of pleasure in sacrifice, as more or less a *normal* component of femininity, which involves eroticized "submission" to the physical pain of sexual intercourse and childbirth, and to the psychological humiliation of social inferiority. Indeed, as Kaja Silverman observes, female masochism in women has often been regarded as non-pathological, as too normal to deserve the elaborate discussions devoted to the male masochist. The evidence for this view: Masochistic men are described as building intricate and intense fantasies, something said to be missing from the more work-a-day female "martyr" complex.[22] Interestingly, many feminist critics writing on masochism have inadvertently continued the tradition of accepting female masochism as the norm (and implicitly an acceptable norm), and as a condition accepted passively by most women. Silverman, for example, focuses on the "subversive" qualities of male masochism, while generally (though not always) consigning feminine masochism to the margins.[23] If, one argument goes, *men* desire pain and suffering, and find fulfillment in it, they are voluntarily *taking on the feminine role* and implicitly declaring that role a more satisfying one (Silverman, 1980). Yet Silverman herself readily admits that the model of femininity adhered to by male masochists has little to do with women, and much to do with male attitudes toward submitting to the demands of culture. As she notes in *The Acoustic Mirror*, women become a place of projection for male attributes rejected by men ("she" is lacking; "she" is submissive). Male masochism would thus be a way for men to acknowledge that these qualities are really their own.

It does seem that we need another way to describe masochism than as "feminizing," since that version of femininity may have very little to do with the femininity women are trying to achieve through their gestures of self-denigration. Perhaps even more importantly, Silverman and others seem to perpetuate the notion advanced by Reik that woman's version of masochism "has the character of yielding and surrender rather than of the rush ahead, of the orgiastic cumulation, of the self-abandonment of man" (Silverman [1988], 36). Even when they are masochistic, we are to believe, men are more "active" than women.[24] By accepting this view we fail to observe just how *active* this "submission" is! Masochism could not have been foisted off on women for so many centuries if its payoff were not enormous, though enormously destructive. Female masochism involves a triumphant conquering of pain, physical and psychological, which "assures" the woman of approval from the idealized man.[25] The pleasure of female masochism is found in this triumphant and active pursuit of recognition for her sacrifice, of admiration for her difficultly acquired femininity.[26] Often, indeed, the male object proves secondary in importance to the woman's glory. This "ironic" masochism certainly does subvert the credo of male superiority, but at what cost?

Both the story and the film are distinctly masochistic versions of the mermaid tale, one that reverses the earlier narratives: the mermaid has learned the *voluntary* renunciation prized in women—she is not being forced (like her legendary Northern European sisters) to live on land, but sadly and *willingly* leaves behind her beloved home and her "whole" body to live vicariously through the prince. But in both story and film, the renunciation is just that: voluntary and *explicitly* active. The implication is that she *could* choose otherwise. However painful and seemingly compulsive her sacrifice may be, the little mermaid leaves us with the recollection of her stubbornness, of her desperation to throw away her fins so that she may attain a dubious happiness. And here is the danger: even though girls *know* that happiness in marriage is at best a fifty-fifty proposition, the intoxication of approval and recognition is so heady and so addictive that they will often pursue what they suspect to be a losing battle, at the expense of other opportunities for education and employment. *The Little Mermaid* is ideologically pernicious in that it does not question the severe limitations on female options, the means by which they can obtain satisfaction in the world, or provide a way out of the desperate need for male approval upon which the mermaid's search is based. But the mermaid's wink at her buddies as she hobbles away from the shore on her new legs, leaning "submissively" on Eric, indicates that she is *playing*.[27] The game is dangerous, and has a compulsive quality, but it *is* play. We may hope that when this game isn't fun any more Ariel may use her stubbornness, if not her beauty, to play another, more interesting one.

Little girls are, like women, drawn to stories of sacrifice and loss for many reasons. These stories resonate with the girls' increasing awareness that growing up will make specific, often frightening, demands on them. They also echo the triumph the growing child experiences in her mastery of her body, and in the more challenging arena of embracing loss as a means of being recognized and approved. Stories like Disney's *The Little Mermaid* also serve, of course, to disguise the extent of damage that these losses will incur, and to promise that male ardor will be more fulfilling than anything else could possible be. Missing, too, is any awareness that when the girl turns away from her mother, whom she loved and with whom she identified, she suffers a blow far deeper than the maturing boy's,[28] a loss that no prince can supplement. Perhaps this is why Ursula, for all her villainy, is a lovable character, whose obesity must be rejected by the girl viewer on aesthetic grounds, but whose ample, maternal folds may also offer vague refuge. Her scathing wit also indicates, at least, that verbal mastery is possible for women. The mermaid fantasy is a means of prolonging the period when girls are allowed free movement and more far-ranging identification, before they find that in order to be a proper woman their bodies and gaits must be constricted, pared down, defin(n)ed.

I claimed earlier that consumer "use" as well as content of the film is important in understanding its ideological dimension. Indeed, the fact that this film is available on videotape, to be played again and again (as children are wont to do with any form of story), gives the girl the option of living again and again every aspect of the mermaid's various losses and acquisitions. She shops for human artifacts, performs, loses her voice and friends and tail and regains them, acquires legs and pretty clothes and takes them off again, leaves her father and returns, marries the prince over and over again, then leaves him for her undersea friends. Ariel is not irrevocably committed to any aspect of the feminine role she takes on. Of course, the decisions made in life have concrete consequences, as both girls and boys need to understand. But girls especially need to know that growth and change are not limited to a prescribed series of irrevocable events. In its own problematic way, *The Little Mermaid* is being used to explore female choice.

We will close with a brief but essential look at the ideological implications of certain literary allusions made in the film. In their shifting of the mermaid story to a father-daughter Oedipal tale, the makers of *The Little Mermaid* have consciously drown upon Shakespeare's *Tempest* (like the makers of *Forbidden Planet* [Wilcox, 1956] before them). It is always important to place the feminist perspective in the context of the often broader issues of ethnicity and nationality when analyzing films. The fact that TLM alludes to *The Tempest* immediately brings many such issues to light. Curiously, the one overt reference to that play also displaces its underlying structure: rather than naming the daughter "Miranda," after the daughter in *The Tempest*, the little mermaid is called "Ariel," after an airy sprite whom Prospero rescued from imprisonment in a tree.[29] Perhaps the Disney writers felt that the fairy-like Ariel (usually represented as male) better captured the essence of the half-animal mermaid. Ursula, of course, is playing both Antonio, Prospero's usurping brother who has taken his dukedom from him, and the (never-seen) misshapen witch, Sycorax, mother of the enslaved and hideous Caliban. In Shakespeare's play, Caliban's enslavement is partially rationalized by his "savagery" and by his attempt to rape Miranda, with the intent of impregnating her—in revenge for his exploitation by Prospero.

The sexual interdiction imposed on Caliban by Prospero may be paralleled to King Triton's hatred of humans, his disgust with the extreme form of exogamy (marrying outside the clan) that a union with men would entail. Thus, Prince Eric would be the unlikely Caliban figure. Another element of the film, however, brings us back to the New World sources of the play. We are presented with another "Caliban," in the form of Sebastian, the musical crab with a Jamaican accent appointed by King Triton to watch (Ariel-like) over his daughter, but who becomes her ally in trying to win the prince. Sebastian is both the happy-go-lucky "native" of these waters when he performs the calypso, "Under the Sea," and the potential victim of genocide during "Les Poissons," "a disturbing and cannibalistic comedy number in which the prince's chef cuts the heads off fish," boils crabs, and chases Sebastian with a knife (Harmetz, C22).

Various elements of the Sebastian character indicate that the political allegory traced by Caribbean critics in Shakespeare's New World (Caribbean) play was integrated almost intact into the Disney version of *The Little Mermaid*. Caliban, he of the misshapen body, is symbolically present in the liminal, "in-between" mermaid herself, who wants to change her monstrous, *"mestizo"* body.[30] Caliban is found, too, in the crab, Sebastian, the Caribbean native obliged to entertain even as his existence is threatened. In his eponymous essay, Robert Retamar reminds us that "Caliban" is Shakespeare's anagram for "cannibal," and that from that word comes the term "carib," the name of the native Caribbean Indians who have been all but wiped out for centuries (6). I have implied in the preceding that *The Little Mermaid*'s "cannibalism," the act of a species devouring or destroying itself, is indirectly aimed at the female body. The painful "cutting" of this body is not really absent from the film. Instead, as Ariel sits at dinner with Eric, unable to speak and barely touching her food, the "fishy" part of her body is being menaced in the kitchen. The cook chops fish with gusto and chases the "Caribbean" Sebastian, while the little mermaid, unaware of the assault her own desire has triggered, and which Sebastian must serve, smiles at her prince.

Works Cited

Advokat, Stephen. "Two video makers target games for girls 6 to 11 years of age." *Arizona Daily Star*. (May 10, 1991), p. E26.

Andersen, Hans Christian. *The Snow Queen and Other Tales*. Trans. Pat Shaw Iversen. New York: Signet, 1966.

Benjamin, Jessica. *The Bonds of Love: Psychoanalysis, Feminism, and the Problem of Domination*. New York: Pantheon Books, 1988.

Benwell, Gwen and Arthur Waugh. *Sea Enchantress*. New York: Citadel Press, 1965.

Bettelheim, Bruno. *The Uses of Enchantment: The Meaning and Importance of Fairy Tales*. New York: Alfred Knopf, 1976.

Boose, Lynda E. "The Father and the Bride in Shakespeare." *PMLA* 97:3 (1982), pp. 325–347.

194 / Split Skins

——— and Betty S. Flowers, ed. *Daughters and Fathers*. Baltimore: The Johns Hopkins University Press, 1988.

Byrd, Robert. "High school girls more likely than boys to see themselves as fat, survey finds." *Arizona Daily Star*. November 1, 1991, p. A12.

Calistro, Paddy. "A Modern Beauty." *L.A. Times*: Fashion/Screen Style Section. November 29, 1991, p. E8.

Camera Obscura 20/21, "The Spectatrix" (May–September 1989).

De Lauretis, Teresa. *Alice Doesn't: Feminism, Semiotics, Cinema*. Bloomington: Indiana University Press, 1984.

Dinnerstein, Dorothy. "*The Little Mermaid* and the Situation of the Girl." *Contemporary Psychoanalysis* 3 (1967), pp. 104–112.

Doane, Mary Ann. *The Desire to Desire: The Woman's Film of the 1940s*. Bloomington: Indiana University Press, 1987.

——— "Film and the Masquerade: Theorizing the Female Spectator." *Femmes Fatales: Feminism, Film Theory, Psychoanalysis*. New York: Routledge, 1991.

Doun, Liz. "Perfection: Teen-agers' quest leads to plastic surgery." *Arizona Daily Star*. September 24, 1991, pp. B5, 7.

Foucault, Michel. *The History of Sexuality, Volume I: An Introduction*. Trans. Robert Hurley. New York: Vintage, 1980.

Freud, Sigmund. *Collected Papers*. Five Volumes. Ed. James Strachey. Trans. Joan Riviere. New York: Basic Books, 1959.

——— " 'A Child is Being Beaten': A Contribution to the Origin of Sexual Perversions" (1919). *CP* 2, pp. 172–201.

——— "Female Sexuality" (1931). *CP* 5, pp. 252–272.

——— "Some Psychological Consequences of the Anatomical Distinction Between the Sexes" (1925). *CP* 5, pp. 186–197.

——— *The Standard Edition of the Complete Psychological Works*. Trans. James Strachey. London: Hogarth Press, 1953–1964.

——— "The Economic Problem of Masochism" (1924). *SE* 19, pp. 157–170.

——— "Femininity" (1933). *SE* 22, pp. 112–135.

——— "On Narcissism: An Introduction" (1914). *SE* 14, pp. 69–102.

——— "The 'Uncanny' " (1919). *SE* 17, pp. 219–252.

Hansen, Miriam. "Pleasure, Ambivalence, Identification: Valentino and Female Spectatorship." *Cinema Journal* 25: 4 (1986), pp. 6–32.

Harmetz, Aljean. "After the Lean Years, a Triumph." *New York Times*. December 11, 1989, pp. C13, 22.

Haskell, Molly. *From Reverence To Rape: The Treatment of Women in the Movies*. Chicago: University of Chicago Press, 1974. 2nd Edition, 1987.

Hollinger, Karen. " 'The Look,' Narrativity, and the Female Spectator in *Vertigo*." *Journal of Film and Video* 39: 7 (Fall, 1987), pp. 18–27.

Johnston, Claire. "Femininity and the Masquerade: *Anne of the Indies*." *Psychoanalysis and Cinema*. Ed. E. Ann Kaplan, New York: Routledge, 1990.

Kaplan, E. Ann. *Women in Film Noir*. London: BFI, 1978, 1980.

Kierkegaard, Søren. *Fear and Trembling* and *The Sickness Unto Death*. Trans. Walter Lowrie. Princeton: Princeton University Press, 1941, 1954.

Lacan, Jacques. *Female Sexuality*. Trans. Jacqueline Rose. Ed. and Intro. Juliet Mitchell and Jacqueline Rose. New York: Norton, 1982.

Lederer, Wolfgang. *The Kiss of the Snow Queen*. Berkeley: University of California Press, 1986.

Lévi-Strauss, Claude. *The Elementary Structures of Kinship*. Trans. James Harle Bell, John Richard von Sturmer, and Rodney Needham, ed. Boston: Beacon Press, 1969.

Marker, Frederick J. *Hans Christian Andersen and the Romantic Theater*. Toronto: University of Toronto Press, 1971.

Mayne, Judith. *The Woman at the Keyhole: Feminism and Women's Cinema*. Bloomington: Indiana University Press, 1990.

Modleski, Tania. *The Women Who Knew Too Much: Hitchcock and Feminist Theory*. New York: Methuen, 1988.

Mulvey, Laura. "Visual Pleasure and Narrative Cinema." Ed. Constance Penley. *Feminism and Film Theory*. New York: Routledge, 1988.

Retamar, Robert Fernández. *Caliban and Other Essays*. Trans. Edward Baker. Minneapolis: University of Minnesota Press, 1989.

Ridgeway, Karen. "Mermaids become the chic of the sea." *USA Today*. November 30, 1989, p. D1.

Riviere, Joan. "Womanliness as a Masquerade." *Psychoanalysis and Female Sexuality*. Ed. Hendrik M. Ruitenbeek. New Haven: College and University Press, 1966.

Silverman, Kaja. "Masochism and Subjectivity." *Framework* 12 (1980), pp. 2–9.

―――― *The Acoustic Mirror: The Female Voice in Psychoanalysis and Cinema*. Bloomington: Indiana University Press, 1988.

―――― "*Histoire d'O*: The Construction of a Female Subject." *enclitic* 7: 2 (1983), pp. 63–81.

―――― "Masochism and Male Subjectivity." *Camera Obscura* 17 (1988), pp.30–67.

―――― *The Subject of Semiotics*. New York: Oxford University Press, 1983.

―――― "White Skin, Brown Masks: The Double Mimesis, or With Lawrence in Arabia." *Differences* 1: 3 (1990) pp. 3–54.

Spillman, Susan. "Creating a 'Mermaid': The Body." *USA Today*. November 30, 1989, p. D2.

Studlar, Gaylyn. *In the Realm of Pleasure: Von Sternberg, Dietrich, and the Masochistic Aesthetic* (Urbana: University of Illinois Press, 1988).

Trites, Roberta. "Disney's Sub/Version of Andersen's 'The Little Mermaid.' " *Journal of Popular Film and Television* 18: 4 (Winter, 1991), pp. 145–152.

Turner, Victor. *A Forest of Symbols: Aspects of Ndembu Ritual*. Ithaca: Cornell University Press, 1967.

Woodward, Kathleen. "Youthfulness as a Masquerade." *Discourse* 11:1 (Fall–Winter 1988–89), pp. 119–142.

Zipes, Jack, ed. *Don't Bet on the Prince: Contemporary Feminist Fairy Tales in North America and England*. New York: Methuen, 1986.

Zwinger, Lynda. *Daughters, Fathers, and the Novel: The Sentimental Romance of Heterosexuality*. Madison: University of Wisconsin Press, 1991.

13

The Big Switch: Hollywood Masculinity in the Nineties

Susan Jeffords

In 1980, Annette Kolodny summarized what she perceived to be the three stages of feminist literary criticism until that point. After describing the first phase of rediscovering "previously lost or otherwise ignored works of women writers,"[1] and the second of establishing a "female counter-tradition" (500), she identifies a third phase of reading literature "as a social institution," (501) in which issues of gender, class, race, and other forms of social difference are understood in terms of the social constructs that shape and give them meaning. While Kolodny's history accurately describes the general emphases of feminist literary criticism until 1980, there is a further development in feminist criticism since that time that is not included in Kolodny's list: the shift from focusing upon women and women's issues to the study of gender, in particular, a shift toward including studies of men and masculinity.

During the 1980s, a "men's movement" was formed, modeled on the second wave of the women's movement in the United States and directed toward reassessing traditional roles and expectations for men's behavior in U.S. society. From this movement sprang discussion groups, therapeutic strategies, men's studies courses, conferences, music, artworks, newsletters, and magazines that took as their subject the question of men's changing roles in U.S. society. While figures like Robert Bly and Sam Keen are among the most prominent of this movement, the list of its contributors includes philosophers, sociologists, psychologists, artists, and Vietnam veterans.[2] Largely a movement oriented towards and encouraged by white, middle-class men, the men's movement gained, through the late 1980s, a wide degree of public attention and credibility.

Among feminist scholars, there existed some division as to the importance of the men's movement to addressing the issues of women and their socio-cultural environments. While most feminists agree that men should begin to take responsibility for assessing their own participation in the structures of gender oppression in this country, there is some disagreement about the role that feminists, especially feminist scholars, should play in that process. And while the majority of feminist research in this country continues to focus on the important questions of women's labor, reproductive rights, histories, racial and ethnic identities, economies, politics, and so on, there is an increasing understanding that many of the issues that affect women's lives cannot be adequately understood without a companion understanding of the intricate interrelationships between the constructions of women's and men's lives by and through the gender system.

This does not mean, however, that feminist scholars interested in questions of gender and masculinity envision themselves as participants in the men's movement. Instead, feminist discussions of masculinity generally take the shape of analyzing the ways masculinity is presented, how it is embedded in cultural narratives, how its structures and representations affect and shape the experiences of women and men, or what kinds of psychoanalytic narratives it offers.[3] As a continuation of these efforts, I would like to offer the following analysis of Hollywood filmic presentations of masculinity in the 1980s and the changes suggested by a group of 1991 films about how masculinity is to be understood.

1991 was the year of the transformed U.S. man. There's hardly a mainstream Hollywood film from that year with a significant male role that does not in some ways reinforce an image that the hard-fighting, weapon-wielding, independent, muscular, and heroic men of the eighties—Rambo (Sylvester Stallone), Colonel Braddock (Chuck Norris), Dirty Harry (Clint Eastwood), John McClane (Bruce Willis), Martin Riggs (Mel Gibson), Indiana Jones (Harrison Ford), Superman (Christopher Reeve)—have disappeared and are being replaced by the more sensitive, loving, nurturing, protective family men of the nineties. In 1991 films like *Regarding Henry* (Mike Nichols), *Terminator 2: Judgment Day* (James Cameron), *One Good Cop* (Heywood Gould), *Doctor* (Randa Haines), *The Fisher King* (Terry Gilliam), *City Slickers* (Ron Underwood), *Switch* (Blake Edwards), even Walt Disney's *Beauty and the Beast*, a changed image of U.S. masculinity is being presented, an image that suggests that the hard-bodied male action heroes of the eighties have given way to a "kinder, gentler" U.S. manhood, one that is sensitive, generous, caring, and, perhaps most importantly, capable of change. It is, as Janet Maslin says of *Regarding Henry*, that the films contribute to "a coming cinematic vogue," in which the male characters are "ready to reassess the mad excesses of 80's materialism from an aggressively mellow 90's point of view."[4] This is the man of the nineties, U.S. gender culture's response to feminism, civil rights, and a declining Cold Warrior validation. While eighties men may have muscled their way into our hearts, killing anyone who got in the way, nineties men are going to seize us with kindness and declarations that they are changed, "new men."

One of the most important features of these films is their portrayal of male bodies. Eighties films gave audiences close-ups of Rambo's throbbing biceps (though it was admittedly hard to tell exactly what they were at the time), contrived plot opportunities for Chuck Norris to remove his shirt (it always seemed to be hot in the movies where he lived), a naked and powerful Arnold Schwarzenegger lit by the afterglow of a post-nuclear future, a Martin Riggs whose entire body was a "lethal weapon" (especially lethal to women—evey woman he had sex with got killed), and an astoundingly durable Bruce Willis, whose body withstood broken glass, explosions, beatings, and falls from airplanes to still catch the bad guys. When, in *Lethal Weapon* (Richard Donner, 1987), the evil mercenaries declare with arrogance that "there are no heroes anymore," audiences are triumphant as Martin Riggs crashes through the door and puts a halt to their drug-smuggling and kidnapping days. Having withstood the expert torture of the foreign Endo, Riggs's lethal body appears to remind audiences that, if there is anything heroic left in American culture, it rests in male bodies like these.[5]

But there's no one crashing through the doors in 1991. Instead, many nineties Hollywood men get doors slammed in their faces, or they are forced to stand patiently outside them while the women inside decide whether to see them or not. (The teapot and chipped cup can get into Beauty's room, but the Beast cannot.) What has happened to those lethal bodies that could have kicked down any door? (Or think of the fascination so many eighties action-adventure films had with men smashing through plate glass windows—*Stick, Lethal Weapon 2, Die Hard, Terminator,* and so on; nothing could stop these men.) What, in other words, happened to the male body in 1991? Or, perhaps more directly, what happened to the manhood shaped by that body, the masculinity that it seemed nothing could stop?

To answer these questions, let me move back one year, to a 1990 film that shows explicitly the transitions between the manhood of the eighties and this "new" manhood of the nineties—*Kindergarten Cop* (Ivan Reitman). As in so many cases, Arnold Schwarzenegger seems to have tapped into the tempo of U.S. culture slightly ahead of his compatriot hero-actors. *Kindergarten Cop* in fact makes possible the changes Schwarzenegger's character will undergo in *Terminator 2,* where he plays a protective and nurturing robot instead of the relentlessly lethal one he created for *Terminator* (James Cameron, 1984). For in *Kindergarten Cop,* Schwarzenegger doesn't just act as if the changes have already taken place (in

Terminator 2 it's already been reprogrammed at the start of the movie), he lets us witness how and why they happen. He offers a cultural key to the refiguring of U.S. manhood in the nineties.

At the beginning the the film, John Kimball *is* the eighties man, the lethal weapon *par excellence*. He's a tough, unshaved, brutal, determined police officer who holds the single-minded goal of imprisoning Cullen Crisp, an expert drug-dealer and murderer who is backed up by his evil, overprotective mother. When legal police procedures prevent his partner from detaining the only witness to Crisp's crime, Kimball chases after her on his own, breaking down doors, blowing away furniture with a special-make shotgun, and brutalizing anyone who comes between him and his witness. For Kimball, as for all eighties action-adventure heroes, the legal system is only an impediment to getting things done and putting criminals away. Kimball is a loner, a single-minded law officer who writes the rules as he goes along, a tough guy who needs no family or partners, and a brutal, violent, and unfeeling man. He is, in other words, the typical eighties hero.

But by the end of the film, Kimball has given up being a police officer in favor of teaching kindergarten. He has broken through his emotional barriers to tell Joyce, another teacher, that he doesn't want to lose her or her son, Dominic. He feels guilty when he punches an abusive father and promises from now on to use the law to get such men. His life is most threatened, not by another super-macho, special combat male enemy (like Mr. Joshua in *Lethal Weapon*), but by a determined mother who is out to revenge the death of her son. And his life is saved, not by a fancy weapon or an effective body blow, but by his partner, a short woman with a baseball bat. What happened to turn that relentless, law-making, brutalizing cop into a nurturing, playful, and loving kindergarten teacher?

It takes only one word: Family. John Kimball, the cop, once had a wife and child, but his wife left him many years ago and has since remarried a "nice man" who now raises Kimball's son. One of the reasons Kimball devotes his life to police work is simply that he has no other life to which to go. He has, audiences are invited to psychologize, used the violence and confrontation of his job to block out the pain he feels about the loss of his family. It is only when he is reintroduced to children (who are coincidentally about the age of his son when they were separated), that he begins to remember this pain and realize how the loss has affected his life. When his police assignment invites him not only to have contact with another mother and son but to guard and protect them from the sadistic Crisp, Kimball's lost-family emotions are given full play, and he learns that he does not want to lose yet another opportunity to have a family. Consequently, when all the bad guys are caught and Kimball's battle wounds have begun to heal, he returns, not to the police station to tag yet another criminal, but to his newly found family and the life of a full-time father, both as parent and as kindergarten teacher. The message? The emotionally whole and physically healed man of the eighties wants nothing more than to be a father, not a warrior/cop, after all.

Kindergarten Cop anticipates the endings of many 1991 films that are resolved through a man's return to his family. When the character played by Billy Crystal in *City Slickers* finds himself on a cattle ranch and discovers the meaning of life, the "one thing" he learns is that he must return to his family, accompanied by his own "child," a calf that he birthed on the trail and subsequently saved from the slaughterhouse. Michael Keaton's character in *One Good Cop* is excused for the crime of theft that he committed and is welcomed back onto the police force because he took the money in order to provide a house for his family. Steve Brooks (Perry King/Ellen Barkin) gains a pardon for his treatment of women and entrance into heaven when s/he gives birth to a daughter in *Switch*. And even though the Terminator "dies" in *Terminator 2*, it does so to insure the survival of its new family, Sarah and John Connor. In these films, families provide both the motivation for and the resolution of changing masculine heroisms.

In addition to laying the outline for the male transformation of the nineties, *Kindergarten Cop* identifies how the issues of manhood are to be addressed and defined in the next decade. One of the clearest messages to come out of *Kindergarten Cop* is that the tough, hard-driving, violent, and individualistic man of the eighties is not like that by choice. Kimball was, like the police officer of *One Good Cop*, the radio announcer of *The Fisher King*, the lawyer of *Regarding Henry*, or even the machine-programmed Terminator, trying to do his job, and doing it the way the job had been defined by a social-climbing, crime-conscious, techno-consumer society. The problem all these men confront in their narratives is that they did their jobs too well, at the expense of their relationships with their families. Spending so much time tracking criminals and making money left little time for having, let alone raising, children or relating to, let alone meeting, women. And, as *Kindergarten Cop* makes so clear, while these men were doing their jobs, they were unhappy, lonely, and often in pain.

Retroactively, the men of the eighties are being given feelings, feelings that were, presumably, hidden behind their confrontational violence. While eighties action-adventure films gloried in spectacular scenes of destruction, nineties films are telling audiences that these men were actually being self-destructive. (The extent to which audiences are responding to this message can be seen in the difference between many female viewers' reactions to Mel Gibson's character in *Lethal Weapon*: in 1988, they spoke of Gibson's sex appeal; in 1992, they are touched by Martin Rigg's expressions of pain at his wife's death.) At the cost of their personal and family lives, eighties heroes were rescuing armies, corporations, and ancient artifacts. Now, they're out to save themselves.

But didn't they bring all this loneliness and suffering on themselves? Weren't they the ones who picked up the guns and went for the high-powered jobs? Weren't they the ones who spent time at the office (or firing range) instead of home? According to these films, not exactly. To return to one of the prototypical action-adventure sequences of the eighties, the *Rambo* films, at the beginning of each narrative, Rambo is minding his own business when someone else—either government or local law enforcement—forces him to engage in his heroic acts. In *Rambo 3* (1988) he even refuses, until the Soviets make the issue, as they say in *Lethal Weapon 2*, "personal"—situations in which the heroes can't turn their backs on their friends and family. So even the narratives that the nineties films are challenging had already carved out a space for their heroes that allowed them always to be reacting to some outside force rather than acting from their own internal needs for violence or action. In each case, it was their jobs, their nations, or their friends who made it necessary to enter into these violent confrontations. It was not, these films conclude, the wishes of the men themselves.

But many nineties films go even farther than this, suggesting that it wasn't just the jobs or social obligations that brought these men to betray their own feelings and families. It was, in an odd way, their very bodies themselves, those heroic exteriors that made it possible for them to do what other people couldn't. One of the plot features of a number of nineties films is a discovery by the male lead that his body has failed him in some way, whether through wounds, disease, or programming. The body that he thought was "his," the body he had been taught to value as fulfilling some version of a masculine heroic ideal—suddenly that body became transformed into a separate entity that was betraying the true internal feelings of the man it contained. *Robocop 2* (Irvin Kershner) led the way here in 1990 by showing the distress brought about in its hero's life by the conflicts between Robocop's bullet-proof exterior and his memories of his family. The indestructible body that was to make Robocop invincible led not to a machine-like insensitivity but to deep pain and isolation at the loss of love. *Robocop* makes clear that behind the tough bodies of these male heroes lies, not cheap insensitivity and lusty brutality, but a caring, troubled, and suffering individual. In 1991, though the Terminator had been reprogrammed to protect John Connor and had been ordered not to hurt humans, it had to destroy itself, not because it was afraid that its "feelings" for humanity would change, but because a piece of its body—

a computer chip—could be used to rebuild Skynet and destroy all human life. And though the Beast wanted love and companionship, its horrific body and mystical curse doomed it to live alone and unloved until someone could see past that body to the "true" man inside. But what 1991 films provide that *Robocop* did not is a happy ending, where the betrayed body is transformed, either back to its "original" loving owner, or into a body that is now in tune with the internal goodness that the film's narrative has revealed. One of the best examples of this theme of bodily betrayal and internal revelations is in Blake Edwards's 1991 comedy, *Switch*.

As even a brief summary of the plot reveals, *Switch* competes with *Beauty and the Beast* for the prize of the most extreme body transformation of 1991. Steve Brooks, practiced and successful womanizer, is killed by three women he had affairs with. While the male half of God is willing to admit Steve into Heaven, the female half insists that he prove himself worthy or go to Hell. At the advice of the Devil, they send him back to life with the command that he find "one female who truly likes Steve Brooks," with the catch that he is returned as a woman. Through his experiences "as a woman," Steve Brooks learns how difficult it is for a woman to live and work in a sexist environment. When s/he is raped by Steve's best friend (non-consensual sex), s/he becomes pregnant and gives birth to a daughter who, as you might have guessed, truly likes Steve Brooks, and he goes to heaven.

Like Robocop and the Beast, Steve Brooks is betrayed by his own body. Confined in the stereotypical form of a swinging bachelor, Steve fulfills its edicts by treating women only as sexual conquests, using them for his own pleasure, for the gratification of his clients and business associates, or for the promotion of the products his advertising firm contracts to sell. He doesn't know that the women he uses are miserable, or that they universally hate him. It seems that no one ever taught Steve Brooks any differently. Steve's curse is twofold: he must find a female who likes him, and he must learn to think differently about women. In order to do this, he has to change.

When Steve first returns to life as a woman, he views his body as he had those of all the women he had known: as an object. Appraising himself in a mirror, Steve, now Amanda ("A-Man-da"), describes him/herself to Walter: "I'm blond, about 5' 7", and built like a brick shithouse." And when s/he meets Walter in a bar, s/he says that s/he's Amanda "in the flesh. And what about that flesh, huh? So what do you think? Did you get a good look at my legs?" But after having an idea stolen by his/her boss, having construction workers ogle her/him, and learning that *no* woman likes the way she had been treated by Steve, Amanda tells a co-worker who comes on to her/him, "I'll tell you why I'm so pissed off, buddy-boy! I'm sick and tired of being treated like a piece of meat!" For the first time in the movie, audiences are to believe, Steve Brooks is actually *in* a woman's body. S/he has begun the transformation that will gain Steve Brooks entrance into heaven.

As the film goes on, Amanda becomes more of a woman. S/he experiences what it is like to have sex only for a man's desire. Awakening after a drunken night with Walter, he informs her that they had sex. Because s/he has no recollection of the event, Amanda declares that Walter raped her while s/he was unconscious. And in the film's climactic representation of what it must be like to inhabit a woman's body, Amanda feels the pains of childbirth. At that moment, when s/he realizes that his/her daughter likes her/him, s/he undergoes a miraculous transformation: through Amanda, Steve Brooks gives birth to his new self and enters heaven.

To insure that the film is challenging categories of gender and not of sexuality, Steve Brooks is consistently coded as heterosexual. When Amanda tries to have sex with Sheila Faxton in order to secure a multi-million dollar account for the firm, s/he is unable to do so, even though the experience of having sex with a woman would have been familiar to him/her as Steve. But as Margo, the women who killed Steve, explains to Steve/Amanda: "You are a macho homophobic. . . . And gay, male or female, scares the living hell out of you." And while the plot twist of date-rape helps to create the image of Amanda's raised consciousness about being a woman, it also insures that Amanda can become pregnant without having to have sex with a man, a far too explicitly homosexual scene for the film to depict. Though there is no hesitation about showing Amanda and Sheila kissing, Walter and Amanda/Steve can never kiss. The film's anxiety is explicitly about male and not female homosexuality, indicating that the film is less about its ostensible topic of "women's liberation" than about masculine identity. Steve Brooks is, after all, still a man in a woman's body, not really a woman at all.

The date-rape scene is important for another reason. Narratively, the scene is meant to be the capping instance of Steve Brooks's education about how women feel. Not only has he had to learn about what it feels like to be ogled at, pawed, and propositioned, but he now must learn what it is like to have a man take advantage of a woman's body without her consent and solely for the gratification of his own desires. He must learn, in other words, about what he has done to other women. But the amnesia at the center of this scene—Walter remembers having sex, but Amanda remembers nothing—makes its message complicated. Certainly, it would be difficult for Steve Brooks to remember having sex with his best male friend, even if he is in a woman's body. But Steve's lessons about what it feels like to be in a woman's body stop short here when he can't remember the most significant confrontation in the film between male and female bodies—sex that is unwanted by a woman can still be forced by a man.

Now, if Walter, the "good" man of the film, can commit date-rape, then what are audiences to imagine about Steve Brooks, the "bad" man of the plot, who made his reputation by using every woman he met? We can, I think, only surmise that Steve Brooks was himself at some time guilty of date-rape, principally because, as the Gods tell us, he never cared about the feelings of the women he was with. If Walter is made to hear Steve's/Amanda's outraged anger about the unwanted sex, why is Steve Brooks let off with no reprimand or even recognition here?

Because, this and other films tell us, Steve Brooks does not have to take responsibility for his past actions. He only has to change in the present and future in order for a happy ending to occur. The logic seems indisputable: because they've been trapped in bodies not of their own making, men don't have to take responsibility for the acts those bodies have committed—the terror they have applied, the profit they have gained, or the consequences their acts have had on others. Steve Brooks does not set about making amends to the women he has harmed. In fact, the film goes to lengths to show that the women he has known are themselves often shallow and self-serving as well, as in the case of the model who had sex with Steve in order to get on the cover of a magazine. The plots suggest that it is the men themselves who have suffered the most from their behaviors, having their lives taken away from them and placed in different bodies. Consequently, they're not called upon to repair the damage they've done—it's not, after all, all that severe. They have only to become *aware*, of themselves and their needs to change.

Transformations are certainly nothing new in Hollywood cinema. From vampire movies to alien takeovers, movies have been populated by people whose bodies have ceased to become their own and whose minds are being controlled by an external force. In most cases, much of the horror-effect these films produce is that these possessed bodies look no different than the "normal" ones that people inhabited before. From the early Cold War era *Invasion of the Body Snatchers* (1956) to the late Cold War era *Alien* (1979), much of these films' suspense surrounded the effort to try and tell if and when someone had been transformed.

Not so with these new body shifters. Here, it is the external body that is drastically changed, while the internal self remains the same. That self changes only as it learns, by living in its transformed body, how to love and how to produce love in another.

But while women in those earlier horror films were just as subject as men to being taken over by a pod, or infested with an alien creature, these new transformations happen only to men. More specifically, heterosexual white men, the men whose profit from traditional masculinities seems most threatened by the changing economic and social marketplace that typifies U.S. culture of the nineties. What Elayne Rapping calls these "white boy adventures"[6] suggest that it is largely white men who have suffered from the burdens of traditional masculinities, and white men who have to be given this extra help in learning how to change themselves into "better" people.

And while many 1991 films by black male directors about black men's lives emphasize families and masculinities as well—*Boyz N the Hood* (John Singleton), *Straight Out of Brooklyn* (Matty Rich), *Jungle Fever* (Spike Lee)—the thematics of internalization and bodily betrayal are not present as they are in Hollywood films about white male leads, largely because the action-adventure heroism of the eighties was never meant to figure black men's bodies in the first place. While, for example, Martin Riggs (Mel Gibson) *is* the "lethal weapon" in the films named for his body, Roger Murtaugh's body (Danny Glover) is never depicted as "lethal" at all. Audiences' first shot of him is in a bathtub, surrounded by his loving family, all of whom tell him he looks old. And Riggs has to insist that Murtaugh shoot, not to maim, but to kill, since the enemies you maim always come back to haunt you. Under Riggs's tutelage, Murtaugh is able, at the end of *Lethal Weapon 2*, to fire point blank and kill the chief enemy of the film, Argen Rudd, a South African diplomat whose immunity, Murtaugh declares, has just been "revoked." The safe, non-lethal, aging image of an African-American police officer who kills only when provoked by true evil is an appealing screen character for white mainstream audiences who can be assured that assimilated black men will enforce rather than challenge U.S. systems. Murtaugh does not have to "discover" his feelings for or through a family, since he has one intact at the beginning of the film. His job, or, more pointedly, his masculinity, has not taken him away from his family, largely because, such films imply (the *Die Hard* series is another example), he has not been out saving countries, artifacts, or corporations. He has not, in other words, been carrying the white man's burden, or, by implication, his masculinity.

There is, consequently, a dangerous racial subtext to all this Hollywood body shifting and internal reform. As has historically been the case in dominant U.S. cultures, masculinity is defined in and through the white male body. Action films of the eighties reinforce these assumptions in their characterizations of heroism, individualism, and bodily integrity as centered in the white body. And though nineties films repudiate many of the characteristics of that body—its violence, its isolation, its lack of emotion, and its presence—it does not challenge the whiteness of that body, nor the "special" figuration that body demands. If, these films suggest, there is a body that has been betrayed, victimized, burdened by the society that surrounds it, it is not the body of color, the body that has been historically marked by the continuous betrayals of a social, political, and cultural system that has marginalized and abused it. It is, instead, the body of the white man who is suffering because he has been unloved.

So what's so wrong with all this? Obviously, I've been objecting throughout this essay to the idea that men should be viewed as special victims of U.S. gender cultures. But isn't it possible that these films have a positive message as well? Wouldn't it seem logical for a feminist to approve of films that insist that white men must change? That they must give up their violence, physical intimidation, insensitivity, and dominance? Isn't it possible that male viewers would look upon these films as providing confirmation of some men's sense that they would like to alter their lives but don't quite know how? Or that female viewers would gain a sense from these films that they *do* have something to teach men and that men might listen?

Yes, I'm sure that these impressions run through these films, and that the narratives of masculine transformation may well supply an alternative for many viewers to the current gender systems that operate in this country. I know that many men view positively films about crises and changes in masculinity that women do not often see in the same ways. Many men, for example, responded in different ways than women to Brian DePalma's 1989 film, *Casualties of War*. While most women I talked to identified with Oanh, the Vietnamese woman kidnapped and raped by several U.S. soldiers during the Vietnam War, many men identified with Private Eriksson, the only man who refused to participate in the rape and who eventually testified against his fellow soldiers. Many men described the film as offering the possibility that men could maintain moral and ethical positions that necessitated denying not only other men but many of the traditional codes of masculinity—violence, the possession of women, comradeship, loyalty. Though I do not share these film experiences, I understand that many men do seek in films possible models for or confirmations of their own desires for change. The lessons learned about sexism by Steve Brooks, the recognition in *City Slickers* that family is more important than male-bonding, *Terminator 2*'s awareness of male participation in the production of nuclear warfare, John Kimball's commitment to children rather than criminals—each of these can be viewed as a positive experience for many male viewers who are struggling with similar issues in their own lives.

At the same time, for me, as a feminist viewer, these films hold a different message. Donna Haraway explains in an interview that "the image of the sensitive man calls up, for me, the male person who, while enjoying the position of unbelievable privilege, also has the privilege of gentleness."[7] And this is finally what troubles me most about these films and the cultural arguments they represent: that the transformations undergone by white male characters do nothing to address the consequences of the privileges associated with white U.S. masculinities. When restored to his human form, the Prince/Beast retains his castle and holdings and the class, economic, and social profits that accompany them. And in *Switch*, Amanda steps quickly into Steve Brooks's former job, arguing for an increased salary because she, unlike Steve, can give the boss a "hard-on." There is no discussion of the circumstances that so often prevent women from holding jobs like Steve Brooks's or that place them in the positions more usually associated with women in the film, that of secretary, model, or waitress.

Finally, these men do not have to take responsibility for their past actions, or acknowledge the systemic structures that so often dictate the treatment of men and women as socially, economically, and culturally different. Their histories as men are limited to their personal sufferings at the hands of traditional codes of masculinity, and their messages of change remain at the level of individualized experience within the interpersonal realm. Steve Brooks never apologizes to the women he has harmed. John Kimball never repudiates his brutal cop tactics (he does acknowledge that it's inappropriate to use violence in front of children). *One Good Cop* ends with the reinstatement and acceptance of an embezzling police officer who gets to keep the house he bought with drug money. And the Terminator has simply been reprogrammed; the problem is not the Terminator's but Sarah Connor's, who almost gets killed by the T1000 because she assumes—based on his bodily image—that the Terminator is the "same" as it was before. In these scenes, Sarah Connor is the audience's emblem. Like her, we are to learn that, if we want to have a future, we cannot judge men by their bodies alone.

Perhaps more importantly, their futures after transformation are left, to say the least, vague. Steve Brooks finally enters Heaven, and John Kimball enters the idyllic world of Astoria, Oregon. The Beast dances off into a Disney future, and *The Fisher King*'s male heroes become naked cloud-watchers in the middle of Central Park. In none of these scenarios does there seem the promise that these revised men will do anything to alter the social structures that affected them and the people surrounding them. Instead, it is understood that they will devote their times to improving their personal lives and the stability of their families. Just as they have abandoned the external bodies that defined them in the eighties, these new men of the nineties are turning away from the external concerns of government, law, international drug cartels, militarism, and crime that occupied their time and energy in the eighties. Their focus now is on the improvements of their "internal" selves: their health, their emotions, their families, and their homes.

It is just this divided interpretation of these films that poses one of the most important issues for feminist criticism. Critics such as Teresa de Lauretis, Trinh T. Minh-ha, Chandra Mohanty, and Cherrié Moraga have been insisting for some time that feminist interpretations take into account the differing positionalities and often contradictory identifications that women of varied racial, ethnic, sexual, social, economic, geographical, and political contexts bring to cinematic experiences. These same kinds of arguments must be explored as well in relation to the varied experiences of men and women as they interact with the cultural messages conveyed through Hollywood's visions.

14

Between Apocalypse and Redemption: John Singleton's *Boyz N the Hood*

Michael Eric Dyson

By now the dramatic decline in black male life has become an unmistakable feature of our cultural landscape—though of course the causes behind the desperate condition of black men date much further back than its recent popular discovery. Every few months, new reports and conferences attempt to explain the poverty, disease, despair, and death that shove black men toward social apocalypse.

If these words appear too severe or hyperbolic, the statistics testify to the trauma. For black men between the ages of 18 and 29, suicide is the leading cause of death. Between 1980 and 1985, the life expectancy for white males increased from 63 to 74.6 years, but only from 59 to 65 years for black males. Between 1973 and 1986, the real earnings of black males between the ages of 18 and 29 fell 31 percent as the percentage of young black males in the workforce plummeted 20 percent. The number of black men who dropped out of the workforce altogether doubled from 13 to 25 percent.

By 1989, almost 32 percent of black men between 16 and 19 were unemployed, compared to 16 percent of white men. And while blacks comprise only 12 percent of the nation's population, they make up 48 percent of the prison population, with men accounting for 89 percent of the black prison population. Only 14 percent of the white males who live in large metropolitan areas have been arrested, but the percentage for black males is 51 percent. And while 3 percent of white men have served time in prison, 18 percent of black men have been behind bars.[1]

Most chillingly, black-on-black homicide is the leading cause of death for black males between the ages of 15 and 34. Or to put it another way: "One out of every 21 black American males will be murdered in their lifetime. Most will die at the hands of another black male." These words appear in stark white print on the dark screen that opens John Singleton's masterful new film, *Boyz N The Hood* (1991). These words are both summary and opening salvo in Singleton's battle to reinterpret and redeem the black male experience. With *Boyz N The Hood* we have the most brilliantly executed and fully realized portrait yet of the coming-of-age odyssey that black boys must undertake in the suffocating conditions of urban decay and civic chaos.

Singleton adds color and depth to Michael Schultz's groundbreaking *Cooley High* (1975), extends the narrative scope of the Hudlin Brothers' important and humorous *House Party* (1990), and creates a stunning complement to Gordon Parks's pioneering *The Learning Tree* (1969), which traced the painful pilgrimage to maturity of a rural black male. Singleton's treatment of the various elements of contemporary black urban experience—gang violence, drug addiction, black male-female relationships, domestic joys and pains, friendships—is subtle and complex. He layers narrative textures over gritty and compelling visual slices of black culture that show us what it means to come to maturity, or die trying, as a black male.

Singleton's noteworthy attempt to present a richly hued, skillfully nuanced portrait of black male life is rare in the history of American film. Along with the seminal work of Spike Lee, and the recently expanded body of black film created by Charles Burnett, Robert Townsend, Keenan Wayans, Euhzan Palcy, Matty Rich, Mario Van Peebles, Ernest Dickerson, Bill Duke, Charles Lane, Reginald and Warrington Hudlin, Doug McHenry and George Jackson, and Julie Dash, Singleton symbolizes a new generation of black filmmakers whose artistic visions of African-American and American life may influence understandings of black worldviews, shape crucial perceptions of the sheer diversity of black communities, and address substantive racial, social, and political issues.

A major task, therefore, of African-American film criticism is to understand black film production in its historical, political, socio-economic, ideological, and cultural contexts. Such critical analysis has the benefit of generating plausible explanations of how black film developed; what obstacles it has faced in becoming established as a viable and legitimate means of representing artistic, cultural, and racial perspectives on a range of personal and social issues; the ideological and social conditions which stunted its growth, shaped its emergence and enabled its relatively recent success; the economic and political forces which limited the material and career options of black filmmakers, and constrained the opportunities for black artists to flourish and develop in a social environment hostile to black artistic production.

Another task of African-American film criticism is to provide rigorous tools of analysis, categories of judgment, and modes of evaluation that view the artistic achievements of black filmmakers in light of literary criticism, moral philosophy, feminist theory, intellectual history, cultural studies, and poststructuralist theory. African-American film criticism is not a hermetically sealed intellectual discourse that generates insight by limiting its range of intellectual reference to film theory, or to African-American culture, in interpreting the themes, ideas, and currents of African-American film. Rather, African-American film criticism draws from the seminal insights of a variety of intellectual traditions in understanding and explaining the genealogy, scope, and evolution of black artistic expression. In short, black film criticism does not posit or constitute a rigidly defined sphere of academic analysis or knowledge production, but calls into question regimented conceptions of disciplinary boundaries while promoting the overlapping and interpenetration of diverse areas of intellectual inquiry.

Finally, African-American film criticism is related to the larger task of sustaining a just, enabling, but rigorous African-American cultural criticism that revels in black culture's virtues, takes pleasure in its achievements, laments its failed opportunities, and interrogates its weaknesses. African-American cultural criticism is intellectually situated to disrupt, subvert, and challenge narrow criticisms or romantic celebrations of black culture. A healthy African-American cultural criticism views black folk not as mere victims in and of history, but as its resourceful co-creators and subversive regenerators. It understands black people as agents of their own jubilation and pain. It sees them, in varying degrees and in limited manner, as crafters of their own destinies, active participants in the construction of worlds of meaning through art, thought, and sport that fend off threatening enclosure by the ever-enlarging kingdom of absurdity. In this light, African-American film criticism pays attention to, and carefully evaluates, the treatment of crucial aspects of black culture in black films. Singleton's film addresses one of the most urgent and complex problems facing African-American communities: the plight of black men.

We have only begun to understand the pitfalls that attend the path of the black male. Social theory has only recently fixed its gaze on the specific predicament of black men in relation to the crisis of American capital, positing how their lives are shaped by structural changes in the political economy, for instance, rather than viewing them as the latest examples of black cultural pathology.[2] And social psychology has barely explored the deeply ingrained and culturally reinforced self-loathing and chronic lack of self-esteem that characterizes black males across age group, income bracket, and social location.

Even less have we understood the crisis of black males as rooted in childhood and adolescent obstacles to socio-economic stability, and moral, psychological, and emotional development. We have just begun to pay attention to specific rites of passage, stages of personality growth, and milestones of psycho-emotional evolution that measure personal response to racial injustice, social disintegration, and class oppression.

James P. Comer and Alvin F. Poussaint's *Black Child Care*, Marian Wright Edelman's *Families in Peril*, and Darlene and Derek Hopson's foundational *Different and Wonderful* are among the exceptions which address the specific needs of black childhood and adolescence. Jewelle Taylor Gibb's edited work, *Young, Black and Male in America: An Endangered Species* has recently begun to fill a gaping void in social-scientific research on the crisis of the black male.

In the last decade, however, alternative presses have vigorously probed the crisis of the black male. Like their black independent film peers, authors of volumes published by black independent presses often rely on lower budgets for advertising, marketing, and distribution. Nevertheless, word-of-mouth discussion of several books has sparked intense debate. Nathan and Julia Hare's *Bringing the Black Boy to Manhood: The Passage*, Jawanza Kunjufu's trilogy *The Conspiracy to Destroy Black Boys*, Amos N. Wilson's *The Development Psychology of The Black Child*, Baba Zak A. Kondo's *For Homeboys Only: Arming and Strengthening Young Brothers for Black Manhood*, and Haki Madhubuti's *Black Men: Obsolete, Single, Dangerous?* have had an important impact on significant subsections of literate black culture, most of whom share an Afrocentric perspective.

Such works remind us that we have too infrequently understood the black male crisis through coming-of-age narratives, and a set of shared social values that ritualize the process of the black adolescent's passage into adulthood. Such narratives and rites serve a dual function: they lend meaning to childhood experience, and they preserve and transmit black cultural values across the generations. Yet such narratives evoke a state of maturity—rooted in a vital community—that young black men are finding elusive or all too often, impossible to reach. The conditions of extreme social neglect that beseige urban black communities—in every realm from health care to education to poverty and joblessness—make the black male's passage into adulthood treacherous at best.

One of the most tragic symptoms of the young black man's troubled path to maturity is the skewed and strained state of gender relations within the black community. With alarming frequency, black men turn to black women as scapegoats for their oppression, lashing out—often with physical violence at those closest to them. It is the singular achievement of Singleton's film to redeem the power of the coming-of-age narrative while also adapting it to probe many of the very tensions that evade the foundations of the coming-of-age experience in the black community.

While mainstream American culture has only barely begun to register awareness of the true proportions of the crisis, young black males have responded on the last decade primarily in a rapidly flourishing independent popular culture, dominated by two genres: rap music and black film. The rap music of Run D.M.C., Public Enemy, Boogie Down Productions, Kool Moe Dee, N.W.A., Ice Cube and Ice T., and the films of Spike Lee, Robert Townsend, and now Matty Rich and Mario Van Peebles, have afforded young black males a medium to visualize and verbalize their perspectives on a range of social, personal, and cultural issues, to tell their stories about themselves and each other while the rest of America consumes and eavesdrops.

John Singleton's new film makes a powerful contribution to this enterprise. Singleton filters his brilliant insights, critical comments, and compelling portraits of young black male culture through a film that reflects the sensibilities, styles, and attitudes of rap culture.[3] Singleton's shrewd casting of rapper Ice Cube as a central character allows him to seize symbolic capital from a real life rap icon, while tailoring the violent excesses of Ice Cube's rap persona into a jarring visual reminder of the cost paid by black males for survival in American society. Singleton skillfully integrates the suggestive fragments of critical reflections on the black male predicament in several media and presents a stunning vision of black male pain and possibility in a catastrophic environment: South Central Los Angeles.

Of course, South Central Los Angeles is an already storied geography in the American social imagination. It has been given cursory—though melodramatic—treatment by news anchor Tom Brokaw's glimpse of gangs in a highly publicized 1988 TV special, and mythologized in Dennis Hopper's film about gang warfare, *Colors* (1988). Hopper, who perceptively and provocatively helped probe the rough edges of anomie and rebellion for a whole generation of outsiders in 1969's *Easy Rider*, less successfully traces the genealogy of social despair, postmodern urban absurdity and longing for belonging that provides the context for understanding gang violence. Singleton's task in part, therefore, is a filmic demythologization of the reigning tropes, images, and metaphors that have expressed the experience of life in South Central Los Angeles. While gangs are a central part of the urban landscape, they are not its exclusive reality. And though gang warfare occupies a looming periphery in Singleton's film, it is not the defining center.

Unquestionably, the 1991 urban rebellions in Los Angeles following the Rodney King verdict have given new poignancy to Singleton's depiction of the various personal, social and economic forces which shape the lives of the residents of South Central L.A. His film was an incandescent and prescient portrait of the simmering stew of social angers—aimed at police brutality, steeply declining property values, poverty and virile racism—

which aggravate an already aggrieved community and which force hard social choices on neighborhoods (do we riot in our own backyards; do we maliciously target Korean businesses, especially since the case of Latasha Harlins, a black teenager murdered by a Korean grocer, who was simply given five years' probation; and do we destroy community businesses and bring the charge of senseless destruction of resources in our own community when in reality, before the riots, we were already desperate, poor and invisible, and largely unaided by the legitimate neighborhood business economy?) amounting to little more than communal triage. Singleton's film proves, in retrospect, a powerful meditation upon the blight of gang violence, hopelessness, familial deterioration and economic desperation which conspire to undermine and slowly but surely destroy the morale and structure of many urban communities, particularly those in South Central L.A.

Boyz N The Hood is a painful and powerful look at the lives of black people, mostly male, who live in a lower middle-class neighborhood in South Central Los Angeles. It is a story of relationships—of kin, friendship, community, love, rejection, contempt, and fear. At the story's heart are three important relationships: a triangular relationship between three boys, whose lives we track to mature adolescence; the relationship between one of the boys and his father; and the relationship between the other two boys and their mother.

Tre (Cuba Gooding, Jr.) is a young boy whose mother Reva Devereaux (Angela Bassett), in an effort to impose discipline upon him, sends him to live with his father across town. Tre has run afoul of his elementary school teacher for challenging both her authority and her Eurocentric curriculum. And Tre's life in his mother's neighborhood makes it clear why he is not accommodating well to school discipline. By the age of ten, he has already witnessed the yellow police tags that mark the scene of crimes and viewed the blood of a murder victim. Fortunately for Tre, his mother and father both love him more than they loved each other.

Doughboy (Former N.W.A. rapper Ice Cube, in a brilliant cinematic debut) and Ricky (Morris Chestnut) are half-brothers who live with their mother Brenda (Tyra Ferell) across the street from Tre and his father. Brenda is a single black mother—a member of a much-maligned group that, depending on the amateurish social theory that wins the day, is vilified with charges of promiscuity, judged to be the source of all that is evil in the lives of black children, or at best stereotyped as the helpless beneficiaries of the state. Singleton artfully avoids these caricatures by giving a complex portrait of Brenda, a woman plagued by her own set of demons, but who tries to provide the best living she can for her sons.

Even so, Brenda clearly favors Ricky over Doughboy—and this favoritism will bear fatal consequences for both boys. Indeed in Singleton's cinematic worldview both Ricky and Doughboy seem doomed to violent deaths because—unlike Tre—they have no male role models to guide them. This premise embodies one of the film's central tensions—and one of its central limitations. For even as he assigns black men a pivotal role of responsibility for the fate of black boys, Singleton also gives rather uncritical "precedence" to the impact of black men, even in their absence, over the efforts of present and loyal black women who more often prove to be at the head of strong black families.

While this foreshortened view of gender relations within the black community arguably distorts Singleton's cinematic vision, he is nonetheless remarkably perceptive in examining the subtle dynamics of the black family and neighborhood, tracking the differing effects that the boys' siblings, friends, and environment have on them. There is no bland nature versus nurture dichotomy here: Singleton is too smart to render life in terms of a Kierkegaardian either/or. His is an Afrocentric world of both/and.

This complex set of interactions—between mother and sons, between father and son, between boys who benefit from paternal wisdom or maternal ambitions, between brothers whose relationship is riven by primordial passions of envy and contempt, between environment and autonomy, between the larger social structure and the smaller but more immediate tensions of domestic life—define the central shape of *Hood*. We see a vision of black life that transcends insular preoccupations with "positive" or "negative" images and instead presents at once the limitations and virtues of black culture.

As a result, Singleton's film offers a plausible perspective on how people make the choices they do—and on how choice itself is not a property of autonomous moral agents acting in an existential vacuum, but rather something that is created and exercised within the interaction of social, psychic, political, and economic forces of everyday experience. Personal temperament, domestic discipline, parental guidance (or its absence), all help shape our understanding of our past and future, help define how we respond to challenge and crisis, and help mold how we embrace success or seem destined for failure.

Tre's developing relationship with his father, Furious Styles (Larry Fishburne), is by turns troubled and disciplined, sympathetic and compassionate—finely displaying Singleton's open-ended evocation of the meaning of social choice as well as his strong sensitivity to cultural detail. Furious Styles's moniker vibrates with double meaning, a semiotic pairing that allows Singleton to signify in speech what Furious accomplishes in action: a wonderful amalgam of old-school black consciousness, elegance, style, and wit, linked to the hip-hop fetish of "dropping science" (spreading knowledge) and staying well informed about social issues.

Only seventeen years Tre's senior, Furious understands Tre's painful boyhood growth and identifies with his teen aspirations. But more than that, he possesses a sincere desire to shape Tre's life according to his own best lights. Furious is the strong presence and wise counselor who will guide Tre through the pitfalls of reaching personal maturity in the chaos of urban childhood—the very sort of presence denied to so many in *Hood*, and in countless black communities throughout the country.

Furious, in other words, embodies the promise of a different conception of black manhood. As a father he is disciplining but loving, firm but humorous, demanding but sympathetic. In him, the black male voice speaks with an authority so confidently possessed and equitable wielded that one might think it is strongly supported and valued in American culture, but of course that is not so. The black male voice is rarely heard without the inflections of race and class domination that distort its power in the home and community, mute its call for basic respect and common dignity, or amplify its ironic denial of the very principles of democracy and equality that it has publicly championed in pulpits and political organizations.

Among the most impressive achievements of Singleton's film is its portrayal of the neighborhood as a "community." In this vein Singleton implicitly sides with the communitarian critique of liberal moral autonomy and atomistic individualism.[4] In *Hood* people love and worry over one another, even if they express such sentiments roughly. For instance, when the older Tre crosses the street and sees a baby in the path of an oncoming car, he swoops her up, and takes her to her crack-addicted mother. Tre gruffly reproves her for neglecting her child and insists that she change the baby's diapers before the baby smells as bad as her mother. And when Tre goes to a barbecue for Doughboy, who is fresh from a jail sentence, Brenda beseeches him to talk to Doughboy, hoping that Tre's intangible magic will "rub off on him."

But Singleton understands that communities embody resistance to the anonymity of liberal society as conceived in Aristotle via MacIntyre. His film portrays communities as more heterogenous, complex, and diverse, however, than the ideal of consensus that grounds MacIntyre's conception of communities, which is at least partially mediated through a common moral vocabulary. Singleton's neighborhood is a community precisely because it turns on the particularity of racial identity, and the contradictions of class location, that are usually muted or eradicated in mainstream accounts of moral community. Such accounts tend to eliminate racial, sexual, gender, and class difference in positing the conditions that make community possible, and in specifying the norms, values, and mores which regulate moral discourse and that structure communal behavior. Singleton's film community is an implicit argument for the increased visibility of a politics of difference within American culture, a solemn rebuke to the Capraesque representation of a socially and economically homogenous community.[5]

The quest for community represented in Singleton's film is related to the quest for intellectual community facilitated by certain modes of African-American cultural criticism. By taking black folk seriously, by taking just measure of their intellectual reflections, artistic perceptions, social practices, and cultural creations, the black cultural critic is seeking both to develop fair but forceful examination of black life, and to establish a community of interlocutors, ranging from high-brow intellectuals to everyday folk, whites and people of color alike, who are interested in preserving black culture's best features, ameliorating its weakest parts, and eradicating its worst traits.

Of course, specific moments of black cultural criticism also help shed light on aspects of black artistic production that may be overlooked or underestimated in much of mainstream criticism. A crucial role for African-American cultural criticism is to reveal historical connections, and thematic continuities and departures between black films and issues debated over time and space in African-American society. By doing so, the black cultural critic illumines the material interests of black filmmakers, while drawing attention to the cultural situation of black film practice. Singleton's depiction of community provides a colorful lens on problems which have long plagued black neighborhoods.

Singleton understands that communities, besides embodying the virtuous ends of their morally prudent citizens, also reflect the despotic will of their fringe citizens who threaten the civic pieties by which communities are sustained. *Hood*'s community is fraught with mortal danger, its cords of love and friendship under the siege of gang violence, and by what sociologist Mike Davis calls the political economy of crack.[6] Many inner-city communities live under what may be called a "juvenocracy": the economic rule and illegal tyranny exercised by young black men over significant territory in the black urban center. In the social geography of South Central L.A., neighborhoods are reconceived as spheres of expansion where urban space is carved up according to implicit agreements, explicit arrangements, or lethal conflicts between warring factions.

Thus, in addition to being isolated from the recognition and rewards of the dominant culture, inner-city communities are cut off from sources of moral authority and legitimate work, as underground political economies reward consenting children and teens with quick cash, faster cars, and sometimes, still more rapid death.[7] Along with the reterritorialization of black communal space through gentrification, the hegemony of the suburban mall over the inner city and downtown shopping complex, and white flight and black track to the suburbs and exurbs, the inner city is continually devastated.

Such conditions rob the neighborhood of one of its basic social functions and defining characteristics: the cultivation of a self-determined privacy in which residents can establish and preserve their identities. Police helicopters constantly zoom overhead in *Hood*'s community, a mobile metaphor of the ominous surveillance and scrutiny to which so much of poor black life is increasingly subjected. The helicopter also signals another tragedy, that *Hood* alludes to throughout its narrative: ghetto residents must often flip a coin to distinguish Los Angeles' police from its criminals. After all, this was Darryl Gates's L.A.P.D., and the urban rebellion following the Rodney King verdict, with the thousand tales of social misery reported by black men of every age and economic group across the country, only underscores a long tradition of extreme measures that police have used to control crime and patrol neighborhoods.[8] As Singleton wrote after the rebellion:

> "Anyone who has a moderate knowledge of African-American culture knows this was foretold in a thousand rap songs and more than a few black films. When Ice Cube was with NWA (Niggas With Attitude), he didn't write the lyrics to 'Fuck tha Police' just to be cute. He was reciting a reflection of reality as well as fantasizing about what it would be like to be on the other end of the gun when it came to police relations. Most white people don't know what it is like to be stopped for a traffic violation and worry more about getting beat up or shot than paying the ticket. So imagine, if you will, growing up with this reality regardless of your social or economic status. Fantasize about what it is to be guilty of a crime at birth. The crime? Being born black . . . By issuing that verdict, the jury violated not only Rodney King's civil rights, not only the rights of all African Americans, but also showed a lack of respect for every law-abiding American who believes in justice." (Singleton, 75)

Furious's efforts to raise his son in these conditions of closely surveilled social anarchy reveal the galaxy of ambivalence that surrounds a conscientious, community-minded brother who wants the best for his family, but who also understands the social realities that shape the lives of black men. Furious's urban cosmology is three-tiered: at the immediate level, the brute problems of survival are refracted through the lens of black manhood; at the abstract level, large social forces such as gentrification and the military's recruitment of black male talent undermine the black man's role in the community; at the intermediate level, police brutality contends with the ongoing terror of gang violence.

Amid these hostile conditions, Furious is still able to instruct Tre in the rules of personal conduct and to teach him respect for his community, even as he schools him in how to survive. Furious says to Tre, "I know you think I'm hard on you. I'm trying to teach you how to be responsible. Your friends across the street don't have anybody to show them how to do that. You gon' see how they end up, too." His comment, despite its implicit self-satisfaction and sexism (Ricky and Doughboy, after all, do have their mother Brenda), is meant to reveal the privilege of a young boy learning to face life under the shadow of fatherly love and discipline.

While Tre is being instructed by Furious, Ricky and Doughboy receive varying degrees of support and affirmation from Brenda. Ricky and Doughboy have different fathers, both of whom are conspicuously absent. In Doughboy's case, however, his father is symbolically present in that peculiar way that damns the offspring for their resemblance in spirit or body to the despised, departed father. The child becomes the vicarious sacrifice for the absent father, though he can never atone for the father's sins. Doughboy learns to see himself through his mother's eyes, her words ironically recreating Doughboy in the image of his invisible father. "You ain't shit," she says. "You just like yo' Daddy. You don't do shit, and you never gonna amount to shit."

Brenda is caught in a paradox of parenthood, made dizzy and stunned by a vicious cycle of parental love reinforcing attractive qualities in the "good" and obedient child, while the frustration with the "bad" child reinforces his behavior. Brenda chooses to save one child by sacrificing the other—lending her action a Styronian tenor, Sophie's choice in the ghetto. She fusses *over* Ricky; she fusses *at* Doughboy. When a scout for USC's football team visits Ricky, Brenda can barely conceal her pride. When the scout leaves, she tells Ricky, "I always knew you would amount to something."

In light of Doughboy's later disposition toward women, we see the developing deformations of misogyny. Here Singleton is on tough and touchy ground, linking the origins of Doughboy's misogyny to maternal mistreatment and neglect. Doughboy's misogyny is clearly the elaboration of a brooding and extended *ressentiment*, a deeply festering wound to his pride that infects his relationship with every woman he encounters.

For instance, at the party to celebrate his homecoming from his recent incarceration, Brenda announces that the food is ready. All of the males rush to the table, but immediately before they begin to eat, Tre, sensing that it will be to his advantage, reproves the guys for not acting gentlemanly and allowing the women first place in line. Doughboy chimes in, saying, "Let the ladies eat; 'ho's gotta eat too," which draws laughter, both from the audience with which I viewed the film, and the backyard male crowd. The last line is a sly sample of Robert Townsend's classic comedic sendup of fast-food establishments in *Hollywood Shuffle* (1987). When his girlfriend (Regina King) protests, saying she isn't a "ho," Doughboy responds, "Oops, I'm sorry bitch," which draws even more laughter.

In another revealing exchange with his girlfriend, Doughboy is challenged to explain why he refers to women exclusively as "bitch, or 'ho, or hootchie." In trying to reply, Doughboy is reduced to the inarticulate hostility (feebly masquerading as humor) that characterizes misogyny in general: " 'cause that's what you are."

"Bitch" and "ho," along with "skeezer" and "slut," have by now become the standard linguistic currency that young black males often use to demonstrate their authentic machismo. "Bitch" and equally offensive epithets compress womanhood into one indistinguishable whole, so that all women are the negative female, the seductress, temptress, and femme fatale all rolled into one. Hawthorne's scarlet A is demoted one letter and darkened; now an imaginary black B is emblazoned on the forehead of every female.

Though Singleton's female characters do not have center stage, by no means do they suffer male effrontery in silent complicity. When Furious and Reva meet at a trendy restaurant to discuss the possibility of Tre returning to live with his mother, Furious says "I know you wanna play the mommy and all that, but it's time to let go." He reminds her that Tre is old enough to make his own decisions, that he is no longer a little boy because "that time has passed sweetheart, you missed it." Furious then gets up to fetch a pack of cigarettes as if to punctuate his self-satisfied and triumphant speech, but Tre's mother demands that he sit down.

As the camera draws close to her face, she subtly choreographs a black women's grab-you-by-the-collar-and-set-you-straight demeanor with just the right facial gestures, and completes one of the most honest, mature, and poignant exchanges between black men and women in film history.

> It's my turn to talk. Of course you took in your son, my son, our son and you taught him what he needed to be a man, I'll give you that, because most men ain't man enough to do what you did. But that gives you no reason, do you hear me, no reason to tell me that I can't be a mother to my son. What you did is no different from what mothers have been doing from the beginning of time. It's just too bad more brothers won't do the same. But don't think you're special. Maybe cute, but not special. Drink your café au lait. It's on me.

Singleton says that his next film will be about black women coming of age, a subject left virtually unexplored in film. In the meantime, within its self-limited scope, *Hood* displays a diverse array of black women, taking care not to render them as either mawkish or cartoonish: a crack addict who sacrifices home, dignity, and children for her habit; a single mother struggling to raise her sons; black girlfriends hanging with the homeboys but demanding as much respect as they can get; Brandi (Nia Long), Tre's girlfriend, a Catholic who wants to hang on to her virginity until she's sure it's the right time; Tre's mother, who strikes a Solomonic compromise and gives her son up rather than see him sacrificed to the brutal conditions of his surroundings.

But while Singleton ably avoids flat stereotypical portraits of his female characters, he is less successful in challenging the logic that at least implicitly blames single black women for the plight of black children.[9] In Singleton's film version, it is not institutions like the Church that save Tre, but a heroic individual—his father Furious. But this leaves out far too much of the picture.

What about the high rates of black female joblessness; the sexist job market which continues to pay women at a rate that is seventy percent of the male wage for comparable work; the further devaluation of the "pink collar" by lower rates of medical insurance and other work-related benefits, all of which severely compromise the ability of single black mothers to effectively rear their children?[10] It is the absence of much more than a male role model and the strength he symbolizes that makes the life of a growing boy difficult and treacherous in communities such as South Central L.A.

The film's focus on Furious's heroic individualism fails, moreover, to account fully for the social and cultural forces that prevent more black men from being present in the home in the first place. Singleton's powerful message, that more black men must be responsible and present in the home to teach their sons how to become men, must not be reduced to the notion that those families devoid of black men are necessarily deficient and ineffective. Neither should Singleton's critical insights into the way that many black men are denied the privilege to rear their sons be collapsed to the idea that all black men who are present in their families will necessarily produce healthy, well-adjusted black males. So many clarifications and conditions must be added to the premise that *only* black men can rear healthy black males, that it dies the death of a thousand qualifications.

In reality, Singleton's film works off the propulsive energies that fuel deep, and often insufficiently understood tensions between black men and black women. A good deal of pain infuses relations between black men and women, recently dramatized with the publication of Shahrazad Ali's infamous and controversial underground best-seller, *The Blackman's Guide to Understanding the Blackwoman*. The book, which counseled black women to be submissive to black men, and which endorsed black male violence toward women under specific circumstances, touched off a furious debate that drew forth the many unresolved personal, social, and domestic tensions between black men and women.[11]

This pain follows a weary pattern of gender relations that has privileged concerns defined by black men over feminist or womanist issues. Thus, during the civil rights movement, feminist and womanist questions were perennially deferred, so that precious attention would not be diverted from racial oppression and the achievement of liberation.[12] But this deference to issues of racial freedom is a permanent pattern in black male-female relations; womanist and feminist movements continue to exist on the fringe of black communities.[13] And even in the Afrocentric worldview that Singleton advocates, the role of black women is often subordinate to the black patriarch.

Equally as unfortunate, many contemporary approaches to the black male crisis have established a rank hierarchy that suggests that the plight of black men is infinitely more lethal, and hence more important, than the conditions of black women. The necessary and urgent focus on the plight of black men, however, must not come at the expense of understanding its relationship to the circumstances of black women.

At places, Singleton is able to subtly embody a healthy and redemptive vision of black male-female relations. For instance, after Tre has been verbally abused and physically threatened by police brutality, he seeks sanctuary at Brandi's house, choreographing his rage at life in South Central by angrily swinging at empty space. As Tre breaks down in tears, he and Brandi finally achieve an authentic moment of spiritual and physical consummation previously denied them by the complications of peer pressure, and religious restraint. After Tre is assured that Brandi is really ready, they make love, achieving a fugitive moment of true erotic and spiritual union.

Brandi is able to express an unfettered and spontaneous affection that is not a simplistic "sex-as-proof-of-love" that reigns in the thinking of many teen worldviews. Brandi's mature intimacy is both the expression of her evolving womanhood and a vindication of the wisdom of her previous restraint. Tre is able at once to act out his male rage and demonstrate his vulnerability to Brandi, thereby arguable achieving a synthesis of male and female responses, and humanizing the crisis of the black male in a way that none of his other relationships—even his relationship with his father—are able to do. It is a pivotal moment in the development of a politics of alternative black masculinity that prizes the strength of surrender and cherishes the embrace of a healing tenderness.

As the boys mature into young men, their respective strengths are enhanced, and their weaknesses exposed. The deepening tensions between

Ricky and Doughboy break out into violence when a petty argument over who will run an errand for Ricky's girlfriend provokes a fistfight. After Tre tries unsuccessfully to stop the fight, Brenda runs out of the house, divides the two boys, slaps Doughboy in the face and checks Ricky's condition. "What you slap me for?," Doughboy repeatedly asks her after Ricky and Tre go off to the store. She doesn't answer, but her choice, again, is clear. Its effect on Doughboy is clearer still.

Such everyday variations on the question of choice are, again, central to the world Singleton depicts in *Hood*. Singleton obviously understands that people are lodged between social structure and personal fortune, between luck and ambition. He brings a nuanced understanding of choice to each character's large and small acts of valor, courage, and integrity that reveal what contemporary moral philosophers call virtue.[14] But they often miss what Singleton understands: character is not only structured by the choices we make, but by the range of choices we have to choose from—choices for which individuals alone are not responsible.

Singleton focuses his lens on the devastating results of the choices made by *Hood*'s characters, for themselves and for others. *Hood* presents a chain of choices, a community defined in part by the labyrinthine array of choices made and the consequences borne, to which others must then choose to respond. But Singleton does not portray a blind fatalism or a mechanistic determinism; instead he displays a sturdy realism that shows how communities affect their own lives, and how their lives are shaped by personal and impersonal forces.

Brenda's choice to favor Ricky may not have been completely her own—all the messages of society say that the good, obedient child, especially in the ghetto, is the one to nurture and help—but it resulted in Doughboy's envy of Ricky, and contributed to Doughboy's anger, alienation, and gradual drift into gang violence. Ironically and tragically, this constellation of choices may have contributed to Ricky's violent death when he is shot by members of a rival gang as he and Tre return from the neighborhood store.

Ricky's death, in turn, sets in motion a chain of choices and consequences. Doughboy feels he has no choice but to pursue his brother's killers, becoming a more vigilant keeper to his brother in Ricky's death than he could be while Ricky lived. Tre, too, chooses to join Doughboy, thereby repudiating everything his father taught, and forswearing every virtue he has been trained to observe. When he grabs his father's gun, but is met at the door by Furious, the collision between training and instinct is dramatized on Tre's face, wrenched in anguish and tears.

Though Furious convinces him to relinquish the gun, Furious's victory is only temporary. The meaning of Tre's manhood is at stake; it is the most severe test he has faced, and he chooses to sneak out of the house to join Doughboy. All Furious can do is tensely exercise his hands with two silver balls, which in this context are an unavoidable metaphor for now black men view their fate through their testicles, which are constantly up for grabs, attack, or destruction. Then sometime during the night, Tre's impassioned choice finally rings false, a product of the logic of vengeance he has desperately avoided all these years; he insists that he be let out of Doughboy's car before they find Ricky's killers.

Following the code of male honor, Doughboy kills his brother's killers. But the next morning, in a conversation with Tre, he is not so sure of violence's mastering logic anymore, and says that he understands Tre's choice to forsake Doughboy's vigilante mission, even as he silently understands that he is in too deep to be able to learn any other language of survival.

Across this chasm of violence and anguish, the two surviving friends are able to extend a final gesture of understanding. As Doughboy laments the loss of his brother, Tre offers him the bittersweet consolation that "you got one more brother left." Their final embrace in the film's closing moment is a sign of a deep love that binds brothers; a love that, however, too often will not save brothers.

The film's epilogue tells us that Doughboy is murdered two weeks later, presumably to avenge the deaths of Ricky's killers. The epilogue also tells us that Tre and Brandi manage to escape South Central as Tre pursues an education at Morehouse College, with Brandi at neighboring Spelman College. It is testimony to the power of Singleton's vision that Tre's escape is no callow Hollywood paean to the triumph of the human spirit (or, as some reviewers have somewhat perversely described the film, "life-affirming"). The viewer is not permitted to forget for a moment the absurd and vicious predictability of the loss of life in South Central Los Angeles, a hurt so colossal that even Doughboy must ask: "If there was a God, why he let motherfuckers get smoked every night?" Theodicy in gangface.

Singleton is not about to provide a slick or easy answer. But he does powerfully juxtapose such questions alongside the sources of hope, sustained in the heroic sacrifice of everyday people who want their children's lives to be better. The work of John Singleton embodies such hope by reminding us that South Central Los Angeles, by the sheer power of discipline and love, sends children to college, even as its self-destructive rage sends them to the grave.

Works Cited

Anderson, Elijah. *Streetwise*. Chicago: University of Chicago Press, 1991.

Bellah, Robert N., Richard Madsen, William N. Sullivan, Ann Swidler, and Steven M.

Tipton. *Habits of the Heart: Individualism and Commitment in American Life*. Berkeley: University of California Press, 1985.

Carson, Clayborne. *In Struggle: SNCC and the Black Awakening of the 1960s*. Cambridge, Mass.: Harvard University Press, 1981.

Cottingham, Clement. "Gender Shift in Black Communities." *Dissent* (Fall, 1989), pp. 521–525.

Davis, Mike and Sue Riddick. "Los Angeles: Civil Liberties between the Hammer and the Rock." *New Left Review* (July-August, 1988), pp. 37–60.

Dyson, Michael Eric. "As Complex As They Wanna Be: 2 Live Crew." *Z Magazine* (January, 1991), pp. 76–78.

———. "Performance, Protest and Prophecy in the Culture of Hip-Hop." *The Emergency of Black and The Emergence of Rap*. Ed. Jon Michael Spencer. Durham: Duke University Press, 1991, pp. 12–24.

———. "Rap, Race and Reality." *Christianity & Crisis* (March 16, 1987), pp. 98–100.

———. "Tapping Into Rap." *New World Outlook* (May–June, 1991), pp. 32–35.

———. "The Culture of Hip-Hop." *Zeta Magazine* (June, 1989), pp. 44–50.

———. "2 Live Crew's Rap: Sex, Race and Class." *The Christian Century* (January 2–9, 1991), pp. 7–8.

Ferrara, Alessandro. "Universalisms: Procedural, Contextual and Prudential." *Universalism vs. Communitarianism: Contemporary Debates in Ethics*. Ed. David Rasmussen. Cambridge, Mass: MIT Press, 1990, pp. 11–38.

Gardner, Jim. "Taking Rap Seriously: Theomusicologist Michael Eric Dyson on the New Urban Griots and Peripatetic Preachers (An Interview)." *Artvu* (Spring, 1991), pp. 20–23.

Gibbs, Jewelle Taylor, ed. *Young, Black, and Male in America: An Endangered Species*. Dover: Auburn House Publishing Company, 1988.

Harding, Vincent. "Toward a Darkly Radiant Vision of America's Truth: A Letter of Concern, An Invitation to Re-Creation." Ed. Charles H. Reynolds and Ralph V. Norman. *Community in America: The Challenge of Habits of The Heart*. Berkeley: University of California Press, 1988, pp. 67–83.

hooks, bell. *Ain't I A Woman?: Black Women and Feminism*. Boston: South End Press, 1981.

Jaynes, Gerald David and Robin Williams, Jr., eds. *A Common Destiny: Blacks And American Society*. Washington, D.C.: National Academy Press, 1989.

Lorde, Audre. *Sister/Outsider*. Freedom: The Crossing Press, 1984.

MacIntyre, Alisdair. *After Virtue*. Notre Dame: University of Notre Dame Press, 1981.

Malveaux, Julianne. "The Political Economy of Black Women." *The Year Left 2—Toward A Rainbow Socialism: Essays on Race, Ethnicity, Class and Gender*. Ed. Mike Davis, Manning Marable, Fred Pfeil, and Michael Sprinker. London: Verso, 1987, pp. 52–72.

Nonini, Don. "Everyday Forms of Popular Resistance." *Monthly Review: An Independent Socialist Magazine* (November, 1988), pp. 25–36.

Singleton, John. "The Fire This Time." *Premiere* (July 1992): 74–75.

Walker, Alice. *In Search of Our Mother's Garden*. New York: Harcourt, Brace and Jovanovich, 1983.

Wallace, Michele. *Invisibility Blues: From Pop to Theory*. London: Verso, 1990.

Wilson, William Julius. *The Truly Disadvantaged: The Inner City, the Underclass, and Public Policy*. Chicago: University of Chicago Press, 1987.

15

Making Cyborgs, Making Humans: Of Terminators and Blade Runners

Forest Pyle

Bodies and Machines: Deconstruction at the Movies

Cinema has a way of leaving the images of certain faces and bodies permanently inscribed in our memories: just as no one who has seen them is likely to forget the faces of Maria Falconetti in *The Passion of Joan of Arc* or Charles Bronson in *Once Upon a Time in the West,* no one is likely to forget the imposing body of Arnold Schwarzenegger moving relentlessly across the screen of *The Terminator.* Perhaps no aspect of the cinema is more powerful—or more potentially troubling—than its capacity to confront viewers with such moving bodies and faces, larger than life, images projected in motion and in time. Of course, the cinematic attention to the effects (special and otherwise) of bodies in motion stretches across film genres, from the action-adventure picture to the classical Western to hard-core pornography. But something curious happens when the bodies in motion turn out to be "cyborgs." This is the case for a subgenre of science fiction films that have achieved considerable critical and popular attention over the past decade, science fiction films which, often with distinctly dystopian tone and premise, make the "cyborg"—hybrid of human and machine—their thematic and formal focus. What we find in movies such as *Blade Runner* (Ridley Scott, 1982) and the *Terminator* series (James Cameron, 1984; 1991) are unsettled and unsettling speculations on the borders that separate the human and the nonhuman.

The collisions—and collusions—between human and nonhuman do not originate with these films, of course: the opposition between human and cyborg is but a contemporary and more mechanical mutation of a motif that extends at least to *Frankenstein.* Nonetheless, these films rework the opposition inherited from Romanticism in some important ways, drawing attention to a deep instability, by turns compelling and disorienting, present in our attempts to distinguish and define the human from its other. *Blade Runner* and the *Terminator* series not only reflect upon the threats to humanity posed by unchecked technological developments, they raise even more probing questions about the consequences of our definitions of the human. These films demonstrate that when we make cyborgs—at least when we make them in movies—we make and, on occasion, unmake our conceptions of ourselves.

To appreciate the stakes involved in the concern over the distinction between human and nonhuman in science fiction film, one could look to the often rancorous debates of contemporary cultural theory where the curricular role of the humanities, the status of humanism, and the notion of the "human" have revealed themselves to be tightly knotted and highly contentious issues. However removed these debates are from real life, including the curious real life of Hollywood production, the clamor and alarm that have accompanied them make it appear that much more than the value of the traditional Western Humanities curriculum is being questioned: indeed, it often seems as if humanity itself has been put at risk by a variety of critical methodologies—primarily imported, but with some domestic hybrids—oriented around a critique of humanism. Nowhere have the disputes and misunderstandings raged more than on the terrain of what is called "deconstruction."[1] None of the recent modes of analysis stands more accused of an anti-humanist nihilism, charged with a malevolent disregard for human agency, cast in the role of a "terminator."

In the context of these films, three pertinent aspects of deconstructive analysis should be emphasized. The activity most commonly identified with deconstruction is the location in a textual system of a decisive, even founding opposition, such as that between the "organic" and the "mechanical." In the course of critical interrogation, the opposition is disclosed to be both asymmetrical and unstable, rendered "undecidable" at some decisive if often unexpected moment: the presumed superiority of "organic" over "mechanical," for instance, is upset at a moment in the text which reveals that the "organic" *needs* the "mechanical" or proves them to be inextricable. The point of deconstruction, then, is not to decode a film's meaning or even to "unmask" its "ideologies"; decoding and unmasking presume a secure position of knowledge outside the unstable oppositions under consideration and immune from the effects they generate. Instead—and this is the second aspect of deconstruction to be stressed—the viewer finds the opposition between spectator and spectacle to be unstable, begins to acknowledge his or her complicity with the object under consideration, and acknowledges that the extent of the complicity may never be fully acknowledged, since there turns out to be no place free from the critical complications that ensue. In the case of a film such as *Blade Runner*, for example, we may start out with our assumptions of a clear distinction between human and machine intact; but through its representation of the hybrid figure of the cyborg, the film "plays" on a borderline that we come to see as shifting and porous, one than begins to confuse the nature of the opposition and the values we ascribe to it.[2] In the course of the film, our own position as viewer does not remain unaffected. What results, as I will argue below, is the sense that we too have become implicated in the "deconstruction" of the oppositions we have just witnessed.

It is by no means necessarily the case that a film (or its director, writers, actors, producers) conceives such a "deconstruction" to be its overt or implicit project. Deconstruction—and this is the third point to be stressed—marks the moment in which aspects of the text's *performance* conflict with the themes it declares or develops.[3] A deconstructive analysis of film would confront the tensions and consequences generated by moments of visual or rhetorical excess that cannot be accommodated by the narrative demands of plot or reconciled with the film's thematics: the proliferation of point-of-view shots in a film, for instance, can establish a perspective that remains at odds with the development of the film's story or theme.

In *Blade Runner* we are confronted with a curious sort of visual excess: heavily allegorized shots (and scenes) which cannot be squared with the symbolic or mythological references they invite. When the cyborg Roy Batty impales his hand with a nail near the end of the film, the shot establishes a visual symbolic association to Christ on the cross, an association bolstered by other visual metaphors, such as the dove released to a suddenly blue sky at Roy's death. But though such images draw on that symbolic repertoire, the association with the Christian narrative inevitably conjured by the shots is invalidated by the film's own narrative logic: Roy inserts the nail into his palm solely in order to prolong his life, to defer his "time to die." Roy is in this and every regard far from Christ-like: he has, of course, just murdered the "father" (Tyrell) who played his god and maker. What the film leaves us with are allegorical shots severed from their mythological sources, empty allegories that cannot be redeemed by the Christian narrative.

While the deconstructive attention to the rhetorical and performative capacities of language has been accused of dissolving all worldly matters into textual fictions, one can construe very differently deconstruction's emphasis on the "text," on properties of language and the tendency of language to exceed human mastery. In the work of Paul de Man, for instance, the "confusion of linguistic with natural reality" is held to be both a perpetual occurrence and another name for ideology. Deconstruction thus "upsets rooted ideologies [such as the ideology of humanism] by revealing the mechanics of their workings," mechanics which are themselves textual (*RT,* 11). This may mean, for instance, opening the fundamental opposition between human and inhuman to such a deconstruction by stressing the cinematic "languages" that form it in the first place. According to de Man, there are aspects and operations of language that are irreducibly mechanical and that disallow the organic models we traditionally attribute to it. That which we most want to be our own, that which we may believe to be most human—language—is thus from this deconstructive perspective an insistently *nonhuman* and even mechanical operation.

For an analysis of film and for the films under consideration this has particular relevance, because deconstructive analysis discloses the ways by which mechanical and rhetorical features of language always underwrite and potentially undermine our concept of the human. We can often discern an awareness of this aspect of cinematic language in the statements of some of the cinema's early practitioners, struggling as they were with formal and technical as well as theoretical matters. One of the founders of Soviet cinema, Lev Kulesov, in what has become a famous declaration, asserted that film must be regarded at its most basic level as a language: "The shot must operate as a sign, a kind of letter."[4] Deconstructive analysis works not only to recover the importance of the shot as "a kind of letter," it attends to the instances at which this "letter" may undo the narrative and thematic structures that are its effects, its "projections." What often gets obscured by the more hostile responses to deconstruction is its critical attention to the means and modes by which the recognition of such figural constitution, the insistence of the cinematic "letter," is actively forgotten or recuperated by the course of the film. Indeed, we will find that the wavering balance between memory and forgetting is central to any understanding of *Blade Runner*. And certainly one measure of the massive popular success of the *Terminator* series is the effectiveness of its recuperations of the tensions and instabilities the films generate: their ability to recover an "entertainment" by restoring the oppositions between human and machine that have been threatened.

There has been considerable and perhaps inevitable resistance to a theoretical approach that does not presume the "human" to be a nontextual foundation, one that regards the "human" as a concept/metaphor subject to the effects that befall all such elements of language: Derrida, de Man, and those influenced by their work have been accused of nothing less than "inhumanity," as if the critique and displacement of certain governing concepts and assumptions were themselves a threat to the race. David M. Hirsch, a shrill and prominent voice in the chorus of denunciation, claims that deconstruction "seek[s] to blind and deafen readers to all that is human."[5] I mark the most inflammatory issue in the debates surrounding deconstruction, because it goes to the heart of matters that resonate with considerable visual and thematic complexity in *Blade Runner* and the *Terminator*s.

It is important not to confuse deconstruction with destruction or nihilistic termination or even demystification: it is best understood in the context of film as the attempt to *read* moving pictures: such a reading is not to be confused with traditions of "close reading" associated with the New Criticism which took both the subject and object of reading to be stable (if complex) entities. A deconstructive reading is itself an unstable but productive *activity*, one which forces us to confront the constructedness of certain concepts, such as the human, that we may have presumed to be stable essences and that we may have preferred not to look much into. The point is not, therefore, to "deconstruct" movies "from the outside" but to bring "deconstructive" questions to bear upon them in order to understand how the films are *already* soliciting or working on the more significant oppositions. It is not, therefore, merely a matter of taking theory to the movies but of apprehending how movies project considerable theoretical light of their own on the screen of our concerns. It thus may be the case that when theory leaves the movie theater, it does not leave unchanged—particularly when that theory is called deconstruction.

It is certainly the case that the issues raised by deconstruction regarding the instability of the concept of the human are evident in films such as *Blade Runner* and both *Terminator*s; these films take the technological threat to the human as their narrative point of departure and make that threat into the occasion for a cinematic treatment and exploration of the status of the human. Each of the films takes up a consideration of the relationships between human and technology, moreover, not simply in the stories they tell but by their presentation of the spectacle of movies. Of all media, film would seem most likely to confirm de Man's insistence on the mechanical aspects of a text, for film foregrounds most insistently its reliance on the apparatus from the economics of production to the mechanics of projection. But this feature, the necessity of the apparatus, is through a variety of conventions susceptible to naturalization. Each of these films—and perhaps any of the recent science fiction dystopias— returns the problem of the apparatus to the viewer in the stories they tell and by the form of visual spectacle. And each of these films asks in its own way what happens when the status and fate of the human becomes intertwined with the technologically reproduced image of the cyborg.

"If you want to live"

Nothing less than the very fate of the human race is at stake in James Cameron's *The Terminator*. The film's justly celebrated and gruesomely nightmarish opening scene depicts a post-apocalyptic world in which the humans who have survived nuclear holocaust are engaged in a pitched battle for survival with machines that "got smart" and now recognize all humans as threats to their existence. The machines send a combat-model cyborg back through time with the intention of "terminating" the mother of John Conner, future commander of the human resistance. The humans follow suit by sending a "lone warrior," Kyle Reese, back through time to protect Sarah Conner from the terminator and thus to preserve the inception of the rebellion.

The opposition between protagonist and antagonist is established early in the film by the depictions of their arrival to the present. Schwarzenegger's body and motion are a cluster of signs—sculpted "Aryan" invulnerability—which immediately resonate historically as "man-machine." These signs must however be supplemented by crucial point-of-view shots: the terminator's apparent inhumanity must be confirmed not only by our seeing him (such looks could be deceiving), but by seeing for ourselves how he sees. This seals the distinction, for the point-of-view shots reveal that the terminator does not "see" images but merely gathers "information."

If omnipotence is registered cinematically as inhumanness, the simplest of negative markings, relative physical weakness, identifies Kyle Reese as human (who doesn't need the point-of-view shot to establish any further identification). This empty marker is filled out in the course of the movie as the mechanical physical superiority of the cyborg is contrasted to the positive human capacity to improvise. Reese becomes distinguished by his ability to master or "hotwire" technology through improvisation and *bricolage,* mobile forms of thinking and acting which the movie tells us are reserved for the human.[6] What *The Terminator* defines as fundamentally human is the routing of technological mastery into a rebellious subjectivity, a heroism capable of resistance and even self-sacrifice.

The Terminator is cluttered with images and elements of contemporary (and low) technology which, even when incidental to the plot, lend the film its visual density and contribute to the motif of a pervasive—and invasive—penetration of technology. The elements of contemporary technology that the film puts on display—answering machines, blow driers, phone systems, junked cars, toy trucks—are neither ominous nor advanced. What they collectively signify, however, is the interference these technologies pose to human communication and human agency. These are interferences that are open literally and figuratively to manipulation by the terminator and that must thus be recuperated by human vigilance.

Sarah Conner's initial bewilderment when confronted by this mechanized world made hostile functions both as a plot device which heightens the film's suspense and as an allegory of our potential enslavement to and possible liberation from technology. Constance Penley has challenged such an interpretation of *The Terminator*, arguing that the traces of technology that punctuate the movie do not support such an opposition: "the film does not advance an 'us against them' argument, man versus machine, a Romantic opposition between the organic and the mechanical," says Penley, for this is a cyborg, "part machine, part human."[7] But if the film displays the thorough interpenetration of human and machine or depicts their hybridization, its narrative logic is bent upon fulfilling a fundamentally humanist fantasy, that of human mastery over the machine. Critics who have interpreted the film as politically progressive have stressed that it attributes the human capacity for mastery to the woman, Sarah Conner, who is not only the bearer of human potential, the mother of humanity's savior, but the character that the film represents as achieving agency. When Sarah flattens the terminator between the plates of the hydraulic press, she does not become, as Penley claims, machine-like; rather, she gets to make good on what the film has constructed as our collective desire to crush the threatening technological other. The fantasy is thus a comprehensive one, for not only does it pose as two victories over the machine—ensuring the victorious *future* resistance (Reese suggests that humans in 2029 are poised to win) by achieving a human triumph in the present—it presents the possibility of human mastery over time itself, a theme which becomes a prominent motif in the sequel. *The Terminator* is in this sense about the reassertion of sheer and absolute human agency, "the triumph of the will."

We note during the course of this cinematic triumph the progressive physical revelation of the terminator's inhumanness. The movie proceeds to unmask the cyborg, to reveal visually that the semblance is indeed an illusion, that beneath the flesh and tissue there is nothing human. But in another sense, the machine that gets revealed is all-too-human, the embodiment of a host of human fears. This is played out in the film through the vehicle of suspense in the protracted ending. Reese's pipe bomb blows up the terminator's truck, and when the terminator is engulfed in fire, Reese and Sarah embrace in what looks like an ending. The relief is premature, of course, for the terminator emerges from the flames, metal frame intact, and the machine that we see resembles the murderous machines that haunted the film's opening scenes and that haunt Reese's "flashbacks" of the future. The concluding scenes are the film's most harrowing in part because we suddenly recognize that this technological other is nothing less than our own quite "human" images and fears. The war zone of the future is literally a nightmare, Reese's and our own, populated by pop cultural preconceptions of dinosaurs, mechanical Tyrannosaurus Rex and flying Pterodactyls, while the humanoid terminators stripped of their flesh spook us with the ghoulish childhood fears of the animated skeleton. At this moment the opposition between human and nonhuman established by the film is given a twist, for though we see the terminator as more inhuman than ever—all fleshly human resemblance seared away—its "inhuman" mechanical otherness is simultaneously felt to be a human projection.[8] When the human opposition *to* the machine finally triumphs in *The Terminator,* the opposition *between* human and cyborg begins to appear as the human projection it always was.

"Do Androids Dream . . . ?"

Something much less apocalyptic than the fate of the race is at stake in Ridley Scott's *Blade Runner.* The execution, or "retirement," of cyborgs or "replicants" is portrayed as part of the business of law enforcement in the Los Angeles of 2019. Deckard is recruited back into service as a "blade runner" when four replicants escape to earth after an "off-world" skirmish in which a score of humans are killed. Though the replicants are depicted as ruthless and deadly, the threat is nothing of the order of *The Terminator:* this is but a minor slave uprising, and nothing suggests that the world is threatened. But from the outset, from the moment of Deckard's initial reluctance, the film conveys the sense that while "retirement" may be more or less routine, it is a very messy business. The historical analogy is established when Deckard's boss describes the replicants as "skin jobs," cop parlance which Deckard likens to the language which, as the "history books" tell us, referred to black men as "niggers." Deckard is coerced into taking the assignment, nonetheless, and begins the job of detecting and terminating the replicants.

The film's action of detection and termination might appear on first sight as the mirror image of the logic we witness in *The Terminator:* "blade runners" are, after all, "terminators" of a sort who seek and destroy cyborgs, such as the terminator. But the depiction of the cyborg in *Blade Runner* takes us in a very different direction. Though the film's plot suggests that the cyborgs pose no real threat of extinction, the movie itself introduces a very real and troubling threat—not so much to the characters in the film, but to the stability of the notion of the human that underwrites our actions, beliefs, meanings. Everything in the course of Deckard's "detection" of the replicants leads him—and his audience—to a self-detection of a different and disturbing sort: namely, the recognition of the undecidable nature of the opposition between human and its technological double.

The film thus begins to ask of humans what Walter Benjamin asked of the work of art in his highly influential essay of 1936. How, asked Benjamin, is the status of the work of art affected by the advent of its technological reproducibility? He argues that though the work of art has always been "in principle" "reproducible," the development of new technologies—most dramatically that of film—shattered the "aura" and "authenticity" which surrounded the "original."[9] One could indeed interpret the necessity of the replicants' extinction in light of this logic: they are too close, the very fact of their duplicity too disquieting, and because they pose a threat to the very "aura" of the "original"—the authentic human—the cyborg must thus be eliminated. Eric Alliez and Michel Feher describe the threat of replication in terms which, echoing Benjamin, bring to our attention the "postmodern" condition of this relationship:

> Thus it becomes imperative to maintain formal distinctions between men and machines even if the real differences tend to blur. Here we find the explanation for the four-year life span given to the replicants. As machines, they could remain efficient for more than four years. This time limit, then, does not represent a technological limit, but is rather an imposed level of tolerance beyond which the men/machine interface becomes uncontrollable. . . . Beyond this threshold, that which allowed one to distinguish between model and copy, between subject and object, disappears.[10]

The film itself, then, appears to confirm Benjamin's understanding of the fate of the "original" and in the process confirms de Man's assertions with which we opened about the collapse of the foundational concept "human": "there is," de Man asserts extemporaneously, "in a very radical sense, no such thing as the human" (*RT*, 96). *Blade Runner* delivers us to the point of such an awareness, one that is resisted in the name of "humanism": that the "human" is an *effect* of an opposition which at certain anxious and decisive moments cannot be sustained.

The film has attracted opposing interpretations, of course; most notably that it depicts the threat an autonomous technology poses to humanity. Thomas B. Byers, for instance, sees the film as a cautionary tale that "warn[s] us against a capitalist future gone wrong, where such [human] feelings and bonds are so severely truncated that a quite literal dehumanization has become perhaps the gravest danger."[11] While no one is likely to read *Blade Runner* as a celebration of late capitalism, it is not clear that the film reserves such a distinctly human space outside the logic of mechanization. Rather, technological reproducibility is taken by the film to be the condition of things. It would not seem, moreover, that "dehumanization" is the "gravest danger" proposed by the film, for much that is both grave and dangerous in *Blade Runner* goes by the name of the human. Far from preserving an essential and organic human dimension which can be opposed to the dehumanized replicants, the film tends to undo that opposition. This undoing is performed not by extending humanity to the replicants—their "superhuman" and "mechanical" qualities are visible to the end—but by disclosing the distinction to be unviable.

The blade runner's means of "detecting" a replicant is significant in this regard: the "Voight-Kampf" test examines the dilation of capillaries in the eye during interrogation. The detective's eye establishes the difference between human and replicant by looking into the eye of his subject, though judgment is made only by way of the mechanical device which measures what the detective cannot see for himself. The motif of the eye and its gaze runs throughout the movie: the eye superimposed over the city in the film's opening shot, the eye magnified in the "Voight-Kampf," the eye of the owl perched in Tyrell Corporations Headquarters, the eyes genetically engineered and grown in the subzero lab, the lenses of various microscopes, the photograph enhancers, the gaze of panopticon devices and advertising projections, even the eyes of Tyrell himself, shielded by thick spectacles and blinded in the Oedipal inversion of Roy's dramatic patricide. All this literal and symbolic attention to eyes, this ubiquity of the gaze, only serves to underline the failures of seeing, for it turns out that one can never tell the difference by looking. Rachael's questions about the "Voight-Kampf" test are pertinent: "have you ever tried that thing on yourself?," she asks of Deckard, "ever retired a human by mistake?"

But because one cannot see or detect a difference does not in and of itself prove that such difference is absent: there may well be internal differences unavailable to empirical detection. And the film presents the search for the most essential internal differences and distinctions—self-consciousness, emotion, memory—that would preserve the integrity of the human. Most crucial in this regard is the examination of time and memory, an examination that extends to every aspect of the film's visual and narrative logic. Most immediately, perhaps, the film addresses the memory of its *audience* by working in—and *with*—a style, *film noir,* that cannot help but evoke nostalgia. But the *film noir* effect of this hybrid of the 1940s and the early 21st Century creates a curious effect, since the cinematic nostalgia played out in shadows and muted colors is projected onto the future. The "noirish" resonances work against the grain of a Hollywood nostalgia that is most often the reassuring nostalgia for a morally unambiguous and comforting past. But this does not mean that nostalgia is banished: with *Blade Runner,* we are confronted by the nostalgia for memory itself, for a memory of something more than a film genre, and for a form of remembering that is something other than a cinematic projection.

The replicants' fascination with old photographs—"your beloved photos," as Roy tells Leon—is initially treated by Deckard as a quirky eccentricity: "I don't know why replicants would collect photos. Maybe they were like Rachael, they needed memories." But his encounter with Rachael's simulated past modifies that judgment: for she too has "photographs," documents that prove her past, give testimony. Though Deckard determines the photos to be "fakes," supplied by Tyrell to shore up Rachael's memory "implants" with the illusion of facticity, they prompt Deckard's own poignant reflection over his old photos—photos of absent women—photos that are clearly of another age, figures that within the time-frame of the film Deckard could never have "known." Deckard doesn't give voice here to the recognition we witness: his photos are also "fakes." Why, then, would anyone collect photos? Because photos *are* memories and the film tells us that, *exactly like the replicants,* we need memories to shore up the stories we tell of ourselves. There turns out to be a gap where we expect to find the core of the human; we need photographs to fill that gap, and "humans" no more or no less than "cyborgs" use the photographic image—which is always a stand-in, a "fake"—to supplement what's missing.[12]

As spectators, our own relationship to the film and to its engagement with its *film noir* intertext functions similarly to undermine memory.[13] As we recognize the film's intertextual codes, we gain a sense of knowledge and mastery: "Wary and world-weary detective, shadowy cinematography and shadowy characters, venetian blinds and ceiling fans, dark woman with a dark past: but, of course, it's *film noir.*"[14] On one level, then, this "intertextual" reference or cross-generic play situates the viewer as knowledgeable, capable of mastering cinematic codes and generic traditions. But the security such knowledge should provide fades as we, alongside Deckard, are drawn by the allure of a past we could never know, a memory that could only be a borrowed one. The sense of a "darkness" to Rachael's past that is invited by the *film noir* intertext is revealed not to be a sinister or disreputable act which veils her past in mystery, but a literal darkness. The film, in other words, does not merely deviate from the tradition of *film noir;* the film quotes the genre only to displace its thematic authority: the sense of "mystery" is revealed to be an effect of our faith in the distinction between replicant and human. *Blade Runner* disrupts that faith by insisting on the inability of memory to restore the presence of what is past, an inability shared by all who live and remember in this movie.

The rhetorical question asked by Gaff near the film's end—"Too bad she won't live! But then again, who does?"—speaks directly to the matter of a movie that has, so it seems, effectively presented the deconstruction of its presiding opposition between the human and the machine. But it also seems that the movie cannot tolerate to conclude under the sign of such undecidability, at least not in its studio release, for the suspended conclusion—one which has suspended oppositions—is supplemented by Deckard and Rachael's escape in the final scene. They have not only escaped the oppressive atmosphere and dangerous blade runners of the city, they have escaped the film's disorientations, to the liberating blue sky and romantic green world of the "North." It's the most transparent of gestures, of course, and however much it fails to respect the director's cut (the ending as well as Deckard's voice-over were demanded by the producers over Ridley Scott's objections), it demonstrates that the film has generated such a knot of visual and thematic intricacy that it can be "stabilized" only by recourse to such a pastoral gesture. The film has thus reached a limit of sorts, a limit that reveals that in *Blade Runner,* when humans make cyborgs, it means the unmaking of the human through an anxious recognition that both were assembled in the first place.

"Trust Me"

When James Cameron returns to the distinction between human and cyborg in *Terminator 2: Judgment Day,* the opposition is given a new turn and a new terminator, both of which initially appear designed to make "*T2*" more fully an action-adventure movie and to make the opposition between human and other more stable. In Cameron's sequel, a second terminator has been sent by "Sky Net" to eliminate the young John Conner. Schwarzenegger returns in *T2* as a terminator, but one sent by Commander Conner in 2029 to protect himself from termination in 1991. The two warring terminators are neither identical nor equal, however, for as Schwarzenegger explains to the young John Conner, the second terminator, a "T–1000," is technologically superior: no longer a cybernetic organism, "living tissue over metal endoskeleton," the T–1000 is composed exclusively of liquid metal. *T2* thus gives us both a new terminator and a new opposition: the "moving-parts" mechanism of the older terminator (to whom John endearingly refers at one point as "lug nuts") is posed against the advanced technology of its amorphous and wholly inorganic adversary. The film replays Hollywood's apparently compulsive drive to up the technological ante and, by the same token, allegorizes the confrontation of a postmodern technology with a modernist one. That token is then given an interesting turn, for *T2* depicts a "modernist" triumph over the very technology—dazzling, amorphous, uncanny, postmodern—that marks the film as different from its predecessor.

While the T–1000 is not technically a cyborg, it possesses the capacity to replicate any animate or inanimate object of its own mass, including a human, and to mimic the human voice. This ability provides the film with its violently uncanny moments of doubling, when the copy confronts and then kills the original. But *T2* backs away from the more radically disorienting possibility implicit in such technology: namely, that we might *never* know beforehand who the terminator is. Instead, the moments of such doubling punctuate the otherwise continuous (assumed) "identity" of the terminator. This identity is not of course entirely reassuring, since the terminator "is" an L.A. cop. The T–1000's capacity for "shape-changing" establishes visually an opposition that recurs throughout the film thematically as well: the opposition between mechanical mimicry and genuine learning. While the T–1000 belongs purely and exclusively to the logic of machines, the older "Cyberdyne Systems model 101" comes equipped with a "learning computer." Early in the film, John Conner asks the terminator whether it could "learn stuff [it] hadn't been programmed with, so [it] could be, you know, more human, and not such a dork all the time." The terminator replies that the more contact he has with humans, the more he learns. There would seem to be nothing more human than "learning"—particularly a moral and ethical learning—and *T2* cultivates further than its predecessor this humanist position.

The film even revises the equation of resistance with humanity implied in *The Terminator:* sheer resistance leads to the excesses of Sarah Conner, who has become physically formidable and has acquired from mercenaries, ex-Green Berets, *contras,* and other dubious sources the soldier and survival skills displayed by Reese in the first film. Her zeal leads her to attempt the execution of Myles Dyson, the computer engineer responsible for developing the computer chip recovered from the first terminator into the advanced Sky Net computer system that, in "one possible future," becomes "self-aware" and commits genocide. Poised to execute Dyson, she refrains, but must be taught by her son the same lesson he teaches the terminator: "you can't go around killing people." Nothing would appear more laudably "humanist" than the film's emphasis on learning such lessons, its insistence on a human agency informed by moral principles, its rejection of a closed future: "No fate but what we make" is the refrain passed from John to Reese to Sarah to young John and, perhaps, to the audience itself.

But though the film appears to deepen the distinction between human and machine, setting the moral and ethical principles of a human education against the threatening autonomy of a mutatable technology, it achieves this distinction by way of a hybrid intermediary that upsets the stability of the opposition. The cyborg can learn, and it seems to acquire—to earn—from its contact with humans nothing less than genuine human subjectivity. The film's overt humanist thematics are thus made tenuous when it is revealed that the cyborg terminator is indispensable to the opposition: both for the story of the human opposition *to* the machines and for the conceptual opposition *between* human and machine. In one sense, the cyborg is benevolent only because of its complete obedience; at the same time, however, the opposition between human and machine is placed at the mercy of the cyborg. The instability is suggested by Sarah Conner's rhapsody on the cyborg as she watches him play with her son.

"The terminator would never stop," she says, "it would always be there, and it would die to protect him." What had in the first film defined the terminator's terror, the sheer thoughtless relentlessness of its drive to terminate, is reinscribed here as trust and reliability: the terminator thus becomes in Sarah's estimation the "best father."

The cyborg has thus been "humanized," capable of learning and, crucially, of dying. In the first film, as Sarah flattens the terminator in the hydraulic press, she declares, "You're terminated, fucker!" She now gives voice to a belief in the capacity of the terminator not merely to be terminated but to experience "death." This is confirmed by the film's ending: after the spectacular extended meltdown of the T–1000, one in which the history of its replicated victims reappear in a Dante-like procession, the Schwarzenegger terminator sacrifices himself in order to prevent the possibility that any prototypes or computer chips from this deadly technology would remain to provoke the catastrophe that has just been rescinded. Paradoxically, the act is his most fully "human" act of the film, for to subject himself to the vat he refuses for the first time his master's order, who implores him to stay behind.[15] As Sarah lowers him into the vat—he cannot "self-terminate"—the terminator's mechanical hand makes the rhetorical gesture of human triumph: the victorious "thumbs up." It is an easy visual cliché, of course, but it is emblematic of the deep interweaving of human and machine. However much the film may want to extricate itself from the logic of machines, the knotting of human and cyborg is inextricable: in *Terminator 2,* the triumph of humans and humanism is made dependent on the humanizing of cyborgs.

Human Gestures, Mechanical Hands

I want to return in closing to the issues with which we opened, to the critical possibilities opened by a deconstructive reading and to the resistance it has provoked. I hope that it has become evident that far from seeking to "blind and deafen its readers to all that is human" (Hirsch), deconstruction opens a critical questioning of the ways by which the sounds and visions of cinema operate, and the ways by which such sounds and visions get tangled up with our notions of the human. If the concept of the human proves to be less stable than before, it is not because of a nihilistic disregard for human beings, but because questions are raised by the films themselves that, if looked into, can only shake up the oppositions between human and machine that are deeply and problematically embedded in our culture.

An image from each of these films can serve as a coda to our discussion. In each film, the "death" or "termination" or "retirement" of cyborgs is accompanied by gestures of the hand: the hand of the first threatening terminator extended toward Sarah's neck as she terminates him in the hydraulic press; the hand of Roy Batty in *Blade Runner* closing "Christ-like" over the nail he has inserted as his "time to die" approaches; the triumphant "thumbs up" of the second terminator. Each is a "human" gesture made by a "mechanical" hand, and each gesture points towards a humanism that the films may hope to affirm, but only by way of the insistence of mechanical hands which bind the human deeply to its other, even in termination.

16

Genericity in the Nineties:
Eclectic Irony and the New Sincerity

Jim Collins

Perhaps the most useful way to begin discussion of "genre film" in the early 1990s is to look at representative scenes in two quite recent Westerns, each representing in its own way how "genericity" works in contemporary American culture. In *Back to the Future III* (1990) Marty and Doc ride through the desert in what is supposed to be 1885, charging across the landscape in their disabled DeLorean time machine, sitting side-by-side atop the car, drawn by a team of horses. This configuration of drivers, horses, and desert is made to resemble not just any stagecoach in any old Western, but *the* stagecoach, namely John Ford's *Stagecoach* (1939)—a parallel made explicit by replicating one of the most famous shots of Ford's film almost exactly. The DeLorean "stagecoach" is pulled through Monument Valley, framed in a high angle shot, moving diagonally through the frame, accompanied by soundtrack music that is remarkably similar to the "original." The second scene comes from *Dances With Wolves* (1990). After John Dunbar has taken part in a buffalo hunt and begun his initiation into the tribe, he contemplates the Sioux tribe moving across the horizon, silhouetted against a spectacular sunset, a picturesque vision of an unspoiled West. Dunbar says in a voice-over that he had never encountered a people so completely connected to their environment—"The only word that came to mind was harmony"—at which point we see not the Sioux, but Dunbar framed perfectly in the midst of a magnificent sunset, situated just as heroically and just as harmoniously within that landscape.

I choose these scenes because they represent two divergent types of genre film that co-exist in current popular culture. One is founded on dissonance, on eclectic juxtapositions of elements that very obviously don't belong together, while the other is obsessed with recovering some sort of missing harmony, where everything works in unison. Where the former involves an ironic hybridization of pure classical genres in which John Ford meets Jules Verne and H. G. Wells, the latter epitomizes a "new sincerity" that rejects any form of irony in its sanctimonious pursuit of lost purity. Despite their apparently antithetical perspectives, both types of genre films have emerged within the past decade as reactions to the same cultural milieu—namely, the media-saturated landscape of contemporary American culture. The goal of this article is to try to make sense of how these popular films make sense of our cultural existences and in so doing to explore the changing forms and functions of "genericity" in postmodern popular culture.

I use the term "genericity" here because I want to address not just specific genre films, but genre as a category of film production and film-viewing. Traditionally, Hollywood studios subdivided their annual production into specific genre films that, if nothing else, served as a useful way of striking a balance between product standardization and differentiation. Maintaining certain formulas that would stabilize audience expectations and, by extension, stabilize those audiences, was obviously in Hollywood's best interests. But how does the category of genre "work" today when popular entertainment is undergoing such a massive recategorization brought on by the ever-increasing number of entertainment options and the fragmentation of what was once thought to be a mass audience into a cluster of "target" audiences?

Genre Films/Genre Theories: Life on the New Frontier

Just as generic texts have been a staple of the culture industries, genre theory has been all-pervasive within the criticism industries. Film scholars and social historians have tried to explain the cultural significance of the Western, the melodrama, and other popular genres since the 1940s, and they have employed a number of critical methodologies to explain the popularity of genres and what that popularity suggests about "mass consciousness." One of the most commonly used approaches once film study began to acquire a certain degree of rigor in the 1960s was myth study, i.e. reading popular narratives as the secularized myths of modern societies. This work depends on two interconnected assumptions: 1) films function as explanatory narratives told by multiple storytellers in multiple versions; and 2) out of this storytelling certain patterns emerge that reflect how the "mass consciousness" feels about any number of issues at a given time. The genre-as-myth approach most often incorporated the work of French anthropologist Claude Lévi-Strauss, whose analysis of myth in primitive cultures provided a theoretical framework for investigating just how popular stories could be interpreted as a symbolic working-out of a given culture's core values and its most pressing social problems. The most frequently borrowed principle of Lévi-Strauss's methodology was his notion of "structuring antinomies," the binary oppositions around which the conflicts of any number of films were structured. This approach was used in reference to the musical and other genres (see Altman and Feuer), but it was most influential in the study of the Western. Jim Kitses, for example, in his introduction to *Horizons West* (1969), presents a table of antinomies that he believes are central to understanding the genre (Wilderness vs. Civilization, Individual vs. Community, Nature vs. Culture, etc.) and Will Wright (1975) traces the evolution of the Western by charting the changing configuration of the antinomies from the 1940s through the 1960s.

By the 1970s, however, this view that classical genres owe their success to their mythical dimensions came under closer scrutiny. John Cawelti, for example, argued that by the late 1960s–early 1970s, genre films ceased to function as pure, unalloyed myth, and that four types of what he calls "generic transformation" appeared: the burlesque, in which the conventions of the classical genre are pushed to absurd lengths and played for laughs, e.g. *Blazing Saddles* (1974); the nostalgia film, in which the glorious myths of Hollywood's Golden Age are revisited sentimentally, e.g. *True Grit* (1978); demythologization, in which the lessons of these classical genre films are revealed to be destructive and deluding, e.g. *Little Big Man* (1970); and affirmation of the myth for its own sake, in which the original myth is seen as antiquated, but nevertheless significant in its own way, e.g. *The Wild Bunch* (1979). The chief strength of Cawelti's overview is that it recognizes that Hollywood films could not be considered "pure myth" by the late 1960s, since all four forms of generic transformation frame the classical-genre-film-as-myth at one remove, from a self-conscious perspective in the present, clearly distanced from the imagined Golden Age. The chief limitation of Cawelti's argument is his explanation of why these transformations happened when they did. His contention that "generic exhaustion" occurred largely because a new generation of filmmakers and film-viewers (having grown up with television where older Hollywood films were ubiquitous) had acquired a degree of sophistication that made the old stories just that—old stories that failed to describe "the imaginative landscape of the latter half of the 20th century." Surely this increasing sophistication, the result of a fast-developing cinematic cultural literacy, was a major factor in shaping the changes in genre films by the late 1960s–early 1970s, but that explanation doesn't really address the interconnectedness of technological and demographic changes that accompanied those changes in cinematic literacy. The advent of television didn't increase just the average film-viewer's stock of stored narrative memories, it actually changed which genres were given highest priority by Hollywood, initially by triggering the industry's move to Cinemascope, Technicolor, and stereophonic sound that resulted in the greater prominence of the Western and historical epic. But by the late 1960s, television's impact on genre films was felt in another way. The ambiguity of television in American homes by the 1960s caused a profound shift in the nature of the film-going public. Families tended to stay home and watch television and would venture forth only rarely for special-event blockbusters. A new target audience emerged—namely, the youth audience, or more specifically a college-age audience—who by the late 1960s wanted a different form of entertainment, and to a certain extent received it in the form of "counter-cultural" films like *The Graduate* (1967), *Medium Cool* (1970), *Zabriske Point* (1970), *The Strawberry Statement* (1970), *Five Easy Pieces* (1970), which were marketed as a kind of genre unto themselves alongside the generic transformation films like *Bonnie and Clyde* (1967), *Little Big Man* (1970), etc. If genre-films-as-myth changed, it was due to the interconnectedness of social, technological, and demographic changes that gave rise to target myths for target audiences, a development that has serious ramifications for any claim that popular films reflect some sort of unitary, *mass* consciousness in some abstract sense.

If we are to understand the cultural context of genericity in the late 1980s–early 1990s, we need to examine the current set of pre-conditions formed by the interplay of cultural, technological, and demographic factors. Neither *Back to the Future III* nor *Dances With Wolves* fits any of Cawelti's categories particularly well—hardly surprising given the changes that have occurred in popular entertainment since the publication of his essay in 1978. The four types of generic transformation that were simultaneously at work in the 1960s and 1970s may have differed in regard to degree of respect shown a particular genre, but in each case the transformation is one that remains within the confines of a specific genre, whereas the eclectic, hybrid genre films of the eighties and nineties, like *Road Warrior* (1981), *Blade Runner* (1982), *Blue Velvet* (1986), *Near Dark* (1988), *Who Framed Roger Rabbit?* (1988), *Batman* (1989), *Thelma and Louise* (1991), all engage in specific transformation *across* genres. Just as these eclectic films were a new development in genericity in the 1980s, so too is the "new sincerity" of films like *Field of Dreams* (1989), *Dances With Wolves* (1990), and *Hook* (1991), all of which depend not on hybridization, but on an "ethnographic" rewriting of the classic genre film that serves as their inspiration, all attempting, using one strategy or another, to recover a lost "purity," which apparently pre-existed even the Golden Age of film genre.

Just as television changed the nature of popular entertainment in the 1950s and 1960s, a whole range of technological developments had a massive impact on the shape of genre films in the 1980s and 1990s. In his essay in this collection, Tom Schatz quotes the astounding increase in VCR ownership that developed in tandem with comparable developments in cable television, premium movie channels, and further refinements in both television monitors (specifically, simultaneous display of multiple channels and remote control) and playback options with the introduction of videodiscs and CD video. These interdependent developments cannot be reduced to any one overall effect. Some of the most significant ramifications of this new media technology have been: the exponential increase in the sheer volume of images that were transmitted to/playable in the average household, a comparable increase in software (titles available on videotape, disc, etc.), and parallel developments that allow for both the faster accessing and greater manipulability of that reservoir of images. The ever-expanding number of texts and technologies is both a reflection of and a significant contribution to the "array"—the perpetual circulation and recirculation of signs that forms the fabric of postmodern cultural life.

That a seemingly endless number of texts are subject to virtually immediate random access inevitably alters the relationship between classic and contemporary when both circulate alongside one another simultaneously. This simultaneity does not diminish the cultural "status" of the former so much as it changes its possible functions, which has far-reaching implications for how genre, and by extension popular culture, function in contemporary culture. The evolution of genre is traditionally conceived as a three-stage pattern of development: an initial period of consolidation in which specific narratives and visual conventions begin to coalesce into a recognizable configuration of features corresponding to a stable set of audience expectations. This period is followed by a "Golden Age," in which the interplay of by now thoroughly stabilized sets of stylistic features and audience expectations is subject to elaborate variations and permutations. The final phase is generally described in terms of all-purpose decline, in which the played-out conventions dissolve either into self-parody or self-reflexivity (end-of-the-West Westerns from *The Man Who Shot Liberty Valance* [1962] to *The Shootist* [1976]).

This three-stage model, however, doesn't adequately explain the reemergence of the Western, primarily because that resurgence is in many ways unprecedented. Rather than conceiving of the return of the Western as some kind of "fourth stage," it is perhaps more profitable to see this "renaissance" phase in terms of technological and cultural changes that have produced a set of circumstances in which the central function of genericity is in the process of being redefined. The "recyclability" of texts from the past, the fact that once-forgotten popular texts can now be "accessed" almost at will changes the cultural function of genre films past *and* present. The omnipresence of what Umberto Eco has called the "already said," now represented and recirculated as the "still-being-said" is not just a matter of an ever-accumulating number of texts ready to be accessed, but also involves a transformation of the "cultural terrain" that contemporary genre films must somehow make sense of or map. If genre films of the 1930s and 1940s functioned as the myths of Depression-era and war-time American culture, how do they function when they come back around as "classics" or just campy old movies? How does the "cultural work" of these genre films change, especially when these mythologies of earlier periods now co-exist alongside the "new" genre films and the mythologies they activate?

This situation is described quite effectively by Lestat, the vampire narrator of Anne Rice's *The Vampire Lestat*. As the novel opens, Lestat explains that he came back from the dead because he was awakened by the "cacophony in the air"—the radio and television waves that penetrated even his coffin underground. Upon resurfacing, one of the things that he finds most surprising about life at the end of the 20th Century is that

> the old was not being routinely replaced by the new anymore . . . In the art and entertainment worlds all prior centuries were being "recycled" . . . In grand fluorescent-lighted emporiums, you could buy tapes of medieval madrigals and play them on your car stereo as you drove ninety miles an hour down the freeway. In the bookstores Renaissance poetry sold side by side with the novels of Dickens or Ernest Hemingway. Sex manuals lay on the same table with the Egyptian Book of the Dead. . . . Countless television programs poured their ceaseless flow of images into every air-cooled hotel room. But it was no series of hallucinations. This century had inherited the earth in every sense. (8–9)

The ever-expanding array to which this "inheritance" gives rise alters not just the circumstances of *representation*, but also, just as fundamentally, the *to-be-represented*, the "raw" experience of daily life, which now comes to us already framed in multiple ways, *always already* so highly mediated. The fact that the old is not replaced by the new anymore does not just change the historical development of specific genres, it also changes the function of genre films, which, if they can still be said to be engaged in symbolically "mapping" the cultural landscape, must do so now in reference to, and *through* the array that constitutes the landscape. Rice's vampire is a case in point. Lestat's monstrosity is inseparable from his media personality—we're allegedly reading his best-selling memoirs that he composes on his word-processor when he is not otherwise engaged in recording his best-selling albums or making his rock videos—all of which play globally. If the genre texts of the 1960s are distinguished by their increasing self-reflexivity about their antecedents in the Golden Age of Hollywood, the genre texts of the late 1980s–early 1990s demonstrate an even more sophisticated hyperconsciousness concerning not just narrative formulae, but the conditions of their own circulation and reception in the present, which has a massive impact on the nature of popular entertainment.

When the Legend Becomes Hyperconscious, Print the . . .

Two scenes from Robert Zemeckis's *Back to the Future III* are useful examples of this emergent type of genericity. In this film we follow the adventures of Marty and Doc on the Western frontier in the 1880s, but we are also encouraged to take simultaneous delight in the intertextual adventures that *Back to the Future* engages in as it negotiates the array, the endless proliferation of signs that constitutes the postmodern frontier. When the characters travel back in time to the Old West, their trip is actually a voyage into the Old Western, a point made most explicitly in the scene where Marty attempts to drive back to the 1880s to rescue Doe from certain death. His avenue to the past is the film screen, a metaphor literalized by his driving the time machine through a drive-in movie screen in order to reach the past. The screen, then, is a portal to a 19th Century that can exist only in the form of images, in the form of cinematic reconstructions, and their very materiality is overtly foregrounded by the text, a point made especially explicit by the fact that the drive-in happens to be located within Monument Valley. Once back in the Old Western, when the painted image of Indians gives way to the real Indians(!) who chase the DeLorean across the desert, Marty looks into his rearview mirror to check their location. This point of view shot is perhaps the most representative shot in the film because it synthesizes in a single image the relationship between past and present and between genre and postmodern culture. This image, a close-up of the mirror, taken from Marty's perspective, frames the approaching Indians perfectly—we see "history," but only as an image from the rearview mirror of the present. The literalizing of yet another metaphor concerning the visibility of the past from the present foregrounds once again, in comedic terms, one of the main themes of postmodern historiography—that history can exist for us now only in forms of representation, that we construct the significance of the past only as we frame it in the present. This, of course, has led to charges of trivialization of history (Sobchack), i.e., evil postmodern culture has "reduced" the world to images that it then cannibalizes, as if "History" were somehow accessible to us without the mediation of representation, and as such possesses some kind of "sanctity" that cannot be treated ironically through such juxtapositions. In this foregrounding of time-travel as a process inseparable from the production of images, *Back to the Future*

III, resembles Julian Barnes *History of the World in 10½ Chapters*, in which the narrator states, "We cling to history as a series of salon pictures, conversation pieces whose participants we can easily reimagine back into life, when all the time it's more like a multi-media collage. . . . The history of the world? Just voices echoing in the dark; images that burn for a few centuries and then fade; stories, old stories that sometimes seem to overlap; strange links, impertinent connections " (240).

Within the Old West of *Back to the Future III*, we enter a narrative universe defined by impertinent connections, no longer containable by one set of generic conventions. We encounter, instead, different sets of generic conventions that intermingle, constituting a profoundly intertextual diegesis, nowhere more apparent than in the shot of the DeLorean time machine being pulled through the desert by a team of horses, the very co-presence of John Ford and H. G. Wells demonstrating the film's ability to access both as simultaneous narrative options, each with a set of conventions that can be recombined at will. This simultaneity of options, each subject to a kind of random access, is epitomized by the scene in which Marty prepares for his final slowdown with the villain. While practicing his draw in the mirror, dressed as Clint Eastwood in *A Fistful of Dollars* (1966), he calls up a few tough-guy lines, opting first for Eastwood's "Make my day" from his Dirty Harry/hard-boiled incarnation (*Dirty Harry*, 1971), then Travis Bickle's "Are you talkin' to me?" routine from *Taxi Driver* (1976). The simultaneous accessibility of the Spaghetti Westerner, the Hard-Boiled Cop, and the Urban Psychopath as potential heroic poses functions as a more sophisticated version of the print-outs that the Terminator sees before his eyes in Cameron's 1984 film, a menu of relevant lines that can be selected according to immediate need. The fact that the hero's choices are all cinematic quotations reflects not just the increasing sophistication of the cinematic literacy of *Back to the Future*'s audiences (and the profoundly intertextual nature of that literacy), but also the entertainment value that the ironic manipulation of that stored information now provides.

In contemporary popular culture, we see both the menu and its misuse; while the Terminator's options are all *appropriate* to a given situation, Marty's options are all *appropriated* from divergent contexts, all relevant insofar as they serve as macho poses, but inappropriate in that they purposely confuse time and genre. The Dirty Harry and Travis Bickle quotations are latter-day manifestations of the conventional gunfight, anachronisms in relation to the 1880s, but flashbacks in reference to the 1990s. Their co-presence in this scene reflects not the alleged "collapse of history," but a simultaneity that functions as a techno-palimpsest, in which earlier traces can be immediately called up, back to the surface to be replayed, or more precisely, recirculated. The act of appropriation problematizes distinctions between appropriate and inappropriate, as well as the stability of the categories of shared information that we might call cultural literacy. The categories are inappropriate only in reference to the topoi of the Old Western, but entirely appropriate to a culture in which those topoi are one of a series of push-button options. This foregrounded, hyperconscious intertextuality reflects changes in terms of audience competence and narrative technique, as well as a fundamental shift in what constitutes both entertainment and cultural literacy in the "Information Age."

Contemporary film criticism has been utterly unable to come to terms with these very profound changes in the nature of entertainment because this hyperconscious eclecticism is measured against 19th-Century notions of classical narrative and realist representation. The indictment drawn up by critics on the "left" and "right," who are always horrified by this unmanageable textuality that refuses to play by the old rules, always takes the same form—hyperconscious eclecticism is a sign of (choose one): a) the end of "Narrative"; b) the end of "the Real," "History," etc.; c) the end of art and entertainment for anyone other than overstimulated promiscuous teenagers; d) a sign of all-purpose moral and intellectual decay. All of this has been caused by: a) the all-purpose postmodern malaise that is hell-bent on recycling the detrius of Western Civilization instead of presenting us with the "really Real," "History," etc.; b) the overwhelming desire for perpetual stimulation that makes reading "Great Books" or watching "fine films" passé; c) shorter attention spans caused by television, advertising, rock music, and permissive child-raising; d) unbridled greed in people who have read neither (choose one) Aristotle or Marx; e) technology in the hands of people described in d). What is also left out of these pronouncements is the possibility that the nature of entertainment, narrative, art, identification may be undergoing significant reformulation due to widespread changes in the nature of information distribution, access, and manipulability. That this simply doesn't exist as an option reveals the tenacity with which social critics from Allen Bloom to Jean-Louis Baudrillard still cling to notions of art, epistemology, and signification that were developed, at the very latest, in the 19th Century. The following quotations suggest the common concerns, as well as the hysterical tenor, of condemnations of the new *zeitgeist*.

> Picture a thirteen-year-old sitting in the living room of his family home, doing his math assignment while wearing his headphones and watching MTV. . . . A pubescent child whose body throbs with orgasmic rhythms, whose feelings are made articulate in hymns to the joys of onanism or the killing of parents. . . . In short, life is made into a nonstop, commercially prepackaged masturbatory fantasy. (Bloom, 74–75)

Essentially a youthful crowd, this audience does not have very sophisticated tastes or expectations when it comes to narrative. Given that lack, they may never ask for strong, persuasive storytelling when they grow up. What we get . . . is not narrative as it has been traditionally defined, but a succession of undifferentiated sensations . . . there is in fact no *authentic* emotional build-up, consequently no catharsis at the movie's conclusion . . . . For in most movies today the traditional function has been inverted. Instead of the major dramatic incidents growing *naturally* out of the story, that is, out of the interaction of plausible characters with a recognizable moral and physical landscape, the opposite occurs. . . . [W]e are left without consoling coherences of old-fashioned movie narrative, left with anarchy, picking through the rubble it leaves in its wake, wondering what hit us. (Schickel, 3–4)

We rarely see the kind of panoramic composition that once allowed a generous impression of quasi-global simultaneity . . . and that also, more subtly enriches the frame in most great movies, whose makers have offered *pictures,* composed of pleasurable "touches" and legible detail. These moving tableaux often, as André Bazin argued, gave their viewers more choice, and required some (often minimal) interpretive attention. Only now and then and in films that don't come out of Hollywood—Terry Gilliam's *Brazil,* Stanley Kubrick's *Full Metal Jacket*—do we perceive such exhilarating fullness. In contrast, today's American movies work without or against the potential depth and latitude of cinema, in favor of that systematic overemphasis deployed in advertising and all other propaganda. (Miller, 52)

The all-purpose complaint about overstimulation is framed by Richard Schickel in reference to its devastating impact on narrative, but what exactly is in crisis—narrative, or just traditional notions of narrative that depend on coherence, plausibility, *authentic* emotional build-up, *natural* outgrowths, and catharsis? This list of requirements grows out of conventions first developed in classical tragedy (and codified most obviously in Aristotle's *Poetics*) and then expanded in realist theater and literature of the 19th-Century. According to this definition, virtually all modernist and postmodernist stories are deficient narratives. The only acceptable film narratives would appear to be those that are simply cinematic versions of 19th-Century models. Cultural changes that have occurred in the 20th Century apparently should have no impact on the well-made narrative. But even if we bracket this problem and ignore the obvious condescension in the dismissal of viewers less "sophisticated" than Schickel, the most serious problem with his narrative complaint has to do with yet another stipulation—the "recognizable moral and physical landscape" that characters must inhabit. This definition simply dismisses another possibility—that the popular narratives of the 1980s and 1990s present a moral and physical landscape in a state of previously unfathomable change and that these stories just might be an attempt to make the chaotic, dissonant cultures of the later decades of the 20th Century somehow more manageable through their presentation of a new mediated landscape that can be successfully mapped out only by contemporary media, and not some antiquated notion of the well-made play. The alternatives that Schickel offers—classical narrative or anarchy—are uncannily similar to the binary, either/or, all-or-nothing opposition proposed by Matthew Arnold in *Culture and Anarchy;* culture can only be "Culture" if it imitates the culture of any time *other than* the present.

Mark Cripsin Miller's condemnation of contemporary film style is cast in the same nostalgic mode, but his presuppositions regarding what films supposedly "worked" in the good old days are even more problematic. Schickel's nostalgia is for old-fashioned storytelling that did indeed exist (and still does to a far greater extent than he is willing to allow), but Crispin Miller pines for an imaginary film-viewing state that never existed, based as it is on Bazin's now-discredited assumptions concerning the relationship among the camera, reality, and the spectator. Miller's thesis concerning the negative impact that advertising has had on filmmaking is a rhetorically powerful argument, but his grand alternative—how film used to work—is founded on a thoroughly outdated understanding of filmic representation. By invoking Bazin's idealist theory of representation, in which true cinematic geniuses allow the photographic plate to capture the "real" in an unmediated way, thereby allowing truth to leap directly onto the celluloid strip, Miller posits an authentic or genuine form of representation against which all other types of film practice will be automatically judged deficient. The problem here, of course, is the notion of film as unmediated reality, a "fullness" that spectators were able to contemplate, free to formulate their own interpretations out of the essential ambiguity of the filmic image. One of the main themes of film theory since the late 1960s has been the rejection of this sort of idealism, and a number of theorists have been investigating the various stylistic, institutional, and ideological apparatuses that intervene between camera and "reality," and then between image and spectator, all of which demonstrate that these relationships are never as unmediated as Bazin imagined them to be. Miller's sweeping rejection of Hollywood filmmaking depends on his appeal to a "classic" film style as imagined by an antiquated film theory developed in the 1950s to describe the masterpieces of the 1930s and 1940s. It is hardly surprising that such an approach would provide only a blindered view of recent filmmaking, unable to come to terms with the highly "mediated" nature of our contemporary cultural existences and the images needed to represent them. The "exhilarating fullness" of this world is due to the fact that the real now comes to us always already "imaged" in any number of ways, the "depth and latitude" of contemporary cinema depending on the negotiation of that thickness of representation, those sedimented layers of images that define the cultural significance of any subject matter.

In all such attacks on current popular films that decry their avoidance of traditional narrative and authentic representation, one finds the same assumption—that the increasing sophistication of the media produces a sensory overload in which individual viewers are overstimulated into numbness, reachable only through blunt appeals to animal appetites. But these technophobic denunciations of media "overload" never even begin to address the distinguishing features of recent popular narratives, namely the attempts to encounter directly that "overload," that semiotic excess, and turn it into a new form of narrative entertainment that necessarily involves altering the structure and function of narrative. Tim Burton's *Batman* is a useful example here, because it epitomizes these attempts to incorporate the array that now forms the "imaginative landscape" of contemporary cultural life, and the criticism devoted to this film by Schickel and Miller epitomizes just as explicitly the failure of the anti-quated paradigms they use to evaluate it. Miller dismisses *Batman* as part of the "cartooning" of Hollywood, and Schickel cites it as one more example of deficient narrative, of visual pyrotechnics instead of plot— "Its story—the conflict between its eponymous hero and the Joker for the soul of Gotham City—is all right, kind of fun. But that is not what the movie is primarily about. It is about—no kidding—urban design" (14). But Burton's film is about far more than urban design. It presents a decidedly "old-fashioned" plot, but it also situates the adventures of Batman and the Joker within the mediated culture of the present and makes their manipulation of the images that surround them a crucial part of the conflicts between them.

Batman is not just vaguely symptomatic of how popular narratives try to envision the array—its main characters actively engage in different strategies of image play. Throughout the film, we see the Joker in his headquarters, producing "cut-ups" from the photographs that surround him, and then in a later scene at the museum he defaces one painting after another either by painting over the original or writing his name over the surface. His "hijacking" of signs is more explicit in his seizure of the television signal when he interrupts scheduled programming with his own parodic advertisements. Batman's appropriation of images works according to a quite different dynamic. Like the Joker, Batman seems to spend a significant amount of time watching television, and like his adversary he is shown surrounded by images that he manipulates for his own purposes. Just as Joker is practically engulfed by the photographs he cuts up, the first sequence in the Batcave presents Batman in front of a bank of monitors, surrounded by footage of his guests that his hidden cameras have recorded, images that he "calls up" (rather than "cuts up") in order to summon a reality that escaped his purview the first time around. While the Joker's manipulations of images is a process of consistent deformation, Batman engages in a process of retrieval, drawing on a reservoir of images that constitutes the past. The tension between abduction and retrieval epitomizes the conflicting but complementary processes at work in the film—a text that alternately *hijacks* and *accesses* the traditional Batman topoi. German Expressionism, Gaudi's *Sagrada Familia* Cathedral, Hitchcock films, etc.

The foregrounding of disparate intertexts and the all-pervasive hyperconsciousness concerning the history of both "high art" and popular representation has become one of the most significant features of contemporary storytelling. Narrative action now operates at two levels simultaneously—in reference to character adventure and in reference to a text's adventures in the array of contemporary cultural production. That this self-referentiality should emerge as a response to that array is comparable to parallel developments in other disciplines. Mark Poster's recent essay on modes of information is a very productive attempt to specify the impact of new technologies on the nature of information, but it also reveals the necessity of dealing with the second half of the problem—the need to specify emerging forms of textuality used to negotiate the array. He argues:

> . . . the complex linguistic worlds of the media, the computer and the database it can access, the surveillance capabilities of the state and the corporation, and finally the discourse of science are each realms in which the representational function of language has been placed in question by different communicational patterns, each of which shift to forefront the self-referential aspect of language. In each case, the language in question is constituted as an intelligible field with a unique pattern of wrapping, whose power derives not so much from representing something else, but from its internal linguistic structure. While this feature of language is always present in its use—today, meaning increasingly sustained through mechanisms of self-referentiality and the non-linguistic thing, the referent, fades into obscurity, playing less and less of a role in the delicate process of sustaining cultural memory. (72)

While Poster wisely acknowledges that there is a plurality of discontinuous modes of information each with its own historical peculiarities, he still maintains that his self-referentiality necessarily means the loss of the "really Real" referent—a loss which has only devastating effects on communication and subjectivity; "instead of envisioning language as a tool of a rational autonomous subject intent on controlling a world of objects for the purpose of enhanced freedom, the new language structures refer back upon themselves, severing referentiality and thereby acting upon the subject and constituting it in new and disorienting ways" (75). But do these new structures sever referentiality or just redefine the nature of referentiality? The notion of the referent posited here presupposes that this self-referentiality necessarily replaces any other kind of referentiality, but this argument offers no compelling reason to assume that self-referentiality, *ipso facto,* cancels out other types of referentiality. The self-referentiality that is symptomatic of communication in techno-sophisticated cultures, is a recognition of the highly discursive, thoroughly institutionalized dimension of all signs. At this point these signs become doubly referential, referring to a "really real" world, but also to the reality of the array, which forms the fabric of day-to-day experience in those very cultures. It is the individual negotiations of the array that form the delicate process of not just maintaining but constantly rearticulating cultural memories.

This "double referentiality" is the basis of the strategies of *rearticulation* discussed in the essays by Ann Cvetkovich, Cathy Griggers, Sharon Willis, and Ava Preacher Collins in this volume. The individual voguers in *Paris is Burning* (1990), Callie Khouri's screenplay for *Thelma and Louise* (1991), and Jim Jarmusch's use of Elvis in *Mystery Train* (1989), all recognize the inseparability of these two levels of referentiality in regard to notions of gender and racial difference, the nature of sexual preference, and the determination of cultural value. All such distinctions are patterns of signs, conventionalized in such a way that they are now taken to be "real" and therefore must be exposed as such through strategies of rearticulation that change that real by foregrounding mechanisms of referentiality. *Thelma and Louise* addresses the reality of the subjugation of women through its concerted reworking of the reality of the buddy film and the Western, repeatedly emphasizing the interconnectedness of gender difference and cinematic representation. Willis states this very succinctly: "We women were raised on the same cinematic and televisual images and stories that men were, and we were identifying, perhaps with more resistance, or more intermittence, but identifying all the same, with the same male figures and masculine scenarios as our male contemporaries. This must be the framework in which images of women raiding those nearly worn-out stories, trying on those clichéd postures might have the effect of 'newness,' and might challenge our readings of those postures themselves, as it might challenge our analysis of process and the effects of identification in our histories as consumers of popular culture." Rather than disorientation, these strategies of rearticulation that reflect a hyper-consciousness about the impact of images on social categorization are a process of fundamental *reorientation* conducted on and through that double referentiality.

The divergent, often conflicting ways in which recent narratives rearticulate conventional structures of popular genres has become a distinguishing feature of contemporary textuality, but there is no uniform politics of rearticulation anymore than there is a single aesthetic of rearticulation. The ironic, hyperconscious reworking of the array varies, from the flat-out comedic parody of *Back to the Future III* to the more unsettling, ambivalent parody of *Blue Velvet,* to the explicit hijacking of signs in a film like *Thelma and Louise.* While stakes and strategies may differ profoundly, they do have one thing in common—the recognition that the features of conventional genre films that are subjugated to such intensive rearticulation are not the mere detritus of exhausted cultures past: those icons, scenarios, visual conventions continue to carry with them some sort of cultural "charge" or resonance that must be reworked according to the exigencies of the present. The individual generic features then, are neither detritus nor reliquaries, but *artifacts* of another cultural moment that now circulate in different arenas, retaining vestiges of past significance reinscribed in the present.

In their frustration of the homogeneity and predictability considered the prerequisite for "genericity," these hybrid popular narratives present a paradoxical situation in which we encounter texts composed entirely of generic "artifacts" that contradict, as an assemblage, the function of genre as coordinator of narrative conventions and audience expectations. I use the term artifact here because the individual icon or semantic feature acquires a kind of different status, not really the same element as before, since it now comes back with a set of quotation marks that hover above it like an ironic halo. But neither is it really an exhausted piece of debris ready to be camped up. Finding an analogous sort of transformation is difficult because this transformation process is, to a great extent, unprecedented. One could point to the transformation/transportation that a tribal artifact undergoes when it is placed in the museum, when, for example, the ceremonial mask or door-lock becomes revalued as minimalist sculpture once it is solidly ensconced not just behind the glass, but with the institutional frameworks that guarantee its new value. Rather than the figural becoming merely functional, the poetic degraded to common prosaic speech, here the functional acquires a figural status, becoming marked as a special kind of expression that can no longer be taken literally. Generic artifacts, like tribal artifacts, acquire new discursive registers unforeseen in their initial contexts, but they differ in regard to stability of the rearticulation. Where the new value given to the mask is anchored within the discursive formation that is museum art, the generic artifact remains unanchored, subject to multiple transformations, multiple transportations while still retaining vestiges of the original semantic and syntactic relationships that once gave it a precise generic value.

When the legend becomes hyperconscious, print the array.

And the Only Words that came to Mind were "the New Sincerity"

Getting an adequate picture of contemporary genericity depends on our ability to recognize widespread changes in what constitutes narrative action and visual entertainment, but these ironic, eclectic texts are not the "whole story," or more appropriately, are not the *only* story. Another type of genre film has emerged since the late 1980s, which is also a response to the same media-sophisticated landscape. Rather than trying to master the array through ironic manipulation, these films attempt to reject it altogether, purposely evading the media-saturated terrain of the present in pursuit of an almost forgotten authenticity, attainable only through a sincerity that avoids any sort of irony or eclecticism. Films such as *Dances With Wolves, Hook,* and *Field of Dreams,* all fix this recoverable purity in an impossible past—impossible because it exists not just before the advent of media corruption, but because this past is, by definition, a never-never land of pure wish-fulfillment, in which the problems of the present are symbolically resolved in a past that not only did not, but could not exist.

In *Dances With Wolves,* that lost authenticity is situated in a West before the Western "got to it." In other words, the narrative of *Dances* focuses on the life of Native Americans before the arrival of the white man, a period traditionally ignored by the Western film. For most of the film, the only white man on the scene is John Dunbar, and he takes on the role of proto-ethnographer, rather than that of settler. His chief activity, observing and cataloguing the Sioux way of life, respects the purity of that tribe's existence. Dunbar's journal is all-important in this regard, since it serves as a guarantee of the authenticity of his position as ethnographer and as a symbol of his difference from other white men—a point made especially obvious when his journal is literally used as toilet paper by a pair of the most repulsive cavalrymen.

But *Dances With Wolves* makes this pre-history of the Western the site of another project—beyond an ostensible desire to depict the previously undepicted—in which the problems of White America of the 1990s are first diagnosed and then solved in the imaginary of that pre-history. The film repeatedly attempts to "demythologize" the classic Western, whether by inverting conventions or presenting what *really* happened. The manifest destiny ideology that floated implicitly or explicitly throughout virtually all classic Westerns concerned with the settling of the West is here rewritten as a ruthless imperialism. The traditional structuring antinomy, Civilization vs. Savagery, is mobilized here, but the polarities are reversed as the Sioux become the model civilization. This reversal is most apparent in the final scene in which the heroic Indian warriors recapture Dunbar, now one of their own, and kill off a few soldiers (now defined as savages) in the process. But at the same time, this rewriting of the history of the

Western expansion from the perspective of Native Americans is far from an end in itself. The other major project of the narrative, John Dunbar's self-actualization, is thoroughly intertwined with that rewriting; the virtues of the Sioux of the 1860s are expressed in terms of another ideology generated by White America, specifically a "New Age" mentality that becomes increasingly prominent in the second half of the film, when Dunbar "finds himself." The Sioux language may be respected here in an unprecedented manner through the use of subtitles, but the content of their speech is remarkably similar to what my students called the "California speak" of the present.

The complicated, conflicted agenda of the New Sincerity genre becomes apparent in the "harmony scene" mentioned in the introduction to this essay. After Dunbar takes part in the buffalo hunt and the celebration afterward, he watches the tribe move on the next day. The scene begins with a long pan across a breathtaking sunset—a tableau shot in the tradition of the classic Western, in which the Sioux are exquisitely silhouetted as dark figures on the crest of the horizon against the purple sky. This extremely painterly composition, when combined with Dunbar's voice-over, accords the figures an almost divine status: "It seems everyday ends with a miracle here. And whatever God may be I thank God for this day. To stay any longer would have been useless. We had all the meat we could possibly carry. We had hunted for three days, losing half-a-dozen ponies, and only three men injured. I'd never known a people so eager to laugh, so devoted to family, so dedicated to each other, and the only word that came to mind was harmony." When we first see Dunbar, it is from the side, observing the tableau from the distance in a completely different light zone. But as the scene progresses, his point of view shots of this awe-inspiring, harmonious spectacle alternate with shots of Dunbar, now framed by exactly the same majestic purple sunset. As he waves to his companions, he has been virtually united with them, set in harmony with them through the lighting and his Sioux chest-protector. Once this solidarity is established, there is a pause in the voice-over, and the last shot of the Sioux is followed by a low-angle close-up of Dunbar that monumentalizes him still further as he says, "Many times I'd felt alone, but until this afternoon I'd never felt completely lonely."

The progression here exemplifies the interdependency of the rewriting of history and the process of self-actualization in which the former repeatedly gives way to the latter. The voice-over praises the Sioux, but in the images they are framed as a decorative cluster of Noble Savages, with only the sympathetic White Man receiving the big close-up. Paradoxically, this scene, while it locates authenticity in the pre-history of the Golden Age of the Western, uses the Native American in a way that is remarkably similar to that employed by early 19th-Century European fiction such as

Chateaubriand's *Atala, or the Love of Two Savages in the Desert* (1801), which virtually defied the Noble Savage. The ultimate "authenticity" here depends upon another exigency—whether the plight of the Noble Savage of the past can serve as a satisfactory site for the narcissistic projections of alienated Europeans in the present. This dimension of *Dances With Wolves* becomes particularly apparent later in the film, when Dunbar reflects on the battle with the Pawnee, a battle without a "dark political agenda." "I felt a pride I'd never felt before. I'd never really known who John Dunbar was. Perhaps the name itself had no meaning, but as I heard my Sioux name being called over and over, I knew for the first time who I really was." In *Back to the Future III*, the rearview mirror tableau of "Indians!" emphasized the artifice of any cinematic travels into history, that all Westerns are finally nothing more than highly conventionalized representations of an imaginary West. *Dances With Wolves* avoids any such ironic constructions in its attempt to locate the authentic vision of the past; nonetheless, the seemingly unmediated tableau becomes another kind of mirror, the idealized imaginary in which the troubled hero sees himself, a mirror in which he is magically healed, in harmony, although only in this unrecoverable past.

Dances With Wolves contains a number of distinguishing features of this New Sincerity genre film: the move back in time away from the corrupt sophistication of media culture toward a lost authenticity defined simultaneously as a yet-to-be-contaminated folk culture of elemental purity, and as the site of successful narcissistic projection, the hero's magic mirror; the foregrounding not only of the intertextual, but of the "Urtextual," in which an originary genre text takes on a quasi-sacred function as the guarantee of authenticity; the fetishizing of "belief" rather than irony as the only way to resolve conflict; the introduction of a new generic imaginary that becomes the only site where unresolvable conflicts can be successfully resolved. While it is well beyond the scope of this essay to catalogue all the instances of this emergent configuration or to detail its various permutations, I hope a brief analysis of two representative films, *Hook* and *Field of Dreams*, will suggest how this configuration functions in other texts.

Spielberg's continuation of the Peter Pan story foregrounds all of these emergent conventions, and the differences between the Disney version and the Spielberg versions of J. M. Barrie's book throw the changing stakes of the New Sincerity genre film into sharp relief. While the former establishes the opposition between childhood and adulthood, the latter adds a level of hyper-self-awareness regarding the role film plays in constructing that difference, only to provide an imaginary transgression that takes the form of an ideal synthesis of the two. The indictment of media-saturated culture is omnipresent—the portable phone and camcorder are two major obstacles between Peter (now the lawyer as pirate) and his own children. The demonization of the camcorder involves one of the most interesting contradictions within the New Sincerity—that even though the search for lost purity and authenticity may depend on dazzling special effects and the blockbuster budgets they entail, there is nevertheless a free-floating technophobia. We know that Peter is a miserable failure as a father because he sends an assistant to videotape his son's baseball game, willfully foregoing the authentic, "unmediated" experience of watching his son's game "in person." The opposition between an authentic "live-ness" seen as superior to an artificial technology is emphasized repeatedly in the opening scenes. The family goes to a school play to see one of the children perform as Wendy in a theatrical production of *Peter Pan,* which appears to charm everyone in the diegetic audience except Peter. When the family arrives at Wendy's London townhouse, she tells the children the story of Peter Pan, the tale-telling "primal scene" accentuated in much the same way as the reading of *Peter Pan* in a comparable scene in *E.T.* (1982). In the earlier Spielberg film, the transmission of the "Ur-story" is set up in a mis-en-abîme structure—while the mother reads the "clap your hands if you believe" passage to her daughter, the son and E.T. sit transfixed in the dark, listening unobserved in the closet just as the theater full of parents and children listen unobserved in the dark. The fore-grounding of the Ur-text in *Hook* becomes most explicit when Wendy hands the adult Peter "the book"—apparently the first edition of Barrie's book, which, she tells Peter, was not fiction at all, but Barrie's transcription of the children's actual adventure, made possible by the fact that Barrie was their next-door neighbor. Once back in the world of children's fantasy, Peter regains his lost purity by recovering his childish delight in the elemental among the Wild Boys—a folk culture par excellence—leading to a resolution that can be effected only in *the* never-never land. Peter succeeds as a father only by recovering the lost child within him, thereby fusing two contradictory desires in one impossible composite: the desire to become the consummate father and the desire to return to the bliss of childhood outside of any paternal control.

The determination to resolve the unresolvable in a never-never land that is available neither in the present nor the past, but in an imaginary pre-history or originary moment takes an even more fanciful form in *Field of Dreams.* The film begins with a brief family history of the main character, Ray Kinsella, accomplished through family photos and voice-over narra-tion. The main point of this section is that Ray and his father, once close, especially in their love of baseball, broke irreconcilably during his teenage years. His father had "died" when his beloved White Sox threw the World Series in 1920 and later died an embittered shell of a man, old before his time. Once this troubled family history is established, the action in the present begins with Ray hearing voices in his cornfield. The field, like the Western landscape, is doubly fetishized as the yet to be corrupted pre-industrial, agrarian paradise ("Is this heaven?" "No. It's Iowa."), and as the site of narcissistic projection, here taken to an even greater extreme as the land actually talks directly to Ray about his private psycho-drama. The Ur-text in this film is likewise taken to more elaborate lengths; the lost text becomes the lost team as the Black Sox magically reappear in the dream diamond in the midst of the cornfield. The purity of this "text" is emphasized through explicit comparison to the corrupt present. Shoeless Joe waxes rhapsodic about the elemental joys of the game, the "thrill of the grass," the fact that he would have played just for meal money (unlike the soulless mercenaries of contemporary major league baseball, of course). Within this eulogizing of the game, baseball as it was played by Shoeless Joe and company becomes a folk-cultural activity—an organic and, at the same time, mystical ritual. Grafted onto this nostalgia for baseball the way it used to be is a parallel nostalgia for the 1960s, and Ray believes he must "ease the pain" of Terence Mann, the famous counter-cultural writer who becomes a kind of proxy father-figure for Kinsella, first in the 1960s (after he reads Mann's *The Boat Rocker* he stops playing catch with his biological father), and then explicitly in the 1980s when they travel together in search of their dreams. The connection between the America of the late teens and the late 1960s is articulated by Terence Mann during his "People Will Come" speech near the film's conclusion—both periods are collapsed into mere passing moments along-side the eternal game that represents an eternal childhood.

> Ray, people will come, Ray. They'll come to Iowa for reasons they can't even fathom. They'll turn in to your driveway not knowing for sure why they're doing it. They'll arrive at your door, as innocent as children, longing for the past. . . . They'll find they have reserved seats somewhere along the baselines where they sat when they were children and cheered their heroes, and they'll watch the game and it'll be as if they dipped themselves in magic waters. The memories will be so thick they'll have to brush them away from their faces. People will come, Ray. The one constant through all the years, Ray, has been baseball. America has rolled by like an army of steamrollers. It's been erased like a blackboard, rebuilt and erased again. But baseball has marked the time. This field, this game, it's part of our past, Ray. It reminds us of all that once was good and could be again. Oh, people will come, Ray, people will definitely come.

Mann's oration perfectly describes the appeal of the New Sincerity. Like this mythical game, these films offer the recovery of lost purity, the attempt to recapture the elemental simplicity of childhood delight in a magical state that yields its perfect resolutions of the otherwise impossible conflict. Once Kinsella's proxy father departs with the players to document their stories and what is "out there," Ray finally reunites with his real father—but his father as a young man, a young baseball player years before he becomes a father. Generational tensions dissolve in this imaginary realm where boys can once again play catch with their fathers before their fathers became fathers, an impossible temporality that allows boys to reconcile with their lost fathers only when they're yet to be their fathers.

The two types of genre film that I have discussed here represent contradictory perspectives on "media culture," an ironic eclecticism that attempts to master the array through techno-sophistication, and a new sincerity that seeks to escape it through a fantasy technophobia. That both should appear as responses to media saturation is not surprising, nor is the simultaneity of these responses; the popular narratives of the late 1980s and early 1990s articulate a profound ambivalence that reflects the lack of any sort of unitary mass consciousness. Both types of these genre films involve a meta-mythological dimension, in which the cultural terrain that must be mapped is a world already sedimented with layers of popular mythologies, some old, some recent, but all co-present and subject to rearticulation according to different ideological agendas. These emergent forms of genericity do not mark the beginning of post-postmodernism or late postmodernism, especially since the latter might turn out to be as much of a misnomer as Late Capitalism. One could just as easily argue that what we have seen of postmodernism thus far is really a first phase, perhaps Early Postmodernism, the first tentative attempts at envisioning the impact of new technologies of mass communication and information processing on the structure of narrative. If, following Marshal Berman, we might say that Modernism was a period in which all that was solid melted into air, the current period is defined by a different dynamic, in which all that is aired eventually turns solid, the transitory coming back around as the monumental with a decidedly different cultural status and cultural resonance. Contemporary popular narratives mark the beginning of the next phase, when new forms of textuality emerge to absorb the impact of these changes, and in the process turn them into new forms of entertainment.

Works Cited

Altman, Rick. *The American Film Musical*. Bloomington: Indiana University Press, 1987.

Aristotle. "The Poetics." *Aristotle's Theory of Poetry and Fine Art, with a Critical Text and Translation of the Poetics*. S. H. Butcher. New York: Dover, 1951.

Arnold, Matthew. *Culture and Anarchy*. Cambridge: Cambridge University Press, 1963.

Barnes, Julian. *History of the World in 10½ Chapters*. New York: Knopf, 1989.

Barrie, J. M. *Peter Pan in Kensington Gardens*. London: Hodder and Stroughton, 1906.

Baudrillard, Jean-Louis. "The Implosion of Meaning in the Media and the Information of the Social in the Masses." *Myths of Information: Technology and Postindustrial Culture*. Ed. Kathleen Woodward. Madison: Coda Press, 1980, pp. 137–148.

Bazin, André. *What Is Cinema?* Vols. I and II. Trans. Hugh Gray. Berkeley: University of California Press, 1971.

Berman, Marshall. *All That Is Solid Melts Into Air: The Experience of Modernity*. New York: Simon and Schuster, 1982.

Bloom, Allan. *The Closing of the American Mind: How Higher Education Has Failed Democracy and Impoverished the Souls of Today's Students*. New York: Simon and Schuster, 1987.

Cawelti, John. "*Chinatown* and Generic Transformation in Recent American Film." *Film Theory and Criticism*. Ed. Gerald Mast, Marshall Cohen. New York: Oxford University Press, 1978, pp. 498–511.

Chateaubriand, François René, Vicomte de. *Atala*. Paris: J. Corti, 1950, 1801.

Eco, Umberto. "Postmodernism, Irony and the Enjoyable." *Postscript to The Name of the Rose*. New York: Harcourt Brace Jovanovich, 1984, pp. 65–67.

Feuer, Jane. "The Self-Reflective Musical and the Myth of Entertainment." *Genre: The Musical*. Ed. Rick Altman. London: Routledge and Kegan Paul, 1981, pp. 208–215.

Kitses, Jim. *Horizons West: Anthony Mann, Budd Boetticher, Sam Peckinpah: Studies of Authorship within the Western*. Bloomington: Indiana University Press, 1969.

Lévi-Strauss, Claude. *Structured Anthropology*. Trans. Claire Jacobson, Brooke Grundfest Schoept. New York: Basic Books, 1963.

Miller, Mark Crispin. "Hollywood: The Ad." *Atlantic Monthly*. April, 1990, pp. 49–52.

Poster, Mark. "Words Without Thing: The Mode of Information." *October* 53. Summer, 1990, pp. 63–77.

Rice, Anne. *The Vampire Lestat*. New York: Ballantine, 1984.

Schickel, Richard. "The Crisis in Movie Narrative." *Gannett Center Journal*. Summer, 1989, pp. 1–15.

Sobchack, Vivian. *Screening Space: The American Science Fiction Film*. New York: Ungar, 1980.

Wright, Will. *Six Guns and Society: A Structural Study of the Western*. Berkeley: University of California Press, 1975.

Notes

1. The New Hollywood

1. Recent studies of "classical" Hollywood and the "studio system" include *The Classical Hollywood Cinema: Film Style and Mode of Production to 1960,* David Bordwell, Janet Staiger, and Kristin Thompson (New York: Columbia University Press, 1985); *The Hollywood Studio System,* Douglas Gomery (New York: St. Martin, 1986); and *The Genius of the System: Hollywood Filmmaking in the Studio Era,* Thomas Schatz (New York: Pantheon, 1988).

2. Here and throughout this essay, I will be referring to "*rentals*" (or "rental receipts") and also to "*gross revenues*" (or "box-office revenues"). This is a crucial distinction, since the gross revenues indicate the amount of money actually spent at the box office, whereas rental receipts refer, as *Variety* puts it, to "actual amounts received by the distributor"—i.e., to the moneys returned by theaters to the company (usually a "studio") that released the movie. Unless otherwise indicated, both the rentals and gross revenues involve only the "domestic box office"—i.e., theatrical release in the U.S. and Canada.

   All of the references to box-office performance and rental receipts in this article are taken from *Variety,* most of them from its most recent (January 11–17, 1989; pp. 28–74) survey of "All-Time Film Rental Champs," which includes all motion pictures returning at least $4 million in rentals. Because this survey is continually updated, the totals include reissues and thus may be considerably higher than the rentals from initial release. In these cases I try to use figures from earlier *Variety* surveys for purposes of accuracy.

3. "'Gone With the Wind' Again Tops All-Time List," *Variety* (May 4, 1983), p. 15.

4. "Top 100 All-Time Film Rental Champs," *Variety* (January 6, 1992), p. 86.

5. Eileen R. Meehan, "'Holy Commodity Fetish, Batman!': The Political Economy of a Commercial Intertext," in *The Many Lives of the Batman,* Roberta E. Pearson and William Uricchio, eds. (New York: BFI-Routledge, 1991), p. 62.

6. Christopher H. Sterling and Timothy R. Haight, *The Mass Media: Aspen Institute*

Guide to Communications Industry Trends (New York: Praeger, 1978), pp. 187 and 352. Unless otherwise noted, the statistics on attendance, ticket sales, etc., are from this reliable compendium of statistical data on the movie industry.

7. "All-Time Film Rental Champs," *Variety* (January 11–17, 1989), pp. 28–74.

8. Personal correspondence from Selznick to Louis B. Mayer, September 16, 1953; David O. Selznick Collection, Humanities Research Center, University of Texas at Austin.

9. Rudy Behlmer, ed., *Memo from David O. Selznick* (New York: Viking, 1972), p. 373.

10. See Janet Staiger, "Individualism Versus Collectivism," *Screen* 24 (July–October, 1983), pp. 68–79.

11. Freeman Lincoln, "The Comeback of the Movies," *Fortune* (February, 1955), p. 127.

12. See Robert Vianello, "The Rise of the Telefilm and the Networks' Hegemony Over the Motion Picture Industry," *Quarterly Review of Film Studies* (Summer, 1984) pp. 204–18.

13. See William Lafferty, "Feature Films on Prime-Time Television," in *Hollywood in the Age of Television*, Tino Balio, ed. (Boston: Unwin Hyman, 1990), pp. 235–256.

14. Lincoln, "Comeback," p. 131.

15. Stephen M. Silverman, *The Fox That Got Away* (Secaucus, N.J.: Lyle Stuart Inc., 1988), pp. 323–329.

16. Tino Balio, "Introduction to Part II" of *Hollywood in the Age of Television*, pp. 259–260.

17. Joseph R. Dominick, "Film Economics and Film Content: 1964–1983," in *Current Research in Film* (Norwood, N.J.: Ablex, 1987), p. 144.

18. Lafferty, "Feature Films," pp. 245–248.

19. Michael Pye and Lynda Myles, *The Movie Brats* (New York: Holt, Rinehart and Winston, 1979), p. 236.

20. Carl Gottlieb, *The Jaws Log* (New York: Dell, 1975), pp. 15–19. Note that Dell is a subdivision of MCA.

21. Gottlieb, *Jaws Log*, p. 62.

22. Pye and Myles, *Movie Brats*, p. 232.

23. James Monaco, *American Film Now* (New York: New American Library, 1979), p. 50.

24. Axel Madsen, *The New Hollywood* (New York: Thomas Y. Crowell, 1975), p. 94.

25. Balio, "Introduction to Part I," *Hollywood in the Age of Television*, p. 29.

26. "Theatrical Data" section in "1990 U.S. Economic Review" (New York: Motion Picture Association of America, 1991), p. 3.

27. Dominick, "Film Economics," p. 146.

28. Jennifer Pendleton, "Fast Forward, Reverse," *Daily Variety* (58th Anniversary Issue, "Focus on Entertainment Marketing," October, 1991), p. 14.

29. Michelle Hilmes, "Breaking the Broadcast Bottleneck," in Balio, *Hollywood*, pp. 299–300.

30. See Hilmes, "Breaking," and also Bruce A. Austin, "Home Video: The Second-Run 'Theater' of the 1990s," in Balio, *Hollywood,* pp. 319–349.

31. J. Hoberman, "Ten Years That Shook the World," *American Film* 10 (June, 1985); p. 42.

32. Jim McCullaugh, "*Star Wars* Hikes Demand for Dolby," *Billboard* (July 9, 1977), p. 4.

33. "*Star Wars:* A Cultural Phenomenon," *Box Office* (July, 1987), pp. 36–38.

34. Hoberman, "Ten Years," pp. 36–37.

35. "Behind the Scenes on *Raiders of the Lost Ark,*" *American Cinematographer* (November, 1981), p. 1096. See also Tony Crawley, *The Steven Spielberg Story* (New York: Quill, 1983), p. 90.

36. "Top 100 All-Time Film Rental Champs," *Variety* (January 11–17, 1989), p. 26.

37. Hoberman, "Ten Years," and A. D. Murphy, "Twenty Years of Weekly Film Ticket Sales in U.S. Theaters," *Variety* (March 15–21, 1989), p. 26.

38. Figures from "Theatrical Data" and "VCR and Cable" sections in MPAA's "1990 U.S. Economic Review."

39. Robert B. Levin and John H. Murphy, unpublished case study of Walt Disney Pictures' 1986 marketing strategies, for use in an advertising course taught by Professor Murphy.

40. Richard Natale, "Hollywood's 'new math': Does it still add up?," *Variety* (September 23, 1991), pp. 1, 95.

41. Terry Ilott, "Yank pix flex pecs in new Euro arena," *Variety* (August 19, 1991), pp. 1, 60.

42. John Marcon, Jr., "Dream Factory to the World," *Forbes* (April 29, 1991), p. 100.

43. Figures from "Prints and Advertising Costs of New Features" in MPAA's "1990 U.S. Economic Review."

44. Charles Fleming, "Pitching costs out of ballpark: Record pic-spending spells windfall for tv," *Variety* (June 27, 1990), p. 1.

45. "Week-by-week domestic b.o. gross," *Variety* (January 7, 1991), p. 10.

46. "Video and Theatrical Revenues," *Variety* (September 24, 1990), p. 108.

47. "The Teachings of Chairman Jeff," *Variety* (February 4, 1991), p. 24. Article contains excerpts of the January 11 memo.

48. Charles Fleming, "Megabudgets Boom Despite Talk of Doom," *Variety* (February 4, 1991), pp. 5ff.

49. Geraldine Fabrikant, "In Land of Big Bucks, Even Bigger Bucks," *New York Times* (October 18, 1990), p. C5.

50. William Goldman, *Adventures in the Screen Trade* (New York: Warner Books, 1983), p. 39.

51. "Disney's profits in park: Off 23%," *The Hollywood Reporter* (November 15, 1991), pp. 1, 6.

52. Meehan, "'Holy Commodity," p. 47.

53. John Mickelthwait, "A Survey of the Entertainment Industry," *The Economist* (December 23, 1989), p. 5.

54. For an excellent overview of both the Sony and Matsushita deals, and Ovitz's role

in each, see Connie Bruck, "Leap of Faith," *New Yorker* (September 9, 1991), pp. 38–74.

55. Lawrence Cohn, "Stars' Rocketing Salaries Keep Pushing Envelope," *Variety* (September 24, 1990), p. 3.

56. Spielberg/Hoffman/Williams deal reported in Geraldine Fabrikant, "The Hole in Hollywood's Pocket," *New York Times* (December 10, 1990), p. C7. Nicholson deal in Ben Stein, "Holy Bat-Debt!," *Entertainment Weekly* (April 26, 1991), p. 12.

57. Fabrikant, "The Hole in Hollywood's Pocket," p. C7.

58. Meehan, "'Holy Commodity," p. 52.

59. Mark Crispin Miller, "Hollywood: The Ad," *Atlantic Monthly* (April, 1990), pp. 49–52.

60. Quoted in Hoberman, "Ten Years," p. 36.

61. Richard Schickel, "The Crisis in Movie Narrative," *Gannett Center Journal* 3 (Summer, 1989), p. 2.

62. Schickel, "Crisis," pp. 3–4.

63. Schickel, "Crisis," p. 3.

64. See Joshua Hammer, "'Small Is Beautiful,'" *Newsweek* (November 26, 1990), pp. 52–53, and William Grimes, "Film Maker's Secret Is Knowing What's Not for Everyone," *New York Times* (December 2, 1991), pp. B1+.

2. Reclaiming the Social

1. For a theoretical analysis of the depoliticizing nature of aesthetic discourse, principally as it has been used by Marxists, see Bennett. For an analysis of the depoliticizing of politics, see Grossberg.

2. I have taken this issue up in Giroux, *Border Crossings*.

3. This issue is taken up in great detail in Aronowitz and Giroux.

4. This issue is explored from a variety of contexts in Ferguson, Gever, Minh-ha, and West, eds. See Hall for an analysis of the relationship between culture and politics as part of the new hegemonic thrust in England.

5. Giroux and Trend provide a critical analysis of the conservative assault on education and the arts in the United States.

6. For three excellent collections that address these issues in feminist, postmodern, and postcolonial terms, see Grossberger, Nelson, and Treichler, eds.; Rutherford, ed.; Ferguson Gever, Minh-ha, and West, eds.

7. The chief proponent of this position is Graff. As Bruce Henricksen points out, Graff does not sufficiently "contextualize his model as a class and power-allocating activity"; nor does he move beyond the relativism of a dialogic model in which there is "no firm ground, nothing to believe in but the conversation itself" (pp. 31, 35).

8. The theoretical rationale and specifics of this type of critical pedagogy, one which is linked to the imperatives of defining teachers as transformative intellectuals, and pedagogy as a broader exercise in the creation of critical citizens can be found in Giroux, *Schooling and the Struggle for Public Life*.

9. For an exemplary analysis of critical pedagogy as a form of cultural politics, see Simon.

10. On the radical need to engage "whiteness" as a central racial category in the

construction of moral power and political/cultural domination, see Dyer; West, "The New Cultural Politics," p. 105; Ferguson, Gever, Minh-ha, and West, eds.

11. For another analysis of the relationship between critical pedagogy and the issue of resistance in *Dead Poets Society,* see Peter McLaren.

12. There is a curious "structuring silence" in Keating's refusal to engage or indicate any evidence of the "beat" literature of the 1950s, which appropriated "carpe diem" as a counter-cultural text. Given Keating's hip, iconoclastic pedagogy, it seems inconceivable that a "free-thinking" English teacher would not be aware of the works of "beat" poets and novelists such as Jack Kerouac, William Burroughs, Gregory Corso, Allen Ginsberg, and others.

13. I would like to thank Hilary Radner for her helpful comments about gender relations in this film.

14. I have taken up this issue particularly with respect to the appropriation of Paulo Freire's work and the pedagogy of the popular; see Giroux, "Paulo Freire and the Politics of Post-Colonialism"; see also the various articles in Giroux and Simon eds.

15. For an excellent analysis of the politics of reading formations, see Bennett, *Outside Literature.*

3. Pretty Is as Pretty Does

I would like to thank my colleagues in Communication and Gender Studies at the University of Notre Dame for their patience, support, and suggestions; Tom Schatz, Kathleen Pyne, and Susan White who discussed my ideas with me; my students Megan Wade, Liza Dolen, and Kelly Streit, whose papers on *Pretty Woman* helped me realize the significance of this film; the Feminist Forum of the University of Notre Dame who asked me to lecture on the film; my research assistant Ron Hogan; my co-editors Ava and Jim; and finally Diane Gibbons for her careful reading, comments, and much more than is implied in the term copy-editing.

1. *Variety* reported in January of 1991 that with $81,903,000 in rentals *Pretty Woman* (directed by G. K. Marshall, produced by A. Milchan and S. Reuther, distributed by Buena Vista) ranked second after *Ghost* among films released in 1990. *Forbes* reported in April of 1991 that the film grossed $180 million in the U.S. but over $250 million at foreign box offices.

2. See the work of Claude Lévi-Strauss for an explanation of this concept and the work of Edmund Leach for a discussion of the limits of the validity of this concept.

3. The ideal of the companionate marriage in which men and women are united by the bonds of conjugal love, in which woman theoretically had some role in the choice of her husband, was in part supported by the 18th-century novel; however, in fact, women were legally and materially constrained by their position within the family. See Nancy Armstrong for a discussion of the complexity of these issues.

4. Miriam Hansen explains: "Throughout most of the nineteenth century, public life was a predominantly masculine arena to which women had access only in a highly controlled and dependent form; conversely, the private realm of the family was identified as the domain of an idealized femininity, defined by the cult of domesticity, sexual purity, and moral guardianship" (52). For a discussion of the relationship between the doctrine of separate spheres and the representation of feminine sexuality see the work of Thomas Laqueur.

5. This genre evolves out of the conduct books of the 18th and 19th Centuries, when book publishers began addressing the new middle-class woman rather than the

aristocratic male. In the 1960s, the genre began its final evolution into the full-scale self-help book of the 1980s. For a description of the conduct books of the 18th and 19th Centuries see the work of Nancy Armstrong.

6. Helen Gurley Brown also wrote a sequel to *Sex and the Single Girl* called *Sex in the Office* published in 1964.

7. Helen Gurley Brown did not have a college education nor did she come from a privileged, or even middle-class background. Her instructions were geared towards women like her, whose principle capital was the "self" that they created and mobilized in the office, where their careers began as part of the secretarial pool.

8. See Lois Banner, *American Beauty*.

9. See Stewart Ewen and Elizabeth Ewen, *Channels of Desire: Mass Images and the Shaping of American Consciousness*.

10. *Working Girl* (1988, directed by Mike Nichols, starring Melanie Griffith) also marks this shift in feminine definition. The "Working Girl" of the film's title is sexually attractive but she also has excellent business sense, underlining the qualities of value in the new feminine. She has both the sexually knowledgeable body and the capacity for agency within a public sphere. Again, it would be a mistake to see either *Working Girl* or *Pretty Woman* as marking a break in the Hollywood tradition; both narratives formalize a number of issues surrounding the place occupied by the career woman within contemporary culture, and the way the figure of the career woman mobilizes and immobilizes the codes of feminine representation defined through the binary opposition masculine/feminine. A comparison of the 1932 (directed by John Stahl), the 1941 (directed by Robert Stevenson) and the 1961 (directed by David Miller) versions of *Black Street,* based on a Fannie Hurst novel (1931), offers a very clear illustration of the evolution of the intersecting tropes of chastity and economic autonomy in the production of the feminine position(s) within classical Hollywood narrative.

11. See Ava Collins in "Redressing Cinderella," for a more elaborate discussion of these issues.

12. Feminist critic, Rachel DuPlessis offers a succinct definition of the marriage plot: "What I call a romance or marriage plot is the use of conjugal love as a telos and of the developing heterosexual love relation as a major, if not the only major, element in organizing the narrative action" (p. 200).

13. Huang Mei goes so far as to see the two as virtually synonymous: "the Cinderella theme (or marriage plot)" (p. 119) in *Transforming the Cinderella Dream.* For a popular culture articulation of the issue see C. Dowling, *The Cinderella Complex.*

14. Huang Mei comments: "It is well known that the story of Pamela's Cinderella adventure was originally 'concocted' by Richardson for women, with an eye to teach them to live and write properly. . . ." (p. 26).

15. Tania Modleski comments: "Samuel Richardson's *Pamela,* about a servant girl who marries her master is, as many critics have observed, the 'mother' of popular romances for women" (p. 36).

16. Edward's fistfight with his ex-partner in corporate rape, Phil (Jason Alexander), who assaults Vivian, and from whom Edward must save her, represents Vivian's redemption, her reform that now makes her worthy to be a wife.

17. The 18th-Century novel *Fanny Hill, or, Memories of a Woman of Pleasure* raises a number of interesting problems in this context, too complex to be addressed here.

18. This fantasy is defined in terms of primary narcissism as opposed to secondary narcissism discussed later in the paper. See Laplanche and Pontalis for a fuller discussion of this issue.

19. I discuss the full ramifications of Oedipalization as the recognition of the threat of castration later in the article. See Note 27.

20. For a different reading of the importance of this intertext, see Ava Collins, cited above.

21. My goal here is not to exhaust the phantasmatic paths of the film, which would be impossible by definition, but to sketch out a number of potential paths.

22. Louise Kaplan offers the following definition of fetishism: "The basic requirement or obligatory precondition for sexual arousal is that the pervert have in his possession an inanimate object—a leather boot, a lace handkerchief, a black corset—or that he obtain a sexual partner who is willing to wear the inanimate object. However, beyond these fundamentals are numerous possibilities and variations" (21).

23. This notion of "covering up" is crucial to the importance women's fashions come to play within cinematic mise-en-scène and its relation to narrative desire. Fashion demands that the woman's body be appropriately covered just as the fetishist demands that the foot be covered. At the same time that these coverings cover, their function is also to draw attention to that which they cover.

24. As a child, I found this story very disturbing. First of all it seemed very possible to me, statistically speaking, that the Prince could make a mistake. In an entire country, there had to be at least several girls with equally small feet. Secondly, I found it difficult to believe that the Prince really did not love her if he were only able to recognize her foot size. In adult terms, the implausibility of the plot underlined the arbitrary quality of the fetish and its relationship to the romantic heterosexual paradigm.

25. One of the principle arguments to emerge out of Mulvey's article is the notion that masculinity is implied, defined as such, through the position of looking while femininity is defined through the quality of "to-be-looked-at-ness." Here I am investigating a more subtle articulation of this topos, also taken from the same article.

26. See Note 28 for a discussion of scopophilia.

27. The threat represented by castration is specifically the threat of the father who has shown himself more powerful than the little boy. For the boy to accept the law (society as a system of constraints imposed upon the individual subject) entails an internalization of that threat, represented externally by the female as a sign of the castrated subject. In accepting his position as regulated by paternal law, the boy must renounce his desire for the mother, or rather displace it in recognition of the father's superior claims. He must become like the father, but he can never be the Father because he is always subject to the Law. This process of accepting the law is part of the process of Oedipalization, or the resolution of the Oedipal complex, in which the child's immediate desire was focused on the mother. See Laplanche and Pontalis, for a more complete definition of these terms.

28. Scopophilia is most simply described as: love or desire in seeing, or the desire to see. Mulvey defines the "Scopophilic instinct" as the "pleasure in looking at another person as an erotic subject" (p. 67). The fetish is not necessarily visual (i.e., it could be something the subject touched, or heard, as long as it enabled him to disavow the threat of castration), though it lends itself most easily to visual representation.

29. Mulvey is in fact describing the treatment of Marlene Dietrich in the films of the classical Hollywood director Josef von Sternberg.

30. This wardrobe is part of the deal that Vivian makes with Edward. In addition to giving her money, she also keeps the clothes as part of the profits of her transactions.

31. I discuss the issue of narcissism, consumerism, and feminine pleasure more fully in "Quality Narcissism," *Genders:* 8 (Fall, 1990) and in *Shopping Around: Feminine Culture and the Pursuit of Pleasure* (Routledge, forthcoming).

32. This spread appeared in the April issue of *Vogue,* which was on the newsstands in mid-March, but the interview was done before the film's release.

33. In this sense, Vivian's racial and ethnic identity is crucial. The logic of this narrative demands that Vivian be white. The "moral values" of patriarchal capitalism could not have accommodated a Galatea (or Pygmalion, for that matter) who was African-American, Hispanic, or Asian. The implicit racism of *Pretty Woman* is characteristic of marriage-plot narratives from *Jane Eyre* to *Harlequin Romances.*

34. This regime comes under the rubric of "Je sais bien mais quand même"—I know very well but—in which the process of disavowal is always also a process of admission, of confession, a conscious embrace of a specific discursive ideology. As Jim Collins points out in *Uncommon Cultures:* "Discursive ideologies are the means specific discourses use to provide ample justification for a spectator or reader to formulate a 'quand même' position regarding that discourse" (110). See also Octave Mannoni, *Clefs pour l'Imaginaire ou L'Autre Scène.*

35. If feminine viewers tended to comment on Julia Roberts's outfits while watching the film, masculine viewers seemed to give the same attention to Roberts's doubles, as though they represented the same transformative array that the outfits represented for the female viewer.

36. The use of composite bodies in fashion spreads is also quite common.

4. The Unauthorized Auteur Today

1. *Epuration* refers to the period in France just following World War II when certain personalities in the film world were for a time forbidden to practice their trade because of hints of collaboration with the Nazis. Henri-Georges Clouzot and Artletty were the most famous names taken out of circulation for a time.

2. *Hors Cadre* 8 (Spring, 1990); James Naremore, "Authorship and the Cultural Politics of Film Criticism," *Film Quarterly* 44, no. 1 (Fall 1990); Timothy Corrigan, *A Cinema Without Walls* (New Brunswick: Rutgers University Press, 1991), Naturally none of the authors of these texts wants to return to the critical paradigm of the 1950s and 1960s; all of them complicate the issue, but all of them discuss it too. Naremore does so sheepishly, a bit ashamed to bring it up in these sophisticated days. Corrigan more courageously accords the auteur a role in the new system of textual production that goes by the name postmodernism. Many of the contributors to *Hors Cadre* gladly return to the concept if not the flesh and blood of the author (seen now as split, or absent, or constructed, or as a mere signature) in their efforts to probe ever more deeply into the peculiar, and I would say hybrid, medium known as the cinema.

3. Someone who does not forget this is Jim Hillier whose collection *Cahiers du Cinéma: The 1950s* (Cambridge, Mass.: Harvard University Press, 1988) is indispensible to the history of auteurism.

4. André Bazin, *What is Cinema?*, trans. Hugh Gray, Vol. 1 (Berkeley: University of California, 1968), p. 130.

5. André Bazin, "La Politique des auteurs," in Hillier, *Cahiers du Cinéma.*

6. Peter Wollen, *Signs and Meaning in the Cinema* (London: Secker and Warburg, 1972), p. 168.

7. I am indebted here to Aaron Gerow's unpublished 1991 paper "Spectating in the Postmodern: The Suzuki Seijun Mondai."

8. Competing values complicate the situations, as when filmmakers such as Helke Sander and Tomás Gutiérrez Alea loudly disdain cinema as "art" in the traditional sense, yet are canonized as auteurs who have opened up new options in the social production and reception of cinema.

9. Naremore declared auteurism dead on page 20 of his *Film Quarterly* essay, adding that debates about it (his and mine included, I suppose) were likewise finished.

10. Corrigan, *A Cinema Without Walls*, p. 135.

11. Edward Said, *Beginnings* (Baltimore: The Johns Hopkins University Press, 1975), p. 24.

12. Eric Rohmer relates viewing films to reading books in a library in his *The Taste for Beauty* (Cambridge University Press, 1989), 157.

13. Maseo Miyoshi, *Off Center: Power and Cultural Relations between Japan and the United States* (Cambridge, Mass.: Harvard University Press, 1991), p. 217.

14. Masao Miyoshi notes that the scholarly essay is increasingly being replaced by the transcript of the round-table discussion, the latter satisfying a need for quick summaries of positions, for the illusion of immediacy and of the "event" rather than of reflection, and of course for the illusion of contact with the auteurs of the intellectual sphere.

15. To all appearances, a disproportionate share of the film's $16,000,000 budget went into the final quarter of the movie, complete with daring, but familiar helicopter shots. Our interest in the female characters and their perceptions is swept into the chase, re-masculinized. Still, in its very title *Thelma and Louise* gives a conscience to the rather standard road picture it becomes. The genre perhaps has always contained its own critique, though it may seldom have been so visible.

16. Gilles Deleuze, *Cinema I: The Movement-Image* (tr. by Hugh Tomlinson Minneapolis: University of Minnesota Press, 1989), p. 21.

17. See Cl. Gandelman and N. Greene, "Fétichisme, signature, cinéma," *Hors Cadre* 8 (Spring, 1990), pp. 147–162.

18. Jacques Aumont, *L'Oeil interminable* (Paris, Séguir 1989), and *L'Image* (Paris: Fernand Nathan, 1990); Raymond Bellour, ed., *Cinéma et peinture: Approaches* (Paris: Presses Universitaires de France, 1990), and *L'Entre-image* (Paris: 1990).

19. Pierre Corneu, the director of *Tous les matins du monde,* does not hesitate to discuss the Straub/Huillet *Chronicle of Anne Magdelena Bach* in assessing his own achievement in *Cahiers du Cinéma* 451 (January, 1992). *Tous les matins du monde* grossed more money than any other film in Paris in the first weeks of 1992. While the French may have pushed the notion of the artist-creator the furthest, an international interest in this topos can be seen by scanning recent films such as *Angels at my Table* (Campion, 1991), *Vincent and Theo* (Altman, 1990), *Prospero's Books* (Greenway, 1991), and so on.

20. Marc Le Bot, "L'Auteur anonyme ou l'état d'imposteur," *Hors Cadre* 8 (Spring, 1990), p. 19.

21. Paradoxical because the term "écriture" which has haunted cinema since 1950 at first did so under the spirit of literature. Today those films—specifically Rivette's and Godard's—that take up the struggle of language and expression, increasingly do so under the spirit of painting and art history. This would be Raymond Bellour's point, and I agree with it.

22. *Lire* 193 (October, 1991).

23. Marguerite Duras, *L'Amant de la Chine du Nord* (Paris: Gillimard, 1991), p. 17.

24. The phenomenon is notable enough to have received mention (with a photo!) in *Newsweek*, February 17, p. 8.

5. Loose Canons

1. See especially Aronowitz and Giroux, and Rorty.

2. Popular film was incorporated into the arena of academic study through the development of "the auteur theory," which in its earliest expressions attributed the message or vision of the text to the guiding consciousness and genius of the director, ignoring the highly collaborative nature of filmic production. Dudley Andrew's essay in this volume traces the evolution of this concept and argues convincingly that auteurism still exerts a powerful evaluative force, even if—or perhaps because—it is no longer institutionally reified.

3. The day this paper was sent to press for copy-editing, the feature article on the front page of the *Chicago Tribune* was about the postal service's plans to allow the public to decide which image of Elvis should grace its newest stamp—the Las Vegas Elvis or the youthful, Fifties Elvis. I am quite anxious to see the outcome!

4. Janet Staiger, "The Politics of Film Canons"; see also Dudley Andrew and Gerald Mast.

5. I am indebted to Giroux and Simon for this formulation, which seems to me a crucial one, but which many conservative critics choose to ignore in their "critiques" of left "political correctness."

6. Bernard Gendron's balanced critique of Adorno discusses how Adorno failed to distinguish mass-cultural texts from mass-produced products using Motown music as the example for his analysis.

7. For an in-depth discussion of the strategies of appropriation and their significance for popular culture, see Jim Collins.

8. The notion of appropriation here thus is very different from the type of affiliation that Harold Bloom describes as the "anxiety of influence," in which an author situates his/her work in relation to well-established authors and traditions either to align themselves with that author/tradition or to struggle against it.

6. Spectacles of Death

1. Adam-Troy Castro, "Killer Instinct," *Premiere* (August, 1990), p. 100.

2. Peter Travers, "When Shock Has Value," *Rolling Stone* (March 8, 1990), p. 69.

3. Dave Kehr, "Heartland," *Film Comment* 26 (May–June, 1990), p. 61.

4. Kehr, "Heartland," p. 62.

5. Elliott Stein, "Sexual Adversity in Chicago," *Village Voice* 35:13 (March 27, 1990), p. 59.

6. Both films are also distant cousins to Hitchcock's *Psycho,* although each film takes

the psycho-slasher formula in a radically different direction. Hitchcock's *Psycho* was a landmark film in changing both the horror genre itself and the way that critics thought about horror films in general. Before *Psycho*, American film-viewers had been menaced by an assortment of gothically garbed monsters (*Frankenstein, Dracula, The Wolfman*), a host of irradiated and severely irritated creatures (*Them!, Tarantula, Attack of the Giant Leeches*), and occasional unfriendly visits from extraterrestrials (*It Conquered the World, Invaders from Mars, The Brain From Planet Arous*). *Psycho* presented a pivotal moment in the genre as the first commercially successful and artistically celebrated film to feature a "human monster." Norman Bates, the film's dedicated yet tormented son and knife-wielding transvestite, established a new trend in horror that located monstrosity, not only in human form, but within the context of the American family. In this respect, Freddy and Henry are both cinematic cousins of Norman.

This alone would probably have insured *Psycho*'s fame in the history of the horror film. But *Psycho* did not just change horror films, it became central to new ways of thinking about horror and cinema in general. In the films before *Psycho*, horror criticism had most often been a search for the "symbolic" meaning of various monsters (i.e., Frankenstein = slumbering proletariat of Depression-era America, radioactive ants in *Them!* = American anxiety over nuclear warfare). Produced in 1960 by Hollywood's and academia's most celebrated cinematic artist, Alfred Hitchcock, *Psycho* appeared just as "auteurist"-centered criticism began to flourish and quickly became a key text in authorship studies. As film studies became increasingly influenced by Marxist and psychoanalytic approaches in the late sixties and into the seventies, *Psycho* became an important film in discussing the relationships of vision and power that theorists ascribed to the cinema as a whole. In a period when the Oedipal scenario began to inform almost every discussion of the Hollywood cinema, Norman's tumultuous family history, sinister voyeurism, and bizarre sexual prroclivities made *Psycho* the ideal film for "psycho" analysis.

7. Caryn James, "Dream the Dreams, Scream the Screams," *New York Times* (August 19, 1986), p. C8.

8. Stein, "Sexual Adversity," p. 59.

9. David Bordwell, *Narration in the Fiction Film* (Madison: University of Wisconsin Press, 1985), p. 58.

10. Those interested in pursuing these debates in more detail might consult the following sources. Useful overviews of these issues appear in the following volumes, listed here in increasing order of complexity. Robert Lapsley and Michael Westlake, *Film Theory: An Introduction* (Manchester: Manchester University Press, 1988), Kaja Silverman, *The Subject of Semiotics* (New York: Oxford University Press, 1983), and Rosalind Coward and John Ellis, *Language and Materialism: Developments in Semiology and the Theory of the Subject* (London: Routledge and Kegan Paul, 1977).

11. For more advanced discussions of the process at work in an individual film, see Raymond Bellour, "Hitchcock the Enunciator," *Camera Obscura* 2 (Fall, 1977), pp. 69–94; or Stephen Heath, "Film and System," Parts 1 and 2, *Screen* 16: 1 (Spring, 1975), and *Screen* 16: 2 (Summer, 1975).

12. Christian Metz, *The Imaginary Signifier* (Bloomington: Indiana University Press, 1982), p. 96.

13. Metz, *Imaginary Signifier*, p. 49.

14. Metz, *Imaginary Signifier*, p. 97.

15. Laura Mulvey, "Visual Pleasure and Narrative Cinema," in *Narrative, Apparatus, Ideology,* ed. Philip Rosen (New York: Columbia University Press, 1986), pp. 198–199.

16. Lapsley and Westlake, *Film Theory,* p. 161.

17. For an overview of Brecht's influence in film studies, see George Lellis, *Bertolt Brecht, Cahiers du Cinéma and Contemporary Film Theory* (Ann Arbor: UMI Research Press, 1982). For period debates on Brecht, see Stephen Heath, "From Brecht to Film: Theses, Problems," *Screen* 16:4 (Winter, 1975–76), and all of *Screen* 15:2 (Summer, 1974) [Brecht and Revolutionary Cinema].

18. Jim Collins, *Uncommon Cultures* (New York: Routledge, 1989), p. 109.

19. Carol J. Clover, "Her Body, Himself: Gender in the Slasher Film," *Representations,* 20 (Fall, 1987), p. 190.

20. Clover, "Her Body," p. 191.

21. Clover, "Her Body," p. 221.

22. For purposes of continuity between sequels, usually one teen survives from the film to initiate the action in the next installment of the series.

23. Kehr, "Heartland," p. 62.

24. Travers, "When Shock Has Value," p. 69.

25. The tone of *Henry* is such that the MPAA gave it an "X" rating despite the fact that it features less on-screen violence than most "R"-rated films. Officials at the MPAA stated that the film's tone was "too disturbing."

26. Travers, "When Shock Has Value," p. 69.

27. Kehr, "Heartland," pp. 61–62.

28. Kehr, "Heartland," p. 62.

29. Noël Carroll, *The Philosophy of Horror: or, Paradoxes of the Heart* (New York: Routledge, 1990), p. 35.

30. Castro, "Killer Instinct," p. 100.

7. Hardware and Hardbodies

1. To avoid any confusion, let me state emphatically that I am *not* arguing that films, and popular culture in general, have no political effect or function. That is precisely my point: we cannot analyze their political effects as direct statements transparently conveyed, nor can we fix their meanings in an image or plot. Nor can any wishfulness on our part, however well-intentioned, sanitize cultural representations of the unconscious fantasies they mobilize.

2. This seems to be the appropriate point to introduce the story of this reading's origin. It goes back to an argument I had about *Thelma and Louise* with a friend, Scott Sommer, who is a screenwriter, and who thinks a good deal about what responsible popular cinema might look like. His displeasure in the film had been at least as intense as my enthusiasm for it, and as the argument heated up, our positions become polarized and simplified, so that he wound up having to argue that these were negative and reactionary images, while I had to become a cheerleader for the positive and progressive potential offered by sheer visibility. One of the few interesting points that emerged in this polarized face-off, however, was his suggestion that what he hated about the film was the way it recycled exhausted images and scenarios of bravado that he felt had helped to build a tradition of masculine posturing that men

of his generation are still struggling to overcome. Why, he wondered, should women content themselves with, and even celebrate, a film that picks up an image repertoire that men are trying hard to discard? It occurred to me at that point that he was missing an important piece of the puzzle, the puzzle of *my* reaction to the film, that is, which is this: we women were raised on the same cinematic and televisual images and stories that men were, and we were identifying, perhaps with more resistance, or more intermittance, but identifying all the same, with the same male figures and "masculine" scenarios as our male contemporaries. And this must be the framework in which images of women raiding those nearly worn-out stories, trying on those clichéd postures, might have the effect of "newness," and might challenge our readings of those postures themselves, so it might challenge our analysis of the process and the effects of identification in our histories as consumers of popular culture. This paper owes a good deal to Scott for pushing my argument to the point where my analysis gave way to the personal in an adamant and unequivocal defense of my own pleasure in it. This is where I began to be able to read my own intense ambivalence about the film, and about the issues it raised for spectatorship.

3. Tom Conley has suggested to me that *Thelma and Louise* reads like a long commercial for Coors Light. Based on the Silver Bullet Bar's centrality to the narrative progress, his point is well taken. But it leads to some questions about a competing image: Thelma's obsessive purchase of the tiny one-shot bottles of Wild Turkey to drink on the road. The cumulative effect of this manic accumulation of miniatures points to the excess and its pleasures that seem to drive Thelma and Louise. But where light beers have been sufficiently enough coded as feminine that their advertising aggressively targets male consumers now, the move to Wild Turkey in the film is clearly marked as a move towards a more traditionally masculine style and taste in drinking.

4. One of these is clearly *Butch Cassidy and the Sundance Kid* (1969). By comparison to its male buddy film precursor, however, Thelma and Louise's image is not immediately memorialized as public, as news, the way *Butch Cassidy* memorializes its heroes, framing their immobility on film stock that shades into siena tones. Butch Cassidy and the Sundance Kid are frozen as the figure of a failed masculinity outstripped by the history whose image they become. Thelma and Louise, on the other hand, are suspended as the image of the unfinished.

5. Some of these questions were suggested to me by Elissa Marder in a recent conversation, during which I was groping for my point of departure with *Thelma and Louise*.

6. In this regard, they may recall the national obsession with transformer toys that Susan Willis analyzes in *A Primer for Daily Life* (London and New York: Routledge, 1991). Willis sees in this "vast array of toys whose singular purpose is to transform" "a fitting motto for the late twentieth century capitalism." And that motto is, bluntly put: "Everything transforms but nothing changes" (p. 36). Broadly speaking, these toys suggest a pleasure in pure and perpetual transformation. Willis locates a different manifestation of the consumer drive to transformation that is specifically related to sexual difference in feminine exercise culture. She describes the phenomenon of the aerobicized body as fashion in the following way. "The image of the workout woman articulates the fundamental contradiction between the desire for dramatic transformation shackled to the desire for gender identity, in a society where only one gender needs definition" (p. 76).

7. These complexities disrupt any sense of the coherence of gender identity, foreground its performativity, in the sense that Judith Butler proposes when she suggests that identification be understood as "an enacted fantasy or incorporation." This enactment

makes it clear, she argues, "that coherence is desired, wished for, idealized, and that this idealization is an effect of corporeal signification" *Gender Trouble: Feminism and the Subversion of Identity* [London and New York: Routledge, 1990], p. 136). But the very performativity at the heart of identification gives the lie to any dream of coherence since, as Butler continues, "[s]uch acts, gestures, enactments, generally construed, are performative in the sense that the essence or identity that they otherwise purport to express are fabrications manufactured and sustained through corporeal signs and other discursive means" (p. 136).

8. *Thelma and Louise* and the Cultural Generation of the New Butch-Femme

1. What there is in place of a whole story is repetition and difference. Storytelling as a form of cultural memory is both a defeating of forgetfulness through repetition, and the maintenance of forgetfulness. It is the regeneration of repetition and the death of difference, but equally, it is the death of repetition and the regeneration of differences. No one more than the other, but both together. The story itself—that is, as a genre, as a repetition, and as the act of repetition—is therefore a crucial component of the meaning of any particular memory. Both print and film make these memories easier to mass reproduce and more permanent. Storytelling multiples, but its process of reproduction makes its mechanical iterations less malleable to individuals in the chain of reception and reproduction; the oral circuit of teller>listener>teller is much more distanced, if not short-circuited. That the story once materially mass-reproduced cannot change in its retelling places more emphasis on the reading/rewriting process as the scene of individual agency. But we must also add that under commodity logic any apparatus of representation must not only accommodate differences, it must *produce* them in order to satisfy the performativity criterion of perpetual innovation. Who would pay to see the same movie over and over?

   The exception, of course, is fetish pornography or fetishistic cult films such as *The Rocky Horror Picture Show* (1975), starring, not insignificantly, a young Susan Sarandon. To any viewer "in the know," Sarandon's screen presence bears the valence of a history with cult films in which she pairs with women (or in the case of *Rocky Horror,* a transvestite posing as a woman). Because of the cult film's excess of erotic surplus value, it can elicit repeated monetary exchanges from underground communities within a mainstream network. In this subcultural sense, *Thelma and Louise* bears cult potential with lesbian markets, and it will be interesting to see how it ranks in the next few years on the top-renting video listings.

2. It goes without saying that *Thelma and Louise* will be claimed as readily by "normative" straight readings as by straight-feminist and camp queer ones, exemplifying the cultural differences and contentions amongst these communities.

3. Aberrant readings by definition take an irreverent license with the "authority" of the text, privileging reception aesthetics over textual analysis. In the case of Thelma and Louise's kiss, however, the scene is obviously filmed to toe a delicate line by which it can "pass" as straight even as it represents a tabooed erotic bond between the two female characters. Conversely, the scene can easily pass as non-straight for the discerning viewer—a tactic of ambiguity that produces more rather than fewer proceeds at the box office.

4. This double-narrative strategy of manifestation and containment is exemplified by the whole genre of imprisoned and dead *femmes fatales* in the history of *film noir*.

5. See Seboek's "The Fetish" for a semiotic definition of the fetish as a supervalent sign that invites excessive or "extra" ordinary meanings.

6. See "The Voice of the Code" in Barthes's *S/Z*. In the realist narrative, the code of truth is carried in the hermeneutic code—that of questions, enigmas, and their delays and answers. In detective fiction and the *film noir* detective mystery, this code is typically in the hands of the male detective by film's end (he solves the mystery and makes the appropriate arrest), though the tension of the detective narrative arises from the challenge that the *femme fatale* presents to the "truth" status of both the plot and the male hero. In other words, the *femme fatale* (typically fetishized) challenges the "truth" of the plot (though by film's end she's usually done in by it).

7. One of the signs of *Sweet Sweetback's Baadasssss* Song's radical ideological posture is its refusal of the death sentence on the level of the plot: at film's end the outlaw Sweetback, unlike Thelma and Louise, successfully crosses the border into Mexico—and escapes. Though too radical in too many ways to ever make it mainstream, the film was able to circulate broadly as a porn film (the protagonist's sexual prowess is prodigious). See Mark Allen Reid's "The Black Action Film: The End of the Patiently Enduring Black Hero."

8. If such a reading seems excessive, remember that, by definition, the fetish-sign calls the viewer to attach excessive meaning to it. Not everyone will answer its call. Access to its frozen erotic register, to the pleasure of its subtext, depends upon the point of view of the viewer. Žižek uses the term "looking awry" to suggest this function of the fetish-sign. Its supervalency depends upon a loaded psychic register provided by a viewer who "looks awry," who looks aslant or askew. To the viewer who looks at the sign straight on, so to speak, without any psychic investment, the fetish-sign doesn't mean anything—it's nothing at all (*Looking Awry*, pp. 8–12). It goes without saying that many people will "not see" a camp reading. It also goes without saying that differences between straight and camp readings are sites of social contention.

9. On domestic labor from the point of view of feminist rereadings of Marx, see Gardiner's "Women's Domestic Labour" and Coulson, Magas, and Wainwright's "'The Housewife and her Labour under Capitalism'—A Critique."

10. Though in return she has her first orgasm, which may not be a bad exchange.

9. Taboos and Totems

I would like to thank Eithne Johnson for preparing such an interesting Ph.D. reading list, Beth Wichterich for helping me understand parts of the events, and audiences at the 1991 Nordiskt Filmsymposium (Lund, Sweden), the Women's Research Seminars at the University of Texas at Austin, and the University of Wisconsin-Madison for giving me very valuable responses to drafts of this essay.

1. In this paper I will usually not refer to bisexuality as a sexual preference. However, bisexuality should be considered an implied option throughout.

2. Leslie Larson, "Foster Freeze," [Letter to] *Village Voice* (April 2, 1991) [n.p.—from *Silence of the Lambs* clipping file, Academy of Motion Picture Arts and Sciences Margaret Herrick Library—hereafter SLfile]. Background, descriptions, and debates preceding this can be found in David J. Fox, "Gays Decry Benefit Screening of 'Lambs,'" *Los Angeles Times* (February 4, 1991) [n.p. SLfile]; Michael Musto, "La Dolce Musto," *Village Voice* (February 12, 1991) [n.p. SLfile]; Amy Taubin, "Demme's Monde," *Village Voice* (February 19, 1991), pp. 64, 76–77; Lisa Kennedy, ed., "Writers on the *Lamb*," *Village Voice* (March 5, 1991), pp. 49, 56; Michelangelo Signorile, "*Lamb* Chops," [Letter to] *Village Voice*, (March 12, 1991) [n.p. SLfile]; [Letters to] *Village Voice* (March 19, 1991) [n.p. SLfile]; Elaine

Dutka, "'Silence' Fuels a Loud and Angry Debate," *Los Angeles Times* (March 20, 1991) [n.p. SLfile]; and Michael Bronski, "Reel Politic," *Z Magazine* 4:5 (May, 1991), pp. 80–84.

3. Julie Salamon, "Weirdo Killer Shrink Meets the G-Girl," *Wall Street Journal* (February 14, 1991); Amy Taubin, "Demme's Monde"; Lisa Kennedy, "Writers"; Martha Gever (in Kennedy, ed., "Writers"); C. Carr (in Kennedy, ed. "Writers"); Sheila Benson, "Why Do Critics Love These Repellent Movies?," *Los Angeles Times Calendar* (March 17, 1991); Andrea Kusten, Letters, *Village Voice* (March 19, 1991); Anna Hamilton Phelan, Tammy Bruce, and Phyllis Frank quoted in Elaine Dutka, "'Silence' Fuels a Loud and Angry Debate"; Leslie Larson, "Foster Freeze"; B. Ruby Rich, quoted in Bronski, "Reel Politic"; Maria Magenit, quoted in Bronski, "Reel Politic."

4. If I were explaining something else about the reception of *Silence of the Lambs,* other features and practices in the discourse might be pertinent.

5. Henry Sheehan, "Overcooked Lambs," *Los Angeles Reader* (February 15, 1991), pp. 29–30. These footnotes contain only the sources which I quote from; other reviews were part of my sample.

6. David Denby, "Something Wilder," *New York* 24:7 (February 18, 1991), pp. 60–61.

7. Brian D. Johnson, "The Evil That Men Do," *Maclean's* (February 18, 1991), pp. 51–52.

8. Peter Stallybrass and Allon White, *The Politics and Poetics of Transgression* (London: Methuen, 1986).

9. "A recurrent pattern emerges: the 'top' attempts to reject and eliminate the 'bottom' for reasons of prestige and status, only to discover, not only that it is in some way frequently dependent upon that low-Other . . . but also that the top *includes* the low symbolically, as a primary eroticized constituent of its own fantasy life. The result is a mobile, conflictual fusion of power, fear and desire in the construction of subjectivity: a psychological dependence upon precisely those Others which are being rigorously opposed and excluded at the social level. It is for this reason that what is *socially* peripheral is so frequently *symbolically* central (like long hair in the 1960s)" (Stallybrass and White, *Politics and Poetics,* p. 5).

10. "Cart," "The Silence of the Lambs," *Variety* (February 11, 1991), p. 109.

11. Sigmund Freud, *Totem and Taboo: Resemblances Between the Psychic Lives of Savages and Neurotics* [1918], trans. A.A. Brill (New York: Vintage Books, 1946). "The cannibalism of primitive races derives its more sublime motivation in a similar manner. By absorbing parts of the body of a person through the act of eating we also come to possess the properties which belonged to that person" (p. 107).

12. Denby, "Something Wilder."

13. Johnson, "The Evil."

14. Stephen Harvey, in Kennedy, ed., "Writers." p. 49.

15. Henry Sheehan, "Overcooked Lambs," p. 29; John Powers, "Skin Deep: Jonathan Demme's Chatter of the Hams," *L.A. Weekly* (February 15–21, 1991), p. 27; Stanley Kauffmann, "Gluttons for Punishment," *New Republic* (February 18, 1991), p. 48.

16. J. Hoberman, "Skin Flick," *Village Voice* (February 19, 1991), p. 61.

17. As Hoberman notices, in the original novel, Starling's relation with her mother is a dominant theme. In the film, her mother's death and its meaning to Starling are

repressed, with the film concentrating on Starling's need to deal with her father's death.

18. Terrence Rafferty, "Moth and Flame," *New Yorker* (February 25, 1991), pp. 87–88.

19. Carol J. Clover, "Her Body, Himself: Gender in the Slasher Film," *Representations* 20 (Fall, 1987), pp. 187–228.

20. Starling was widely perceived by the viewers to be unfeminine. She was variously referred to in her role as an FBI recruit. Although Orion's publicity materials described her as "gutsy," repeating verbatim studio handout sheets is taboo among reviewers; equally unsettling might have been the unconscious connection between that adjective and Lecter's idiosyncratic diet. Here, however, Starling is variously relabeled to be "tenacious," "sturdy," "tough," "resourceful," "persistent," "ambitious," "driven." The *Silence of the Lambs* publicity materials, Orion Pictures [SLfile].

21. Thomas Harris, *The Silence of the Lambs* (New York: St. Martin's, 1988).

22. Rafferty, "Moth and Flame."

23. Peter Travers, "Snapshots from Hell: The Silence of the Lambs," *Rolling Stone* (March 7, 1991), pp. 87–88.

24. Denby, "Something Wilder."

25. Chuck Smith, "Hollywood Horror," *Vanguard* (April 19, 1991) [n.p. SLfile].

26. Hoberman, "Skin Flick."

27. Stuart Klawans, "Films," *The Nation* (February 25, 1991), pp. 246–247.

28. Powers, "Skin Deep."

29. Smith, "Hollywood Horror."

30. Richard A. Blake, "Visions of Evil," *America* 64:10 (March 16, 1991), p. 292. *Commonweal*'s reviewer implies the film is about Faust and Mephisto. The *Rolling Stone* headline says the film has "snapshots from hell."

31. Margaret R. Miles, *Carnal Knowing: Female Nakedness and Religious Meaning in the Christian West* (New York: Vintage Books, 1989).

32. Miles, *Carnal Knowing*, pp. 12 and xi.

33. Vincent Canby, "Methods of Madness in 'Silence of the Lambs,'" *New York Times* (February 14, 1991), p. C17.

34. Salamon, "Wierdo Killer."

35. Amy Taubin, in Kennedy, ed., "Writers."

36. Reviewers did at times discuss him not only as monstrous but as alien or an extraterrestrial.

37. In *Alice Doesn't: Feminism, Semiotics, Cinema* (Bloomington: Indiana University Press, 1984), Teresa de Lauretis's analysis of narrativity and gender uses the Oedipal myth with its stories of meeting the Sphinx and the Minotaur tale as part of her argument about patriarchy's construction of desire. This odd coincidence is not particularly troublesome to explain since the equation is widely known through feminist discourse, and Taubin and Hoberman both are familiar with that discourse. We do not need to assume anything more than common social and discursive networks provoked this conjunction of terms.

38. Arnold I. Davidson, "Sex and the Emergence of Sexuality," *Critical Inquiry* 14:1

(Autumn, 1987), pp. 16–48, writes that it was through psychiatry that a split was made between anatomical sex and psychological sex. Medicalization takes over, investigating for visual evidence of gender both externally and internally.

39. Hoberman, "Skin Flick."

40. Barbara Creed, "Horror and the Monstrous-Feminine: An Imaginary Abjection," *Screen* 27:1 (January–February, 1986), pp. 44–70.

41. Sheehan, "Overcooked Lambs."

42. And as psychoanalysis as a discourse begins its dissemination.

43. Klawans, "Films."

44. It was derived from the novel but appears even during publicity generated while the film was in production. Its potency is obvious from the fact that the ad campaign recently won an award for the best movie poster of the year. Eithne Johnson informs me that the posters used Dali's "punning" picture of women to create the skull. Furthermore, moths and butterflies have a long-standing association with the vagina. No reviewer, however, made note of either.

45. Klawans, "Films"; Smith, "Hollywood Horror."

46. Mary Douglas, *Purity and Danger: An Analysis of the Concepts of Pollution and Taboo* (New York: Praeger, 1966), p. 122.

47. Douglas, *Purity,* p. 126.

48. Richard Jennings quoted in Fox, "Gays Decry Benefit Screening of 'Lambs.'"

10. The Powers of Seeing and Being Seen

1. Laura Mulvey, "Visual Pleasure and Narrative Cinema," *Visual and Other Pleasures* (Bloomington: Indiana University Press, 1989), pp. 14–26.

2. See John Fiske, *Television Culture* (London and New York: Routledge, 1987), and E. Ann Kaplan, *Rocking Around the Clock: Music Television, Postmodernism, and Consumer Culture* (New York and London: Routledge, 1987).

3. Susan McClary, "Living to Tell: Madonna's Resurrection of the Fleshly," *Genders* 7 (Spring, 1990), pp. 2, 16.

4. Richard Dyer, *Stars* (London: BFI Publishing, 1979).

5. See, for example, Lynn Hirschberg, "The Misfit," *Vanity Fair* 54:4 (April, 1991), pp. 158–169; Don Shewey, "Madonna: The Saint, The Slut, The Sensation," *The Advocate* 576 (May 7, 1991), pp. 42–51; Carrie Fisher, "True Confessions: The *Rolling Stone* Interview with Madonna" and Steven Meisel, "Flesh and Fantasy," *Rolling Stone* 606 (June 13, 1991), pp. 36–40, 43–50; Adrian Deevoy, "Reveal Yourself," *Us* 156 (June 13, 1991), pp. 16–24. Madonna was featured on the cover of each of these magazines. In addition, MTV broadcast a special featuring an interview with Madonna on May 8, 1991 to coincide with the opening of *Truth or Dare* in New York and Los Angeles.

6. The replication of the "Diamonds Are A Girl's Best Friend" sequence from *Gentlemen Prefer Blondes* in "Material Girl" and of some of Marilyn Monroe's photo sessions in the April 1991 *Vanity Fair* are not the only instances of Madonna reproducing earlier images. Steven Meisel's photographs in *Rolling Stone* are inspired by the work of Brassai; one of the poses at the end of the "Vogue" video is a reproduction of a 1939 Horst photo; the live performance of "Vogue" for the 1990 MTV Music Video Awards borrows from the Stephen Frears's film version of *Les*

Liaisons Dangereuses; and the staging of "Keep It Together" in the Blond Ambition tour is inspired by the film *Cabaret.*

7. Mary Ann Doane, "Film and the Masquerade," *Femmes Fatales* (New York and London: Routledge, 1991), p. 26. See also "Masquerade Reconsidered: Further Thoughts on the Female Spectator" in the same collection.

8. Judith Butler, *Gender Trouble: Feminism and the Subversion of Identity* (New York and London: Routledge, 1989), p. 137.

9. Michael Moon and Eve Kosofsky Sedgwick, "Divinity: A Dossier, A Performance Piece, A Little-Understood Emotion," *Discourse* 13:1 (Fall–Winter, 1990–91), p. 18.

10. Sue-Ellen Case, "Towards a Butch-Femme Aesthetic," *Discourse* 11:1 (Fall–Winter, 1988–89), pp. 61–62.

11. Susan Bordo, "'Material Girl': The Effacements of Postmodern Culture," *Michigan Quarterly Review* 19:4 (Fall, 1990), p. 676.

12. See Kobena Mercer, "Black Hair/Style Politics," in *Out There: Marginalization and Contemporary Cultures,* ed. Russell Ferguson, Martha Gever, Trinh T. Minh-ha, and Cornel West (Cambridge, Mass.: MIT Press, 1990), pp. 247–264. For a similar argument against those who see Michael Jackson's self-transformations as motivated by a desire to be white, see Michèle Wallace, "Michael Jackson, Black Modernisms, and 'The Ecstacy of Communication,'" in *Global Television,* ed. Cynthia Schneider and Brian Wallis (Cambridge, Mass.: MIT Press, 1988), pp. 300–318.

13. See Frigga Haug, *Female Sexualization* (London: Verso, 1986).

14. See, for example, Stuart Hall and Tony Jefferson, eds., *Resistance Through Rituals: Youth Subcultures in Post-War Britain* (London: Unwin Hyman, 1976) and Dick Hebdige, *Subculture: The Meaning of Style* (London and New York: Methuen, 1979).

15. See Teresa de Lauretis, in Bad Object-Choices, eds., *How Do I Look?: Queer Film and Video* (Seattle: Bay Press, 1991).

16. In a recent interview with Norman Mailer in *Vanity Fair,* for example, Beatty for the most part refuses to discuss his sex life, despite Mailer's repeated questions. Although his reputation as a ladies' man has been crucial to his public image, Beatty implies that discussion of his "private" life compromises his seriousness as an artist and professional. Taking refuge in a double standard that tends to grant men the luxury of separating their professional and sexual lives, he stands in marked contrast with Madonna, who, despite the fact that she may have more to lose, seems unthreatened by demands that she discuss both her professional and personal life in interviews. See Norman Mailer, "The Warren Report," *Vanity Fair* 54:11 (November, 1991), pp. 174–180. (Of course, since then Beatty has become—at long last— a husband and father, and for the moment at least the conventional image of domestic bliss has been absorbed into his public image.)

17. bell hooks, "Is Paris Burning?," *Z Magazine* (June, 1991), pp. 60–64. For more sympathetic accounts of *Paris Is Burning* by African-American critics, see Essex Hemphill, *"Paris Is Burning," The Guardian* (July 3, 1991), pp. 10–11; and Jackie Goldsby, "Queens of Language," *Afterimage* 8:10 (May, 1991), pp. 10–11.

18. For a discussion of how Livingston situates herself with respect to gay and lesbian culture, see "Reel to Real: A Conversation Between Jennie Livingston and Todd Haynes," *Outweek* 94 (April 17, 1991), pp. 34–41.

19. See, for example, Diana Fuss, ed., *Inside/Out: Lesbian Theories, Gay Theories* (New York: Routledge, 1991); Christine Stansell and Sharon Thompson, eds., *Powers of Desire: The Politics of Sexuality* (New York: Monthly Review Press, 1984); Susie Bright, *Susie Sexpert's Lesbian Sex World* (San Francisco: Cleis Press, 1990); Mark Thompson, ed., *Leatherfolk: Radical Sex, People, Politics, and Practice* (Boston: Alyson Press, 1991); Joan Nestle, ed., *The Persistent Desire: A Femme-Butch Reader* (Boston: Alyson Press, 1992).

20. Goldsby, "Queens of Language," p. 11.

21. For an excellent discussion of white and avant-garde artists' desires for the oppositionality implicit in non-white and ethnic identities, see Coco Fusco, "Fantasies of Oppositionality," *Afterimage* 16:5 (December, 1988), pp. 6–9. The same kind of analysis could be applied to the relations between gay and straight cultures.

11. Spike Lee and the Fever in the Racial Jungle

1. Although seemingly, the flames of this debate have been fanned by market forces, one can glean the core issues of Amiri Baraka and Lee's differences over the legacy of Malcolm X from the following articles: David Ansen, et al., "The Battle for Malcolm X," *Newsweek* (August 26, 1991), pp. 52–54; Spike Lee, "Who Owns Malcolm X?," *San Francisco Chronicle* (August 21, 1991), E1.

2. For an excellent critique of Lee's entrepreneurial politics and positioning within dominant cinema discourse see Wahneema Lubiano, "But Compared to What?"

3. Film scholar Manthia Diawara succinctly raises the ongoing issue of being trapped by a binary essentialism when he asks, "how might we talk about Blackness without substituting the historical White man as bad object with an historical Black man as good object?" His essay contains an important illumination of the topic, Manthia Diawara, "Cinema Studies, the Strong Thought and Black Film."

4. Here, I credit long discussions about black film with Tommy Lott for helping me to develop this issue. Also relevant to this essay is Lott's fine article which, in part, explores the social construction of blackness in relation to the formation of black cinema discourse: Tommy L. Lott, "A No-Theory Theory of Contemporary Black Cinema."

5. Mas'ud Zavarzadeh, *Seeing Films Politically* (New York: State University of New York Press) pp. 7–8. Here Zavarzadeh urges the critic to go beyond dominant ideology's "own terms" of formalist, aesthetic criticism. He argues that one must explore the suppressed political "tale" under the dominant, narrative surface by not asking "*how* a particular tale means but rather *WHY it means what it is taken to mean.*" He writes that he has found the "political (why) to be a more effective mode of inquiry than the rhetorical (how)."

12. Split Skins

1. Important works initiating and carrying on the debate about the representation of women and female desire in Hollywood cinema include Laura Mulvey's 1975 essay, "Visual Pleasure and Narrative Cinema," Miriam Hansen, "Pleasure, Ambivalence, Identification: Valentino and Female Spectatorship," Karen Hollinger, "'The Look,' Narrativity, and the Female Spectator in *Vertigo*," Teresa de Lauretis, *Alice Doesn't*, Judith Mayne, *The Woman at the Keyhole*, Mary Ann Doane, *The Desire to Desire* and *Femmes Fatales*, Tania Modleski, *The Women Who Knew Too Much*, Gaylyn Studlar, *In the Realm of Pleasure*, and *Camera Obscura* 20/21, a special issue on "The Spectatrix."

2. See Michael Foucault, *The History of Sexuality* (pp. 17–35).

3. *The Little Mermaid* was nominated for Academy Awards for Original Score (by Alan Menken) and Best Song ("Under the Sea," "Kiss the Girl" by Menken and Howard Ashman). The musical score and "Under the Sea" won in their categories. In its first ten days (November 17–26, 1989), the film grossed $16.8 million, and went on to become the highest grossing initial release of an animated feature in film history ($84,355,863), although *Beauty and the Beast* (1991) has since surpassed it. Brian McEntee was head of the animation team on both films.

4. The extremely influential French psychoanalyst, Jacques Lacan, spent his career explicating and elaborating on Freud's writings in an attempt to reform the modern psychoanalytic institutions which had, Lacan believed, wandered too far from Freud's theories. For informative readings of Lacan's work from a feminist perspective, see Jacqueline Rose's and Juliet Mitchell's introductions in *Feminine Sexuality*, as well as Kaja Silverman, *The Subject of Semiotics*.

5. Tyco's *The Little Mermaid* Collectible Figures," made in the People's Republic of China for The Walt Disney Company, are recommended for ages three and up.

6. The version of "The Little Mermaid" to which I refer to this essay is found in Hans Christian Andersen, *The Snow Queen and Other Tales*.

7. Andersen is writing in the same atmosphere that produced Kierkegaard's meditations on the nature of Christianity—Copenhagen of the 1830s and 1840s. The history of the mer-world in Andersen's writing includes his "totally miscarried failure" in 1843 to bring to the theater his 1834 dramatic poem, *Agnete and the Merman*, which disappeared after two "notorious performances" (Marker, p. 47). The poem involves a girl who falls in love with a merman and is forced to leave her home on land to follow him, after which he abandons her. Both of Andersen's mer-folk stories depict a girl's separation from home and parents. The ever-ironic Kierkegaard may be reacting to Andersen's *Agnete* when he includes the "Agnes and the Merman" story in *Fear and Trembling* (pp. 103–109). Strangely, both Kierkegaard and Andersen use the merman tale as an allegory of their broken engagements, though Kierkegaard clearly identifies himself with the seductive merman, while Andersen was said to see himself as the forsaken girl. Thanks to Susan Bernstein, Jeff Wallen, and Peter Fenves for sharing their knowledge of Kierkegaard.

8. In the mermaid diaspora, the Western African gender-ambiguous mermaid/man tradition was also exported to the Caribbean and South America. Thanks to Aníbal Mejía for his useful discussions of the mermaid in Central and South American culture.

9. See E. Ann Kaplan, ed., *Women in Film Noir* for an overview of the *film noir femme fatale*.

10. Steven Spielberg's exorbitantly expensive version of the "Peter Pan" story, *Hook* (Amblin 1991), involves two male-rite-of-passage dilemmas: that of the original "boy who doesn't want to grow up," and that of the man who seems unable to accept his role as husband and father. Not surprisingly, an important moment in the story features three beautiful, neon-haired mermaids who rescue Peter from drowning (by breathing erotically into his mouth), helping to guide him towards his final acceptance that he is "a daddy."

11. Freud's central theory, whose terms are under continual dispute, is that boys find girls both extremely threatening *and* contemptible because girls lack the male genital organ, so important to the male child as a source of feeling and identity. Because

the girl's sexual organs' real difference is ignored, she seems to be "missing" something. The boy who sees her genitalia believes she is "castrated," and that he, too, is in danger of losing his valued penis. It is in cases like this that Freud can most usefully be seen as describing how we have been brainwashed by patriarchal culture. It is only because the penis represents the *social* superiority of males (what Lacan called "phallic" power) that the girl is regarded and regards herself as contemptible. The "castration" theory has extraordinary importance for Freud: it is only the fear of losing their genitals that makes boys pass through the "Oedipal phase," and give up the primordial desire for the mother under the stern order of the father.

12. In *The Elementary Structures of Kinship,* Claude Lévi-Strauss hypothesizes that all societies are held together internally and form external alliances through men "exchanging women." According to this view, the incest taboo would be a practical solution to the social need always to give the woman *away* to another group, performing what is known as "exogamy."

13. See, especially, Bruno Bettelheim, *The Uses of Enchantment*. Feminist readings of fairy tales which implicitly or explicitly critique Bettelheim's rosy view include Zipes, ed., *Don't Bet on the Prince,* and Melissa Murray, et al., *Rapunzel's Revenge* and *Ms. Muffet and Others: Fairy Tales for Feminists,* which contains a rereading of the Northern mermaid myth called "The Selkie."

14. See Roberta Trites, "Disney's Sub/Version of Andersen's 'The Little Mermaid,'" and Dorothy Dinnerstein, "*The Little Mermaid* and the Situation of the Girl." In *The Kiss of the Snow Queen,* Wolfgang Lederer emphasizes the sexual meaning of the "immortality" sought by the mermaid: "We already know that one meaning of immortality is progeny. When the Little Mermaid obtains two legs that she can spread, that are split (have a cleft in between), she has become a sexual woman . . ." (p. 251).

15. In Disney's 1991 cable promotional film "The Making of the Little Mermaid," the animators discuss the way they used human forms as models for *TLM*'s characters. Ursula, the fat sea witch, is explicitly modeled on the 1950 *film noir* "heroine," *Sunset Boulevard*'s Norma Desmond. See also Spillman, "Creating a 'Mermaid': The Body," p. D2.

16. Trites astutely criticizes the film's trivialization of the search for a soul, its making marriage to the prince the sole purpose of the pie-eyed maid. However, her contention that the prince is only interested in Ariel's "appearance" is obviously incorrect, in that the mermaid is unable to seduce him without her voice. Kaja Silverman's claim that the female voice is used in cinema primarily as a means of reminding women of her confinement to her body (*The Acoustic Mirror*) certainly finds confirmation in this film.

17. An anonymous archivist for Disney Studios told me that Ariel had been rated lowest of all of Disney's animated heroines on one critic's scale of self-determination and assertiveness. The "phallic" aspect of the story was inadvertently underscored by the video carton illustration of King Triton's castle, which was said to have penises as turrets (*L.A. Daily News*, "L.A. Life" section, July 29, 1990). *The Little Mermaid, Beauty and the Beast,* and *Father of the Bride* (1991) are part of a recent resurgence of father-daughter stories, featuring possessive fathers, in Hollywood film.

18. *TLM* spun off an enormous range of products associated with the mermaid and aimed at young female consumers (Ridgeway, p. D1). In addition, *The Little Mermaid* is the subject of one of the first two video games targeted exclusively at girls. The

other is a "Barbie" game—the former loosely follows the plot of the movie, while the latter is also a "quest" narrative, in which Barbie must collect accessories for the upcoming ball (Advokat, p. E26).

19. There is, of course, an increased trend towards (moderate) muscularity in female beauty standards in the 1990s. Indeed, ironically, the powerful mermaid seems to fit into the mold of a newer stereotype. However, although muscularity has the benefit of making women stronger and better able to defend themselves, it does not mean that women and men are finding equality through body building. Size, the very thing men want to achieve through "bulking up," is still problematic for women. Since the additional layer of fatty tissue natural to the female body impairs the visibility of muscular conformation, in order to look muscular on the male model and remain slender at the same time, women must still be concerned with removing layers of themselves.

20. Andersen's story, "The Red Shoes," also depicts the difficulty of achieving womanhood, the danger of dying in childhood, and so forth. As in "TLM," the ruling metaphor is that of agonizing pain in walking and dancing. "The Red Shoes" was also (appropriately) made into a ballet (later filmed by Michael Powell). The little mermaid's transformation might well be compared to the art of ballet for women— itself a form of achieving femininity through pain. The late choreographer for the New York City Ballet, George Balanchine, frankly declared that "Ballet is Woman," and with his image of the emaciated body, silicone-injected lips, and waiflike gestures of the prima ballerina, determined the fate of a generation of anorexic ballet dancers. See Calistro (p. E8) for a similar description of Belle in Disney's *Beauty and the Beast*.

21. See Molly Haskell, *From Reverence to Rape* for a thorough discussion of the kinds of sacrifice characterizing different subgenres of women's films.

22. Silverman (1988, p. 36) cites Reik on the "anemic" quality of women's masochistic fantasies.

23. In "*Histoire d'O:* The Construction of a Female Subject," Silverman discusses the inscription of female sexuality through masochism. This is not a description of a sexuality that undermines patriarchal norms. Studlar focuses on male masochism in *In the Realm of Pleasure*, though her recent work takes up female masochism more specifically.

24. Silverman (1988, pp. 61–62) argues briefly for the possibility of subversive female masochism, citing a case in which a woman derives sexual gratification from gynecological exams, thus, from a pretended obedience to the demands of male doctors.

25. It is important to note that the idealized being may in fact be the pre-Oedipal or negative Oedipal mother, even though a man may stand in for that omnipotent being.

26. In *The Bonds of Love*, Jessica Benjamin discusses the erotic charge girls and women get from masochism. Although Benjamin's view of masochism and sexual difference itself seems to me much too optimistic, her argument is certainly worth noting.

27. The "playful" side of acting out feminine submissiveness has been described as the "masquerade" of femininity by authors including Joan Riviere, Mary Ann Doane (1991), and Claire Johnston. Feminine attributes can be put on and taken off like clothing: thus "real" women's femininity is not unrelated to that of transvestites. Also useful in the context of *TLM* is Kathleen Woodward, "Youthfulness as a Masquerade": "[The postmodern body] is the surgically youthful body, the uncanny aging body-in-masquerade" (p. 136).

28. In *The Reproduction of Mothering*, Nancy Chodorow describes in detail the consequences of women taking the role of primary nurturer. For the girl, the closeness felt with a mother who is physically similar to her eventually becomes suffocating. Ursula's size might be read as symbolic of this potential for suffocation of the "daughter." She yearns to escape to the more aloof father, who seems to promise freedom (as does Eric in *The Little Mermaid*). This desire is reinforced by the cultural denigration of women, of which the girl becomes aware at the age of two or three. Tearing herself from the unacceptable, smothering mother, the girl seeks happiness through closeness with boys, then men. But the man, who has been conditioned away from closeness by his own sense of separation from the mother, is unable to offer the woman the intimacy she desires.

29. Shakespeare's Prospero delights in finding the royal suitor for his daughter (the Eric-like Prince Ferdinand), a gesture that has been read as yet another means for a father to hold on to his daughter. Like the other fathers we have seen, *he* wants to decide who will sexually possess her, taking her out of the "normal" circuit of exchange upon which culture is supposedly based. For descriptions of the patterns of exogamy challenging the basic "exchange of women" model offered by Claude Lévi-Strauss, see Lynda Zwinger, *Daughters, Fathers and the Novel*, and Lynda Boose, "The Father's House and the Daughter in It," in *Daughters and Fathers*, and her "The Father and the Bride in Shakespeare." Zwinger and Boose present evidence that fathers from the Biblical era to the present attempt to hold onto rather than exchange daughters.

30. Retamar (p. 4) describes the *mestizo* as a product of "racial intermingling, racial mixture." Ariel's half-and-half appearance seems to imply that she, too, is a composite.

13. The Big Switch

1. Annette Kolodny, "Dancing Through the Minefield: Some Observations on the Theory, Practice, and Politics of a Feminist Literary Criticism," in *Critical Theory Since 1965*, ed. Hazard Adams and Leroy Searle (Tallahassee: Florida State University Press, 1986), p. 499.

2. Robert Bly's *Iron John: A Book About Men* (New York: Addison-Wesley Publishing, 1990) and Sam Keen's *Fire in the Belly: On Being a Man* (New York: Bantam, 1991) have been among the most popular and most controversial of these texts, principally because both figures have inspired many men to take up their philosophies. Sociologist Michael Kimmel was among the first academics to publish books on the questions of men and masculinity in his books, *Changing Men: New Directions in Research on Men and Masculinity* (Beverly Hills: Sage, 1987) and *Men Confront Pornography* (New York: Crown, 1990). Philosopher Harry Brod was instrumental in beginning and influencing many of the men's studies programs that now exist across the country, both through his administrative work and through his books, *The Making of Masculinities: The New Men's Studies* (Boston: Allen and Unwin, 1987) and *A Mensch Among Men: Explorations in Jewish Masculinity* (Freedom, Cal.: Crossing Press, 1988). Among literary scholars, Joseph Allen Boone has published influential work on masculinity in American literature and culture.

3. There have been a number of key feminist publications on questions of masculinity. Among the most influential have been Alice Jardine's edited collection, *Men in Feminism* (New York: Methuen, 1987); the special issue of *Camera Obscura* on "Male Trouble" (vol. 17, May 1988); and the special issue of *Differences* on Male Subjectivity" (vol. 1, no. 3, Fall, 1989). Feminist critics such as Constance Penley,

Tania Modelski, Kaja Silverman, Christine Di Stefano, and Nancy Hartsock have written persuasively and insightfully about the topic of masculinities.

4. Janet Maslin, "In the 90's, the 80's Turn to Junk," *New York Times* (July 14, 1991), p. H9.

5. The extent to which even Martin Riggs can be a "changed man" in the nineties is shown in the 1992 release of *Lethal Weapon 3* (Richard Donner), in which Riggs' female companions no longer die when he falls in love with them. Instead, Riggs is now teamed up with a woman who can fight off five criminals by herself, while Riggs looks on admiringly.

6. Elayne Rapping, "Boys of the Summer," *The Progressive* (November, 1991), p. 36.

7. Constance Penley and Andrew Ross, "Cyborgs at Large: Interview with Donna Haraway," *Technoculture*, eds. Constance Penley and Andrew Ross (Minneapolis: University of Minnesota Press, 1991), p. 19.

14. Between Apocalypse and Redemption

1. These statistics, as well as an examination of the social, economic, political, medical, and educational conditions of young black men, and public policy recommendations for the social amelioration of their desperate circumstances, are found in a collection of essays edited by Jewelle Taylor Gibbs, *Young, Black, And Male in America: An Endangered Species*.

2. William Julius Wilson has detailed the shift in the American political economy from manufacturing to service employment, and its impact upon the inner city and the ghetto poor, particularly upon black males who suffer high rates of joblessness (which he sees as the source of many problems in the black family) in *The Truly Disadvantaged*. For an analysis of the specific problems of black males in relation to labor force participation, see Gerald David Jaynes and Robin M. Williams, Jr., eds., *A Common Destiny* (pp. 301, 308–312).

3. I have explored the cultural expressions, material conditions, creative limits, and social problems associated with rap, in "Rap, Race and Reality," (pp. 98–100); "The Culture of Hip-Hop" (pp. 44–50), "2 Live Crew's Rap: Sex, Race and Class" (pp. 7–8) "As Complex As They Wanna Be: 2 Live Crew" (pp. 76–78), "Tapping Into Rap" (pp. 32–35), "Performance, Protest and Prophecy in the Culture of Hip-Hop" (pp. 12–24), and in Jim Gardner, "Taking Rap Seriously: Theomusicologist Michael Eric Dyson on the New Urban Griots and Peripatetic Preachers (An Interview)" (pp. 20–23).

4. I have in mind here the criticism of liberal society, and the forms of moral agency it both affords and prevents, that has been gathered under the rubric of communitarianism, ranging from MacIntyre's *After Virtue* to Bellah, et al.'s *Habits of the Heart*.

5. I am indebted to Christine Stansell for this characterization of how Singleton departs from Capra's depictions of community in his films.

6. See Mike Davis's and Sue Riddick's brilliant analysis of the drug culture in "Los Angeles: Civil Liberties between the Hammer and the Rock" (pp. 37–60).

7. For an insightful discussion of the relationship between the underground or illegitimate economy, and people exercising agency in resisting the worse injustices and effects of the legitimate economy, see Don Nonini, "Everyday Forms of Popular Resistance" (pp. 25–36).

8. For a recent exploration of the dynamics of social interaction between police as agents and symbols of mainstream communal efforts to regulate the behavior and

social place of black men, and black men in a local community, see Elijah Anderson, *Streetwise* (pp. 163–206).

9. According to this logic, as expressed in a familiar saying in many black communities, black women "love their sons and raise their daughters." For a valiant, though flawed attempt to get beyond a theoretical framework that implicitly blames black women for the condition of black men, see Clement Cottingham, "Gender Shift in Black Communities" (pp. 521–525). Cottingham attempts to distance himself from arguments about a black matriarchy that stifles black male social initiative and moral responsibility. Instead he examines the gender shifts in black communities fueled by black female educational mobility and the marginalization of lower-class black males. But his attempt is weakened, ironically, by a prominently placed quotation by James Baldwin, which serves as a backdrop to his subsequent discussions of mother/son relationships, black male/female relationships, and black female assertiveness. Cottingham writes:

    "Drawing on Southern black folk culture, James Baldwin, in his last published work, alluded to black lower-class social patterns which, when set against the urban upheaval among the black poor from the 1960s onward, seem to encourage this gender shift. He characterizes these lower-class social patterns as 'a disease peculiar to the Black community' called 'sorriness.' 'It is,' Baldwin observes, 'a disease that attacks black males. It is transmitted by Mama, whose instinct is to protect the Black male from the devastation that threatens him from the moment he declares himself a man.'

    Apart from its protectiveness toward male children, Baldwin notes another dimension of 'worriness.' 'Mama,' he writes, 'lays this burden on Sister from whom she expects (or indicates she expects) far more than she expects from Brother; but one of the results of this all too comprehensible dynamic is that Brother may never grow up—in which case the community has become an accomplice to the Republic.' Perceptively, Baldwin concludes that the differences in the socialization of boys and girls eventually erode the father's commitment to family life. (p. 522).

    When such allusive but isolated ethnographic comments are not placed in an analytical framework that tracks the social, political, economic, religious, and historical forces that shape black (female) rearing practices and circumscribe black male/female relations, they are more often than not employed to blame black women for the social failure of black children, especially boys. The point here is not to suggest that black women have no responsibility for the plight of black families. But most social theory has failed to grapple with the complex set of forces that define and delimit black female existence, too easily relying upon anecdotal tales of black female behavior that prevents black males from flourishing, and not examining the shifts in the political economy, the demise of low-skilled, high-waged work, the deterioration of the general moral infrastructure of many poor black communities, the ravaging of black communities by legal forces of gentrification and illegal forces associated with crime and drugs, etc. These forces, and not black women, are the real villains.

10. For a perceptive analysis of the economic conditions which shape the lives of black women, see Julianne Malveaux, "The Political Economy of Black Women" (pp. 53–73).

11. The peculiar pain that plagues the relationships between black men and black women across age, income, and communal strata was on bold and menacing display in the confrontation between Clarence Thomas and Anita Hill during Senate hearings to explore claims by Hill that Thomas sexually harassed her while she worked for him

at two governmental agencies. Their confrontation was facilitated and constructed by the televisual medium, a ready metaphor for the technological intervention into contemporary relations between significant segments of the citizenry. Television also serves as the major mediator between various bodies of public officials and the increasingly narrow publics at whose behest they perform, thus blurring the distinctions between public good and private interest. The Hill/Thomas hearings also helped expose the wide degree to which the relations between black men and black women are shaped by a powerful white male gaze. In this case, the relevant criteria for assessing the truth of claims about sexual harassment and gender oppression were determined by white senatorial surveillance.

12. Thus, it was unexceptional during the civil rights movement for strong, articulate black women to be marginalized, or excluded altogether, from the intellectual work of the struggle. Furthermore, concerns about feminist liberation were generally overlooked, and many talented, courageous women were often denied a strong or distinct institutional voice about women's liberation in the racial liberation movement. For a typical instance of such sexism within civil rights organizations, see Carson's discussion of black female dissent within SNCC, in Clayborne Carson, *In Struggle* (pp. 147–148).

13. For insightful claims and descriptions of the marginal status of black feminist and womanist concerns in black communities, and for helpful explorations of the complex problems faced by black feminists and womanists, see bell hook's *Ain't I A Woman?* Michele Wallace's *Invisibility Blues*, Andre Lorde's *Sister/Outsider*, and Alice Walker's *In Search of Our Mother's Garden*.

14. Of course, many traditional conceptions of virtue display a theoretical blindness to structural factors which circumscribe and influence the acquisition of traditional moral skills, habits, and dispositions, and the development of alternative and non-mainstream moral skills. What I mean here is that the development of virtues, and the attendant skills which must be deployed in order to practice them effectively, is contingent upon several factors: where and when one is born, the conditions under which one must live, the social and communal forces which limit and define one's life, etc. These factors color the character of moral skills which will be acquired, shape the way in which these skills will be appropriated, and even determine the list of skills required to live the good life in different communities. Furthermore, these virtues reflect the radically different norms, obligations, commitments, and socio-ethical visions of particular communities. For a compelling critique of MacIntyre's contextual universalist claim for the prevalence of the virtues of justice, truthfulness, and courage in all cultures, and the implications of such critique for moral theory, see Alessandro Ferrara's essay, "Universalisms: Procedural, Contextual and Prudential" (pp. 11–38). For an eloquent argument that calls for the authors of the communitarian social vision articulated in *Habits of the Heart* to pay attention to the life, thought, and contributions of people of color, see Vincent Harding, "Toward a Darkly Radiant Vision of America's Truth: A Letter of Concern, An Invitation to Re-Creation" (pp. 67–83).

15. Making Cyborgs, Making Humans

One of the greatest pleasures about movie-going is the discussion it provokes. I would like to thank several people who have engaged me in discussion and debate over these films for some time and whose comments have been particularly helpful: C. Lee Taylor, Michael Stamm, Randall McGowen, and the editors of this volume, Hilary Radner, Jim Collins, and Ava Collins.

1. Deconstruction is the name given to a range of critical, philosophical, and literary inquiries and methodological procedures associated with the work of Jacques Derrida and Paul de Man. Their work, the work of those they have influenced, and the range of responses "deconstruction" has provoked comprise an extensive body of discussion. Some of Jacques Derrida's most influential works include: Of *Grammatology*, trans. Gayatri Chakravorty Spivak (Baltimore: The Johns Hopkins University Press, 1976); *Writing and Difference*, trans. Alan Bass (Chicago: University of Chicago Press, 1978); *Margins of Philosophy*, trans. Alan Bass (Chicago: University of Chicago Press, 1982); *The Truth in Painting*, trans. Geoff Bennington and Ian McLeod (Chicago: University of Chicago Press, 1987). Paul de Man's books include: *Blindness and Insight*, 2nd ed., rev. (Minneapolis: University of Minnesota Press, 1983); *Allegories of Reading* (New Haven: Yale University Press, 1979); *The Rhetoric of Romanticism* (New York: Columbia University Press, 1984); *The Resistance to Theory* (Minneapolis: University of Minnesota Press, 1986). Further references to the latter will be included in the text, designated by the abbreviation *RT*.

   The body of secondary material on deconstruction is itself an extensive one. Some important book-length contributions to the discussion include: *Reading de Man Reading*, ed. Lindsay Waters and Wlad Godzich (Minneapolis: University of Minnesota Press, 1989); Jonathan Culler, *On Deconstruction* (Ithaca: Cornell University Press, 1982); Christopher Norris, *Paul de Man and the Critique of Aesthetic Ideology* (New York: Routledge, 1988). Perhaps the most succinct but scrupulous introduction to Derrida's work is Barbara Johnson's "Translator's Introduction" to Jacques Derrida's *Dissemination* (Chicago: University of Chicago Press, 1981). For a lucid and rigorous essay-length introduction to the methods and implications of the work of de Man and Derrida, see Deborah Esch, "Deconstruction" in *Redrawing the Boundaries of Literary Studies in English*, ed. Stephen Greenblatt and Giles Gunn (New York: Publications of the Modern Language Association, 1992).

2. Much of my thinking about the theoretical, cultural, and political importance of the cyborg has been inspired by Donna Haraway's compelling essay, "A Manifesto for Cyborgs: Science, Technology and Socialist Feminism in the 1980's," *Socialist Review* 15:2 (1985), pp. 65–108. And see the "Interview with Donna Haraway" conducted by Andrew Ross and Constance Penley for *Social Text* 25/26 (1990), pp. 8–23.

3. In this regard, deconstruction draws on and complicates the important work of so-called "speech act theory," in particular the work of J. L. Austin. In *How To Do Things With Words* (Cambridge, Mass.: Harvard University Press, 1962), and in other writings, Austin draws attention to an aspect of language that does not state something about the world or represent existing conditions but that *performs* an act. When we make a promise or a wager, when we say "I do" in a marriage ceremony, we are not referring to anything, we are accomplishing the act by saying it. For de Man and Derrida, this *performative* capacity of language cannot be rigorously distinguished from language's *constative* dimension, its capacity to "state" things about the world. The result is a possibly permanent tension or conflict between these dimensions of language. Derrida has explored this most fully in *Margins of Philosophy*, pp. 307–329. De Man's treatments of this tension can be found in *Allegories of Reading*, pp. 119–135, 278–301.

4. Lev Kulesov, *Repeticionnyj metod v kino* (Moscow, 1922); as quoted in Roman Jakobson, "Is the Film in Decline?," *Language in Literature*, ed. Krystyna Pomorska and Stephen Rudy (Cambridge, Mass.: Harvard University Press, 1987), p. 459.

5. David M. Hirsch, *The Deconstruction of Literature: Criticism After Auschwitz*

(Hanover: Brown University Press, 1991), p. 119. Hirsch's virulent denunciation of deconstruction, its philosophical lineage and its company of "fellow travelers" takes off from the disclosures of Paul de Man's wartime writings. From 1939 to 1943, de Man, then in his early twenties, wrote reviews and cultural criticism, primarily for the Belgian newspaper *Le Soir* while under Nazi occupation. Of the many reviews and articles, one—"Les Juifs dans la littérature actuelle"—has come under particularly close scrutiny for its anti-Semitic expressions. For Professor Hirsch—and for many other critics of deconstruction—there exists an essential connection between de Man's early journalistic writings and his mature critical and "deconstructive" work: the disclosures of de Man's "collaborations" in these early writings demonstrate according to Hirsch, that de Man's entire career is one of "prevarication." For critics more sympathetic to the project of deconstruction—and even for many who are not so disposed—the mature work is discontinuous with or even implicitly critical of the formulations which appear in the wartime journalism. The debate over de Man's youthful writings and their possible relationship to deconstruction is itself too intricate to explore here, but it has prompted a substantial body of literature of its own. The reviews and articles Paul de Man published for *Le Soir* and *Het Vlaamsche Land* have been collected and published as *Wartime Journalism, 1939–1943, by Paul de Man*, ed. W. Hamacher, N. Hertz, and T. Keenan (Lincoln: University of Nebraska Press, 1988). An extensive collection of recent critical "responses" to the discovery of the wartime writings and their implications has been published as *Responses: On Paul de Man's Wartime Journalism*, ed. W. Hamacher, N. Hertz, and T. Keenan (Lincoln: University of Nebraska Press, 1989).

6. On this aspect of the film, see Constance Penley's important essay, "Time Travel, Primal Scene and the Critical Dystopia," in *Alien Zone: Cultural Theory and Contemporary Science Fiction Cinema*, ed. Annette Kuhn (London: Verso Books, 1990), pp. 116–127). See also Fredric Jamesons's Marxist analysis of the film: "Progress versus Utopia: Or, Can We Imagine the Future?," *Science Fiction Studies* 9:2 (1982). For a Marxist critique of humanism in the context of recent science fiction cinema, see James H. Kavanagh, "Feminism, Humanism, and Science in *Alien*," in *Alien Zone*, pp. 73–81.

7. Penley, "Time Travel," p. 118.

8. Slavoj Žižek has argued that the terminator is revealed to be nothing more than "the blind mechanical drive" which is distinguished from the human "dialectic of desire." *Looking Awry: An Introduction to Jacques Lacan through Popular Culture* (Cambridge, Mass.: MIT Press, 1991), p. 22.

9. Walter Benjamin, "The Work of Art in the Age of Mechanical Reproduction," *Illuminations*, ed. Hannah Arendt, trans. Harry Zohn (New York: Schocken Books, 1969), pp. 217–252.

10. Eric Alliez and Michel Feher, "Notes on the Sophisticated City," *Zone 1–2*, [n.d.], p. 52. The work of the French critic Jean Baudrillard is most responsible for defining the "postmodern" in terms of the disappearance of the boundary between original and copy. See in particular *Simulations*, trans. Foss, Patton, and Beitchman (New York: Semiotext(e), 1983).

11. Thomas B. Byers, "Commodity Futures," *Alien Zone*, p. 39. *Blade Runner* has been widely and well-written about. See in particular Peter Fitting, "Futurecop: The Neutralization of Revolt in *Blade Runner*," *Science Fiction Studies* 14:3 (1987), pp. 340–354; Yves Chevier, "*Blade Runner*; Or, The Sociology of Anticipation," *Science Fiction Studies* 11:1 (1984), pp. 50–60.

12. Giuliana Bruno has written a valuable essay on the film's linking of history, photography, and mothers. See "Ramble City: Postmodernism and *Blade Runner, Alien Zone*, pp. 183–195.

13. Gerald Prince usefully defines intertextuality as "the relation(s) obtaining between a given text and other texts which it cites, rewrites, absorbs, prolongs, or generally transforms, and in terms of which it is intelligible." *Dictionary of Narratology* (Lincoln: University of Nebraska Press, 1987), p. 46. In the case of *Blade Runner*, the generic patterns of *film noir* would constitute the "intertext" which the film "cites, rewrites, absorbs" and, importantly, "transforms." On the relationship between *Blade Runner* and *film noir*, see Susan Dell and Greg Faller, "*Blade Runner* and Genre: Film Noir and Science Fiction," *Literature/Film Quarterly* 14:2 (1986), pp. 89–100.

14. Annette Kuhn ascribes the effect of "knowing" recognition in *Blade Runner* to the film's processes of "meta-enunciation": the film addresses its spectators doubly, about "events in the narrative, but also about the history of cinema and the conventions of certain film genres" (*Alien Zone*, pp. 145–146).

15. In an important forthcoming article on the *noirish* elements of *Blue Velvet* and *Terminator 2*, Fred Pfeil describes the pivotal moment at which the Schwarzenegger terminator revives after he has been apparently terminated by the T-1000, a moment that tells us that he is indeed human because he has a "soul": "at this very moment of greatest extremity, a small red light begins to shine far, far back in his eye—the sign, we are told, of his back-up power supply kicking in. . . . [I]s it not clear that . . . Arnold, *our* new man, has a core-self—or, if you will, individual soul—and *just enough* of one . . . ?" "Revolting Yet Conserved: Family *Noir* in *Blue Velvet and Terminator 2*."

List of Contributors

DUDLEY ANDREW is Angelo Bertocci Professor of Critical Studies and Director of the Institute for Cinema and Culture at the University of Iowa where he has taught since 1969. After writing three books on film theorists, he authored *Film in the Aura of Art* (Princeton, 1984) and turned to film history with a study of French Poetic Realism, forthcoming from Princeton University Press. He has held a Guggenheim fellowship and numerous awards from NEH. He is currently studying various conceptions of "the Image" in French philosophy and in Japanese cultural criticism.

AVA PREACHER COLLINS is the Director of the Gender Studies Concentration at the University of Notre Dame. She is pursuing a Ph.D. in Comparative Literature at the University of Iowa. Her dissertation, "The Canon Under Fire: (Re)Constructing Cultural Traditions," deals with problems of cultural literacy, taste, and evaluation in the formation of canons.

JIM COLLINS is an Associate Professor in the Department of Communication and Theatre at the University of Notre Dame. He is the author of *Uncommon Cultures: Popular Culture and Post-Modernism* (Routledge, 1989) and the forthcoming *Lost and Found* (Routledge). He has published numerous essays on film, television, and postmodernism.

ANN CVETKOVICH is an Assistant Professor in the Department of English at the University of Texas at Austin. She is the author of *Mixed Feelings: Feminism, Mass Culture and Victorian Sensationalism* (Rutgers University Press, 1992). She has published in *Novel* and *Afterimage*.

MICHAEL ERIC DYSON, formerly a professor of Ethics and Cultural Criticism at Chicago Theological Seminary, is now an Assistant Professor of Afro-American Studies and American Civilization at Brown University. His essays have appeared in numerous books, and in the *New York Times Book Review, Tikkun, The Nation, Social Text, Transition, Cultural Studies, Cultural Critique, Rolling Stone Magazine*, the *Sunday New York Times Arts and Leisure Section*, and Emerge Magazine, which he serves as a contributing editor. He is the author of the forthcoming *Reflecting Black: African American Cultural Criticism* (University of Minnesota Press).

HENRY A. GIROUX is the Waterbury Chair in Secondary Education at Penn State University. He has published widely in the areas of Education and Postmodernism. His most recent works include: *Postmodern Education* (with Stanley Aronowtiz, University of Minnesota Press, 1991) and *Border Crossings: Cultural Workers and the Politics of Education* (Routledge, 1992).

CATHY GRIGGERS is an Assistant Professor in the Department of English's Literary and Cultural Theory Program at Carnegie Mellon University. She has published articles on cinema, popular culture, film theory, and gay and lesbian studies in journals such as *Differences, Semiotica,* and *Postmodern Culture.* She has recently completed a book-length study of transformations in the cultural topography of the feminine within postmodernity, in cultural sites that range from fashion to female predators. She is co-producer of two pedagogical videos, *Discourse/Intercourse* and *Hirohito's Funeral.*

ED GUERRERO teaches black cinema and literature at the University of Delaware. He has written extensively on black cinema for such journals as *Jump Cut, Black American Literature Forum, Discourse* and *Journal of Popular Film and Television.* He has a book on black cinema forthcoming from Temple University Press.

SUSAN JEFFORDS teaches feminist theory in the Department of English at the University of Washington. She is the author of *The Remasculinization of America: Gender and the Vietnam War* (Bloomington: Indiana University Press, 1989). She is author of the forthcoming *Hard Bodies: Hollywood Masculinity in the Reagan Era* (Rutgers) and is currently completing a book on the Persian Gulf War.

FOREST PYLE teaches English literature and Humanities at the University of Oregon. He is the author of *The Ideology of Imagination: Subject and Society in the Discourse of Romanticism* forthcoming from Stanford University Press. The essay in this volume is part of a book-length manuscript, *The Limits of Culture: "From Which One Turns Away,"* on the concept of culture in literature, painting and film. His work has also appeared in *Views Beyond the Border Country: Perspectives on Raymond Williams,* forthcoming from Routledge.

HILARY RADNER is an Assistant Professor of Film and Television Studies in the Department of Communication and Theatre at the University of Notre Dame. Her book, *Shopping Around: Feminine Culture and the Pursuit of Pleasure,* is forthcoming from Routledge. Her work has appeared in *Cultural Studies* and *Genders* and the anthology *Women Writing in Exile* (University of North Carolina Press, 1990). She is currently working on a new manuscript, *Eternal Feminines: Theorizing Heterosexualities.*

THOMAS SCHATZ is G.B. Dealey Professor of Communication in the Department of Radio-Television-Film at the University of Texas at Austin. He is the author of *Hollywood Genres* (Pantheon, 1981), *Old Hollywood/New Hollywood* (UMI Research Press, 1983), and *The Genius of the System* (Pantheon, 1988). He has published numerous essays on film and television, which have been widely anthologized.

JEFFREY SCONCE is a Ph.D. candidate in the Department of Communication Arts at the University of Wisconsin-Madison. He has published in *Wide Angle* and serves as a coordinating editor for *The Velvet Light Trap.* His dissertation is a social history examining concepts of presence and the supernatural in the reception of telecommunications technology.

JANET STAIGER is Associate Professor of Critical and Cultural Studies in the Department of Radio-Television-Film at the University of Texas at Austin. She is the author of

Interpreting Films: Studies in the Historical Reception of American Cinema (Princeton University Press, 1992), and co-author with David Bordwell and Kristin Thompson of *The Classical Hollywood Cinema: Film Style and Mode of Production to 1960* (Columbia University Press, 1985). She is also president of the Society for Cinema Studies.

SUSAN WHITE is Assistant Professor of Film and Literature in the Department of English at the University of Arizona. She received the 1987 Society for Cinema Studies dissertation award for her work on the representation of women in the films of Max Ophuls. Her book, *Max Ophuls and the Figure of Woman*, is forthcoming from University of Illinois Press. She has published in *Arizona Quarterly, Camera Obscura, Quarterly Review of Film, and Video,* and *M.L.N.*

SHARON WILLIS is Associate Professor of French at the University of Rochester, where she also teaches Film, Comparative Literature, and Women's Studies. Her recent articles on film and popular culture have appeared in *Camera Obscura* and the *East-West Film Journal.* Her contribution to this volume is a revised version of part of a chapter from the book she is completing, *Public Fantasies: Sexual and Social Difference in Popular Film.* She is the author of Marguerite Duras: Writing on the Body (University of Illinois Press, 1987). Other articles have appeared in *Diacritics, L'Esprit créateur, Substance,* and *Theater Journal.*